AF323106

Toward a World of Economic Stability

Toward a World of Economic Stability:

Optimal Monetary Framework and Policy

Proceedings of the Third International Conference sponsored by the Institute for Monetary and Economic Studies of the Bank of Japan

edited by Yoshio Suzuki and Mitsuaki Okabe

UNIVERSITY OF TOKYO PRESS

ISBN 4-13-047039-6/47339
ISBN 0-86008-422-1

Contents

Editors' Preface

The Institute for Monetary and Economic Studies of the Bank of
Japan has organized and sponsored an international conference bien-
nially with the view of promoting mutual understanding between economists in academia and those in central banks and international
organizations. This book is the record of the proceedings of the Third
International Conference, "Toward a World of Economic Stability:
Optimal Monetary Framework and Policy," which was held in Tokyo
June 3–5, 1987. The aim of the conference, as the opening address
makes clear, was to identify the causes of economic instability, both
domestic and international, since 1973 and to explore the issue of the
optimal monetary regime and policy for the future.

The Conference consisted of five sessions. The first session com-
menced with the Opening Remarks of Governor Satoshi Sumita of
the Bank of Japan. This was followed by the Keynote Speeches of
Professors James Tobin and Allan H. Meltzer, Honorary Advisers of
the Institute, and by the Introductory Presentation by the Director
of the Institute. The second session examined the causes of domestic
instability in individual countries after 1973—a year marked by the
beginning of the floating exchange rate system and by the first oil price
hike. The third session focused on the causes of international imbalances among major industrial countries in the 1980s. The fourth session
dealt with more normative aspects of the problem: the discussion cen-
tered on the optimal monetary regime and policy management for
economic stability in the future. The final session was devoted to summary presentations and general discussions on the issues which had
emerged as the most important in the preceding sessions.

As the organizers of the Conference, we did not necessarily seek a
well-defined consensus of opinion. Rather, it was hoped that the exchange of differing views would contribute to the enhancement of

mutual understanding among the participants in the Conference. And the fact that this goal was achieved is evident from a reading of the two excellent summary papers by Dr. Andrew Crockett and Professor John B. Taylor, which are the lead papers of this volume. These two papers, in many respects complementary, provide a well-balanced overview of the entire conference, and hence we strongly recommend them to the reader. We would like to take the liberty here, though, of stating our view on what were the key conclusions arrived at by the conference.

First, the principal causes of economic instability, such as increased variability in economic growth and inflation rates in individual countries after 1973, apparently were real shocks on the supply side of the economy, such as the first and second oil price hikes. The implementation of different monetary and fiscal policies in each country in reaction to these supply shocks might explain why these common shocks resulted in dissimilar and sharply contrasting economic performances across countries. However, the transition to flexible exchange rates from a fixed exchange rate system did not by itself necessarily worsen the macroeconomic performances of individual countries. Indeed, that transition was deemed a favorable factor for more stable economic performance.

Second, the fundamental cause of international payments imbalances in the 1980s seemed to lie in the divergence of fiscal policies among the United States, Japan, and the European countries. It was generally recognized that with the significant increase in the international mobility of capital flows such divergences of fiscal policy tended to cause larger fluctuations in exchange rates and therefore greater current account imbalances.

Third, based upon the historical experiences of the major industrial countries, monetary targeting policy was assessed favorably not only as being necessary for clarifying the policy intentions of the monetary authorities, but also as being useful in providing an effective safeguard against political pressures on monetary policy. In order for such monetary targeting policy to be effective in securing economic stability, it was emphasized that the public must be convinced of the credibility of central bank policy, and to obtain such credibility central banks must have a record of success in continuously achieving price stability.

Fourth, concerning proposals to improve the international monetary system, the majority of the participants at the Conference supported the current floating exchange rate system, arguing that, compared with the fixed-rate system, it was superior in fostering the economic stability of individual countries. Meanwhile, a few of the participants supported the ongoing joint interventions in the foreign exchange market.

Fifth, vis-à-vis international payments imbalances, there was some support for the position that these do not really constitute a problem since imbalances are financial capital flows from countries where savings exceed investment to countries where investment exceeds savings; i.e., imbalances reflect internationally efficient resource allocation. However, the majority of participant considered the existence of international payments imbalances to be a serious problem that needs to be addressed. They argued that these imbalances are not sustainable in the long run; in particular they pointed out that a continuation of the large current account deficits of the United States might lead not only to increased protectionism but also to a sharp fall in the dollar, with undesirable effects on the world economy.

Sixth, it was generally recognized that under the flexible exchange rate system with high capital mobility the external transmission effects of fiscal and monetary policies differed significantly. For example, tight fiscal policy would have large external effects, since the increase in net exports resulting from the decline of domestic absorption is enforced by the depreciation of the currency caused by lower domestic interest rates; on the other hand, the net external effects of tight monetary policy would be theoretically ambiguous, since the increase in net exports resulting from the decline of domestic absorption is offset by the appreciation of the currency caused by higher domestic interest rates. Accordingly, many participants underscored the necessity of recognizing these differential transmission effects in international policy coordination. As for fiscal policy, there was general agreement that the U.S. fiscal deficits should be curtailed in due course; however, there existed a wide difference of opinion over whether Japan and the European countries should adopt more expansionary fiscal policies. Also, some participants supported the restructuring of economies to rectify trade imbalances through, for instance, tax reform. And a consensus was evident that the monetary policy of a nation should be managed essentially independently of foreign monetary policies and should focus primarily on the domestic economic conditions of the country.

Seventh, in order to foster the stability of the world economy, which has been characterized by increasing interdependence among the major industrial countries, it was agreed that we need to further explore the possibilities of international policy coordination. In addition, in regard to the framework of international policy coordination, there seemed to be a consensus that even if adopting common and rigid policy rules is not feasible, the institution of some kind of less formal policy coordination would be a positive step.

Finally, we would be remiss if we did not acknowledge the invaluable advice on planning and organizing the conference that we received from many individuals, including particularly Professors James Tobin and Allan H. Meltzer and also Professor Milton Friedman, present Honorary Advisers and former Honorary Adviser, respectively, of the Institute. Our thanks are also extended to all the participants in the Conference; we are especially indebted to those who presented papers or comments at the Conference and commend the uniformly high level of scholarship of their contributions. We would also like to express our appreciation to the staff of the Bank of Japan, particularly those in the Institute, for their devoted efforts to make the conference a success. Because of the extensive cooperation we received, the conference did succeed in clarifying many of the monetary issues that are currently of most interest to policymakers and scholars. It is our hope that the publication of this book will help make the ideas and proposals developed during our Conference into a common asset of those interested in economic stability, optimal monetary regime, and international policy coordination.

Yoshio Suzuki, Director
Mitsuaki Okabe, Chief, Research Division 1

Institute for Monetary and
Economic Studies, Bank of Japan

Opening Remarks

It gives me great pleasure and I am deeply honored to have this opportunity to welcome you with my warmest regards to the Third International Conference of our Bank's Institute for Monetary and Economic Studies.

As many of you may recall, the Institute was established nearly five years ago, in 1982, in commemoration of the centennial of the Bank of Japan. In the following year, it successfully organized the First International Conference on "Monetary Policy in Our Times," and in 1985 it sponsored the Second Conference on "Financial Innovation and Monetary Policy." It is indeed a great honor not only for the Institute but also for the Bank of Japan as a whole that such a large number of distinguished economists from so many parts of the world have once again shown their willingness to participate in this Conference. Distinguished universities, prominent international organizations and, of course, our fellow central banks are all represented. My special thanks go to Professors Tobin and Meltzer, who, as Honorary Advisers of the Institute, have offered us valuable suggestions on the organization of this Conference and have generously agreed to deliver keynote speeches on this occasion, despite their extremely busy schedules.

When we consider contemporary economic history, the year 1973 seems to mark the beginning of a new era. That year saw the start of the floating exchange rate system and was also the year of the first oil price shock. The decade from 1973 was characterized by greater instability in inflation and employment than had previously been experienced in the post-World War II period. Inflationary pressures that had emerged in the 1960s became more intense and spread to a number of countries after the first oil shock. Many of the countries which adopted relatively easy monetary policies thus experienced prolonged stagflation. On the other hand, some of the countries which pursued sharply different macroeconomic policies, notably stringent monetary policy, were successful in restraining recurrent inflation, and subsequently achieved relative economic stability. We saw quite contrasting macroeconomic performances across countries depending crucially on what policies they chose.

By the early 1980s, the problem of protracted inflation was less of a concern for most countries. However, the large international payments imbalances of several major industrial countries, in particular the massive current account deficits in the United States and the correspondingly huge surpluses in Japan and West Germany, constituted a new source of economic instability. Certainly the economic implications of these imbalances are somewhat problematic. But it is undeniable that the persistence of large current account imbalances has presented an increasing threat to the stability of the world economy by inciting trade protectionism, the dangers of which were made evident by the Great Depression in the 1930s. Meanwhile, the floating exchange rate system, which had been originally expected to play a major role in correcting current account imbalances, turned out to be much less effective than had been anticipated. Rather, rapid fluctuations in exchange rates have been another source of instability for the world economy as well as for most national economies.

As I have briefly indicated, the world economy from 1973 until the early 1980s was characterized by significant instability in prices and employment, and in more recent years by large international payments imbalances and highly volatile foreign exchange rates. These observations, therefore, lead us to a fundamental question concerning the monetary system: given the various exogenous shocks such as the first and the second oil crises, does the principal cause of economic instability lie in policy management or in the prevailing monetary regime itself, which is a combination of the fiat money system domestically and the floating exchange rate system internationally?

It is only by carefully investigating the causes of both domestic and international economic instability that we can set out on a course toward a world of economic stability. In the international sphere, the reexamination of the present international monetary system represents an important area of research. In this context, the issue of the increased international mobility of capital would be one of the important topics to be taken up. The discussion may go on to an alternative exchange rate system such as one with fixed rates of some kind, an idea that has recently been proposed by a number of scholars. Or some may argue that it would be better to alter economic policies and maintain the present monetary system. In today's world of international economic interdependence, most countries, large and small, have been strongly influenced by the policies effected by other countries. And no country can be said to enjoy full autonomy in its economic policy. In this situation, the issue of international policy coordination takes on a special importance.

It is easy enough to raise these kinds of issues, but it is not so easy to answer them. What is essential then is closer collaboration between policymakers and the academic community in the search for the optimal monetary framework and policy. It is with this end in view that the Institute for Monetary and Economic Studies of the Bank of Japan has organized this Conference. I sincerely hope that the exchange of views and in-depth discussions that will take place over the next three days will contribute to the understanding of the causes of past economic instability, as well as to the designing of the optimal monetary framework and policy for the future.

SATOSHI SUMITA
Governor
Bank of Japan

Summaries of the Conference

1

Toward a World of Economic Stability: Summing Up

Andrew D. Crockett

In looking back at this conference, it is helpful to begin by recalling the questions and issues that the organizers invited participants to concentrate on. These can be divided into two separate though related aspects of the question of economic instability: first, as an issue in positive economics, the nature and causes of instability; and second, more normatively, how to move toward a world of greater stability. These issues, in turn, were subdivided into their domestic and their international dimensions.

I. The Causes of Domestic Instability

The introductory notes for the conference made the following observation: "When we look back over the past 13 years it is evident that the world economy and most national economies have shown enormous instability in prices, growth, and international payments balances." Two questions are then posed: "Given the shocks, to what extent has the prevailing monetary regime been responsible for instability?" and "Would experience have been better if different policies had been followed?"

As far as the *extent* of instability was concerned, a number of different measures and techniques were introduced to measure instability. Professor Parkin looked at the variability of the growth rate of key variables around a random walk, Professor Fischer provided a careful verbal description of movements in major variables, Professor Meltzer reported results using Kalman filter techniques, and the Bank of Japan's background paper provided a Bayesian approach to trend and variability. Inevitably, there were differences of emphasis in the results presented, depending not only on statistical techniques, but also on country coverage and time periods chosen. Professor Bomhoff, in his commentary, has given a number of insights concerning some of the advantages and disadvantages of the statistical methods used. From a policy viewpoint, however, the principal conclusions are relatively robust.

First, the *average* performance with respect to welfare-relevant variables has been worse in all the major countries since 1973. The average inflation rate and unemployment rate have been higher in all the major countries. Output growth has been lower in all except the two lowest-growth countries (the United States and the United Kingdom), where it is unchanged from earlier experience. As far as balance-of-payments disequilibria are concerned, it is harder to find an unambiguous indicator of "better" or "worse" performance. Nevertheless, as Governor Sumita said in his opening remarks to the conference, payments imbalances have become considerably more troublesome over the past few years.

Next, as far as *instability* of economic performance is concerned (the main focus of the conference), there is evidence that the variability of the major macroeconomic variables has become greater in the post-1973 period. This finding is not quite so uniform across countries, however. Indeed, Japan, for example, has actually had significantly greater stability in key macroeconomic variables since about 1975 as compared with its experience in the 1960s and early 1970s. A fact that received less attention during the conference, however, is that Japan has also had the greatest slowdown in its growth rate between the earlier and the later period. An interesting question would be whether greater stability has been purchased at the cost of the lower average growth rate. To the extent that it has, it would diminish the virtues of the greater stability.

Moving from the measurement to the causes of instability, the organizers of the conference offered three basic factors in their introductory material: external shocks, bad policies, and the monetary regime. In assessing the relative importance of these three factors, their interdependence was well recognized. Not only are all the factors important but they interact. For example, economic policies can create the circumstances that give rise to shocks. It can be plausibly argued that the commodity price increases of the early 1970s owed much to the excess liquidity creation of the late 1960s and early 1970s. Similarly, the monetary regime affects performance not only in its own right but, perhaps more importantly, insofar as it permits or discourages policies that have unstable consequences. Flexible exchange rates may reduce the discipline to pursue a convergent monetary policy; on the other hand, they may also avoid the need for stop-go demand management to protect the balance of payments.

Nevertheless, provided the linkages between the various sources of instability are properly recognized, it is convenient to discuss separately the three factors identified by the conference organizers.

A. Exogenous Shocks

There was wide agreement that the main cause of the greater instability in recent years has been the size and frequency of exogenous disturbances. Professor Parkin's paper concludes that "the major source of variability in output growth in the second half of the 1970s is an increased variability of real shocks hitting the supply side of the economy." Fischer identified three main disturbances that found general agreement in the ensuing discussion. These were: the oil price increase of 1973–74; the second oil shock in 1979–80; and the disturbance associated with the widening of the U.S. fiscal deficit in the 1980s. (It should be noted that while the U.S. fiscal shock can be considered exogenous to *monetary* policy it is certainly not exogenous to policy; therefore it may not be appropriate to refer to it as a supply-side shock.)

Beyond these three main shocks identified by Fischer, other exogenous disturbances were referred to during the course of the discussions. Professor Niehans pointed out that, from the viewpoint of the world outside the United States, U.S. fiscal and monetary policy shifts could be considered an external disturbance to which other countries had to adjust. Professor Sachs noted that the slowdown in productivity growth in most industrial countries, insofar as it was unanticipated and has still not been fully explained, could be considered a change in the economic background contributing to instability. Sachs also drew attention to labor market rigidities, and other speakers referred to the puzzling way the natural rate of unemployment has risen in the European economies. To the extent that there has been an unanticipated shift in the Phillips curve, this too is a change in circumstances with macroeconomic implications.

B. The Monetary Regime

The monetary regime was generally found not to be a major object of blame for the increased instability of recent years. Indeed, a number of speakers felt that exchange rate flexibility had probably helped to reduce the instability of real economic variables, compared with what might otherwise have been the case. It was also pointed out that part of the observed instability in the post-1973 period had been inherited from the fixed exchange-rate regime. The seeds of the inflationary upsurge in the initial years of the floating regime, for example, had been sown by the excess liquidity creation in the final years of the fixed-rate period.

Another important consideration in assessing the contribution of the monetary regime to macroeconomic instability is that an attempt to preserve fixed rates in the face of some of the disturbances that the system has been exposed to recently (for example, fiscal policy divergences) would in fact have made instability greater. To have attempted to resist the appreciation of the dollar in the 1980–85 period through monetary policy would have required more expansionary monetary policy in the United States and more restrictive policy elsewhere. This would have tended to exacerbate the divergences in economic policy that were resulting from fiscal actions.

C. Policy Mistakes

There was no disagreement in the conference that policy mistakes had been made in the post-1973 period, although the extent to which they had been a major cause of instability was debated. Professor Parkin concluded that monetary policy had clearly contributed to the higher level of inflation of recent years, though he doubted whether it had added much to the variability of inflation. More generally, however, it was noted that countries that had enjoyed greater macroeconomic stability seemed to have had more stable policies, Japan being the key example cited in this context. A question raised by Professor Fischer was, why Japan had weathered the second round of oil price increases with less disruption to output than other countries that had similarly stable policies. The consensus of opinion seemed to be that the greater flexibility with which real wages were adjusted in Japan might have had something to do with this outcome.

Although policies were not generally viewed as a major independent source of instability in macroeconomic performance, two caveats are in order. First, policies can be faulted for not adequately offsetting disturbances stemming from other sources. For example, viewed with the benefit of hindsight, the stance of policies was probably too expansionary in the late 1970s, in the face of a slowdown in productivity growth and the apparent increase in the NAIRU in several countries.

This contributed to inflationary pressures and necessitated a sharp policy reversal after the onset of the second round of oil price increases. Second, while monetary policies (the focus of the conference) may have contributed relatively little to instability, the same cannot be said of fiscal policies. Indeed, divergence in fiscal stance between the United States and most other countries since 1981 can be viewed as the key factor behind current imbalances in the world economy.

Before leaving the subject of the causes of instability in domestic economies, it is worth recalling one question raised by the organizers of the conference that was dealt with only in passing: "Have changes in the domestic transmission of policy, if any, affected domestic economic stability under the present regime?" Perhaps one reason why this question was not addressed specifically is that, in a domestic context, most speakers were willing to regard the well-established transmission mechanisms of policy as being still valid. However, it could be argued that the rigidities in factor markets to which Professor Sachs and others referred make domestic economies respond less flexibly to external disturbances. This may constitute part of the reason there appears to have been an increase in the natural rate of unemployment and a serious deterioration in the way in which industrial economies, particularly those of Western Europe, have been functioning. Whether such a phenomenon should be regarded as a change in the "transmission mechanism" of policy is perhaps an open question, however.

II. The Causes of International Imbalances

The introduction to this topic provided by the organizers of the conference again offers three possible explanations of increased imbalances: international differences in saving–investment balances; policy divergences among countries; and increased mobility of international capital. These explanations are by no means mutually exclusive; indeed, in many ways they are intimately linked. Policy divergences, for example, can lead to shifts in domestic saving and investment that in turn spill over, via capital mobility, into exchange rate movements and balance-of-payments shifts. The specific questions that participants in the conference were invited to address were "Has the transmission mechanism (i.e., the international transmission mechanism) changed, in particular the relationship between exchange rates and current account imbalances?" and "How does the variability of exchange rates affect the economy?"

A. Transmission Mechanism

In discussing the transmission mechanism, Professor Niehans began his presentation by noting that there was a "confusing variety" of potential mechanisms offered in the literature. In the conference, however, there appeared to be broad agreement on the main lines of the transmission mechanism that stood behind recent trends. The driving force behind exchange rate shifts is acknowledged to be disturbances affecting the capital account of the balance of payments. This insight of the asset market approach was generally considered a useful way of viewing recent developments. An interesting distinction was drawn between the increased mobility of *financial* capital (or "asset arbitrage," to use Niehans' terminology) and the much more limited mobility of *physical* capital. Since there are substantial lags in the process by which stocks of physical capital respond to changes in desired capital/output ratios, exchange rates and/or interest rates on financial assets may have to move by substantial amounts to maintain financial market equilibrium when something happens to disturb portfolio preferences.

Interpreting recent developments from this perspective, it was widely accepted in the conference that shifts in the stance of fiscal policy, particularly the sharp increase in the U.S. budget deficit and the steady reduction in the German and Japanese deficits, were an important contributing factor to swings in national saving-investment balances. These shifts in saving-investment balances led to incipient interest-rate pressures that generated the exchange rate movements that were observed. These exchange rate movements, in turn, validated the real resource flows that were the counterpart of the underlying shifts in saving-investment behavior.

In all this, there appeared to be a willingness on the part of conference participants to regard exchange rates as the key mechanism in the process and therefore implicitly to answer the conference organizers' question, of whether the transmission mechanism had changed, in the negative. It is true that shifts in saving and investment behavior now loom larger in the interpretation of payments developments, but this in itself does not diminish the role of the exchange rate in the transmission process.

An issue that perhaps was standing behind the question of the role of the exchange rate was whether other factors, such as differential growth rates of absorption or the strength of trade restrictions, now play a relatively larger role in payments trends than previously. To the extent that they do, of course, this would have important implications for the issue of whether further exchange rate changes are needed to correct current imbalances.

With regard to trade restrictions, Professor Komiya pointed out that the balance of payments is a macroeconomic phenomenon that has to be explained in terms of macroeconomic variables. Trade restrictions can have many consequences, which are usually pernicious, but they cannot be held responsible for more than a minor part of the payments surpluses and deficits that now plague the major countries.

Relative rates of income growth are obviously more significant in determining what happens to the balance of payments, but the quantitative results presented in Professor Sachs's paper suggest that differential rates of demand growth can only explain a relatively small part of the shifts in payments positions that have occurred. Several speakers took issue with aspects of Sachs's model, but Professor Fischer noted that the broad results were quite consistent with those derived from most other major internationally linked models, as reviewed, for example, in the 1986 Brookings conference.[1] Last, among non-exchange rate factors affecting trade flows, the debt crisis that developed after 1982 has clearly had an important impact on the import capacity of indebted developing countries, and this may have affected the U.S. position disproportionately, given the concentration of U.S. exports in Latin American markets.

B. Payments Imbalances and Sustainability

The foregoing assessment of recent developments has important implications for the policies needed to correct current imbalances. What it suggests is that differential growth rates, by themselves, will not be adequate to eliminate the large disequilibria that presently exist. In his keynote presentation, Professor Tobin presented some rough calculations that showed a sizable recession in the United States would be required to eliminate the U.S. current account deficit through cutting imports. Likewise, as shown by Professor Sachs's calculations, an acceleration of growth in Germany and Japan, unless it was implausibly large, would go no more than a small part of the way toward eliminating these countries' surpluses.

In this connection, a provocative question was asked by Professor Komiya: "Are the current large imbalances really a problem?" It

[1] Biyant, Ralph C., Dale W. Henderson, Gerald Holtham, Peter Hooper and Steven A. Symansky, eds. "Empirical Macroeconomics for Independent Economies," Brookings, December 1987.

could be argued, for example, that the large capital flows to the United States reflect a recognition on the part of market participants of superior prospects for profitable real investment in the United States. An alternative interpretation, which is perhaps more plausible but has analytically similar implications, is that a change occurred in U.S. savers' time preference. In either interpretation, there has been a sharp reduction in the desire to save relative to the desire to invest in the United States. Thus, it could be argued that the resultant shifts in payments flows are a perfectly efficient reflection of underlying economic forces.

The key to answering the question of whether or not payments imbalances constitute a problem lies in the concept of sustainability. Are the deficits of the United States and the corresponding surpluses of other countries sustainable over the medium term? Professor Tobin, Mr. Frenkel, and others pointed out that if a deficit was not sustainable, then there was by definition a problem that needed to be addressed. The definition of unsustainability, however, is a complex matter, dealt with only briefly in the conference. A first definition would be technical: a situation is unsustainable if it has an inherent explosiveness in it. For example, if a country has a large trade deficit and the interest rate on its external debt is higher than its growth rate of output or exports, then eventually the current account deficit will grow to exceed the gross national product. The difficulty about this definition, however, is that it applies to a small trade deficit too. In fact, it applies to any trade deficit. If the interest rate is higher than the growth rate, service payments on debt will tend to rise, without limit, as a share of GNP. An arithmetical definition of unsustainability is therefore not very helpful as a practical guide to policy assessment.

Mr. Frenkel offered a second type of unsustainability, which might be called market unsustainability. A given payments deficit, by creating an accumulation of assets and liabilities, might at some stage provoke an adverse market reaction, even in situations that were not, in a technical sense, unsustainable. This type of unsustainability is clearly important, and is probably behind the concerns of many observers of the current situation, but it is also a concept that is hard to provide with operational content. One approach would be to calculate the ratio of net foreign assets or liabilities to some relevant scale variable, such as GNP or exports. The larger such a ratio became, the greater, presumably, would be the scope for sudden shifts in sentiment to lead to disruptive movements in market prices. However, Mr. Flemming pointed out that it is not only assets held by foreigners that are potentially available to put pressure on exchange rates. The whole spectrum of assets held in countries with convertible currencies can, at least potentially, be converted into cash and create a threat to the stability of the exchange rate.

A third definition of sustainability might be called political sustainability. This definition would focus on the question, "Is the deficit compatible with other objectives that the authorities of the country are pursuing?" If, for example, the U.S. Government takes action to lower the federal deficit, such action could be considered a collective decision on the part of the American people to save more via a lower federal deficit. If, at the same time, private savings and investment propensities change by less, so that there is no one-for-one offset between public and private spending behavior, macroeconomic equilibrium can only be preserved through a movement in the foreign balance. Thus, an unsustainable external balance can be defined as one that is incompatible with medium-term trends and objectives concerning fiscal policy and private savings and investment.

The issue of sustainability and how to give it operational content is one on which further work could be highly useful, both at the theoretical and at the policy level. The last meeting of the IMF's Interim Committee gave considerable prominence to the concept of sustainability as a means by which standards could be established for appraising the evolution of economic indicators. The forthcoming Venice Summit is also likely to identify sustainability as a means of judging the relative responsibilities of countries in promoting policy coordination. There is still a long way to go before an agreed-upon and useful definition of sustainability for policy purposes can be reached.

III. Optimal Regime and Policy

The final session of the Conference dealt with the more normative issues of the optimal monetary regime (domestic and international) and optimal policies. A number of these issues had, of course, surfaced in the discussions of the causes and extent of instability. Views expressed on the extent to which the current monetary regime had (or had not) contributed to macroeconomic instability clearly have implications for the issue of whether the current regime needs to be changed.

A. Optimal Domestic Policy Regime

It is not possible, of course, to separate fully the question of the optimal international and the optimal domestic monetary regime. The nature of the international monetary regime determines in an important sense the nature of the domestic regime that is desirable. The paper by Professors Fukuda and Hamada was, all agreed, a very neat extension to the international level of the approach followed by Poole in his well-known 1970 paper.[2] Fukuda and Hamada show that it is possible to say something about both the optimal international regime and optimal domestic policy if one knows something about the characteristics of the disturbances that are affecting the economy. The characteristics that are important include whether a disturbance can be considered as affecting the IS curve or the LM curve (a direct analogy with Poole); whether the disturbance is temporary or permanent in nature; whether it is of domestic or foreign origin; and whether it is country-specific or general.

The discussion in the Fukuda-Hamada paper provides many useful insights to policymakers; its practical applicability, however, is limited by several considerations. First, it is usually not possible to identify in advance the source or nature of the disturbances that will affect the economy. Second, different countries may see a disturbance as being of a different nature and may respond differently to it. Third, the authorities may interpret the disturbance as being of a particular kind, but if the market is unaware of the authorities' interpretation, they will be uncertain of the reaction that will ensue.

Should one conclude, therefore, that the authorities should be left with the discretion to analyze the disturbances they face, and respond to them in a discretionary fashion? The answer of the conference to that question was generally in the negative. Professor Meltzer made the point that there is a need to give the market some guidance in order to reduce uncertainty. It was also noted by Professor Taylor that even if the nature of each disturbance could not be clearly identified as it arose, it should still be possible to establish the most common source of disturbances and thereby to devise a policy rule that would be appropriate in the majority of circumstances. Perhaps this is one reason for the attraction of a monetary rule after the mid-1970s. The kinds of problems that seem to have confronted policymakers in the 1960s and early 1970s had been those for which a monetary rule would provide the most effective safeguard.

Another advantage of a rule-based regime was pointed out by Professor Fischer. He noted that monetary growth targets had provided

---

[2] "Optimal Choice of Monetary Policy Instruments in a Simple Stochastic Macro Model." *Quarterly Journal of Economics* 84: 197–216.

the authorities with the necessary political "cover" to raise interest rates to the politically unpopular heights needed to effectively combat the inflation of the early 1980s.

A final advantage of rules as against discretion is that they make the authorities justify their actions. Of course, as Mr. White noted, this advantage from rules seems rather marginal compared with the wide-ranging benefits that early advocates of monetary rules thought could be achieved. Nevertheless, the view of the conference was that it was useful for the authorities to define their actions in terms of identifiable rules, and then to defend them in terms of clear-cut criteria. A monetary rule, for example, would be predicated on the assumption that most disturbances come from shifts in the IS rather than the LM curve. Thus the authorities, if they depart from the rule, would be forced to explain why it is they believe that the LM curve has shifted in a particular case.

If it can be said that the existence of monetary rules has certain advantages, the question then arises of what the rules should be. A number of rules of thumb were tentatively suggested, but the conference did not produce a solid consensus around a particular set of rules. It was generally felt that rules should be relatively simple, so that they are transparent. Professor Barro provided a theoretical and empirical justification for an interest rate rule; and while there was considerable skepticism with this analysis, Professor Tobin pointed out that it was quite possible, and indeed normal, to have an interest rate target as a short-term operating guide to monetary policy, and a monetary aggregate target in a more medium-term framework.

In discussing how rules for monetary aggregates should be formulated, Professor Fischer argued that theory favored multiple monetary targets over a single target, since different monetary aggregates could reveal different aspects of economic performance. Some other speakers felt that multiple targets could cloud the signals, however, and give the authorities a justification to move back toward a more discretionary regime. Professor Meltzer proposed a rule which he termed "activist but nondiscretionary." Under it, the growth rate of money would be adjusted in light of *past* changes in velocity, and every major country would observe the same objective with respect to inflation. In sum, while there was considerable support for the proposition that rules, provided they were not too inflexible, could provide a useful framework for monetary policy, there was a considerable variety of opinion concerning what the rules should be, and how they could be adapted in particular circumstances.

B. Optimal International Policy Regime

As already noted, the question of the optimal international policy regime is not really separable from the domestic policy regime. Putting this consideration on one side, however, there are three main possibilities for the international monetary regime: fixed exchange rates, or some similar system such as target zones; an unmanaged flexible exchange rate system; and an intermediate regime in which policy coordination would be used to limit exchange-rate movements and bring about internationally consistent economic performance. One relatively clear conclusion from the conference was the absence of a strong desire to go back to fixed exchange rates. The analysis presented in the conference papers did not suggest that the variability of exchange rates that has characterized the last 15 years was a principal source of instability in other, more welfare-relevant variables. Furthermore, as noted by Professor Tobin, even if fixed rates were efficient for dealing with certain types of disturbance (as suggested in the Fukuda/Hamada paper) it was not possible to imagine a system in which fixed exchange rates would be the rule *part* of the time. The point about a fixed rate regime is that rates are fixed and economic agents can rely on it. If circumstances are envisaged in which the fixed rates are abandoned, then the advantages of fixity would quickly be undermined.

Another point is that a fixed rate system in which the mechanism by which rates are maintained is not clearly specified can produce destabilizing results. One example would be fixed rates being maintained by monetary policy in circumstances of underlying disturbances caused by divergences in fiscal policies. In such a case (the early 1980s would be an example), subordinating monetary policy to exchange rate considerations would compound the initial policy mistake.

While fixed rates were not viewed with great favor, there was at the same time a recognition that exchange rate flexibility with uncoordinated national policies could create troublesome international imbalances. Some speakers felt this made a persuasive case for coordination, although others expressed considerable scepticism concerning whether coordination was desirable or feasible. The doubts expressed on coordination were of several different kinds. First, political difficulties were cited; it was alleged that countries simply would not be prepared to give up the degree of political sovereignty that was needed to make coordination effective. On the plane of economics, it was pointed out that effective rules for coordination, which would be suitable in a variety of circumstances, were hard to devise. Another objection was that the cost-benefit calculation of economic policy coordination might not be all that advantageous. Studies in the literature tended to show that the potential gains from policy coordination were rather modest compared with the efforts needed to achieve such coordination.

Others, however, pointed out that policy spillovers were important in an increasingly interdependent world, and failure to take them properly into account could have serious adverse consequences. Mr. Henderson and Mr. Frenkel suggested that game theoretic models might underestimate the potential costs of a failure to cooperate. In other words, the absence of policy coordination might not result in optimal noncooperative policies, but rather in positively destructive policies. Protectionism was cited in this regard, as well as the tendency of financial markets to respond disruptively when they sensed the absence of a collaborative approach among the key official players. Professor Tobin concluded that it was too complacent to leave everything to the market.

Policy coordination can cover a variety of possible approaches. There is a broad spectrum of cooperative mechanisms, running all the way from rules that provide fairly mechanical guidance on how to react to different developments, to the simple provision of forums in which information can be exchanged and policies discussed. At the very least, exchange of information would seem to be valuable. This can proceed by gradation into the application of peer pressure and a common approach to the analysis of economic interactions. This seems to be the direction that is being espoused by the major countries. An important subject for additional research by academics, and additional thought by policymakers, is how to steer the middle course between overly mechanical rules on the one side and ineffectual statements on the other. How can one build on the willingness that exists among the major countries to improve the mutual consistency of their policies by developing an analytical structure that is simple enough to be understood and used at a political level, and yet rich enough in its analytical structure to provide useful insights about economic interactions?

2

A Summary of the Empirical and Analytical Results and the Implications for International Monetary Policy

John B. Taylor*

A truly wide array of data, models, and views have been presented in the papers prepared for this conference and in the discussions of the papers. Such a broad scope is entirely appropriate in that the purpose of the conference—the examination of optimal monetary policy for stability in the world economy—requires careful consideration of many different countries, institutions, and events.

But the breadth makes summation difficult. Thanks to the excellent organization of the sessions and the discussions, and the comprehensive statistical analysis prepared by the staff of the Institute for Monetary and Economic Studies, I believe a reasonably coherent and manageable set of results, on which there was considerable agreement, have emerged at the conference. In my view these results deserve careful consideration by policymakers.

I have organized my summary of the results into three main areas. First, I summarize the key *empirical facts of macroeconomic performance* presented in the papers. Second, I summarize some of the *analytical results* developed in the papers and the discussions. Third, I consider the *international monetary policy implications* that might be drawn from the empirical and analytical results.

I. Economic Performance

The conference appropriately began with a presentation of statistical facts about the macroeconomic performance of the major industrial

* This summary was prepared while I was a visiting scholar at the Institute for Monetary and Economic Studies. I am grateful to Dr. Yoshio Suzuki and the staff of the Institute for organizing an excellent conference, and for their gracious hospitality during my visit.

countries during the last 30 years. Most of the analysis was focused on the G-7 countries: Canada, France, Germany, Italy, Japan, the United Kingdom, and the United States. There are a number of key characteristics of these data about which there was rather wide agreement at the conference. I will focus on these areas of agreement, but I will also review the areas of disagreement and attempt to resolve some of this disagreement.

A. The Importance of Supply Shocks in the 1970s and 1980s

An important empirical regularity that emerges from the data is that the main source of disturbances in the period since the early 1970s, in comparison with the period of the 1950s and 1960s, has been from the supply side—real, external shocks affecting the macroeconomies. This fact emerges from Michael Parkin's paper, in which he measures such shocks with the ratio of commodity prices to the general price level, and shows their large impact on output fluctuations. The fact also comes out of the Institute for Monetary and Economic Studies' statistical analysis, in which the variability of such external factors as import prices was shown to increase in the 1970s. It is also emphasized in Stanley Fischer's case study approach, in which he focuses on the two supply shocks of the 1970s and early 1980s. Overall, I think that there is wide agreement that a major source of shocks, at least to the major industrial countries during the period of the 1970s and 1980s, has come from the supply side.

Three remarks might be made about this empirical finding. First, the finding that supply shocks have been a key disturbance in the 1970s and 1980s does not imply that monetary policy has played a small role. I think monetary policy and the differences between monetary policy in the different countries has had a big effect on the transmission of these supply shocks within and between the different economies. The importance of supply shocks should not, for example, be viewed as evidence in favor of a real business-cycle theory, in which monetary policy plays no role. On the contrary, the fact that supply shocks have been so large in the 1970s and 1980s is evidence that monetary factors are important. Monetary policy can explain why similar supply shocks have resulted in dissimilar economic behavior in the different countries hit by these shocks. Technically, the explanation can be put in terms of a distinction between impulse and propagation mechanisms. While it is true that the major impulses have been real shocks, the propagation mechanism has been influenced by monetary policy. Monetary policy has played a role in cushioning the effect of the supply shocks on macroeconomic fluctuations.

Second, there was discussion about whether the productivity slow-downs in the 1970s and 1980s should be included as a significant real supply disturbance affecting economic fluctuations. Jeffrey Sachs, for example, suggested that the productivity slowdown had a big impact on the behavior of the macroeconomies during this period, and may serve as a political-economic explanation for the large deficits and low private saving in the U.S., as people only slowly adjusted their spending to the slowdown in real growth. In the discussion it was argued, however, that the productivity shifts were unlikely to be a source for the large economic fluctuations we have seen, simply be-cause the timing of these shocks has not coincided with the big fluc-tuations. Stanley Fischer mentioned in particular that the big swings in the 1980s were not related to marked productivity slowdowns.

Third, in the discussion it was mentioned that the real supply shocks may not have been entirely exogenous. For example, the likelihood of oil shocks may increase when the world economy is in a boom. In fact, both oil shocks occurred during boom periods in the world economy.

B. Changes in the Magnitude of Economic Fluctuations

The second main point about which there was substantial consensus was that the size of the economic *fluctuations* in output and inflation have been smaller in many countries—by large amounts in some cases—during the 1970s and 1980s, in comparison with the period of the 1950s and 1960s. The breakpoint for this comparison—the early 1970s—coin-cides with three big events and therefore interpretation is difficult. The three events are: the change from fixed to flexible exchange rates, the end of the very high growth periods in Japan and Western Europe, and the start of the period when supply shocks were of greater im-portance.

The most notable reduction in the size of output fluctuations is in Japan. While the Japanese performance is an "outlier," the decline is also noticeable in West Germany and in France. Under the fixed ex-change-rate system, Japan had the largest fluctuations in output among all the countries examined here. Under floating exchange rates Japan had the smallest output fluctuations. Japan moved from the worst, in terms of this measure of performance, to the very best.

This finding emerges from many of the papers presented at the conference. Michael Parkin's paper demonstrates the reduced output variability, as do the statistical time series prepared by the Institute. Allan Meltzer's keynote address emphasized the greater stability in some countries, especially Japan since 1973. Stanley Fischer's study also emphasized the lower output fluctuations in Japan as compared with the other countries, although his study is more of a "cross-country" analysis, looking only at the period since 1973, and not a comparison with the earlier period.

C. Changes in the Variability of the Monetary Instruments

In an effort to make inferences about the cause of the reduction in the variability of economic fluctuations in some countries, several authors examined the variability of the instruments of monetary policy. This examination uncovered the third key observation about which there seemed to be much agreement at the conference: there is evidence that the reduction in macroeconomic variability is associated with the reduction in the variability of the policy instruments—in particular in the reduction in the variability of money growth. Again, the reduction is for the period since 1973 in comparison with the period before 1973. And again, Japan is the best example of this association. The variability of money growth in Japan was lower—much lower—in the post-1973 period than before. The Institute's time series chart on money growth and output growth in Japan shows this most vividly. The association is not so strong in the other countries, but there is no question that the several countries that went from high to low variability of economic fluctuations also tended to go from high to low variability of money growth.

There was some disagreement, however, about whether the evidence showed that *within the same time period*—in particular the 1970s and 1980s—there was an association across countries between the variability of economic fluctuations and the variability of the policy instruments. Stanley Fischer noted in his comparison of four countries that stability of the money supply was not necessarily related to the stability of real output fluctuations. On the other hand, in his paper, Michael Parkin says: "There is a significant relationship across countries between the variability of real output growth and the variability of money growth . . . . The only country dummies that are significant are those for Canada and France in the growth rates. None of the country dummies are significant in the innovations." There appears, therefore, to be some disagreement about whether for the period since 1973 there is any evidence that countries that have had more stable monetary

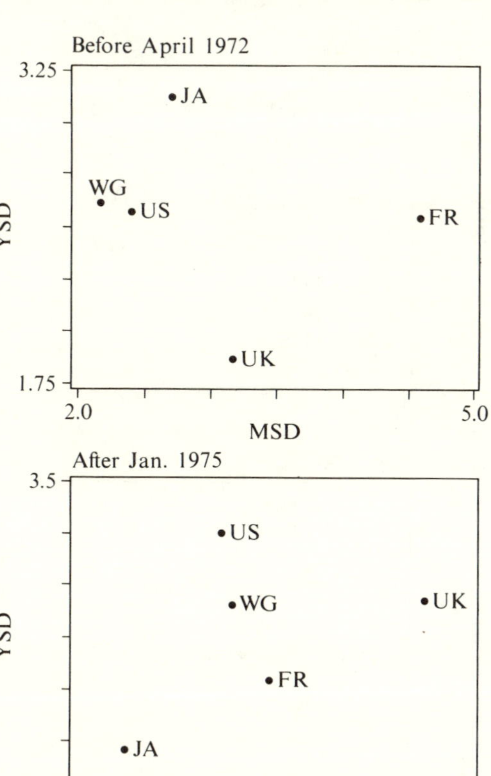

Figure 2.1
Real Output Growth Variability (YSD) and Money Growth Variability
(MSD): before April 1972 and after January 1975.
Source: Institute for Monetary and Economic Studies, Bank of Japan.
Statistical analysis prepared for this paper.

aggregates have also had more stable economic growth.

In order to examine this question in light of this disagreement, it
may be helpful to look at Figures 2.1 and 2.2. Figure 2.1 is based
on variability measures prepared by the Institute for Monetary and
Economic Studies. Figure 2.2 is based on Michael Parkin's growth-rate
variability measure. Both figures are scatter diagrams that illustrate
the relation, across countries and for two different periods of time,
between the variability of real output growth and the variability
of money growth. The two periods are before and after the early
1970s. The top diagram in both Figure 2.1 and Figure 2.2 shows the

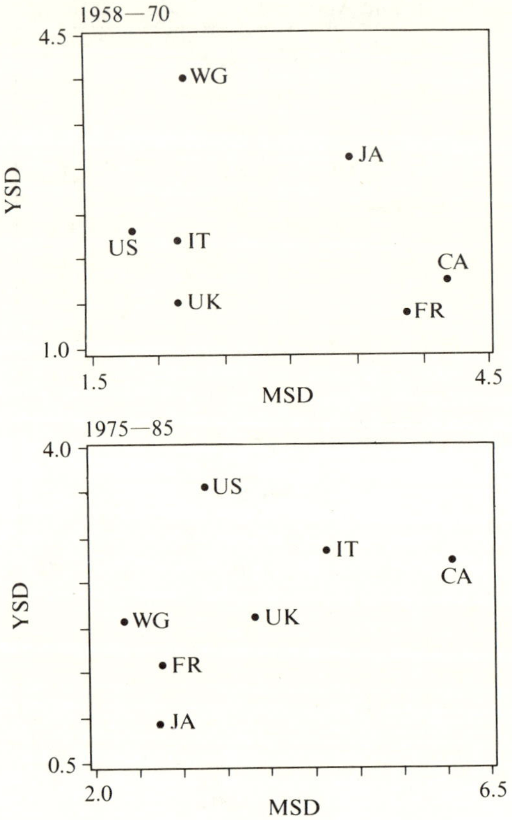

Figure 2.2
Real Output Growth Variability (YSD) and Money Growth Variability (MSD): before 1970 and after 1975.
Source: Michael Parkin's paper in this volume.

variability in the earlier period, while the bottom diagram shows the variability in the later period. Just glancing at these diagrams reveals little systematic relationship between money growth variability and real output variability across the countries during either period. What is evident is the reduction in variability from one period to the next, which I noted above. For example, from the earlier to the later period, the variability both of real output growth and of money growth was reduced in Japan.

Given this visual representation of the data, how then does Michael Parkin come to the conclusion stated above, that "there is a significant relationship across countries between the variability of real output growth and the variability of money growth?" In order to answer this question, I replicated Parkin's pooled time-series and regression results that lead to this conclusion. The dependent variable in the regression is the variance of real output growth, and the key "independent" variable is the variance of money growth. The other independent variables are dummy variables. The regression is a pooling of data over three periods (1958 through 1970, 1971 through 1975, and 1976 through 1985) and over seven countries. Hence, there are 21 data points. Parkin places six dummy variables in the regression for the seven countries and two time dummies for the three time periods, leaving 11 degrees of freedom.

Parkin's finding of a significant relationship among the countries is evident in the significant coefficient for the variance of money growth that he obtains in this pooled regression. However, while only two of the dummy variables are significant, the dummy variables as a group turn out to play a crucial role in his finding. I believe this role of the dummy variables may reconcile the disagreement I have noted.

To show this, I simply ran Parkin's growth rate regression with the country dummies omitted. Without the dummy variables, the significance of the relationship between money growth variability and output growth variability completely disappears. The coefficient for money variability drops from .41 to .13 and the t-statistic drops to the 1.1 value, indicating that the coefficient is insignificantly different from zero. Moreover, the reduction in the R-square falls from 60% to only 11%, showing that almost all of the cross-country explanatory power of the regression has come from the dummy variables.

My point in looking at the regression without the dummy variables is to reconcile Michael Parkin's data with the results presented by Stanley Fischer. Examined in this way, Parkin's data show no "cross-country" relationship between monetary variability and real output variability. In this sense his data are telling the same story as Stanley Fischer's data. The relationship between money variability and real output variability that Parkin's dummy variable regressions show is simply the same reduction in variability within single countries over time that I have already noted. There is no evidence of a significant association across countries during a given time period.

In my view, the dummy variables in Parkin's regressions are not serving simply to let the intercepts differ in a relationship about which there is independent cross-sectional variation. The variation other than that captured by the dummy variables is created by splitting the sample period into three periods. Put somewhat differently, without breaking up his data into different time periods, Parkin could not hope to obtain a cross-country association. In one time period, country dummy variables would of course explain everything!

In my view, therefore, the results should not give the impression that simply by using a more stable monetary instrument policymakers can achieve more stable macroeconomic performance. In this sense I would say that the conclusion of Stanley Fischer on this issue is correct.

In any case, there are, of course, problems with drawing inferences from these associations. James Tobin mentioned that the correlation between instrument variability and output variability could be spurious, and Robert Barro pointed out that the deviations of money growth from the stated monetary targets discussed by Stanley Fischer could simply indicate differences in forecasting abilities at the different central banks.

I think the possibility of spurious correlation is greater when the relationship between instrument stability and output stability occurs over two different points in time. There are many different things that could have changed between those two different periods of time. For a cross section of countries at the same period of time, one might at least hope that the shocks and economic environment are similar across countries, and thereby worry less about spurious correlation owing to omitted factors.

D. Relation between Fiscal and Current Account Deficits

The fourth key fact relating to economic performance is the strong relationship between fiscal deficits and current account deficits in the 1980s. Growing current-account deficits in the U.S. have been associated with growing fiscal deficits. Growing current-account surpluses in Japan and West Germany have been associated with shrinking fiscal deficits. These trends in the 1980s come out most clearly in the Institute's statistical calculations and tend to confirm standard theoretical results in most macroeconomic models.

In Jeffrey Sachs's simulation analysis, he examined whether these changes in fiscal deficits could explain the changes in the current account in the U.S. and Japan in the early 1980s. He concluded that the changes in fiscal deficits could explain virtually all of the changes in the current account during this period. However, Sachs's approach was criticized by several conference participants. Edwin Truman criticized the simulation analysis for ignoring everything else but the fiscal deficits. In particular, he suggested that the movements of monetary policy in the early 1980s were a factor that could not be ignored.

Robert Barro criticized the analysis for focusing only on one period, and for not examining how the model would explain the relationship between fiscal deficits and current account deficits in other periods. Both Allan Meltzer and James Tobin commented that the U.S. fiscal deficit was only part of the explanation of the U.S. current deficit.

Hence, from the results presented at this conference one cannot conclude that changes in government fiscal deficits have been the sole cause of the large current account deficits in the U.S. and the current account surplus in Japan and Germany. But fiscal deficits have certainly been a factor, and reducing the fiscal deficit in the U.S. at this time will certainly improve the U.S. current account.

E. Making Inferences from the Empirical Regularities

What inferences do the data permit concerning macroeconomic policy or macroeconomic behavior? Let me consider three questions.

Fixed versus Flexible Exchange Rates?

It seems safe to say that these results demonstrate that the move to flexible exchange rates since the early 1970s did not necessarily worsen macroeconomic performance. In fact, in some countries the macroeconomic performance has improved dramatically. It is just not possible with these data to make the case that flexible exchange rates have made things worse. My reading of the data is that flexible exchange rates have made things better.

Wage-Price Rigidities or Market Clearing Theories?

Michael Parkin mentioned that the empirical results in his paper showed that "the sticky price theory [i.e., sticky wages or labor contracts] of the cycle is rejected while the class of theories based on market-clearing assumptions is not." Some doubts about the statistical analysis on which this conclusion was based emerged from the discussion, however. As John Scadding and Edward Bomhoff noted, making inferences about the dynamic relations between prices and output in Parkin's statistical analysis is questionable with the second differencing that was used. In addition, it was pointed out by James Tobin that the theories Parkin was testing were originally stipulated as explaining the deviations of real output from normal or natural levels, not as explaining the growth rates.

In fact, some people at the conference pointed out that the data are evidence that sticky wages and prices are playing a role. Professor Yōichi Shinkai and Jeffrey Sachs both pointed out that the greater flexibility of wages in Japan, compared with the U.S. and Europe, could be a reason for the greater output stability in Japan. The importance of nominal wage behavior in explaining why diverse countries performed so differently in the last 10 years was also emphasized in Stanley Fischer's presentation.

In sum, therefore, people seemed to see at least as much evidence in these data in favor of the sticky-wage or -price view of the cycle as against this view.

Do Stable Monetary Instruments Imply Stable Macro Variables?

Finally, as I mentioned above, there was some disagreement about the role of monetary stability in generating real output stability. The reduction in output and inflation variability in Japan is clearly associated with the reduction in monetary variability. But it is clear that merely stabilizing the growth rate of the money supply will not necessarily guarantee stable real output growth. Of the countries examined in the 1970s and 1980s, the U.S. has had one of the best records for small variability of money growth, but one of the worse records for large variability of output growth.

Allan Meltzer emphasized that the lack of a relationship between low variability of money growth and low variability of output growth observed in some countries (in particular the U.S.) must be assessed within a framework that allows for fluctuations in velocity. He also mentioned that the correlation between velocity and money growth was related to the credibility of the central bank. A central bank with high credibility could permit a temporary increase in money growth without consequences for inflation and output.

II. Analytical Results

I will focus on three important theoretical results developed in papers at the conference: the effects of highly mobile capital, the distinction between physical capital mobility and financial capital mobility, and the appropriate policy rule to deal with economies with large "IS" versus large "LM" shocks.

A. The Effects of Highly Mobile Capital

The assumption of nearly perfect international capital mobility has been a key feature of all the theoretical papers presented at the conference, including the Sachs paper, the Niehans paper, and the Fukuda-Hamada paper. There was some discussion about the adequacy of this assumption and its omission of risk premiums. John Makin also noted that there is an asymmetry in arbitrage due to the different tax treatment in the different countries, which is ignored by the perfect capital-mobility assumption. However, no workable alternatives to the simple theoretical assumption of perfect capital mobility were proposed.

What are the implications of the highly mobile capital in these models? Jeffrey Sachs showed in his simulations that monetary policy has a relatively small impact on other countries with highly mobile capital and flexible exchange rates. In his comments on the Sachs paper, Professor Komiya mentioned that this property was also a feature of several other recent studies of perfect capital mobility. I think it is a potentially important result, and have demonstrated it in my own work (Carlozzi and Taylor 1985). It suggests the possibility of conducting monetary policy relatively independently in different countries under flexible exchange rates.

It is also important to note that with perfect capital mobility a fiscal expansion will *appreciate* the currency. This result should be of particular importance now as a large fiscal expansion is being planned for Japan. This result was emphasized by Jeffrey Sachs.

This currency appreciation associated with fiscal expansion was discussed in James Tobin's opening remarks. If in fact there is a fiscal expansion in Japan, then there will be upward pressure on the yen. If this appreciation of the yen is to be avoided, then monetary policy must change. The Bank of Japan can expand, putting downward pressure on Japanese interest rates and the yen, or the Federal Reserve and other central banks can contract. If sterilized intervention has little effect, then these are the only two possibilities. This is the implication of the models. As Tobin said in his keynote address, his view is that the Bank of Japan should expand rather than the Fed contract.

B. Gestation Lags and Physical Capital Immobility

Jürg Niehans's paper began by studying the effects of fiscal policy changes on capital flows, in a model in which physical capital was mobile between countries. However, by introducing gestation lags he also developed results for less-than-complete physical capital mobility caused by the simple fact that capital takes a period of time to build—there is a gestation lag. Niehans also showed that the effects of policy would be quite different if gestation lags were different in different countries. His theoretical analysis focused on a case where one country has no gestation lags and the other country has gestation lags. This is an extreme characterization, of course, and was used for analytical convenience.

More generally, both countries would have gestation lags but possibly of different lengths. Such differences in gestation lags are a potentially important reason why fiscal and monetary policies may have different effects in different countries. If such differences are large, then imposing similar monetary policies on different countries—as would be implied by a strict version of fixed exchange rates—would be suboptimal. Of course, before drawing such an inference one would need empirical evidence for differences in gestation lags.

C. Optimal Policy Rules to Deal with Shocks

Both the Barro and the Fukuda-Hamada papers delve into the question of how policy should respond to disturbances when there are both IS and LM disturbances. As many people pointed out in the discussion, the issues here are similar to William Poole's famous analysis. In the Barro paper, the focus is on the closed economy and the key result is that when shocks to the LM curve are large it is better to smooth out interest rate fluctuations, but when IS shocks are large it is better to let interest rates fluctuate and thereby smooth out the fluctuations in aggregate demand. There is an important innovation in the Fukuda-Hamada paper, in my view, in that this same type of Poole result is shown to hold when there are country-specific shocks to the IS and LM curves. When there are country-specific shocks to LM curves, they show that smoothing interest rates and exchange rates is a desirable objective. When there are large country-specific shocks to the IS curves, then interest rate and exchange rate variability is desirable.

Since the Barro and Fukuda-Hamada results are so reminiscent of the Poole analysis, much of the discussion related the results back to issues associated with the Poole analysis. There were many useful comments that need to be digested by policymakers in order to interpret the results of these papers. Michael Parkin mentioned that when there are only two types of shocks, things are easy. But when there are also supply shocks, one gets more ambiguous results. It is not so easy to make the Poole classification, and in some cases one needs a social welfare function. James Tobin emphasized that the specific time period one is talking about is very important. Are these months, weeks, quarters? He also mentioned that it is not realistic or necessary to think of the responses as one extreme or the other, but rather as a compromise which involves some degree of interest-rate smoothing. William White emphasized that the two-country results are artificial in that the countries are not symmetric, as in the Fukuda-Hamada paper.

In his presentation of the Fukuda-Hamada paper, Mr. Hayakawa mentioned that what is needed is an empirical treatment along the lines of the Barro paper. Such an empirical treatment would address some of the issues mentioned by Parkin, Tobin, and White. In other words, what is needed is a joining up of what Fukuda-Hamada have done and what Barro has done. I have been working on such a research project, one which applies an empirical approach to the optimal policy response in an international setting (Taylor 1987). It might therefore be useful for me to briefly summarize the results of that analysis and relate them to these two papers.

The issue is that in order to make some assessments about the desirability of one international policy regime or another using the Fukada-Hamada approach, one needs an empirical measure of the size of the shocks and the size of the parameters of the model. Barro's approach provides for this in a simple model of a closed economy. Otherwise we will be forever saying, "If this shock is big, do this; if that shock is big, do something else; and don't forget the correlation between the shocks and the relative size of the slopes of the IS and LM curves." An empirical approach gets around this problem in principle by obtaining real-world measures of the parameters and of the shocks.

My empirical approach starts with an quarterly empirical model of the G-7 countries estimated over the last 15 years. I take this model and simulate it over the next 15 years using parameters and the distribution of shocks that I have estimated. I do this simulation over several different regimes, one of which is a flexible exchange-rate regime and another of which is a fixed exchange-rate regime with the U.S. as the center country, and Japan, West Germany, and the other countries using monetary policy to peg the exchange rate.

What I find is that the performance of some countries deteriorates by a large amount under the fixed exchange-rate system in comparison with the flexible exchange-rate system. In particular, the variability of output and prices in Japan and West Germany is much larger under the fixed exchange-rate stochastic simulation than under the flexible exchange-rate simulation. Moreover, one can easily see the reason for this in the simulations: the variability of money growth in Japan and West Germany becomes much larger when exchange rates are fixed with the U.S. as the center country.

These results can explain the empirical observations I noted above, that the variability of output growth in Japan and West Germany was higher in the fixed exchange-rate period of Bretton Woods. The higher variability of money growth during that period is also explained by the simulations. The empirical results confirm the theoretical possibility that the flexible exchange-rate system has given some independence to the monetary authorities. I think the results are also suggestive of what might come out of a linking together of the empirical and theoretical ideas in the Barro and the Fukuda-Hamada papers.

III. Policy Implications

In Figure 2.3 I summarize, in two simple charts, the macroeconomic performances of the United States, Japan, and Europe in the 1970s and 1980s that we have discussed at the conference. The charts show quarterly observations on the *levels* of real output. Since these are the raw numbers, there should be no issues about the method of detrending, or about the focus on levels, rates of change, or deviations. As was mentioned in the discussion, for the purposes of comparing economic performance the levels are perhaps the most reliable indicator.

The top panel of Figure 2.3 is a pairwise comparison of Japan with the U.S., and the bottom panel is a pairwise comparison of Japan with Europe. The charts illustrate rather dramatically the smooth performance of Japan compared with the volatile performance of the U.S. and Europe. Compared with the United States, output in Japan looks as smooth as U.S. potential GNP! It is hard to project any more stability. The most noticeable difference in the chart since the early 1970s between Japan and the U.S. was the big expansion in the U.S. in the late 1970s, followed by the big slump in the U.S. in the early 1980s. Such fluctuations are not noticeable for Japan. This one large swing alone accounts for much of the difference in variability between the U.S. and Japan as reported in the standard deviations.

The bottom chart uses the same scheme to compare Japan with Europe. Again, compared with Japan there was a big expansion in the late 1970s in Europe, followed by a slump in the 1980s. Compared with the U.S., the recovery in Europe was very slow. That slow growth rate in the 1980s contributes to the poor performance in Europe.

A. What Were the Policy Mistakes?

Let me first ask, with reference to these two charts, what were the

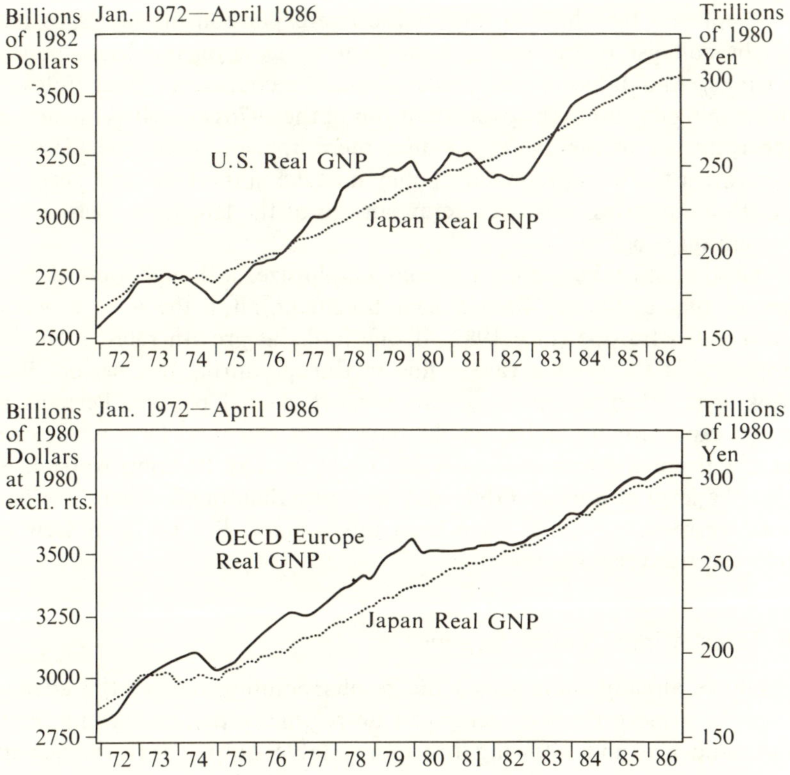

Figure 2.3
Comparison of Real Output Fluctuations in Japan, the United States, and Europe, January 1972 through April 1986.
Source: *OECD Quarterly National Accounts*, No. 4, 1986.

policy mistakes to which people have pointed at the conference? In his paper, Stanley Fischer points to a mistake associated with the U.S. expansion in the 1980s: "In retrospect, it is clear that U.S. monetary policy in the period between the oil shocks was too expansionary, even though money growth rates did not rise much. Rather, the rapid growth and rising inflation were accompanied by an increasing velocity of circulation (the case of the missing money)." Andrew Crockett also emphasized in one of his remarks that policy was too expansionary in the 1977–78 period, perhaps because the slowdown in the trend of potential GNP was not correctly assessed. Edwin Truman, in criticizing Jeffrey Sachs for not including all the important factors in his examination of fiscal policy in the 1980s, said, "The failures of the 1980s echo the failure of the 1970s, and any analysis which ignores this is incomplete," by which he meant the overexpansion in the 1970s led to the collapse in the 1980s. Again, the focus is on this same policy mistake. And James Tobin spoke about the courage of Paul Volcker in bringing an end to the overexpansion of the 1970s as well as in ending the recession of the 1980s. In sum, there appears to be considerable agreement that a big monetary policy mistake in the U.S., and perhaps in other countries, was the overexpansion of the late 1970s before the second oil shock.

Another mistake which I would emphasize, although only a few people such as Stanley Fischer have touched on it, is the slow recovery in Western Europe since 1982. If one looks at growth rates, it might appear that the growth rate is fine in Europe during this period. But looking at absolute levels reveals a more dismal picture. Perhaps a more expansionary policy could have been pursued. Of course, one of the problems with that view, and why it may be controversial, is that the level of normal GNP may be lower than implied here, so that a faster recovery would have been inflationary. But my own view is that the recovery was too slow.

B. International Policy Regime

I have already summarized the results pointing toward the advantages of a more flexible exchange-rate regime in permitting monetary independence and allowing for more stable output performance in some countries. A look at the "policy mistake," discussed above, in terms of the simple picture in Figure 2.3 brings home in a simple, intuitive fashion the fact that the flexible exchange-rate system has been an advantage for some countries. With flexible exchange rates, Japan did not have to go through the boom-bust cycle brought on by the overexpansion of the late 1970s. This simple picture, along with the more formal analysis, indicates to me the advantages of a more flexible exchange-rate regime.

C. Which Policy Rule?

There was surprisingly little debate about the rules-versus-discretion issue at the conference. Allan Meltzer opened the conference with the suggestion that we focus on policy rules, possibly active rules, and there appeared to be no dispute registered.

Unfortunately, there was much less agreement on what the form of the policy rule should be. Allan Meltzer proposed a simple rule for money growth. In my view the rule makes only a very crude correction for velocity, and the fact that it focuses solely on rates of change rather than on levels means that it might generate recoveries that are too drawn out, or booms that are too long or inflationary.

As an alternative, Stanley Fischer mentioned nominal GNP rules. A nominal GNP rule, if strictly adhered to, can also lead to problems if it focuses on rates of change rather than levels. The focus on rates of change in the nominal GNP rule that Fischer attributes to the Bundesbank may have contributed to the slow recovery mentioned above. One needs to have some periods where the nominal GNP growth rate is faster in order to recover adequately from slumps.

I like to think of the ideal policy rule as minimizing the deviations of real output from normal or natural levels, with a correction for inflation. If inflation picks up, the central bank should contract and let the economy drift below normal until inflation dies down. The main difficulty with this rule is determining what is the normal or natural level of output.

D. International Policy Coordination

Finally, what are the policy implications with respect to international policy coordination? If one accepts the view that there are advantages to fluctuating exchange rates, then to some extent the policy coordination issue is easier. There is less need for policy coordination if exchange rates are to fluctuate freely, in the sense that monetary policy can be independent. This doesn't mean, of course, that coordination is not necessary.

Perhaps the most important question for future research is, What should be the appropriate degree of monetary policy coordination when exchange rates are permitted to float? For example, perhaps there should be more systematic coordination with respect to the operating strategies in the different central banks. By operating strategies I simply mean the mechanism through which the short-term interest-rate targets are moved around for the purpose of controlling money growth or nominal GNP. Presently, there is some coordination—occasional telephone calls about changes in the Fed Funds rate—but more could be done on a routine basis. Such coordination would probably require some disclosure of the policy rule that the monetary authorities are aiming for, because the coordination would require statements between central banks about what the policy intentions are.

This coordination would be useful even if policy focused only on domestic goals. Simply announcing your intention for a change in the funds rate or a call money rate to the other central banks on a routine basis and receiving comments would be an important first step. As a more basic first step, perhaps there could be more coordination of the research activities of the staffs of the different central banks.

Finally, with respect to fiscal policy, none of the results of this conference indicate that the coordination of fiscal policy is not important. On the contrary, the joint easing of fiscal policy in Japan and tightening of fiscal policy in the U.S., in order to help address the current account imbalances, was mentioned by many participants at the conference as just the type of coordination that we need now.

References

Carlozzi, Nicholas, and Taylor, John B. 1985. International Capital Mobility and the Coordination of Monetary Policy Rules. In Bandar, Jagdeep S., ed., *Exchange Rate Management under Uncertainty*. Cambridge, Mass: MIT Press.

Taylor, John B. 1987. An Econometric Evaluation of International Monetary Policy Rules: Fixed versus Flexible Exchange Rates. Unpublished manuscript, Stanford University.

Two Keynote Speeches and an Introductory Presentation

3

Are There Reliable Adjustment Mechanisms?

James Tobin

I. Introduction

Once upon a time economics students of my generation learned the theory of international payments adjustment. We marveled at the natural mechanisms which, in principle at least, corrected the imbalances that triggered them. The subjects, even the words, still appear in modern textbooks (e.g. Dornbusch 1980), although they have been swallowed in "open economy macroeconomics," or in what might be called "multi-national macroeconomics" were that subject advanced enough to merit a label. Both the world and the models economists build to model it are vastly more complex than students of my day were led to believe and did believe. Nevertheless, exploiting the license a keynoter has for imprecision and impressionism, I propose to review several possible adjustment mechanisms and to consider their applicability in today's world.

I shall in the end be skeptical that there are any reliable mechanisms. This conclusion, I suspect, is widely shared—if rarely voiced—among economists, and especially among practitioners and policy makers in international finance. Perhaps it is a premise of this very conference. The universal call for coordination of national macroeconomic policies betrays a strong suspicion that absent such coordination the system will not equilibrate itself. The suspicion might be that the natural, automatic mechanisms are weak or perverse, or that they are frequently obstructed and perverted by unconcerted national policies.

With "endogenous politicians," in Assar Lindbeck's phrase, it may be difficult to distinguish policy responses from market responses. Several endogenous politicians are gathering at Venice this month, and effective coordination is not likely to be one of their responses. In the old days, in contrast, the mechanisms of payments adjustment were not thought to leave much room for discretionary national policies, concerted or disparate, for good or for ill.

I shall discuss both short-run and long-run adjustments, to both nominal and real shocks. The two distinctions are interrelated; nominal shocks and adjustments are relatively more important in short runs.

II. *The Necessity of International Price Adjustments*

In those old days to which I referred, the major short-run adjustments to payments imbalances were thought to occur through absolute price changes in deficit and surplus countries, which spelled relative price changes between those countries. Keynesian theory added, in the international context as in the analysis of closed economies, adjustments due to variations of output and effective demand. But for reasons of which I shall remind you below, this mechanism was thought to be inadequate by itself.

Emphasis was concentrated on the adjustments of current accounts, probably because capital movements—other than official settlements and short-term trade finance—were limited by national controls and other barriers. The problem was posed like this: Suppose trade imbalance arises because of changes in comparative advantage—differential changes in tastes, technologies, resources in the trading countries—or because of disparate changes in monetary stocks or velocities. What happens to restore balance?

The oldest and simplest story was the specie flow mechanism of the gold standard, with gold essentially a common international money. Gold would flow from the deficit country to its trading partners in surplus. According to the quantity theory of money, prices would fall in the former country and rise in the latter. If the shock were real, the change in the countries' relative prices would shift international demands for goods and services from surplus countries to the deficit country. These shifts would eliminate the imbalance. If the shock were permanent, the new relative prices would be permanent. Once achieved, they would sustain a new equilibrium in international payments. This story assumes that the countries were producing different goods, imperfect substitutes.

The mechanism is essentially the same in fixed-exchange-rate systems, in which governments, their central banks, and private banking systems augment money supplies beyond national quantities of gold or other international media. Recall the gold exchange system or Bretton

Woods. However, the links to gold or international monetary reserves are looser. Banks and individual agents can substitute local paper money, and central banks and governments can allow or engineer such substitutions. Thus countries—especially and asymmetrically, surplus countries—can postpone or avoid the local price consequences of payments imbalances. "Rules of the game" arose to strengthen the price adjustment mechanism against the capacities and incentives of nations to weaken it. But the rules were informal and frequently honored in the breach.

Banking and central banking make monetary shocks possible. The price adjustment mechanism is supposed to work for them too. A local monetary expansion, or rise in velocity for that matter, raises local prices and generates a trade deficit, which drains gold or other international reserves. The local money supply is restricted until relative international prices are restored to their unchanged equilibrium. The local price increase is mostly, but not entirely, transient. When the adjustment is complete, prices throughout the world have all been raised in the same proportion, the amount necessary to absorb the increment to world money supply due to the initial local monetary shock.

This is essentially the "monetary theory of the balance of payments," even though its modern version was expounded for a one-good purchasing-power-parity world. (That assumption does not seem to me an attractive foundation for international payments theory. It provides no basis for international trade in the first place, except by excess "absorption" in one country and deficient absorption elsewhere. That phenomenon, as well as the neutral adjustment to monetary shock, can be treated without insisting on the "law of one price" in international trade.)

The price adjustment mechanism is also central to the correction of imbalances under floating, market-determined rates of exchange among fiat national currencies. The deficit country's currency depreciates against the surplus countries' currencies. The same changes in international relative prices occur in response to a real shock, possibly but not necessarily without any changes in nominal prices in the several economies. Likewise, in the case of a monetary shock, a local rise in prices robs it of any real domestic consequences, while the exchange depreciation preserves the equilibrium relation of the country's international prices to the rest of the world.

The key to the equivalence is, of course, the assumption that nominal monetary quantities, prices, and exchange rates, are neutral; national moneys are veils; relative and absolute prices are perfectly flexible. It is hard to understand why anyone who believes that assumption—the "classical dichotomy," if you like—prefers one national or international monetary regime to another; cares whether adjustments of international relative prices are made, or prevented, by movements of local prices or of exchange rates; or worries about inflation and deflation.

To this, I am aware, can be voiced the objection that commodity money and fiat money differ. The equivalence just discussed would apply only to alternative regimes with fiat moneys. Under the gold standard, changes in prices of other commodities in one country or in the world do have real effects, via the relative price and production of gold. I think this is not a matter of important substance, except for gold-producing countries.

When classical or Walrasian assumptions supporting the irrelevance of nominal variables are dropped, choices among monetary regimes and international rules of the game become consequential. The case for floating rates was that changes in nominal exchange rates are the quickest and least painful way of bringing about equilibrating changes in international relative prices. The assumption is that the inertia of nominal wage and price paths allows nominal appreciations and depreciations to be real, while the same inertia slows or frustrates the same price adjustments in the fixed-parity regime. Even if discrete changes in parities can be made, they are crisis decisions inviting speculation before and after; they are usually too long delayed; they often undershoot and sometimes overshoot.

Tradeoffs there always are. Flexible rates can emit false as well as true signals. Speculative movements can change relative prices between countries when no change is basically called for, and the volatility of rates can leave traders confused about the relative prices which should enter their calculations and decisions on production, sales, and purchases. Unfortunately "variable peg" regimes, temporarily fixed rates, do not really eliminate these problems. A truly common international currency would do so, but we are far from the commonalities of institutions, laws, taxation, and politics that would make a universal money possible.

III. Obstacles to Price Adjustment Mechanisms

Under floating rates since 1973 nominal exchange rates have moved a great deal, and for the most part real exchange rates have moved with them. Nonetheless I shall argue that the major governments, the economic summit powers, are reluctant to let price adjustment mechanisms work, at any rate to work well enough to handle the tasks that now confront them. In the United States, West Germany (which calls the macroeconomic tune for the European Community and Monetary System), the United Kingdom, and Japan, governments and central banks are quite determined to stick to their nationally chosen paths of domestic price indexes.

The U.K. has for several years geared its monetary policy to hold an exchange rate that puts moderate disinflationary pressure on its prices. Both the big surplus countries, Germany and Japan, are unwilling to deviate from macroeconomic policies that have rewarded them with actual deflation. The United States authorities are afraid of a further depreciation of the dollar because dollar prices of imports and other internationally traded goods would rise.

These attitudes are by no means altogether new. They stood in the way of corrective devaluations and revaluations in the Bretton Woods era. For example, in the early 1960s the United States was running official settlements deficits, though its current account was in surplus. The U.S. inflation rate was only 2% per year, and the economy was not fully employed. Germany and other surplus countries were unwilling either to let their accumulations of reserves show up in higher prices or to revalue their currencies upward. Either course could have given the U.S. a larger trade surplus to match its capital outflows and unilateral transfers. The impasse was not resolved until a less auspicious time, when the Nixon Administration ran out of patience and killed the Bretton Woods system.

An important obstacle to international price adjustment is epidemic confusion between price levels and inflation rates. Once-for-all rises in price indexes do not necessarily spell continuing inflation or acceleration of prices. These one-shot increases often come from shocks that lift particular prices, supply shocks that alter relative prices The oil price hikes of the 1970s, of unhappy memory, are major examples. Likewise, the recent declines when cartel discipline weakened made pleasant headlines. In both cases, the events were not the kind that can regularly recur year after year. The transitional rates of inflation, or of disinflation in 1986, were bound to be temporary. Nonetheless, the OPEC shocks of the 1970s were opposed by monetary restriction as if they were demand-pull inflations.

In 1981–85, the U.S. enjoyed the price-lowering effects of dollar appreciation. Those effects have to be reversed to correct the U.S. trade deficit, but the domestic price index increases due to exchange depreciation scare the Federal Reserve—even though they are once-for-all, even though the upward price adjustments are in effect repayment of downward adjustments borrowed from the rest of the world in the earlier 1980s. The likely policy consequence appears to be that the dollar is to be defended by higher interest rates, holding back an already sluggish economy. One objective is to offset the increases of import prices with extra domestic disinflation. A weightier objective is to guard against the risk that exchange depreciation and higher import prices trigger a price-wage-price spiral.

The examples of the 1970s show that this is not an unreasonable concern. However, running an economy on the assumption that price indexes can never be allowed to rise, regardless of the amount of slack in the economy, regardless of how low the underlying domestic wage and price inflation rates are, is a recipe for stagnation. Moreover, central bank sensitivities to these price shocks are asymmetric. Japan and Europe today, like the U.S. in 1981–85, accept external contributions to disinflation or deflation without engineering compensating expansionary measures. The ratchet effect is to hold down both world inflation and world expansion.

Policy stances are anticipated in the behavior of private agents. That is a lesson of experience as well as of modern economic theory. Financial markets react negatively when monthly inflation news is bad because they have learned that central banks tighten on such news. Indeed, equity markets have become so obsessed by the prospect that central bank concern to prevent or arrest inflation will raise interest rates that they respond negatively to good news about real economic growth and profits, and positively to news of sluggishness and possible recession.

A principal argument for floating rates before 1971 was, as I observed above, that movements of nominal exchange rates would be, compared to movements of domestic nominal wages and prices, a quicker and less painful way of accomplishing necessary changes in international relative prices. This argument assumes, of course, that inertia in nominal wages and prices prevents or delays those adjustments at fixed exchange rates. The same inertia is expected to translate nominal exchange rate movements into effective adjustments in real exchange rates. Clearly this mechanism is disabled to the extent there are quick feedbacks from import prices (in domestic currency) into economy-wide wages and prices. Policies to avoid such feedbacks would improve the adjustment mechanism, just as policies to increase the sensitivity of local prices to market supply/demand conditions would improve the mechanism under fixed rates. Policies to stabilize wage and price paths, to avoid feedbacks from international prices, may be essential to successful devaluations or depreciations. Indexing should be minimized, and at the least exclude compensation for terms-of-trade effects. The case for incomes policies, e.g. guideposts with sticks or carrots to induce compliance, is strengthened under floating rates.

IV. Adjustments in Effective Demand and Absorption

International relative prices are one avenue of adjustment. Variations of output, real income, and employment are another. In the short run, these arise from fluctuations in effective demand, given some inertia or stickiness in nominal wages and prices. A shock that unbalances trade lowers demand in the deficit country, and the consequent decline in incomes and output lowers imports. Likewise the positive impulse to demand in the surplus countries raises their imports. Elementary multiplier theory tells us that these adjustments are far from complete, even if monetary policymakers accommodate them by holding interest rates constant. That is, the multiplier is much lower than the reciprocal of the marginal propensity to import. Imports are only one of the leakages from spending flows; saving and taxes are also important.

What would it take to eliminate a U.S. trade deficit of $150 billion a year, 3.5% of GNP? Assuming a marginal propensity to import of 0.25, twice the average propensity, it would take a GNP contraction of $600 billion, 14%, and raise unemployment well into double-digit rates. To add enough imports to erase its trade surplus, 3% of GNP and 20% of imports, Japan might need a 20% rise of GNP.

In medium and longer runs, further equilibrating mechanisms may come into play. Current account imbalances transfer wealth from deficit to surplus countries; these transfers have both wealth and portfolio effects, some on trade and some on capital movements. Consumption stimulated by the accumulation of wealth leads the surplus country to import more. On the capital account side, the country's appetite for foreign assets diminishes, and the resulting appreciation induces some correction in the trade deficit. The reverse processes in the deficit country strengthen the adjustment.

However, current account imbalances could reflect long-lasting differences among economies in saving propensities, investment opportunities, and growth rates. In this case, there is no guarantee that they will go away, and possibly no economic reason they should. Consider the following scenario: Thrifty country J saves more than it needs for investment, i.e., more than is needed to expand its capital stock given the growth of labor force and the rate of technological progress. Profligate country U, however, needs J's excess saving.

To describe their difference another way, the desired wealth/income ratio in J exceeds its desired capital/output ratio, and the difference is its wealth-owners' demand for stocks of external assets. Both domestic and foreign components of wealth will grow at J's natural rate. On the other hand, in U the desired capital/output ratio exceeds the wealth/ income ratio, the excess being capital owned abroad or in effect mortgaged to foreign creditors. If capital movements are not restricted, the returns to capital in the two countries must be equal (after allowing for trends in the real exchange rate) or anyway stand in such relation that they meet portfolio preferences of savers and borrowers in the two countries. This relationship determines the capital stock in the two countries. The exchange rate path is determined such that a current account imbalance provides the flows that meet the saving and portfolio demands on both sides. The currency of the more rapidly growing country will be appreciating. It is conceivable that a high-saving, fast-growing country eventually owns the whole capital stocks of less thrifty and more sluggish societies, but presumably the behaviors that destine this result would eventually be altered.

Rather than continue on this abstract and speculative line, which I don't really think represents the Japan/United States situation today, I turn to the concrete problems of adjustment we face right now.

V. The Adjustment Processes that Match Flows of Capital and Trade

The gross maladjustments of the 1980s have placed unparalleled burdens on the corrective mechanisms I have been discussing. The main sources of these burdens are first, the internationalization of wealth portfolios and asset markets, and second, the extreme, and extremely different, mixes of monetary and fiscal policies of the major countries. In the 1970s, the sources of the international macroeconomic problems that beset those countries were mainly external and exogenous to them, shocks of unprecedented magnitude in peacetime. In the 1980s, the external environment has been benign; national policies and the failures of coordination are much more to blame for the generally poor economic performance of this decade.

Asset markets began to be internationalized as exchange controls and capital controls were gradually abandoned after World War II.

The pace accelerated tremendously in the last decade. Communications and computer technologies facilitated international transactions and vastly lowered their costs. Multinational banks and financial enterprises multiplied. New international asset markets were born, new instruments and contracts were created, old and new national markets were linked. Deregulation of financial businesses in all countries allowed and encouraged, among other things, a burst of foreign activities. Off-shore money and credit markets in major currencies flourished. The floating exchange rate regime itself generated clients for managing positions in several currencies and countries, including speculators and arbitrageurs in cross-currency financial transactions. Finance in general became a go-go field, enlisting both the best and brightest of young technicians fresh from business schools, and latter-day entrepreneurs and big-time operators; it even became an academic growth enterprise. International finance shared in the phenomenal expansion of the industry and the profession. The sun never sets on currency markets, in which the volume of transactions in New York alone is estimated to exceed $100 billion every business day. Japanese liberalizations of portfolio investment regulations were fateful.

As we all know, a country's capital outflow (inflow) must *ex post* equal its current account surplus (deficit). Market exchange rates, interest rates, and asset values move hour by hour and day by day to convert any *ex ante* deviations from this equality to their *ex post* identity. (Official capital movements, foreign exchange purchases or sales by central banks, may on occasion be factors in this equalization. They have been substantial in recent months, evidently of the same rough magnitude as the U.S. current account deficit.) Over longer short runs, other macroeconomic variables, the ones discussed above, also play important roles.

Exchange rates, interest rates, and asset values can be moved by shocks to international demands for assets in various countries and currencies, as well as by shocks to trade and other current account items. This is the main point in discussing the current situation. Given the liquidity of financial assets in today's worldwide markets, given the intrinsic volatility of the expectations on which asset demands depend, capital account shocks can occur with much greater suddenness than changes in the determinants of trade in goods and services.

A nation's capital inflow or outflow depends positively on the expected returns on its assets relative to those in other currencies and on the expected appreciation of its exchange rate. (I remind you in passing that for an investor concerned ultimately with real returns in his or her own currency, it is the *nominal* interest differential plus the expected appreciation of the *nominal* value of the currency that matters. This reduces to concern for real returns and currency appreciation only if investors' expectations embody purchasing power parity.) The *level* of the exchange rate is much less relevant. We read in the business pages that foreign investors are buying American assets because they are bargains at the present low exchange value of the dollar. They are bargains only if the investors expect the dollar to rise. The level of the exchange rate matters only so far as its variation, like that of any asset price, alters the proportions of the portfolios of risk-averse diversifiers and induces them to shift from relatively appreciated assets.

In formulating exchange rate expectations, an investor with a long horizon will consider how the current rate differs from an equilibrium rate or path of rates. In that consideration, news about the present trade and current account imbalances is quite relevant. Anyone who thinks present U.S. current account deficits are unsustainable—presumably anyone who thinks—will have lowered his or her estimate of the future value of the dollar by observing the glacial pace of improvement of the U.S. trade position in response to the drastic dollar depreciation since mid-1985.

The list of determinants of capital account flows and stocks is different from the list of arguments a model-builder would put in functions explaining exports and imports of goods and services. For the current account, the level of the real exchange rate, in prices or labor costs, would appear, along with the national incomes of trading partners; stocks and returns on internationally held assets would determine the net flows of incomes on those assets.

Supply and demand are, Alfred Marshall taught us, some of us, blades of the same pair of scissors. Yet sometimes one blade may be the cutting edge, sometimes the other. That is the case in currency markets.

It is not too far-fetched to see the inflow of capital into dollar assets in 1981–85 as the driving force in the appreciation of the dollar. The inflow was attracted by relatively advantageous American interest rates, perhaps also by internationally contagious euphoria about the Reagan era. The inflow would have been reinforced, at least in the earlier years of the period, by the appreciation of the dollar itself. Eventually doubts of its continuation, even of its permanence, fed by ministers and central bankers at the Plaza hotel, overtook the markets.

Meanwhile the 1981–85 appreciation, together with the strong recovery of the U.S. economy relative to the stagnation in the rest of the world, brought a trade imbalance and a U.S. current account deficit matching the capital inflow. Qualitatively, the events validated economists' textbooks; quantitatively, they exceeded everybody's prior imagination.

This story is consistent with the common accusation that U.S. trade and current account deficits mirrored its outsized federal budget deficit. However, the reconciliation is more complex than the accusing pundits generally recognize. True, the budget deficit made U.S. interest rates high. But this effect occurred indirectly, through Federal Reserve monetary policy. The Fed did not raise interest rates because the Open Market Committee members were appalled by the budget numbers they read. The chain of events, I think, was more like this: Defense spending and tax cuts stimulated demand and recovery. In order to hold the expansion to a path the Fed regarded as sound and inflation-safe, the Committee kept real interest rates from falling (from their 1980–81 highs) as low as they would have been in a normal pre-Reagan recovery period. Moreover, bond markets came to expect that the deficits were chronic, not just cyclical, and would eventually either lead to inflation or collide with private demands for capital. As a result, long-term bonds yielded premiums above short rates, which made them especially attractive to foreign financial institutions and portfolio managers.

When pundits say that budget correction would have avoided or shut off the capital inflow and the trade deficit, they are right if they add that the Federal Reserve would have had to lower interest rates to keep the economy on the same path of GNP and employment.

Today we face quite a different adjustment problem. The choices available in 1981–83 are not on the menu in 1987–88. The trade deficit is stubborn. Perhaps the J-curve lags are longer than we thought. Most of the J-curve scenario may still be ahead of us. Exporters to the American market have been willing to cut margins in their own currencies rather than lose market shares. In "customer markets," buyers are slow to shift to lower-cost suppliers. Perhaps the long period of dollar overvaluation has crippled U.S. export- and import-competing industries. Some of the effects on competitiveness are irreversible, or anyway will take a long time to overcome. (Young economists are now enchanted by the fashionable, newly discovered word "hysteresis.") Evidently some underlying adverse trends in American competitiveness have proceeded apace, unrelated to but obscured by the overvaluation. Finally, the accumulation of external debt itself is reducing

U.S. net investment income from the rest of the world, which will soon become negative.[1]

Investors and portfolio managers throughout the world have, in any case, plenty of reasons to worry about the real exchange rate necessary eventually to cut the U.S. current account deficit to sustainable size. Given a large deficit that will be with us willy-nilly for some years to come, by what adjustment will the U.S. continue to attract the capital inflows to finance it? There are several possibilities.

One is that the U.S. borrows from foreign governments. After all, they like their trade surpluses and do not want to see the dollar fall in a manner that will eventually threaten their exports. They seem never to have learned how to obtain prosperity and growth driven otherwise than by export demands. Nevertheless, buying up dollars is not a way out that will appeal to the governments of surplus countries indefinitely. Like the creditors of Brazil and Mexico today, they will worry about the prospects of repayment. Nor will official borrowing on a grand scale appeal to the U.S. government. Most important, this course will sooner or later turn off the private participants in the exchange markets. Their resources vastly exceed those of the governments. Once they are turned off, the dollar will fall.

Second, the U.S. could "defend the dollar" by raising its interest rates to entice increasingly skeptical foreign lenders. The Federal Reserve has already moved cautiously in this direction, and is poised to do more. The consequence could be U.S. recession, which while curtailing American imports would have disastrous consequences throughout the world. Third World debtors would face both higher interest charges and diminished export markets.

Third, the dollar could fall until it was low enough to convince investors that its subsequent rise would reward them for holding it. Although Paul Volcker and others are frightened of a "free fall," or "hard landing," overshooting of this kind is precisely the fantasy of rational-expectations economic theorists. Get the bad news over all at once. Markets do not seem to work that way. More likely, the fall occurs over an extended interval, during which expectations and fears of its continuation are destabilizing. No one has a rational basis for calculating the dollar's equilibrium value or the degree of overshooting that determines its floor. Nevertheless, a case can be made that, instead of trying to talk the market into supporting the dollar at its present

---

[1] I am indebted to Paul Krugman and Richard Baldwin, "The Persistence of the U.S. Trade Deficit," forthcoming in *Brookings Papers on Economic Activity*, 1987:1.

rate, the officials of the several countries should welcome a rapid downward jump and intervene with rhetoric and money at a rate from which a rise in the dollar is credible.

Some combination of (2) and (3) seems the most probable chain of events.

The U.S. government, as well as many unofficial commentators, has been urging Japan and Germany, the key European economy, to adopt policies to stimulate domestic demand. Given the slack in their economies and their low, even negative, inflation rates, expansionary policies are obviously desirable. They would benefit those societies themselves and the world as a whole. I have argued that the resulting increase in U.S. exports would be insufficient itself to correct the U.S. trade deficit. Improvement in U.S. competitiveness is essential and will probably entail further dollar depreciation, as well as considerable time.

Meanwhile, expansionary policies in Japan and Europe may or may not facilitate financing of the continuing U.S. current account deficit. Fiscal stimuli, such as Japan has recently announced, would raise interest rates and diminish demands for dollar assets. Monetary expansion would help to "defend the dollar," while retarding the dollar depreciation that may eventually be necessary to correct the trade imbalance. Nevertheless, from a global viewpoint, it is desirable not to raise interest rates in major economies. An attractive compromise would be monetary accommodation of expansions in Japan and Europe, whether fiscally driven or autonomous, holding interest rates outside the U.S. at current levels.

What about that U.S. budget deficit? Isn't it the culprit? Wouldn't its removal solve the problem? As long as the U.S. current account deficit is as stubborn as it now seems, correction of the budget would not avoid the country's need for foreign credit. It would, however, remove a major internal use of the borrowed funds. Here are some round numbers: At the moment U.S. nonfederal saving is $250 billion a year and net national borrowing (current account deficit) is $150 billion. Together they are financing a federal deficit of $180 billion and net private domestic investment of $220 billion. Without a federal deficit but with the same current account deficit and foreign borrowing, the U.S. would have to raise domestic investment and/or reduce internal saving by a total of $180 billion. How? Either by a drastic low-interest monetary policy fostering a mind-boggling investment boom, or by a recession deep enough to cut saving equally severely. (This is an overstatement, because the recession would also cut imports somewhat at the same time. Also, whatever the initial revenue and expenditure measures designed to correct the budget, some of the correction would be nullified by endogenous cyclical effects.) Anyway, the investment boom alternative seems quite unlikely, perhaps impossible. The recession alternative would be disastrous at home and abroad.

The moral is this: Substantial reduction of the federal deficit is an essential part of an ultimate solution, just as it was a major initial source of the problem. But now that the external current account deficit and the equivalent borrowing are more or less frozen into place for some years, it is not prudent to melt the budget deficit much faster than the external deficit can melt. Meanwhile it is, however, prudent to legislate a schedule of measures to be phased in gradually—in my view, mainly revenue increases—that will in the end bring the budget deficit down, not to zero but to, say, 1 or 1.5% of GNP. This legislation would improve the market's view of the future of the dollar and help to attract the financing needed while the external deficit is being corrected.

Reference

Dornbusch, Rudiger. 1980. *Open Economy Macroeconomics*. New York: Basic Books.

4

On Monetary Stability and Monetary Reform

Allan H. Meltzer*

I. Introduction

The organizers of this conference have asked an important question; in my view, one of the most important questions—or more accurately, set of questions—that can be asked of economists. How do we achieve greater stability? How big are the instabilities now, and how many of them are caused, or magnified, by current policy arrangements? Do fluctuating exchange rates augment or buffer shocks arising elsewhere, or are fluctuating exchange rates an independent source of disturbance? Can monetary reforms, domestic or international, increase stability without fiscal reforms, greater stability of trade policy, and, perhaps, either changes in political systems or fewer opportunities for politicians to influence economic events?

Alas, like most big questions, these questions (and others that might be asked) are much easier to pose than to answer. It is not difficult to develop optimal policies for a world in which all prices are flexible, information is costless, policymakers relentlessly pursue the public interest—and only the public interest—and we all agree on the arguments and parameters of a social objective function. The abstract world of economic theory is useful. We rely on it to guide our thinking and to increase knowledge and understanding. Unfortunately, economic analysis has not offered, and probably cannot now offer, more than conditional answers to many of the questions. Some of the answers depend on empirical estimates, while others depend on more compre-

* I am indebted to Eduard Bomhoff, Herbert Buscher, Manfred J.M. Neumann, and Saranna Robinson for supplying some of the data used here.

hensive models than we have yet developed, or on a combination of the two—more comprehensive models and more data analysis.

To answer questions such as these, we need to specify a criterion or objective. I propose to use measures of variability—unanticipated variability—to compare alternative policy arrangements. I take as the proper objective of economic policy the reduction of risk and uncertainty to the minimum level inherent in nature and trading arrangements. Risk and uncertainty are assumed to increase with unanticipated variability.

Critics of fluctuating exchange rates implicitly use variability as a criterion when they decry the variability of exchange rates. Unfortunately, the critics typically err in their use of the criterion by emphasizing the variability of real or nominal exchange rates. Variability of either nominal or real exchange rates is not evidence that an economy experiences excessive risk or bears an excess burden. The benefits of relative price changes are known to often exceed the costs. Despite greater variability of real exchange rates, or even as a result of such variability, fluctuating exchange rates may permit a country to reach an optimum.

To measure variability, I use the variance of unanticipated changes in output and the general price level. These measures are relevant for decisions to hold domestic or foreign assets or to hold money or real capital, so they affect the rate of interest, the intertemporal allocation of resources, and the size of the capital stock. Excessive variability of output and prices contributes to the variability of returns, thereby raising the required rate of return on private investment above the minimum rate of return that society could reach.

Since past efforts to determine analytically whether fixed or flexible exchange rates are Pareto superior have been inconclusive, I have taken an empirical approach. In the following section, I restate some of the main arguments for fixed and fluctuating exchange rates and discuss the importance of variability. Both exchange rate systems can be operated under an inflexible rule, a flexible rule, or with different degrees of discretion. Variability and uncertainty are affected by the choice between a rule and discretionary action. On this issue also, I present some evidence. The evidence suggests that discretionary action is likely to increase variability and uncertainty.

The empirical findings suggest that uncertainty can be reduced by developing rules for monetary policy. I propose a rule to increase domestic price stability while reducing exchange rate variability. A conclusion summarizes principal findings.

II. Fixed Versus Fluctuating Exchange Rates

Fixed exchange rates require the government to relinquish control of money and fix a relative price. Fluctuating exchange rates typically require a government monopoly to control the stock of money. Generally, economic theory supports neither price-fixing nor monopoly. For these reasons alone, conclusions from theoretical work about the proper exchange regime can at most be qualified and conditional. Small, open economies are said to benefit more from fixing than from floating, but not much has been done to establish a dividing line. The small open economy model helps to explain why Holland, Belgium, and Luxembourg choose to peg their exchange rate to the Deutsche mark or why many countries in Central America peg to the U.S. dollar. The model has much less to say about the optimal choice of regime in the United Kingdom, the European Monetary System, Japan, and the United States. It does not explain why Britain, the United States, and Japan have fluctuating rates while Germany, France, and Italy have adjustable, pegged rates within the bloc of countries known as the European Monetary System (EMS) and fluctuating rates outside the bloc. The model has little to say about the risk of relative price changes, about the comparative cost of changing exchange rates instead of changing income and price levels, or about the risk of sudden policy changes.

In a comprehensive system of fixed exchange rates, some means of determining the growth of world reserves must be agreed upon. This is the n-country problem, a standard problem of price determination involving the choice of a numeraire to set, in this case, the world price level. In practice, this is a difficult problem involving comparison of the costs of holding commodities, the gains from seigniorage, the cost to the public of foregoing domestic concerns to maintain international price stability, and some thorny political issues. Formal analysis of several of these issues has not produced firm conclusions. We must rely on less than fully formal analyses.

A useful starting point for discussion of exchange rate systems is Milton Friedman's (1953) "The Case for Flexible Exchange Rates." Friedman considers a world in which changes in trade and payments occur continuously in response to unanticipated real and nominal changes. Adjustment to these shocks requires changes in relative prices and changes in the relative demands for assets denominated in different currencies. Friedman, and much subsequent analysis, considers four ways of adjusting, of which two are most relevant:

countries can allow exchange rates to clear the market, or they can hold exchange rates fixed and wait until prices and money wages adjust. Where the adjustment of some relative prices and real wages is sluggish, as in most modern economies, fixed exchange rates necessarily introduce changes in the demand for labor and unemployment as part of the process of adjustment.

Flexible exchange rates do not avoid all changes in domestic unemployment when major trading partners experience changes in technology or change policy. But flexible exchange rates avoid some changes in internal prices and incomes. The clearest, but not the only, example is the adjustment to an anticipated foreign inflation. The perceived costs of an inflation, anticipated as to occurrence but uncertain in magnitude and timing, became so large in the 1970s that many central bankers and governments changed their views about the relative costs of fixed and fluctuating rate systems. Flexible exchange rates can also increase stability if prices or money wages adjust slowly and there are frequent changes in relative rates of productivity growth at home and abroad.

To a considerable extent, the case in favor of fluctuating exchange rates rests on the greater stability of prices and output that can be achieved at times by allowing exchange rates to adjust prices relative to production costs and foreign prices. An added advantage claimed for fluctuating rates is that fewer resources are invested in holding commodity reserves or foreign exchange, so more saving is available for investment in physical capital. As far as I know, the latter argument has not been challenged; the greater resource cost of fixed rate systems is generally accepted.[1]

Against the benefits claimed for fluctuating exchange rates, proponents of fixed, or fixed-but-adjustable, rates offer three main arguments. First is the claim that fluctuating exchange rates increase the instability of output. The main evidence of increased instability is usually the greater variability of real exchange rates. Second, fluctuating rates are said to reduce trade. The reason given is that exporters and importers face increased uncertainty about prices of traded goods, or they must pay the cost of hedging against uncertainty. Third, fluctuating exchange rates are said to cause greater variability of prices and inflation. The argument is that fluctuating exchange rates work by changing prices of foreign goods relative to prices of domestic goods

---

[1] Some possible exceptions are papers that claim that price stability can be achieved using commodity money systems without holding commodities. McCallum (1985) finds these arguments invalid.

and by changing product prices relative to costs of production. These changes in relative prices affect the price level and, particularly in countries with money wages indexed to the price level, trigger price adjustment and inflation.

The claims and counterclaims are well known by now. Advocates of fluctuating rates point out that price and output variability is caused by shocks and policies. Advocates of fixed rates respond that fluctuating exchange rates amplify the responses in two ways. First, they claim that there is destabilizing speculation under fluctuating exchange rates. Second, they argue that fluctuating rates free countries from the discipline of a fixed-rate system, so they pursue more expansive monetary policies and experience more inflation.

Support for these last conjectures is, at best, weak. There is not much evidence of a relation between the exchange rate regime and the rate of inflation. Inflation was a principal reason for ending the fixed exchange rate regime, and disinflation has been carried out in many countries under fluctuating exchange rates. Countries have learned to use crawling pegs and adjustable pegs to reconcile differences in inflation with fixed real exchange rates. If alternating periods of inflation and disinflation are a greater problem under one type of regime than under the other, much of the cost arises from variability and uncertainty. The issue is, again, one of relative uncertainty.

Mussa's (1986) comprehensive study of the variability of *ex post* real exchange rates shows that the short-term variability of bilateral exchange rates is higher under fluctuating rates, often substantially higher. His finding is that the more rapid adjustment of nominal exchange rates, under a fluctuating rate regime, is not matched by a corresponding increase in the speed of price adjustment. Mussa notes, however, that his findings have no clear welfare implications. Nominal exchange rate changes have real effects, but these effects are the result of the slow, gradual adjustment of prices. He notes that his work does not show that fluctuating exchange rates increase the social cost of the monetary system relative to a system in which exchange rates are fixed permanently or relative to a system with discrete changes in currency parities. Exchange rate data cannot resolve the issue. We want to know whether uncertainty about variables such as output and the price level is increased or reduced, whether there are efficiency losses such as might occur if trade were more restricted under one system than another, or whether there is some evidence of an excess burden.

Studies of the effects of exchange rate variability on trade and capital movements have not produced evidence of a reliable effect. Surveys by Farrell (1983) and by the IMF (1984) report that the evidence is weak or inconclusive. If there is an effect of variability on trade, it has been hard to detect reliably. Farrell notes that many of the studies that have been done fail to distinguish between anticipated and unanticipated changes or between persistent and transitory changes, thereby increasing the difficulty of interpreting the empirical work.

One reason for the absence of demonstrable effects on trade may be that relevant measures of variability have not increased markedly. There is a tendency in discussions of fluctuating rates to jump from the finding of increased variability of real exchange rates to the conclusion that uncertainty has increased. An alternative interpretation is that the variability of real exchange rates reduces the response of prices and output to changes in the environment.

III. Rules, Discretion, and Forecast Accuracy

Models incorporating rational expectations show that every policy is a choice of rule; the only purely discretionary policy is haphazard or random action. Complete discretion is dominated by systematic policy that permits people to learn and to anticipate future actions. Proponents of discretion typically do not favor random or haphazard policies; they favor authority to deviate from a rule or to change the rule when, or if, available information suggests to the policymaker that it is desirable to do so. As always, there are type 1 and type 2 errors; discretionary action may increase or decrease variability and uncertainty. Kydland and Prescott (1977) show that, in general, deviations from a rule reduce welfare.

Empirical comparisons of rules and discretion are difficult to make. There are many different rules to compare to the history of discretionary changes in rules or departures from rules. Further, a change from the discretionary action we have experienced to a rule would affect expectations and structural parameters, so it is difficult to design experiments that sharply discriminate between the history of discretionary action and behavior that would occur under a particular rule.

If the information available to the policymaker is more reliable than the information available to the public, public agencies may have some advantage in forecasting the future, and when making discretionary changes based on such forecasts. Some of the information may be obtained from other governments under conditions which prevent release. Meltzer (1987) summarizes some quarterly and annual inflation forecasts and real output growth by the Federal Reserve and by private forecasters. There is some evidence from work by Lombra and Moran (1983) that the Federal Reserve made smaller errors in quarterly forecasts during 1970–73, but the advantage is small and is not found for annual forecasts.

A notable finding of the comparison of forecast errors is the low accuracy of the forecasts made by each of the forecasters. Forecast errors for output growth are so large relative to quarterly changes that it is not possible for any forecaster, on average, to distinguish reliably between a boom and a recession, either in the current quarter or a year in advance. Forecasts included in the study were made using all or most of the techniques commonly in use, including judgment, econo-

Table 4.1   Root Mean Square Errors of Forecast (annual rates in percent)

	Current Quarter		Year or Four Quarters Ahead	
Real GNP Growth	Value or Range	Median	Value or Range	Mean (M) or Median (Md)
U.S. 1980/2–1985/1[a]	3.1–4.4	3.8	2.2–3.4	2.7 (Md)
U.S. Federal Reserve 1970–73[b]	2.1	n.a.	3.5	n.a.
U.S. 1970/4–1983/4[c]	2.8–3.6	3.0	—	—
German Council of Economic Experts 1969–86[d]			1.9	n.a.
German Council of Economic Experts 1978–86[d]			0.7	n.a.
Dutch Central Economic Plan 1953–85[d]			3.2	n.a.
Dutch Central Plan 1975–85[e]			2.0	n.a.
OECD 1968–79[f]			1.4–4.4	2.3 (M)
Naive OECD 1968–79 (random walk)[f]			2.8–4.5	3.8 (M)
Nominal GNP Growth				
U.S. Federal Reserve, 1967–82[g]		5.5	5.7	n.a.
U.S. Federal Reserve, 1973–82[g]		6.1	6.2	n.a.
U.S. 1970/4–1983/4[c]	3.5–4.3	3.8		

Notes: n.a. = not applicable, single forecaster
[a] 12 econometric and judgmental forecasts from McNees (1986).
[b] from Lombra and Moran (1983).
[c] from Zarnowitz (1986), 4 forecasters.
[d] supplied by Herbert Buscher; see Neumann and Buscher (1985); forecasts are for one year ahead.
[e] Central Economic Plan, various years for one year ahead.
[f] Smyth (1983); 7-country RMSE.
[g] Federal Reserve "green" books.

metric modeling, and time series analysis. The errors from the best forecasts using each method, and from most forecasters, are sufficiently close on average to suggest that the remaining errors are close to the minimum we are likely to achieve with current techniques and models. Remaining errors may be random variation caused by unanticipated real shocks, changes in expectations, and perceived or actual changes in foreign countries.

The information on forecast accuracy and the value of forecasts in Meltzer (1987) comes from the United States, so it may not be general. Table 4.1 shows root mean square forecast errors, for forecasts of real or nominal GNP (or GDP) growth, by governmental and private forecasters in different countries. The first two rows summarize results reported in Meltzer (1987). For comparison, row 3 shows that quarterly forecasts for the U.S. over a longer period have somewhat lower errors than the forecasts for more recent years. The median value of the root mean square error is about equal to the average annual rate of growth, however, so it remains true that, on average, forecasters cannot distinguish between a boom and a recession in the current quarter.

Annual forecast errors for Holland and Germany show a decline in the variability of forecast errors for output under the current system of preannounced monetary growth, adjustable pegged rates within the EMS, and fluctuating rates against other major currencies.[2] For Germany, forecasts are relatively accurate. The root mean square error is less than one-half the average growth rate for the period 1978–86. It remains true, however, that policymakers who rely on forecasts to determine the time for discretionary changes will mistake booms and recessions. For this reason alone, discretionary action based on forecasts is likely to increase variability.

Smyth (1983) studied the accuracy of OECD forecasts for seven countries—the United States, Japan, Germany, France, the United Kingdom, Italy, and Canada—for the years 1968–79. He found no correlation between the errors and the year of the forecast, suggesting that forecast accuracy has not improved significantly but did not worsen after major currencies adopted the fluctuating rate system. Zarnowitz (1986) reports a similar result.

Smyth reports the results of several tests. He used Theil's decomposition to show that most of the errors for output growth and inflation are random. He also compared the accuracy of forecasts to a naive

---

[2] Data for seven additional German forecasters are available, but I have not computed the root mean square errors for each forecaster.

model, the latter a random walk using preliminary data for the preceding year to forecast real output. Table 4.1 shows the comparison. The OECD forecast for each country is more accurate than the random walk, but, Smyth notes, all of the improvement is in the years 1974–76, following the first round of oil price increases. Information about the oil shock was available to private individuals as well as to public bodies, so the mechanical procedure probably overstates the error that people would have made. The results for other years suggest that any private information available to the OECD could not be translated into greater forecast accuracy.[3]

Several economists have proposed that central banks adjust monetary policy to correspond to forecasts of nominal GNP growth and, recently, some have urged coordinated adjustments in other countries. Many of the proposals for international policy coordination, target zones, or stabilization of world money growth or exchange rates depend on forecasts of nominal GNP growth. Table 4.1 presents some evidence on the quality of these forecasts.

The Federal Reserve's record of forecasting nominal GNP growth four quarters ahead has a root mean square error (RMSE) approximately equal to 60% of average nominal growth of GNP under both fixed (1967–72) and fluctuating (1973–82) exchange rates. The relative size of these errors makes it appear unlikely that discretionary policy action based on forecasts of GNP, or efforts to coordinate policy based on forecasts of GNP growth, are likely to reduce variability and uncertainty.[4] For comparison, I have included forecast errors for the current quarter made by private forecasters and by the Federal Reserve. The Federal Reserve forecasts are less accurate than private forecasts, suggesting that any information available to the staff and not made public did not improve forecast accuracy during the period considered.

An additional problem with Federal Reserve forecasts is that they are biased. Mean absolute errors four quarters ahead and for the current quarter are 5.4% and 5.2%, respectively; mean errors are very

---

[3] Comparison of the root mean square error (RMSE) of forecast to the average growth rate for 1968–79 shows that the ratio of RMSE to average growth ranges from 0.35 (France) to 0.95 (U.K.). The mean for the seven countries is 0.78. An alternative measure of the value of forecast is the ratio of RMSE to the standard deviation of real growth. These ratios range from 0.57 (U.S.) to 1.03 (Japan). The results again suggest that, on average, forecasts cannot distinguish reliably between booms and recessions.

[4] The forecasts are made in January for the current quarter and four quarters ahead. Forecasts are revised periodically, so other periods may show more or less accuracy.

similar. A plausible reason is that the Federal Reserve consistently underestimated inflation during these years. This systematic error may have occurred because of unwillingness to recognize the inflationary consequences of past policies, or may be the result of adaptive forecasts that adjust slowly to new information. Whatever the reason for the bias, the presence of persistent bias, lower accuracy than private forecasters, and large errors relative to the mean rate of change gives little support to proposals for nominal GNP targeting, policy coordination, target zones, or other discretionary actions based on forecasts of this kind. If the aim of policy is to reduce, rather than augment, variability and uncertainty, discretionary action based on forecasts or rules that rely on forecasts is unlikely to achieve that goal.

Table 4.2 shows measures of forecast accuracy for inflation. The root mean square errors are smaller than for real growth, reflecting the lower variability of inflation rates. The errors are broadly similar to those reported in Meltzer (1987) for the U.S., and generally between 1% and 2% at annual rates. The OECD root mean square forecast error for each of the seven countries is less than the average rate of price change; the ratio of RMSE to average rate of change is 0.2 to 0.6. Naive forecasts, based on a random walk, are less accurate for

Table 4.2 Root Mean Square Errors of Forecast for Inflation (annual rates in percent)

	Current Quarter		Year or Four Quarters Ahead	
	Value or Range	Median	Value or Range	Mean (M) or Median (Md)
U.S. 1980/2–1985/2[a]	1.4–2.2	1.6	1.1–3.3	1.6(Md)
U.S. Federal Reserve 1970–73[b]	1.4	n.a.	3.4	n.a.
U.S. 1970/4–1983/4[c]	2.0–2.6	2.2		
U.S. 1980/2–1985/1[c]	1.4–2.0	1.8		
Germany, Council of Economic Experts, 1969–86[d]			1.4	n.a.
Germany, Council of Economic Experts, 1978–86[d]			0.7	n.a.
Dutch Central Economic Plan, 1953–85[e]			1.1	n.a.
Dutch Central Economic Plan, 1975–85[e]			0.5	n.a.
OECD, 1968–79[f]			1.2–4.6	3.0(M)
OECD, 1968–79 (random walk)[f]			2.2–7.3	4.3(M)

Notes: See Table 1.

six of the seven countries. This suggests that inflation forecasts may be more useful to private and public decision-makers than forecasts of real growth. It is less clear that inflation forecasts can be used to reduce the variability of the price level.

The data in Tables 4.1 and 4.2 support some preliminary conclusions about fluctuating exchange rates and about discretionary policy action. First, the shift to fluctuating exchange rates has not been followed by lower forecast accuracy. Forecast errors for rates of change of prices and output are a relevant measure of uncertainty faced by decision-makers. These data suggest that the change in monetary regime has not increased uncertainty. Second, the size of forecast errors for growth and inflation, particularly the former, are large relative to the average change. Discretionary actions conditioned on forecasts are more likely to increase variability and uncertainty than to reduce uncertainty to the minimum inherent in nature and trading practices.[5]

IV. Variability under Fixed and Fluctuating Exchange Rates

In earlier work, using quarterly data for the years from the 1960s to the 1980s, I compared the variability of unanticipated changes in prices, output, money, velocity, and exchange rates under fixed and fluctuating rates for five countries—Canada, Germany, Japan, the United Kingdom, and the United States. Meltzer (1985, 1986a) reports these findings and the interrelation among current and lagged values of unanticipated changes in these variables. The results suggest that some countries were able to reduce the variability of unanticipated changes in prices or output, or both, during the fluctuating exchange-rate period. Further, I found little relation between unanticipated changes in nominal exchange rates and unanticipated changes in prices and output. Exchange rate variability did not appear to be a main source of uncertainty about (or of unanticipated changes in) prices and output.

The quarterly data used in previous work may give excessive weight to short-termm ovements. One reason is that the organized futures and forward markets are more active for short- than for long-term maturities. These markets can be used to reduce the cost of variability. It

---

[5] Smyth (1983) also studied the accuracy of trade balance forecasts. These were least accurate, a possible warning to those setting or coordinating policies to reduce the U.S. trade deficit.

seems useful to extend the analysis to see whether annual data give different results.

To compute measures of variability and uncertainty under fixed and fluctuating exchange rates, I again use the multi-state Kalman filter, discussed by Bomhoff (1983) and Kool (1983), to compute forecast errors for real output (GNP or GDP) and the price level.[6] The forecasts, like those reported in Tables 4.1 and 4.2, use only information available at the time of the forecast and are based on annual data for 1950 to 1985. Fluctuating exchange rates begin in 1973.

Countries differ in size and in choice of monetary regime. Two countries, Germany and Denmark, are members of the European Monetary System. They have fixed, but adjustable, exchange rates within the group and fluctuating rates against other major countries. The remaining four countries have fluctuating exchange rates, but they differ in the degree to which they have intervened to affect the exchange rate. The six countries were subject to similar shocks, such as the oil shocks of the 1970s and the relatively large devaluation and subsequent revaluation of the dollar from 1978 to 1984. Each country has an independent fiscal policy and differs in product mix, in technology, and in other ways that may affect variability.

The multi-state Kalman filter computes the univariate forecast error for each year from past values, and subdivides the error into transitory and permanent changes in level and permanent changes in growth rate. The statistical model used for these computations treats each of the errors as independent. Let ε, γ, and ρ be, respectively, the transitory error in level, the permanent error in level, and the permanent error in the growth rate. These errors are given by:

$$X_t = \bar{X}_t + \varepsilon_t \tag{1}$$

$$\bar{X}_t = \bar{X}_{t-1} + \hat{X}_t + \gamma_t \tag{2}$$

$$\hat{X}_t = \hat{X}_{t-1} + \rho_t \tag{3}$$

where X_t, $\bar{X}_t$, and $\hat{X}_t$ are the level, permanent or expected level, and permanent or expected growth rate of X.

The statistical model cannot assign causality to the change in exchange rate regime as a reason for the reduction or increase in forecast error. Reduced, or increased, variability can occur for reasons unrelated to the change in monetary arrangements. The forecast errors can be used, however, to reject the hypothesis that the change from fixed to fluctuating exchange rates increased excess burdens, as mea-

---

[6] See also Meltzer (1985, 1986a) for a discussion of the procedure.

Table 4.3   Root Mean Square Errors, 1970–85 (annual rate in percent)

		Real Income	Growth	Price Level	Inflation
Denmark	1952–72	2.5	2.3	2.4	2.3
	1973–85	1.9	1.9	1.3	1.5
Germany	1952–72	2.3	2.1	1.8	1.7
	1973–85	1.8	1.7	0.7	0.4
Japan	1952–72	1.9	1.8	1.9	1.8
	1973–85	1.8	1.8	2.6	2.6
Sweden	1952–72	1.7	1.6	2.5	2.4
	1973–85	1.8	1.8	1.5	1.5
U.K.	1952–72	1.6	1.5	1.7	1.6
	1973–85	2.1	2.1	4.1	4.1
U.S.	1952–72	1.3	1.2	2.8	2.6
	1973–85	2.3	2.3	1.4	1.4

sured by the variability of unanticipated changes in prices and output.

Table 4.3 shows the root mean square errors of forecasts under fixed and fluctuating exchange-rate regimes. The errors are computed for levels of real income and prices, for rates of growth of output, and for rates of price change. The errors for the levels are the sum

$$\sqrt{V(\varepsilon) + V(\gamma) + V(\rho)} \qquad (4)$$

where V is the variance of the error. The errors for growth and inflation omit $V(\varepsilon)$, the variance of the transitory error in the levels of output and prices.

Many of the errors lie in the neighborhood of 2%, not very different from the forecast errors reported in Tables 4.1 and 4.2 but higher than the best forecasts in some countries. The errors in the earlier tables are for forecasts of growth and inflation, but most shocks are durable, so ε is generally small, and the two sets of errors are often identical at the level of accuracy reported in Table 4.3.[7]

Comparison of the fixed and fluctuating exchange-rate periods provides no support for the claim that fluctuating exchange rates increased variability and uncertainty. Only one of the six countries, the U.K., shows increases in uncertainty for both prices and output. Two countries, Denmark and Germany, show reductions in all measures, with relatively large reductions in price level (or inflation) uncertainty

---

[7] The errors are from univariate models, so in principle efficiency can be increased. Meltzer (1985, 1986a) estimates vector autoregressions (VAR) using unanticipated changes to money, output, and prices, in part to measure the efficiency loss from the univariate model. The reduction in forecast errors is often small. Since the VARs use data for the entire sample period to compute the error in each period, they overstate the reduction in forecast error that would be achieved in practice.

during the fluctuating exchange-rate period. Despite the oil shocks of the 1970s, price level and inflation uncertainty declined in four of the six countries under fluctuating exchange rates.

The reduction in uncertainty for Germany is highly suggestive. Germany has preannounced rules for money growth and exchange rates. The exchange rate rule is an adjustable peg against currencies in the European Monetary System and fluctuating rates against other currencies. To provide information about its policy and about expected inflation, the central bank announces targets for central bank money, a measure very similar to the monetary base. While the targets are not always achieved, the record suggests that the government and the central bank are constrained by the targets. The Bundesbank, unlike the Federal Reserve, does not systematically exceed its money growth target. Money growth is generally within the target range.

The two rules appear to have increased stability relative to other countries and relative to the fixed exchange-rate regime. The Bundesbank raised the credibility of its announced disinflationary policy by holding money growth to a preannounced disinflationary path through the late 1970s and the 1980s. Deviations from the path, for example to support the dollar in 1978, induce a smaller flight from money if the public believes the deviations are transitory. Further, the government has been willing to revalue the mark rather than import inflation from the countries in the EMS with more inflationary policies.

Denmark, and other countries in the EMS, can pursue independent monetary policies, if they choose to do so. Since they bear most of the cost of such policies under the adjustable exchange-rate system, they have an incentive to follow stabilizing policies. Denmark appears to have reduced variability and uncertainty relative to its experience under the Bretton Woods agreement. These data suggest that, despite the oil shocks of the 1970s and the variability of real exchange rates for the dollar, Denmark was able to reduce uncertainty by the choice of policy, in this case membership in the EMS.

The United States is the only country showing a relatively large increase in uncertainty about output and its rate of growth. Inspection of the detail shows that much of the increase is the result of a substantial increase in the forecast error for the permanent growth rate of output. A plausible explanation of the increased uncertainty about output and its rates of growth, relative to the past and relative to other countries in the table, is the frequent change in the thrust of U.S. monetary and fiscal policies in the past decade. Frequent policy changes make the current and maintained rates of growth difficult to forecast, leading to frequent changes in the expected return to capital

Table 4.4 Mean Absolute Errors for Output in Japan and the U.S. (annual rate in percent)

	Japan			United States		
	ε	γ	ρ	ε	γ	ρ
1950–72	0.5	1.0	1.2	0.3	0.6	0.7
1960–72	0.5	1.1	1.4	0.2	0.6	0.7
1973–85	0.1	0.6	0.9	0.3	1.0	1.7
1973–85*	0.1	0.3	0.2	0.3	0.9	1.7

* Omitting year with largest error: 1974 for Japan, 1984 for U.S.

invested in the United States. These, in turn, cause changes in the demand for U.S. assets and in real exchange rates.

Japan shows no reduction in output uncertainty, and increased price uncertainty, following the shift to fluctuating exchange rates. This is misleading. Removing one large error for prices and output changes the results. For output, the forecast error made at the time of the 1974 oil shock is more than five times the mean absolute error. For prices, the forecast error for 1975, when the Bank of Japan changed to a policy of monetary targets and disinflation, is more than four times the mean absolute error.

Table 4.4 compares the size of errors in forecasts of output for Japan and the United States in different periods by type of error. The table shows that the errors for the fixed exchange-rate period are not affected by starting the period in 1950. Mean errors are not much different if the period 1960–72 is used instead.

For Japan, the three computed values of the mean absolute errors for 1973–85 decline, but for the United States, all three increase following the adoption of fluctuating exchange rates. Omitting the year with the largest forecast error substantially reduces the mean absolute error for output (and prices) in Japan and the RMSE for Japan. Thus, omitting 1974 reconciles the annual results for Japan with the results reported using quarterly data in Meltzer (1985). For the United States, the largest error occurs in 1984. Omitting this year slightly reduces the mean absolute error but does not alter the direction of change or the conclusion that output uncertainty increased in the U.S. under fluctuating rates. Since increases are not observed for other countries, we can reject the hypothesis that the increased output uncertainty is a consequence of the fluctuating exchange-rate system.

A plausible, but not fully tested, hypothesis is that the increased variability and uncertainty in the U.S. is the result of more frequent changes in U.S. policy than in the policies of Germany, Japan, or Sweden. Under the fixed exchange-rate regime, these countries absorbed many of the shocks emanating from the U.S. Under fluctuating rates, they can avoid some of the shocks. During the 1970s and 1980s, several countries adopted and sought to implement medium- or long-term strategies for economic policy. The U.S. repeatedly changed the direction of tax, defense, energy, and monetary policies in response to changes in economic activity and popular sentiment.[8] It should not be surprising, given the inaccuracy of forecasts, that frequent policy changes can create an excess burden, raising social costs and increasing the real rate of interest by imposing a risk premium. Mascaro and Meltzer (1983) find evidence that this occurred in the 1980s.

Two main conclusions emerge from these comparisons. First, as already noted, there is no evidence that a system of fluctuating exchange rates necessarily increases uncertainty. Second, in the U.K. and the U.S. uncertainty about output or the price level is higher than in earlier periods. To the extent that the variabilities in the U.S. and the U.K. affect other countries, uncertainty in these countries also is not at the minimum inherent in nature and trading arrangements.

V. A Rule to Reduce Variability

In *A Tract on Monetary Reform*, Keynes (1923) considered two types of rules—rules for domestic price or internal stability, and rules for exchange rate or external stability. He favored internal price stability, but, here and in his later work, he recognized the advantages of reducing both internal and external instability. He recognized also that each country operating alone must sacrifice either internal or external stability unless some country adopts a credible rule for achieving price stability.

Countries operating together can individually achieve internal price stability (or reduce instability) and collectively reduce instability of the exchange rate. Keynes's argument recognizes that stability is a public good and that there are costs of providing stability. One of his main arguments against the classical gold standard is that under this standard the social cost of exchange rate stability is higher than can be achieved under alternative arrangements. Throughout his life he proposed alternatives. The Bretton Woods agreement was Keynes's last effort to solve the problem of internal and external stability.

---

[8] A result of the greater certainty (reduced uncertainty) about policy may be greater stability of the demand for money, or velocity.

In practice, countries have achieved neither price nor exchange rate stability in the postwar period. Excess burdens, measured by the variability of unanticipated changes in prices and output, appear to be lower than during the interwar period or under the classical gold standard,[9] but, as noted in the preceding section, variability can be reduced further by an appropriate rule.

Policy rules differ on many dimensions. McCallum (1984) makes the useful distinction between activist and discretionary rules.[10] An activist policy rule permits the policymaker to respond to events in the economy, or in other economies. The responses follow a rule; they are predictable by private individuals. Hence the changes do not increase the unanticipated component in output and prices. Since all changes are made in accordance with a rule, they are nondiscretionary.

A second characteristic distinguishes activist rules that rely on forecasts of future values from rules that make policy action conditional on observed values. The data summarized in Tables 4.1 and 4.2 give no reason to believe that a rule making action conditional on forecasts reduces uncertainty. Policies based on forecasts appear to be a less effective means of reducing variability and uncertainty than (some) rules that constrain policy action to a more predictable path.

A rule to achieve price stability must choose between the stability of the actual or anticipated price level.[11] Permanent productivity changes, and other permanent changes in the level of output, affect the price level. A rule that calls for stability of the actual price level requires the policymaker to reverse all changes in the price level. A rule that maintains stability of the anticipated price level allows the actual price level to adjust as part of the process by which the economy adjusts real values to unanticipated supply shocks. Once adjustment is complete, real values are the same under either rule. Differences arise during the adjustment, however. To maintain stability of actual prices, the policymaker must know the proper amount by which to change money and other nominal values, so he must know structural parameters including the size of the real wealth effect, the magnitude of the productivity shock, and the price elasticity of aggregate supply. The public must have confidence that the policymaker knows these magnitudes. Such confidence would be misplaced. We simply do not know and,

[9] Meltzer (1986b) compares the different regimes from 1890 to 1980 for the United States. Additional computations for other countries generally support this conclusion.

[10] Dornbusch and Fischer (1978, Chapter 10) make a similar distinction.

[11] If the optimal rate of inflation is non-zero, the rule should distinguish between actual and anticipated inflation.

after several decades of empirical work in macroeconomics, we should not expect to learn these values with enough precision to improve on market adjustment of the price level to one-time shocks.

Furthermore, there is no reason why current owners of nominally denominated assets should not share in the gains and losses resulting from changes in productivity or supply shocks. One of the main benefits of price stability is that stability of anticipated prices reduces uncertainty faced by transactors, thereby lowering the risk of long-term investment. This is, of course, the argument stressed by proponents of the classical gold standard. Another main benefit is that individuals who save for retirement (or for the distant future) have less reason for concern about the form in which assets are held and less reason to fear that the real value of accumulated saving will be altered by unanticipated inflation. Stability of the anticipated price level reduces these risks.

The rule I propose is activist, but nondiscretionary. No use is made of forecasts when setting policy variables. The rule recognizes that, within a period relevant for policy, the trend growth of output is not a fixed value but varies stochastically. The rule has two parts.

The first achieves stability of the anticipated domestic price level by setting the current growth rate of the monetary base (b_t) equal to the difference between a moving average of the growth rate of domestic output ($\bar{y}$) and a moving average of the rate of growth of base velocity ($\bar{v}$). Since forecasts cannot distinguish, on average, between booms and recessions, the rule adjusts b_t in response to the most recent past values of $\bar{y}$ and $\bar{v}$ that are known reliably. Formally, the rule sets

$$b_t = \bar{y}_{t-1} - \bar{v}_{t-1}.$$

The second part of the rule reduces variability of exchange rates. This requires major trading countries—the United States, Germany, Japan, and perhaps the U.K.—to adopt the same rule for stability of the anticipated domestic price level. The rate of growth of the monetary base would differ with the experience of each country and would change over time. Anticipated and actual exchange rates would be subject to change in accordance with changes in relative productivity growth; rates of growth of intermediation; differences in rates of saving, in expected returns to capital, in labor-leisure choice; or other real changes. Prices would continue to fluctuate, but anticipated domestic price levels would be constant in all countries that follow the rule, so the rule eliminates this source of short-term instability in real and nominal exchange rates, and of long-term changes in nominal exchange rates. The remaining changes in real exchange rates facilitiate the efficient allocation of resources in response to changes in tastes and technology at home and abroad.

To complete the rule, we have to choose the period over which moving averages of output and base velocity are computed. In the past, I have suggested a three-year moving average. In practice, a longer or shorter period may provide more stability. Empirical studies can help to determine the length of the period used to compute the moving averages.

Smaller countries could choose to import enhanced price and exchange-rate stability by fixing their exchange rates to a basket of the currencies of major countries or to one of those currencies. They would not be required to do so. There are no international exchange-rate agreements under the rule. Each country would choose its own course. If all countries—large and small—choose independent policies, or make frequent discretionary changes, uncertainty will not be at a minimum. Everyone must accept greater variability of exchange rates, if large countries fail to supply stability.

The proposed rule has some additional advantages:

(1) Costs of monitoring are relatively low. The public can observe, and the central bank can control, the monetary base with very little error. Departures from the rule can be observed quickly, so the principal effect of deviations from the rule is on the exchange rate and not on aggregate real demand.

(2) The rule does not adjust to short-term, transitory changes in level, but it adjusts fully to permanent changes in growth rates of output and intermediation (or other changes in the growth rate of velocity) within the term chosen for the moving averages.

(3) The rule is adaptive and modestly counter-cyclical, particularly if recessions last for several quarters. If there is an unanticipated decline in real growth, the moving average rate of output growth falls, but not as much as the growth rate of current output. Hence growth of the monetary base declines much less than the growth of output in recessions and rises less than the growth of output in expansions.

(4) The rule reflects the difficulties of forecasting and uses certain knowledge about quantitative magnitudes.

VI. Conclusions

Through most of the postwar period, the international financial system has been based on the U.S. dollar. The dollar served as the principal reserve currency, or store of value, and the principal standard for deferred payments. For a time, the dollar standard provided exchange rate stability with relatively low inflation in major trading countries, although formal devaluation or revaluations of the mark, the French franc, the pound, and other currencies occurred from time to time.

The period of relative stability ended with the inflation of the 1960s. For the past 20 years, domestic and international monetary policy has provided neither price nor exchange rate stability. As measured by the variability of unanticipated changes in prices and output, however, uncertainty has not increased, and in some cases has decreased. Computations for Germany, Denmark, and Japan suggest that uncertainty can be reduced further if countries adopt monetary rules for internal and external stability.

Neither discursive argumentation nor formal analysis has resolved major issues about the relative costs and benefits of fixed and fluctuating exchange rates for individual countries. Comparisons of policy rules and discretionary action have been advanced by the development of dynamic models with rational expectations, but many countries have not agreed on the type of rule or even accepted the principle that a rule or a medium-term strategy increases welfare.

On the other hand, some countries—notably Germany and Japan—have been reluctant to deviate from their policy rules or to alter their policies. They have remained committed to price stability, or low inflation, in the face of substantial changes in nominal and real exchange rates and exhortations from other countries. Those urging discretionary changes in the monetary policy of these countries often rely on forecasts. Others emphasize the value of stability and the advantage of rules.

To advance the discussion of policy rules and discretionary action, and of fixed and fluctuating exchange rates, beyond the point at which they are usually left, I introduced two types of data. One shows the forecasting record of private and public bodies. The other uses the variability of annual forecast errors in prices and output as measures of uncertainty, under fixed and fluctuating exchange rates, for several countries.

The forecasting record gives little reason to believe that variability and uncertainty would be reduced by discretionary action based on forecasts or by policy rules conditioned on forecasts.[12] Forecasts, whether based on econometric models, statistical models, judgment, or some combination of these methods, are so wide of the mark that, on average, they cannot distinguish reliably between booms and recessions in the current quarter or a year ahead. Further, comparison of Federal Reserve and OECD forecasts and private forecasts shows that public agencies have not been able to use confidential information to improve forecast accuracy. Federal Reserve forecasts of nominal GNP growth have been less accurate and show substantial bias, while errors by private forecasters appear to be unbiased.

The data suggest that the shift from fixed to fluctuating exchange rates was not followed by a general rise in uncertainty about prices and output, as is often suggested in policy discussions. In some countries both measures of uncertainty are lower under fluctuating than under fixed exchange rates. Of the six countries studied, only one shows an increase in both price and output uncertainty under fluctuating exchange rates.

Two lessons can be drawn from this experience. First, fluctuating exchange rates do not of necessity increase uncertainty for private decision makers.[13] Second, the two countries that adopted rules for internal and external stability—Germany and Denmark—reduced uncertainty absolutely and relative to other countries studied.

Based on these findings, I propose a rule to increase price and exchange rate stability that does not require agreements to take coordinated policy action. The rule is simple to follow and easy to monitor. Each major country—Germany, Japan, the United States, and perhaps the United Kingdom—achieves domestic price stability on average by setting the rate of growth of the monetary base equal to the difference between the moving average of past real output growth and past growth of base velocity. If each country adopts a compatible rule, the rule reduces variability of exchange rates arising from differences in expected rates of inflation.

The rule may not be optimal. We know little about the structure of optimal rules. Perhaps the papers at this conference will improve our understanding and point us toward research leading to an optimal rule.

---

[12] In a recent paper, Zarnowitz (1986) finds that forecast accuracy has not improved since the 1950s and that forecasts are less accurate for recession than for expansions.

[13] I have not attempted to reconcile the reduced variability of unanticipated changes in prices and output with the increased variability of *ex post* real exchange rates. Financial markets may effectively buffer the real economy from these shocks. Whether this occurs and whether the result approaches optimality remains open.

Meanwhile, we have reason to believe that uncertainty can be reduced, if we have the wisdom and the will to adopt more stable policies and a common rule.

References

Bomhoff, E. 1983. *Monetary Uncertainty*. Amsterdam: North-Holland.

Dornbusch, R., and Fischer, S. 1978. *Macroeconomics*. New York: Mc-Graw-Hill.

Farrell, V., with DeRosa, D.A., and McCown, T.A. 1983. Effects of Exchange Rate Variability on International Trade and Other Economic Variables: A Review of the Literature. *Staff Studies*, 130: 1–21. Board of Governors of the Federal Reserve System.

Friedman, M. 1953. The Case for Flexible Exchange Rates. In Friedman, M., ed., *Essays in Positive Economics*. Chicago: University of Chicago Press, pp. 157–203.

International Monetary Fund. 1984. *Exchange Rate Variability and World Trade*. Washington, D.C.: IMF.

Keynes, J.M. 1923. *A Tract on Monetary Reform*. Vol. 4 of *The Collected Writings of John Maynard Keynes*. London: Macmillan and St. Martin's Press for The Royal Economic Society (1971).

Kool, C. 1983. Forecasts with Multi-State Kalman Filters. App. 1 to Bomhoff, E., *Monetary Uncertainty*. Amsterdam: North-Holland.

Kydland, F.E., and Prescott, E.C. 1977. Rules Rather than Discretion: The Inconsistency of Optimal Plans. *Journal of Political Economy*, 85: 473–92.

Lombra, R., and Moran, M. 1983. Policy Advice and Policymaking at the Federal Reserve. In Brunner, K., and Meltzer, A.H., eds., *Carnegie-Rochester Conference Series on Public Policy*, 13: 9–68. Reprinted in Brunner, K., and Meltzer, A.H., eds., *Theory, Policy and Institutions*. Amsterdam: North-Holland, p. 385–444.

Mascaro, A., and Meltzer, A.H. 1983. Long- and Short-Term Interest Rates in an Uncertain World. *Journal of Monetary Economics*, 12: 485–518.

McCallum, B.T. 1984. Monetary Rules in the Light of Recent Experience. *American Economic Review, Papers and Proceedings*, 74: 388–96.

———— 1985. The 'New Monetary Economics', Fiscal Issues and Unemployment. In Brunner, K., and Meltzer, A.H., eds., *Carnegie-Rochester Conference Series on Public Policy*, 23: 13–45.

McNees, S.K. 1986. The Accuracy of Forecasting Techniques. *New England Economic Review*, Federal Reserve Bank of Boston, p. 20–31.

Meltzer, A.H. 1985. Variability of Prices, Output and Money under Fixed and Fluctuating Exchange Rates: An Empirical Study of Monetary Regimes in Japan and the United States. *Bank of Japan Monetary and Economic Studies*, 3: 1–46.

———— (1986a). Size, Persistence and Interrelation of Nominal and Real Shocks. *Journal of Monetary Economics*, Jan. pp. 161–94.

———— (1986b). Some Evidence on the Comparative Uncertainty Experienced under Different Monetary Regimes. In Campbell, C.D., and Dougan, W.R., eds., *Alternative Monetary Regimes*. Baltimore: The Johns Hopkins University Press, pp. 122–53.

——— (1987). Limits of Short-Run Stabilization Policy. *Economic Inquiry*, 25: 1–13.

Mussa, M. 1986. Nominal Exchange Rate Regimes and the Behavior of Real Exchange Rates: Evidence and Implications. In Brunner, K., and Meltzer, A.H., eds., *Carnegie-Rochester Conference Series on Public Policy*, 25: 117–213.

Neumann, M.J.M., and Buscher, H.J. 1985. Wirtschaftsprognosen im Vergleich: Eine Untersuchung anhand von Rationalitätstests. *IFO-Studien*, v. 31: 183–201. Berlin: Dunker and Humblot.

Smyth, D.J. 1983. Short-run Macroeconomic Forecasting: The OECD Performance. *Journal of Forecasting*, 2: 37–49.

Zarnowitz, V. 1986. The Record and Improvability of Economic Forecasting. *Economic Forecasts*, 3: 22–30.

5

The Macroeconomic Performance of Five Major Countries: An Introductory Presentation

Yoshio Suzuki

This presentation was prepared by the Institute for Monetary and Economic Studies for the purpose of providing in the first session a set of statistical indices to the participants of the Conference that measure the instability of a number of national economies since 1973 and also to quantify the international imbalances in the 1980s. The causes of these two phenomena will be major topics in succeeding sessions. In papers presented at this Conference, some authors, particularly Professors Michael Parkin and Stanley Fischer, refer to a similar array of statistics. Nevertheless I think it is still worthwhile to present the data that we have compiled since they will serve as a factual base for the issues that will be taken up later in the Conference and will also be useful as a reference point when comparable data are introduced by other participants in the ensuing sessions.

The Introductory Presentation is based on two sets of materials: The first is a series of figures,[1] and the second is a series of tables with an attached technical appendix on Bayesian trend estimation. In order to assess the extent of domestic instability and of international imbalances for both before and after 1973, which was the year of transition to a floating exchange rate system with fiat currencies, we have chosen thirteen macroeconomic indicators. They are of four types: indicators for stabilization policy goals, those for monetary and fiscal policy, those for external shocks, and those for exchange rates. The indicators for stabilization policy goals are the real growth rate, the unemployment rate, the inflation rate, and the ratio of current account surplus or deficit to GNP. Those for macroeconomic policy are the ratio of the government deficit to GNP, the money growth rate, the real

---

[1] The figures are not reproduced in this volume, except for those illustrating real and nominal exchange rates. The data presented in the deleted figures are summarized in the following tables.

short-term rate, and the real long-term rate, although to what extent the real long-term rate is sensitive to policy is a matter of some debate. Indicators for external shocks are the increase in real exports, the terms of trade, and the increase in import prices, although again to what extent they are exogenous to the domestic economy is open to some question. Finally, exchange rate indicators are the nominal rate and two kinds of real exchange rates, all vis-à-vis the U.S. dollar.

For reasons of tractability, we assembled the data for only five major countries, the U.S., Japan, West Germany, France, and the U.K. Then we estimated for the five countries, using a Bayesian approach, trends and deviations from trends of these indicators, except for the nominal and real exchange rates. These data are presented in Tables 5.1–5.5. In calculating the averages, we omitted figures for 1973 and 1974 because we wish to abstract from the transitional effects caused by the shift to a new exchange rate system. A technical appendix on the estimation technique employed appears after the tables.

We carefully compared the average trends and the deviations from trends of the eleven indicators for the five countries during the floating exchange rate regime with those from the era of the Bretton-Woods agreement, and we found that the following statistical observations

Table 5.1.   Japan

	Average of Trend			Standard Error of Deviation from Trend		
	~72/IV (A)	75/I~ (B)	(B)–(A)	~72/IV (A)	75/I~ (B)	(B)–(A)
Real Growth Rate	9.39	4.15	–	3.12	0.93	–
Unemployment Rate	1.59	2.27	+	0.19	0.14	–
Inflation Rate						
('83/I~)	4.70	5.43(2.43)	+	2.12	1.55	–
Current Account/						
GNP	0.24	1.23	+	0.86	0.98	+
Government						
Deficit/GNP	−0.68	−6.60	–	0.72	0.75	+
Monetary Growth						
Rate	18.33	11.44	–	2.71	1.36	–
Real Short-term						
Rate	7.71	5.82	–	2.43	2.06	–
Real Long-term						
Rate	3.27	4.96	+	1.27	0.53	–
Real Export	12.87	10.49	–	7.26	8.41	+
Terms of Trade						
(1980=100)	217.83	120.07	–	3.16	5.94	+
Import Price	1.67	3.93	+	5.77	21.97	+

Table 5.2. United States

	Average of Trend			Standard Error of Deviation from Trend		
	~72/IV (A)	75/I~ (B)	(B)–(A)	~72/IV (A)	75/I~ (B)	(B)–(A)
Real Growth Rate	3.01	3.01	0	2.57	3.00	+
Unemployment Rate	4.94	7.41	+	0.78	1.11	+
Inflation Rate ('83/I~)	2.44	7.09(3.35)	+	0.57	0.80	+
Current Account/ GNP	0.42	−0.85	−	0.25	0.62	+
Government Deficit/GNP	−0.84	−3.32	−	1.17	1.47	+
Monetary Growth Rate	7.65	9.51	+	2.40	2.09	−
Real Short-term Rate	2.86	6.72	+	0.59	1.36	+
Real Long-term Rate	0.93	4.38	+	0.43	0.99	+
Real Export	5.90	4.86	−	8.01	7.41	−
Terms of Trade (1980=100)	145.10	113.36	−	1.97	3.99	+
Import Price	2.64	7.89	+	2.77	8.90	+

Table 5.3. United Kingdom

	Average of Trend			Standard Error of Deviation from Trend		
	~72/IV (A)	75/I~ (B)	(B)–(A)	~72/IV (A)	75/I~ (B)	(B)–(A)
Real Growth Rate	2.36	2.36	0	1.87	2.36	+
Unemployment Rate	2.08	7.45	+	0.25	0.37	+
Inflation Rate ('83/I~)	5.11	10.17(7.47)	+	1.33	4.77	+
Current Account/ GNP	−0.25	0.12	+	0.97	1.57	+
Government Deficit/GNP	−0.79	−4.19	−	1.19	1.65	+
Monetary Growth Rate	6.97	14.79	+	3.17	3.63	+
Real Short-term Rate	4.53	8.11	+	1.51	2.24	+
Real Long-term Rate	1.37	2.68	+	1.10	2.36	+
Real Export	3.48	3.48	0	6.39	8.63	+
Terms of Trade (1980=100)	97.01	95.67	−	2.08	1.47	−
Import Price	4.18	9.47	+	3.93	6.55	+

Table 5.4. West Germany

	Average of Trend			Standard Error of Deviation from Trend		
	~72/IV (A)	75/I~ (B)	(B)–(A)	~72/IV (A)	75/I~ (B)	(B)–(A)
Real Growth Rate	4.38	2.00	−	2.61	2.32	−
Unemployment Rate	0.97	6.27	+	0.27	0.33	+
Inflation Rate ('83/I~)	2.91	3.80(2.01)	+	1.56	1.34	−
Current Account/ GNP	2.13	2.34	+	0.85	0.81	−
Government Deficit/GNP	−0.42	−1.99	−	0.55	0.58	+
Monetary Growth Rate	12.79	7.20	−	2.17	2.17	0
Real Short-term Rate	3.68	5.12	+	1.64	2.32	+
Real Long-term Rate	2.47	4.12	+	0.49	0.37	−
Real Export	5.55	5.55	0	5.55	6.68	+
Terms of Trade (1980=100)	102.73	104.10	+	2.50	3.38	+
Import Price	−0.41	3.33	+	3.17	7.91	+

Table 5.5. France

	Average of Trend			Standard Error of Deviation from Trend		
	~72/IV (A)	75/I~ (B)	(B)–(A)	~72/IV (A)	75/I~ (B)	(B)–(A)
Real Growth Rate	4.64	2.43	−	2.54	1.57	−
Unemployment Rate	2.52	7.17	+	0.17	0.28	+
Inflation Rate ('83/I~)	5.00	9.77(6.81)	+	1.58	1.02	−
Current Account/ GNP	−0.19	−0.25	−	0.58	1.18	+
Government Deficit/GNP	−0.27	−1.86	−	1.29	1.60	+
Monetary Growth Rate	13.05	11.91	−	4.59	2.44	−
Real Short-term Rate	5.21	8.44	+	1.73	1.89	+
Real Long-term Rate	0.38	2.40	+	0.39	0.45	+
Real Export	9.09	5.07	−	7.07	7.08	+
Terms of Trade (1980=100)	105.50	103.00	−	2.00	3.53	+
Import Price	6.34	6.34	0	5.07	9.18	+

characterize the differences in macroeconomic performance under the two systems.

First, with respect to indicators for stabilization policy goals:

A. The average trends in the rate of unemployment and the rate of inflation rose in all five countries.

B. The average trend in the real growth rate was constant for the lower-growth group, the U.S. and the U.K., but it declined for the higher-growth group, Japan, West Germany, and France; the growth rate differential between the two groups disappeared except in the case of Japan, where it is still higher.

C. The deviations from the trends of the inflation rate and the real growth rate in the U.S. and the U.K. increased, while they decreased in Japan, West Germany, and France, implying that the macro-economies in these three countries became more stable in terms of fluctuations of the inflation rate and the real growth rate.

D. Concerning the ratio of current account surplus or deficit to GNP, the deviation from trend increased in all countries except West Germany, and the average trend showed a growing gap in the 1980s between surpluses in Japan and West Germany and deficits in the U.S.

Second, for indicators for fiscal and monetary policies:

A. The average trend in the ratio of the government deficit to GNP rose in all five countries in the 1970s, but in the 1980s the trend in Japan and West Germany started to decline, while in the U.K. it leveled off, and in the U.S. and France it continued to rise.

B. In Japan, West Germany, and France, the average trend in the money growth rate gradually declined, and in Japan and France the deviation from trend also decreased; however, in the U.S. and the U.K. the average trend in the money growth rate increased and in the U.K. the deviation from trend also increased.

C. Both the average trend and the deviation from trend of the real short-term rate of interest increased in all countries except Japan, where they decreased.

D. The average trend in the real long-term rate of interest rose in all five countries, but the deviation from trend narrowed in Japan and West Germany while it widened in the U.S. and the U.K.

Third, for indicators for external shocks:

A. The deviation from trend for all three indicators—i.e., the change in real exports, the terms of trade, and the import price change—

increased in all countries except for the change in real exports in the U.S. and the terms of trade in the U.K., whose deviations decreased.

B. The average trend of the change in real exports declined, for the terms of trade it deteriorated, and for the inflation rate of import prices it rose in all five countries except for the terms of trade of the U.K., which improved in the 1980s.

Finally, for indicators for the exchange rates (Figures 5.1 and 5.2):

A. Since 1973, in terms of the U.S. dollar, the nominal exchange rates of the Japanese yen, the Deutsche mark, the French franc, and the

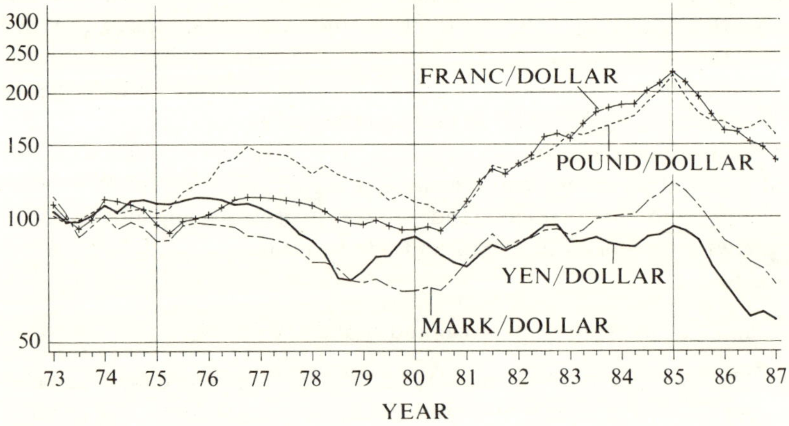

Figure 5.1
Nominal Exchange Rate (1973 = 100; semi-log scale)

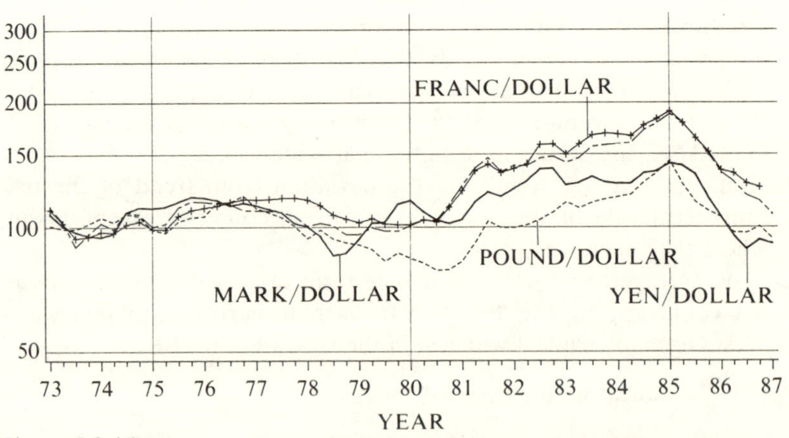

Figure 5.2 (a)
Real Exchange Rate (A): Deflated by GNP deflator

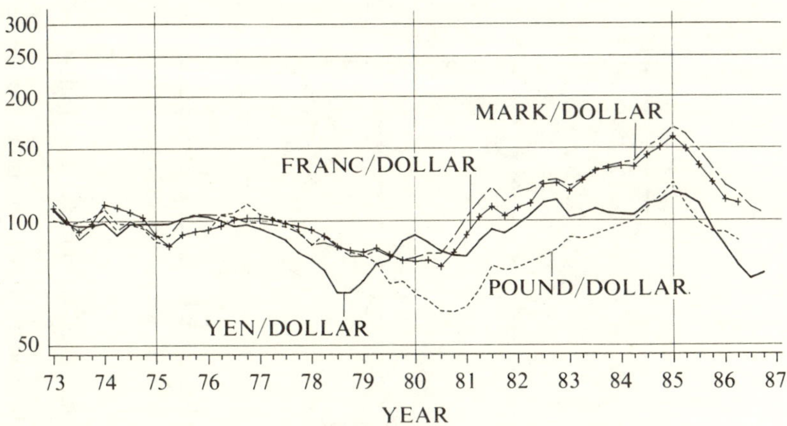

Figure 5.2 (b)
Real Exchange Rate (B): Deflated by WPI (industrial products)

pound sterling have undergone two waves of medium-term fluctuation; as a trend, the yen and the mark have appreciated, while the franc and the pound have depreciated.

B. Real exchange rates, calculated using either the GNP deflator or the WPI for industrial products, were very stable in the 1970s, particularly the WPI-deflated exchange rates. However, in the 1980s the real exchange rates of these four currencies against the dollar depreciated sharply until 1985, when the Plaza Agreement was reached; and then they appreciated dramatically to approach their 1970s levels, which suggests that PPP holds in the long run. Presently, against the dollar, the real exchange rates of the yen and the pound sterling have appreciated, and those of the Deutsche mark and the franc have depreciated relative to their 1973 levels; but deviations from the 1973 benchmarks are very small.

These are the statistical regularities we observed in the thirteen macroeconomic indicators for the five countries. These indicators provide measures of domestic instability and international imbalances under the two exchange rate regimes.

Conclusion

Our analysis of the data indicates that external price and income shocks were no doubt larger after 1973 than before 1972, and that

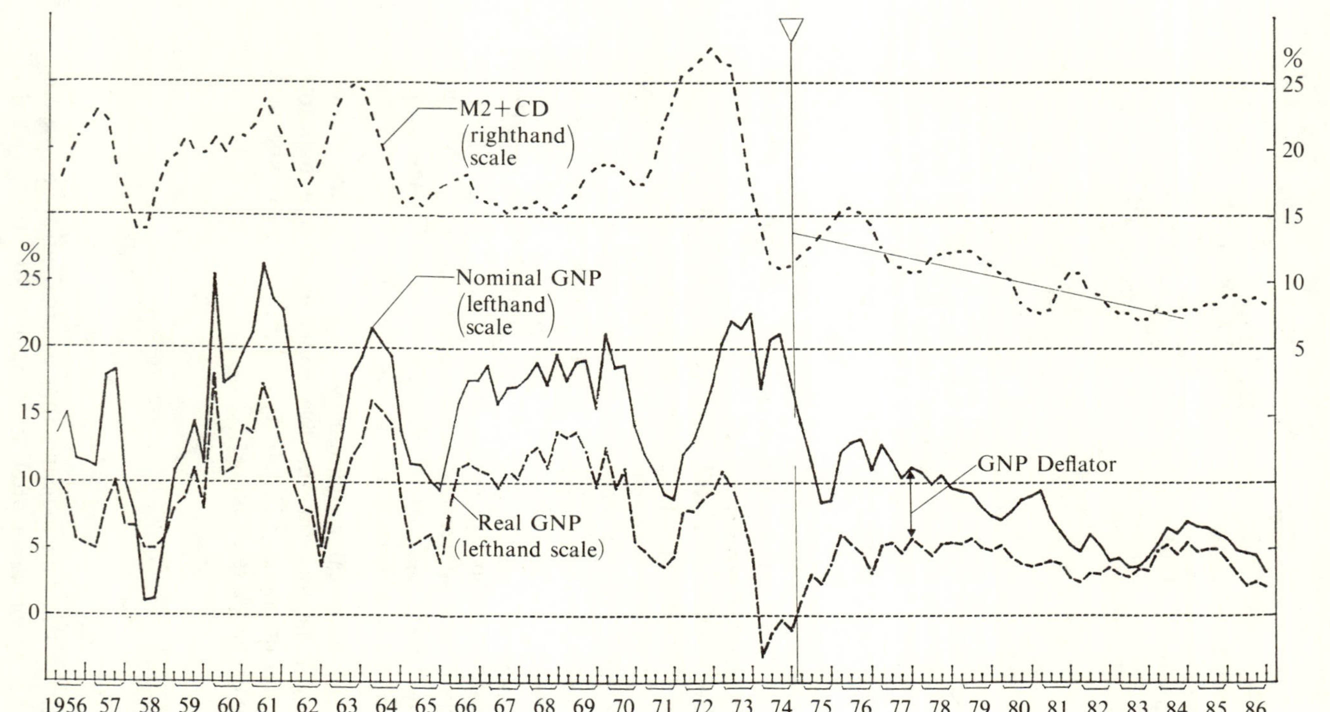

Figure 5.3
Money Stock and GNP (Nominal and Real) in Japan
Notes: 1. Growth rates of money stock and GNP are calculated not against the previous quarter, but against the same quarter the previous year.

2. "M_2 + CD" data (before first quarter 1979, "M_2" data) are averages of end-of-month observations. For example, the first quarter is an average of the data at the end of January, February, and March.

these shocks have been to some degree responsible for the increased domestic instability in the five countries. However, with respect to common external shocks, the extent of induced domestic instability has varied across countries. In those countries where fluctuations of policy variables decreased, the variability of the inflation rate and the real growth rate also decreased. In Figure 5.3 we have provided a representative example. As you can see, since 1975 the money growth rate in Japan has become more stable and the uncertainty associated with it has also decreased due to the announcements of targets. And since 1976 there has been an accompanying decrease in the variability of the inflation and real growth rates.

However, note that at the same time the average growth rates for the more successfully stabilized economies—including Japan—declined. Whether this is due to the cost of stabilization policy or owes to other factors such as the implicit costs of the floating exchange rate system, a deterioration of the terms of trade, worldwide high real interest rates, and reductions in exploitable technology gaps remains to be determined.

Among other points of interest is the surprising stability of real exchange rates in the long run. Also surprising are the wide swings of real exchange rates in the medium run, particularly in the 1980s, a period that has seen the emergence of large international imbalances and substantial divergences among countries in fiscal policy with respect to the levels of government deficits.

This has been a brief summary of our empirical work; the implications of our data will likely be discussed in the following sessions. We hope you will find this presentation to be of some use in the analyses of issues that will be raised at the Conference.

Technical Appendix: Trend Estimation with Bayesian Approach

This estimation method is Bayesian in nature and makes extensive use of Akaike's Information Criteria (AIC). The main features of this approach are listed below. For a more detailed explanation please refer to Kitagawa and Gersch (1984) and Naniwa (1985). A software package for this estimation procedure has been written by Kitagawa (1985).

i) In standard time series analysis, the trend is modeled by a polynomial of specified degree, e.g., a straight line or a quadratic function. In contrast, this approach assumes the trend is stochastic and does not use the standard technique in estimating the trend.

ii) The word stochastic does not imply that the trend changes in a simply random manner. Rather, the trend is assumed to follow a smooth stochastic process. In this sense the approach is Bayesian.

iii) AIC is used to specify the degree of the so-called smoothness prior. Depending on the degree of the smoothness prior, the trend could, for instance, be a straight line or a bumpy line.

iv) The estimation procedure is as follows:

    (a) The observed time series is decomposed into trend, stationary, and error components.

    (b) Each component is represented by a state space model in which the information necessary to characterize the system is incorporated in the state vector.

    (c) The model is estimated using recursive Kalman filtering and smoothing techniques.

    (d) The results are evaluated using AIC. The specification which has the smallest AIC is judged to fit the data best.

    (e) The stationary component is modeled as an AR (autoregressive) process and is estimated simultaneously with the trend.

References

Kitagawa, G., and Gersch, W. 1984. "A Smoothness Prior-State Space Modeling of Time Series With Trend and Seasonality," *Journal of the American Statistical Association*, Vol. 79, No. 386.

Kitagawa, G. 1985. "TIMSAC-84 Part 1," in *Computer Science Monographs*, No. 22, ed. M. Ishida, Institute of Statistical Mathematics.

Naniwa, S. 1986. "Trend Estimation via Smoothness Prior-State Space Modeling," *Monetary and Economic Studies*, Vol. 4, No. 1.

The Causes of Domestic Instability since 1973

6

Monetary Policy and Aggregate Fluctuations

Michael Parkin

This paper* investigates the fluctuations of aggregate real output and the price level in the world[1] economy and in the national economies of the seven major industrial countries (Canada, France, Germany, Italy, Japan, United Kingdom, and United States) over the period 1958 to 1985.[2] The main goal of the investigation is to establish the contribution of monetary policy to output and price level fluctuations. In particular, it seeks to discover the extent to which monetary policy contributed to aggregate economic performance in the era of floating exchange rates since 1973.

The decision to study the world aggregate economy as well as the economies of the seven major industrial countries was based on two considerations. First, closed economies are simpler than open economies, and the world aggregate economy is the best empirical entity available to us that approximates a closed economy.[3] Second, before trying to understand the sources of variability in the aggregate performances of individual countries it seems useful to establish the patterns in the average performance of all countries.

The paper begins by describing the cycles in output and inflation and examining the changing cyclical patterns in the mid-1970s. It then examines a descriptive macroeconomic model that is consistent with

* This is a revised version of a paper prepared for the Third International Conference of the Institute for Monetary and Economic Studies, Bank of Japan. I am grateful to, but in no way implicate, Stanley Fischer, John Scadding, William H. White, John Taylor, and James Tobin for comments on an earlier draft.

[1] The world is defined as the countries whose data are collected and summarized by the International Monetary Fund and published in *International Financial Statistics* as world aggregates.

[2] Not all variables cover the entire period; some begin in 1960 and some end in 1984.

[3] The data available exclude the Soviet Union and most COMECON countries.

a variety of alternative deeper structures and that provides an interpretation of the data on output, prices, and monetary policy. Though the model is descriptive, it contains enough structure to enable us to discriminate between sticky price Keynesian and rational expectations, market-clearing, explanations of aggregate fluctuations. It does not enable us to distinguish, at the world aggregate level, between real business cycle theories on the one hand and monetary theories on the other hand.

Three main conclusions emerge from this study of world aggregate macroeconomic performance. First, the sticky price theory of the cycle is rejected while the class of theories based on market-clearing assumptions is not. Second, the major source of increased variability in output growth in the second half of the 1970s is an increased variability of real shocks hitting the supply side of the economy. Third, the rise in inflation in the 1970s had its origin in increased money supply growth rates in the late 1960s and early 1970s. Real, supply-side, shocks as well as financial innovations and changes in velocity made virtually no contribution to the rise in inflation.

The next section studies the individual countries, examining differences in their output and inflation performances. The main purpose in studying the individual countries is to reveal whether differences in national monetary policies can account for differences in national macroeconomic performances. It turns out that they can.

The seven countries fall into three groups: Canada and the United States, whose aggregate real fluctuations have increased in amplitude since the mid-1970s; Japan, and to a lesser extent Germany and the United Kingdom, the amplitude of whose cycles has decreased in recent years; and France and Italy, for whom the amplitude of aggregate fluctuations has remained constant. There are clear differences in the monetary policies pursued in these three country groups. In the first group, monetary policy has become more volatile under floating exchange rates. In the second, and in particular in Japan, monetary policy has become more stable and predictable; while in the third (and to some degree in Germany and the U.K.), the relevant parameters of monetary policy have not changed much under flexible exchange rates compared with the earlier fixed exchange rate period.

The main conclusion reached is that the major sources of fluctuations in world and national aggregate real economic activity are real shocks. But monetary shocks have also been important in some countries and in particular in Canada and the United States where they have accentuated the fluctuations of output and inflation. Stable and highly predictable monetary policies, in particular in Japan, have contributed to the stabilization of real output even in the face of larger shocks emanating from the supply side of the world economy.

I. The World Economy

The growth rate of world aggregate real Gross Domestic Product (as computed by the International Monetary Fund) is set out in Figure 6.1 (a). Two features of the data shown in that figure are striking. First,

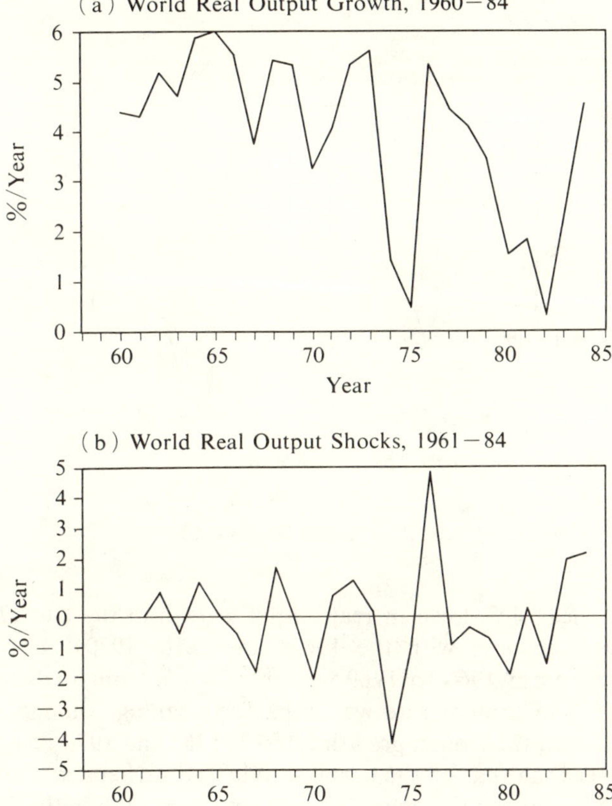

Figure 6.1
World Real Output Growth (a); World Real Output Shocks (b)

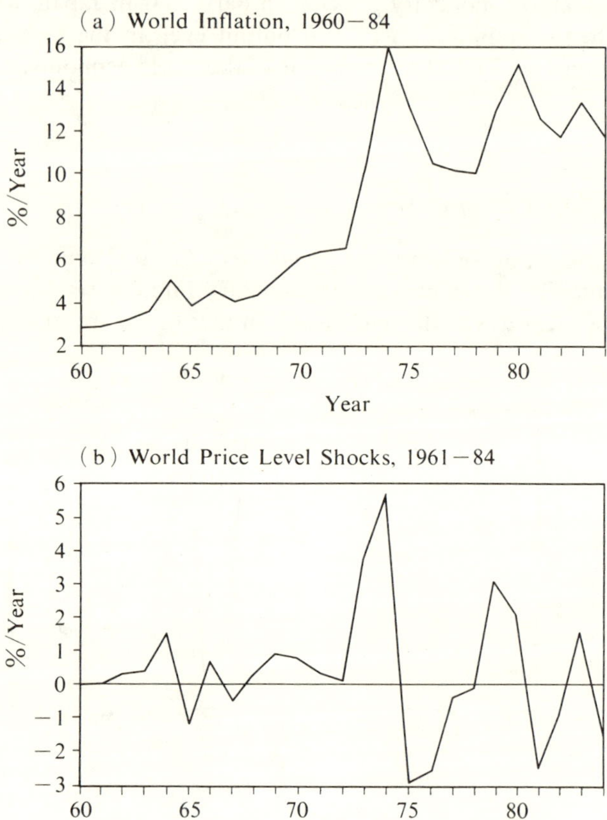

Figure 6.2
World Inflation (a); World Price Level Shocks (b)

there is a clear slowdown in real output growth in the late 1970s and
the 1980s compared with the 1960s and early 1970s. The average
growth rate from 1960 to 1969 was 4.9% while from 1970 to 1984 it
was 3.2% The growth rate was apparently falling, though, even in
the 1960s, with the trough growth rates of 1967 and 1970 being succes-
sively lower than that of 1963. The second and perhaps more dramatic
feature of the data is the increased volatility of growth in the 1970s and
1980s. The variance of output growth in the decade to 1969 was 0.8%,
while from 1970 onward that variance was 3.4%.

The growth rate of world output is quite well described as a random walk. Figure 6.1 (b) adopts this interpretation and plots the innovations in world output (measured as the absolute change in the percent growth rate). The increased volatility of output is more strongly visible at this level of differencing. The variance of the innovations from 1960 to 1970 was 1.5% while from 1971 to 1984 it was 4.7%.

Figure 6.2 shows world inflation (measured as the rate of change in the Gross Domestic Product deflator). The strong rising trend in the 1960s and early 1970s and much increased volatility in the 1970s and 1980s are clearly visible in these figures. The variance of inflation in the 1960s was 1.1% while in the 1970s and 1980s it increased to 7.8%. The variances of the innovations (measured as the absolute changes in the percent inflation rate) for those two same periods are 0.6% and 7.5% respectively.

Why have fluctuations in aggregate output and prices increased in amplitude in the 1970s and 1980s compared with the 1960s? Is the increased volatility in the world averages attributable primarily to real shocks, especially those associated with commodity and energy prices in the early and middle 1970s? Or has the increased volatility in output and prices arisen as a consequence of the abandonment of the Bretton-Woods gold exchange standard and adoption of fiat money standards with flexible exchange rates with a consequential rise in the variability of money supply growth rates?

An attempt at answering these questions will begin by an examination of the contemporaneous relations between the growth rates of output, prices, and the money supply and then by an analysis of the causality (in the Granger sense) relations among the variables.

A. Contemporaneous Relations

In addition to producing data on world aggregate real GDP and the price level, the IMF produces five world aggregate money series— reserve money, narrow money, broad money (defined as money plus quasi-money), the income velocity of money plus quasi-money, and the ratio of reserve money to money plus quasi-money (the inverse of the broad money multiplier).

Two identities help us organize these data and, as it turns out, provide a partial answer to the questions posed above. The first is the income expenditure identity which, in growth rates, is

$$\Delta y + \Delta p = \Delta m + \Delta v \tag{1}$$

where all the variables are logarithms and y is real output, p is the

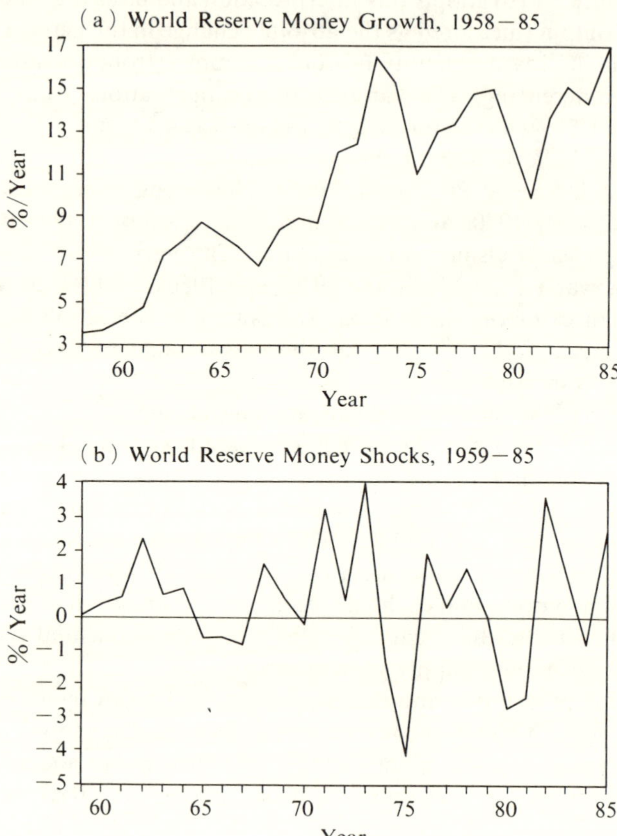

Figure 6.3
World Reserve Money Growth (a); World Reserve Money Shocks (b)

price level, m is the money supply, v is velocity, and Δ is the difference operator. The second identity is that relating the money supply to the monetary base and is

$$\Delta m = \Delta mb + \Delta mm \tag{2}$$

where again the variables are logarithms and mb is the monetary base and mm the money multiplier.

Figures 6.3, 6.4, 6.5, and 6.6 plot the monetary variables in a manner comparable with the data for output and the price level in Figures 6.1 and 6.2, and Table 6.1 summarizes data for all six variables organized in terms of the two identities.

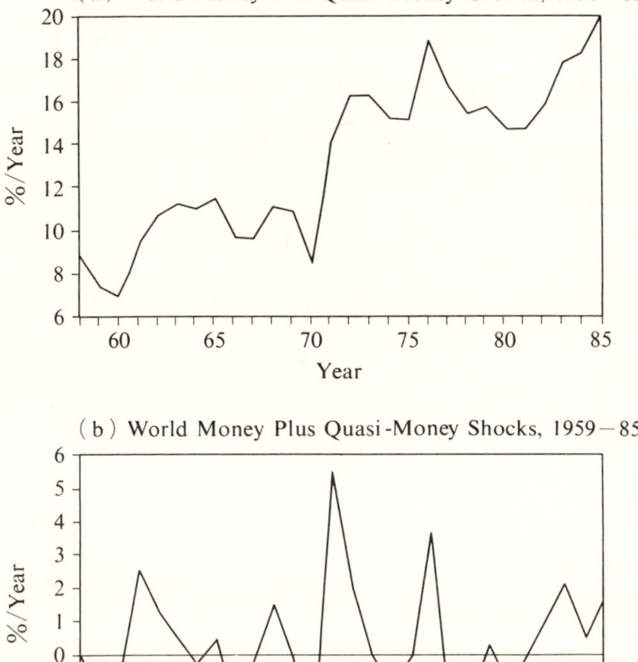

Figure 6.4
World Money Plus Quasi-Money Growth (a); World Money Plus Quasi-Money Shocks (b)

First consider the means. The rise in inflation from 4.2% in the 1960s to 11.5% in the 1970s and 1980s is associated with a rise in the growth rate of the money supply and with an approximately constant rate of change of velocity. The rise in the growth rate of the money supply is associated with a rise in the growth rate of the monetary base and with virtually no change in the rate of change of the money multiplier. Thus, despite massive financial deregulation and innovation in the world aggregate data, the rates of change of velocity and of the money multiplier were little different in the 1970s and 1980s from what they had been in the 1960s, and the higher inflation rate of the

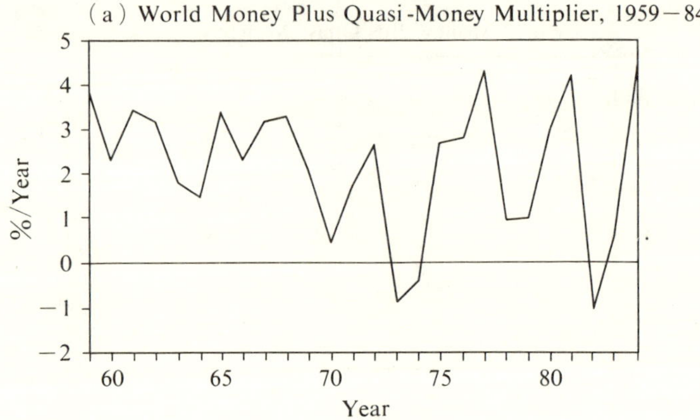

(a) World Money Plus Quasi-Money Multiplier, 1959—84

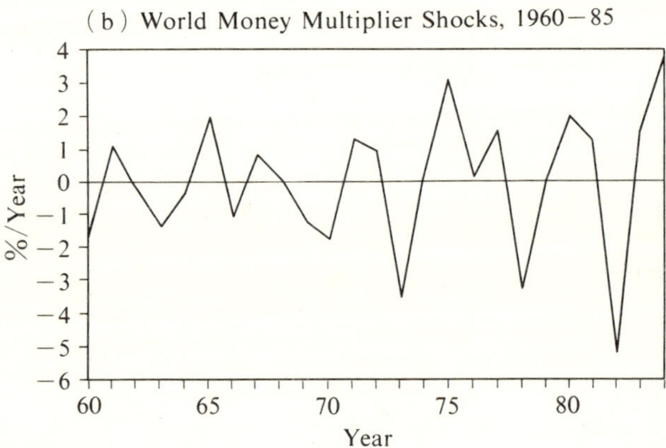

(b) World Money Multiplier Shocks, 1960—85

Figure 6.5
World Money Plus Quasi-Money Multiplier (a); World Money Multiplier Shocks (b)

later period is associated exclusively with a higher growth rate of the money supply and of monetary base.

Next, consider the variances. The most striking differences between the two sub-periods are in output growth and inflation. The variance of output growth increased four-fold and that of inflation almost eight-fold. Where did this increased variability come from? What are the associated changes in the variances of nominal aggregate demand and the monetary variables? First, the variability of the money supply and that of the monetary base are virtually identical in the two sub-periods. The money multiplier and velocity each became more variable. The

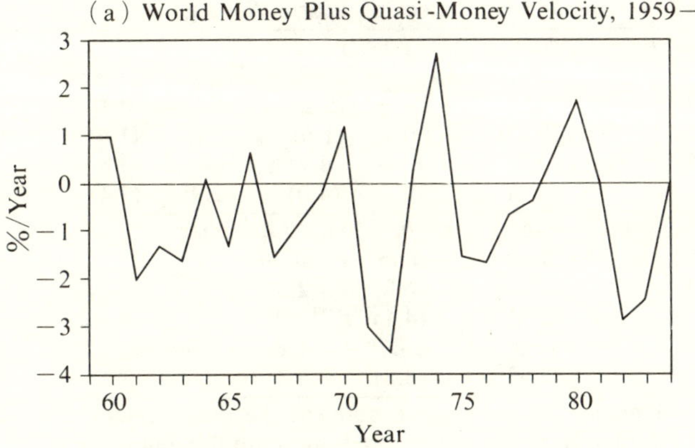

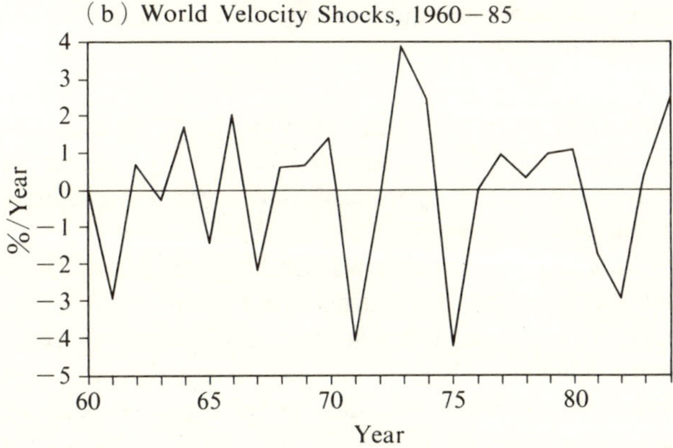

Figure 6.6
World Money Plus Quasi-Money Velocity (a); World Velocity Shocks (b)

money multiplier rather more than tripled in variability and velocity somewhat more than doubled. Negative covariation, however (not visible in the table), between money base growth and the multiplier resulted in the aggregate growth rate of the money supply being no more variable in the 1970s and 1980s than it had been in the 1960s. Further, negative covariation between velocity and money growth resulted in a smaller rise in the variability of aggregate nominal demand than in velocity itself. In fact, the variance of nominal aggregate demand was only 2.5 times larger in the 1970s and 1980s than it had been in the 1960s.

The data in Table 6.1 are consistent with the hypothesis that the

Table 6.1   Means and Variances of World Aggregates

(a) *Income, Prices, Money, and Velocity*

	Δy	$+$	Δp	$=$		Δmqm	$+$	$\Delta vmqm$
1960–1970	4.9	+	4.2	=	9.1 $\cong$	9.7	–	0.4
	(0.8)		(1.1)		(1.6)	(2.3)		(1.4)
1971–1984	3.2	+	11.5	=	14.7 $\cong$	16.3	–	0.8
	(3.4)		(7.8)		(4.0)	(2.9)		(3.4)

(b) *Money, Reserve Money, and the Money Multiplier*

	Δmqm	$=$	Δmb	$+$	Δmm
1960–1970	9.7	$\cong$	6.8	+	2.5
	(2.3)		(4.1)		(0.9)
1971–1984	16.3	$\cong$	13.7	+	1.8
	(2.9)		(3.8)		(3.3)

Notes: 1. Identities do not hold exactly in the data because second-order interaction terms are ignored and data for p and y run from 1960 while other variables run from 1958.

2. mqm is money plus quasi-money, and $vmqm$ is the velocity of money plus quasi-money.

increased variability of output and prices in the 1970s and 1980s was generated by increasingly severe supply and velocity shocks. The data are not consistent with the hypothesis that increased output and inflation variability were generated by increased variability in money supply growth. The data in Table 6.1 are also consistent with the hypothesis that the increase in inflation arose from an increase in the money supply growth rate and not from an increase in the growth rate of velocity. They are also, though, consistent with the hypothesis that the increase in inflation was caused by supply shocks which in turn were accommodated by increased money supply growth. It is to discriminate between these two possible directions of causation and to shed further light on the underlying sources of aggregate fluctuations that I now turn to an examination of the causality relations among the variables.

B. Causality

The contemporaneous relationships among real output, inflation, and the monetary variables are revealing but a deeper understanding of the processes at work can only be obtained by specifying and testing models that have some temporal structure. A model that is consistent with a variety of alternative deeper structures and one that conveniently specializes to three well-known models of the business cycle is the following.

First, aggregate demand, which is restricted to have unit elasticity, is given by

$$y_t^d = m_t + v_t - p_t \qquad \text{(aggregate demand)} \qquad (3)$$

where m is now the monetary base and v is the velocity of circulation of the monetary base.

Aggregate supply is given by

$$y_t^s = y_t^* + \gamma(p_t - a(L)E_{t-\tau}p_t) + u_t \qquad \text{(aggregate supply)} \qquad (4)$$

where y_t^* is "natural" output, $E_{t-\tau}$ is an expectation conditional on information available at $t - \tau$, $a(L)$, with $\sum a_i = 1$, is a polynomial L that operates on τ and u is an unforecastable real technology shock. Aggregate supply shocks are in part real and in part arise from price level forecast errors. The price level forecast errors have been written in what appears to be a complicated and cumbersome way to accommodate two alternative theories of aggregate fluctuations. If $a(L) = 1$ and $\tau = 1$, the aggregate supply function is that suggested by Lucas (1972, 1973). The more general case is the aggregate supply function proposed by Fischer (1977), and is in the spirit of (though not identical to) those of Phelps and Taylor (1977) and Taylor (1979, 1980).

If γ is zero so that price level forecast errors have no effect on aggregate supply, the specification is consistent with that proposed by the proponents of real business cycle theory such as Kydland and Prescott (1982), Long and Plosser (1983), and King and Plosser (1984).

The goods market clears to determine actual output

$$y_t^d = y_t^s = y_t \qquad \text{(equilibrium)} \qquad (5)$$

The monetary sector is described by the two stochastic processes:

$$\Delta v_t = \lambda \Delta m_{t-1} + x_t \qquad \text{(financial technology)} \qquad (6)$$

$$\Delta m_t = \alpha - \beta \Delta p_{t-1} + z_t \qquad \text{(monetary policy)} \qquad (7)$$

The evolution of financial technology (6) reacts to recent changes in monetary base and incorporates a univariate process x_t. Money base growth, (7), reacts to the most recently observed inflation rate and, aside from that reaction, follows a stochastic process z.

It will be convenient to decompose the stochastic processes x and z into the component which is forecastable on information available at $t - 1$ and that which is unforecastable. Specifically let us define that decomposition as:

$$x_t = \hat{x}_t + \xi$$

$$x_t = \hat{z}_t + \varepsilon.$$

The random variables u, ξ, and ε are distributed independently of each other. They are not identically distributed over time, however. Indeed, a principal purpose of this investigation is to explore sources of increased variance in output and inflation.

These five equations may be solved for the paths of output, inflation, and money growth (with velocity growth being given as a linear combination of those three). The solution set out below is for the case in which $a(L) = 1$ and $\tau = 1$. The restrictions implied by that special case solution will be tested subsequently. The more general solution incorporating the Keynesian sticky-wage approach would incorporate distributed lags of all the innovations associated with the lag operator polynomial $a(L)$.

The solution for the special case is

$$y_t = y_t^* + \frac{\gamma}{1 + \gamma}\,(\varepsilon_t + \xi_t) + \frac{1}{1 + \gamma}\,u_t \tag{8}$$

$$\Delta p_t = \alpha + x_t + \hat{z}_t - \beta\Delta p_{t-1} + \lambda\Delta m_{t-1} + (y_{t-1} - y_t^*)$$
$$+ \frac{1}{1 + \gamma}\,(\varepsilon_t + \xi_t - u_t) \tag{9}$$

$$\Delta m_t = \alpha + z_t - \beta\Delta p_{t-1} + \varepsilon_t. \tag{10}$$

Equation (8) says that fluctuations in output around its natural rate are random. The variance of output deviations is

$$\mathrm{Var}(y_t - y_t^*) = \left(\frac{\gamma}{1 + \gamma}\right)^2 (\sigma_\varepsilon^2 + \sigma_\xi^2) + \left(\frac{1}{(1 + \gamma)^2}\right)\sigma_u^2.$$

Notice that money affects output in the sense that innovations in both financial technology (ξ) and money supply growth (ε) generate innovations in output. Output is not, however, caused (in the Granger sense) by money or velocity. The variance of output is higher, the higher the variance of the growth rate of nominal aggregate demand (with a weight $[\gamma/(1 + \gamma)]^2$), and is greater, the greater the variance of the real shocks (with a weight of $1/(1 + \gamma)^2$). In the case of the real business cycle with $\gamma = 0$, output variability is simply σ_u^2, the variance of real supply shocks.

The inflation rate is autocorrelated and is also correlated with the previous period's money supply growth rate. The variance of the unforecastable component of inflation is given by:

$$\text{Var}(\Delta p) = \left(\frac{1}{1 + \gamma}\right)^2 (\sigma_\varepsilon^2 + \sigma_\xi^2 + \sigma_u^2)$$

Even if $\gamma = 0$ (real cycle theory), price variability is related one-for-one with the variability of both nominal demand and aggregate supply. Notice also that regardless of the value of γ (because of the assumption of unit elasticity of aggregate demand) supply shocks have an identical (but opposite sign) effect on output and prices. The money supply evolves according to equation (7) and is correlated with previous-period inflation.

Covariations between inflation and output fluctuations are of ambiguous sign and given by

$$\text{Cov}(y - y^*, \Delta p) = \frac{\gamma}{(1 + \gamma)^2}(\sigma_\varepsilon^2 + \sigma_\xi^2) - \frac{1}{(1 + \gamma)^2}\sigma_u^2.$$

Clearly,

$$\text{Cov}(y - y^*, \Delta p) \gtrless 0 \text{ as } \gamma \gtrless \frac{\sigma_u^2}{\sigma_\varepsilon^2 + \sigma_\xi^2}.$$

The Keynesian formulation of the model, not explicitly written above, involves distributed lags of the random variables ε, ξ, and u and a more complex distributed lag (based on the lag polynomial $a(L)$) in the interaction of inflation and money growth. In the Keynesian model, the lagged money innovations in the output equation imply that money Granger-causes output.

To estimate and test the model whose solutions are set out as equations (8), (9), and (10), it is necessary to introduce some additional hypotheses about the stochastic processes y^* (the evolution of natural output) and $\hat{x}$ and $\hat{z}$, (the stochastic processes governing velocity and money supply growth). The solutions can be written more compactly in the following form:

$$y_t = z_{1t} \tag{8a}$$

$$\Delta p_t = \alpha - \beta \Delta p_{t-1} + \lambda \Delta m_{t-1} + z_{2t} \tag{9a}$$

$$\Delta m_t = \alpha - \beta \Delta p_{1-1} + z_{3t} \tag{10a}$$

where

$$z_{1t} \equiv y_t^* + \frac{\gamma}{(1 + \gamma)}(\varepsilon_t + \xi_t) + \frac{1}{(1 + \gamma)}u_t$$

$$z_{2t} \equiv \hat{x}_t + \hat{z}_t + (y_{t-1} - y_t^*) + \frac{1}{(1 + \gamma)}(\varepsilon_t + \xi_t))$$

and $z_{3t} \equiv z_t$.

Two alternative assumptions are made about the stochastic processes z_i ($i = 1, 2, 3$). Assumption 1 is that Δz_1, z_2, and z_3 are independently and unidentically distributed random variables. Assumption 2 is that $\Delta^2 z_1$, Δz_2, and Δz_3 are identically and independently distributed. With these alternative assumptions and using the formulations written as (8a), (9a), and (10a), vector autoregressions using either the first differences (assumption 1) or the the second differences (assumption 2), output, prices, and money were run and the restrictions implied by (8), (9), and (10) imposed and tested.

One further modification, however, was made to the equations. We know from the above examination of the variables that there was a large rise in the variance of output and prices in the 1970s. We also know that there was virtually no change in the variance of money supply growth (monetary base growth in this case). In terms of the model set out above, the increased variance of output and prices would have to be interpreted as an increase in the variance of either u or ξ. Both u and ξ are technological variables and so each could, in principle, be affected by the same underlying shocks.

To permit variability in u (and possibly ξ) two variables were constructed, designed to capture the major sources of real shocks. The first is the rate of change of the relative price of commodities and the second is the rate of change in the relative price of petroleum. These two variables are shown in Figure 6.7. It turns out that the relative price of commodities on the average (which average, incidentally, excludes petroleum prices) performs better than the relative price of petroleum itself. Notice that the sharp rise in relative commodity prices occurred a year earlier than that in petroleum prices and was associated primarily with the prices of food and beverages.

Defining the change in relative commodity prices as Δr and treating that relative price change as a proxy for unobservable real shocks to technology and endowments, the equations describing the evolution of output, prices, and the money supply become

$$\Delta^d y_t = \delta \Delta r_{t-1} + w_{1t} \tag{11}$$

$$\Delta^d p_t = \alpha - \beta \Delta^d p_{t-1} + \lambda \Delta^d m_{t-1} + \mu \Delta r_{t-1} + w_{2t} \tag{12}$$

$$\Delta^d m_t = \alpha - \beta \Delta^d p_{t-1} + w_{3t} \tag{13}$$

for $d = 1, 2$, and where w_i were assumed to be i.i.d. random disturbances.

Estimation of (11), (12), and (13) as a general vector autoregressive

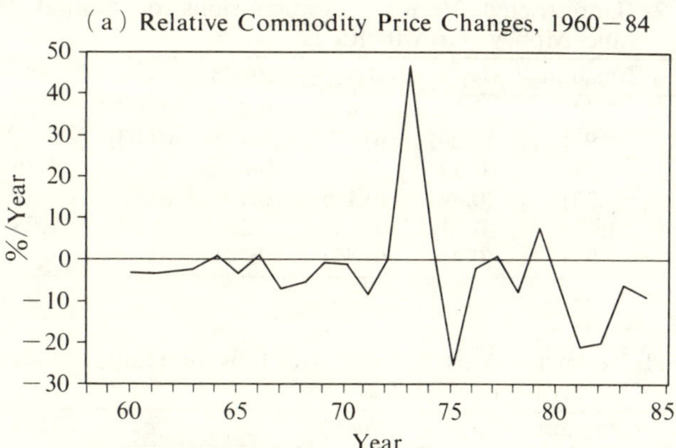

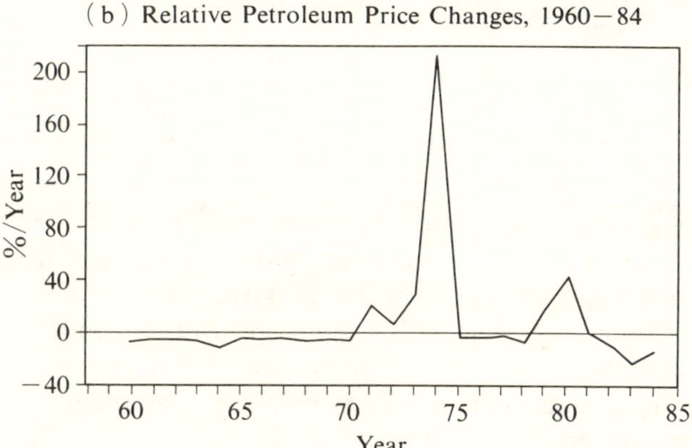

Figure 6.7
Relative Commodity Price Changes (a); Relative Petroleum Price Changes (b)

system gave the estimates set out in Table 6.2a for the first difference case and in Table 6.3a for the second difference case. The estimates of the restricted systems are in Table 6.2b and 6.3b. The *F*-statistic reported against each equation in Tables 6.2b and 6.3b is the one relevant for the restrictions imposed.

Choosing between the first and second difference formulation is not easy on the basis of the small samples with which we are dealing. On one critical issue, though, the two sets of results give the same answer: that is the directions of causation. In neither formulation does money growth Granger-cause output. Under both formulations money growth

Table 6.2a Unrestricted Vector Autoregressions of Output, Inflation, and Money (Growth Rates)

Equation	Constant	Δy_{t-1}	Δp_{t-1}	Δm_{t-1}	Δr_t	σ_w^2	Q(11)
Δy_t	3.92	0.16	−0.41	0.24	0.07	1.20	13.70
	(1.97)	(0.30)	(0.17)	(0.17)	(0.03)		
Δp_t	0.25	−0.39	0.33	0.68	0.05	1.36	10.80
	(2.23)	(0.34)	(0.19)	(0.19)	(0.03)		
Δm_t	3.43	−0.42	−0.44	1.20	0.06	1.78	12.61
	(2.92)	(0.45)	(0.25)	(0.24)	(0.04)		

Table 6.2b Restricted Vector Autoregressions of Output, Inflation, and Money (Growth Rates)

Equation	Constant	Δp_{t-1}	Δm_{t-1}	Δr_t	σ_w^2	Q(11)	$F(n_1,n_2)$
Δy_t	6.32	−0.30	—	−0.03	1.23	17.56	1.58
	(0.57)	(0.06)		(0.02)			(2,18)
Δp_t	−1.86	0.49	0.61	0.03	1.36	9.71	1.27
	(1.22)	(0.14)	(0.18)	(0.03)			(1,18)
Δm_t	3.12	—	0.75	—	1.88	10.48	1.90
	(1.38)		(0.12)				(3,18)

does Granger-cause inflation. There are, though, some contradictions between the two formulations. In the growth rate form, lagged inflation has a strong and significant but negative effect on output growth. In second differences that effect is not present. Second, in the first difference form inflation is autoregressive with a positive coefficient while in the second difference form inflation is autoregressive with a negative coefficient.

The effects of the real shocks, proxied by the rate of change in the relative price of commodities, has an effect of correct sign in both cases. It also corroborates the unit elasticity assumption in aggregate demand since, in each case, the positive effect on the price level is equal to the negative effect on output. In the first difference case that effect is small and not significant (at the 5% level), while in the second difference formulation the effect is larger and strongly significant.

In broad terms it seems to me that the second difference formulation of the model hangs together better and makes more sense than the first difference form. In the case of the money growth equation the difference form almost certainly has a unit root, and imposing that root in the second difference form appears appropriate in terms of both the goodness of fit and the plausibility of the counterinflationary effect found in that form. The output equation makes more sense in

Table 6.3a Unrestricted Vector Autoregressions of Output, Inflation, and Money (Changes in Growth Rates)

Equation	Constant	$\Delta^2 y_{t-1}$	$\Delta^2 p_{t-1}$	$\Delta^2 m_{t-1}$	Δr_t	σ_w^2	Q(11)
$\Delta^2 y_t$	−0.34	−0.11	−0.02	0.07	−0.10	1.45	12.15
	(0.38)	(0.24)	(0.26)	(0.19)	(0.03)		
$\Delta^2 p_t$	0.73	−0.38	0.64	0.53	0.12	1.41	12.49
	(0.37)	(0.23)	(0.25)	(0.19)	(0.03)		
$\Delta^2 m_t$	0.75	−0.30	−0.96	0.16	0.02	1.47	15.44
	(0.38)	(0.24)	(0.26)	(0.20)	(0.04)		

Table 6.3b Restricted Vector Autoregressions of Output, Inflation, and Money (Changes in Growth Rates)

Equation	Constant	$\Delta^2 p_{t-1}$	$\Delta^2 m_{t-1}$	Δr_t	σ_w^2	Q(11)	$F(n_1, n_2)$
$\Delta^2 y_t$	0.30	—	—	−0.10	1.35	11.24	0.07
	(0.29)			(0.02)			(3,17)
$\Delta^2 p_t$	0.67	−0.41	0.40	0.10	1.47	10.57	2.58
	(0.38)	(0.21)	(0.18)	(0.03)			(1,17)
$\Delta^2 m_t$	0.67	−0.72	—	—	1.43	11.37	0.61
	(0.31)	(0.15)					(3.17)

the second difference form with lagged inflation not playing a significant role. Interpreting the lagged inflation term in the first difference form is just about impossible. There are plenty of models that predict such an effect, but not in the absence of a lagged money growth effect. The presence of a lagged inflation effect and the absence of the lagged money growth effect suggest an inappropriate statistical formulation of the equation and favors the second difference case. It is less easy to choose between the two inflation equations. Consistency with the output of money growth equations, though, again points in favor of the second difference form.

What is clear is that this extremely parsimonious second difference representation of the time series behavior of output, prices, and the money supply is a remarkably good one. It also enables us to interpret the data on means and variances presented in Table 6.1. According to this model, world aggregate output became more variable in the 1970s and 1980s as a result of being hit by real shocks that were of much larger amplitude than those experienced earlier. Aggregate output fluctuations were not of higher variance as a result of more variable monetary policy.

Monetary policy produced the inflation of the 1970s. The growth rate of the money supply is itself a random walk with slight drift—

notice that the intercept in the money growth equation is positive and significant. Monetary policy reacts to inflation but does not fully offset inflationary shocks (coefficient of -0.7).

The effect of real shocks on output and the price level, particularly in 1973, were important. According to the estimated coefficient, a 1% rise in the relative price of raw materials has about a one-tenth of 1% effect on output (negative) and on the price level (positive). The actual rise in the relative price of raw materials in 1973 was close to 50%, so this single shock produced a 5% rise in prices and fall in output.

The conclusion to which we are led by this characterization of the world aggregate economy reinforces the conclusion based on contemporaneous correlations. The data are not consistent with a Keynesian sticky price model but are consistent with equilibrium models of both the real and monetary varieties. Are these conclusions borne out by the data describing national aggregate performance?

II. Country Fluctuations

The aggregate fluctuations of the seven major industrial countries (growth rates and changes in growth rates) are set out in Figures 6.8 through 6.14. In common with the world aggregate, the growth rates of all seven countries declined over the sample period. Unlike the world aggregate, however, the amplitude of the cycle did not increase in each and every country. In France and Italy (with the exception of the 1974–76 episode) the variability of output appears to have been roughly constant. Canada and the United States had a much higher degree of variability in the late 1970s and 1980s than earlier. Germany and the United Kingdom—and, more strikingly, Japan—experienced lower variability.

The average growth rates and their variances as well as the average innovations and variances are set out for three sub-periods in Table 6.4. Three sub-periods have been used to separate out the ambiguous period during which the Bretton-Woods system was collapsing but prior to which the flexible exchange rate system had settled down. The data in Table 6.4 give a more precise measure of the changed volatility in the individual countries than the pictures just considered.

Table 6.5 sets out similar data for inflation. The country variability of inflation is less striking than that of real output growth, and there is a much less than perfect correlation between these two variables across

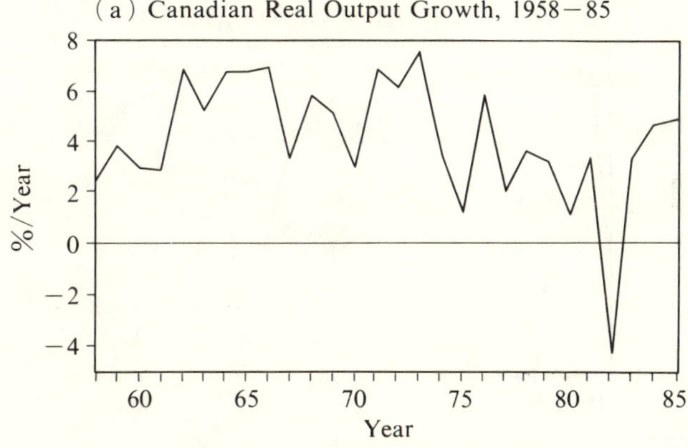

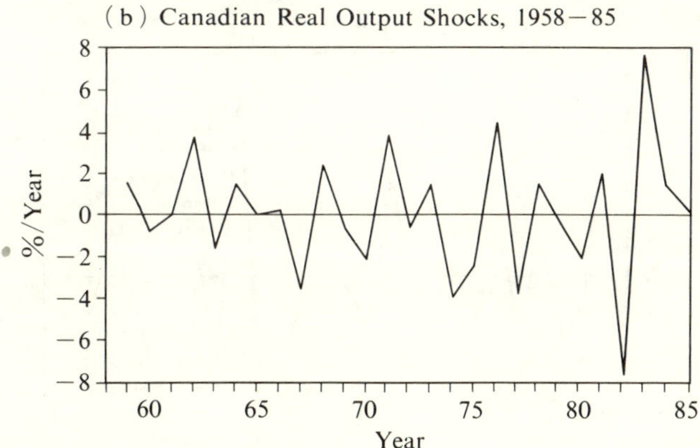

Figure 6.8
Canadian Real Output Growth (a); Canadian Real Output Shocks (b)

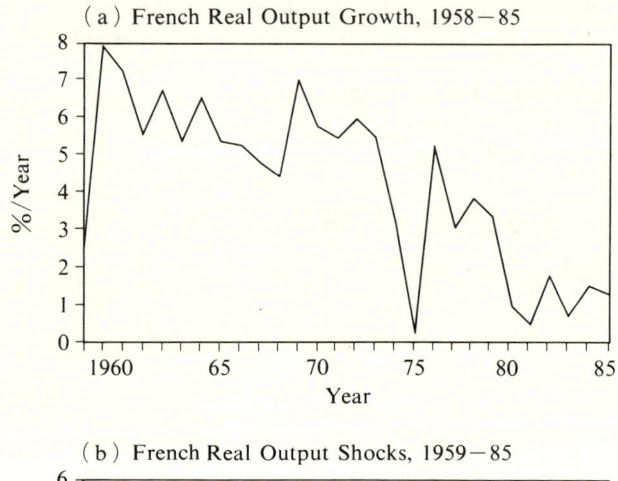

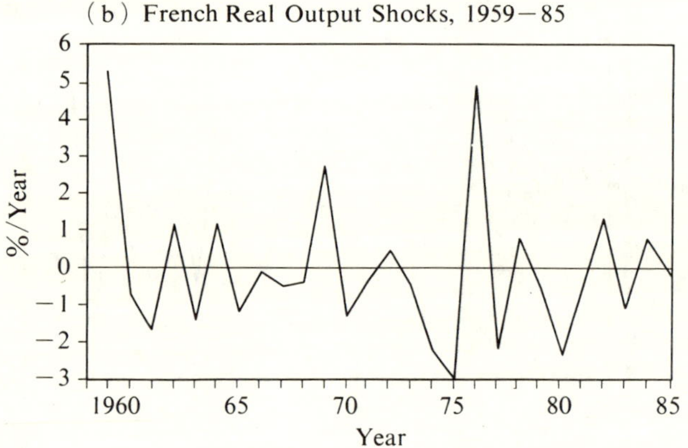

Figure 6.9
French Real Output Growth (a); French Real Output Shocks (b)

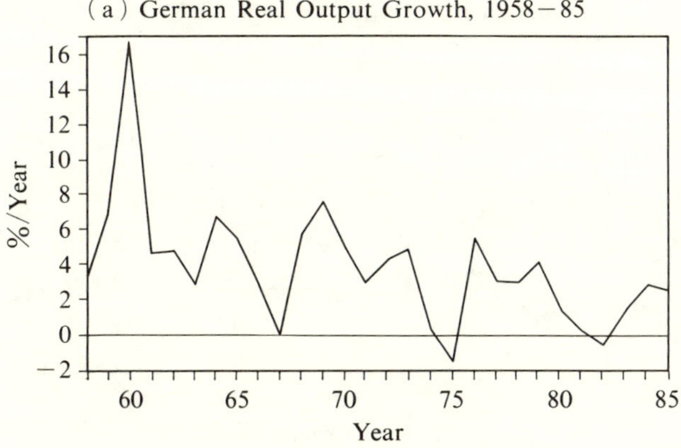

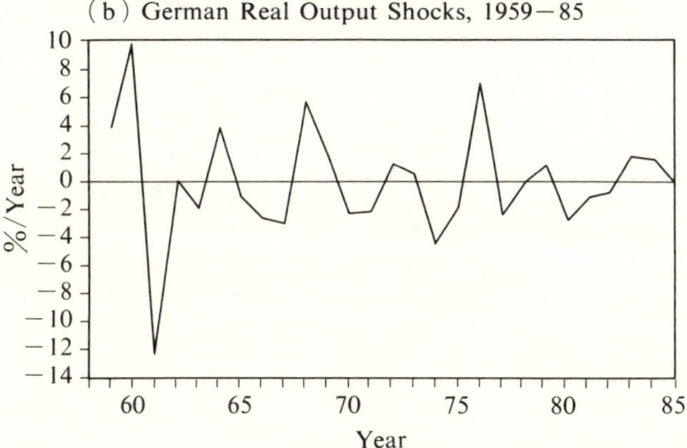

Figure 6.10
German Real Output Growth (a); German Real Output Shocks (b)

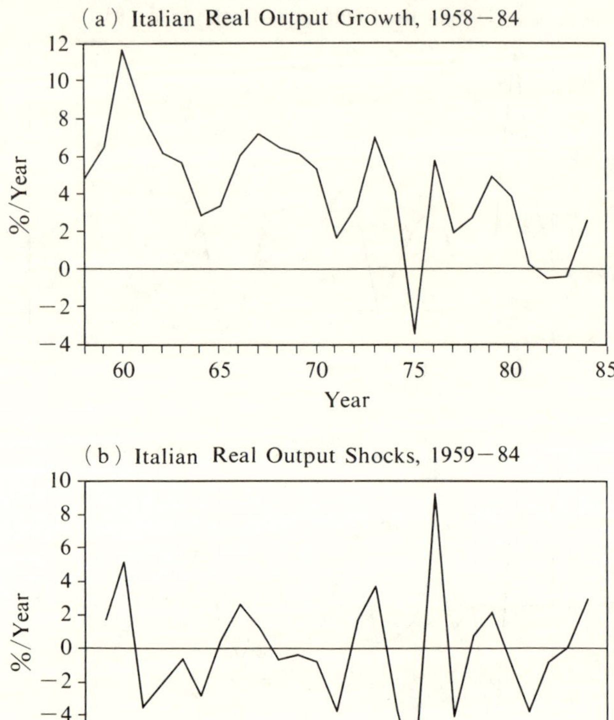

Figure 6.11
Italian Real Output Growth (a); Italian Real Output Shocks (b)

(a) Japanese Real Output Growth, 1958—85

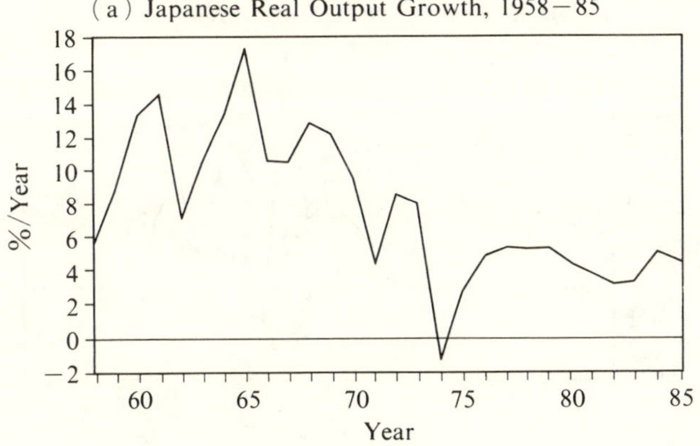

(b) Japanese Real Output Shocks, 1959—85

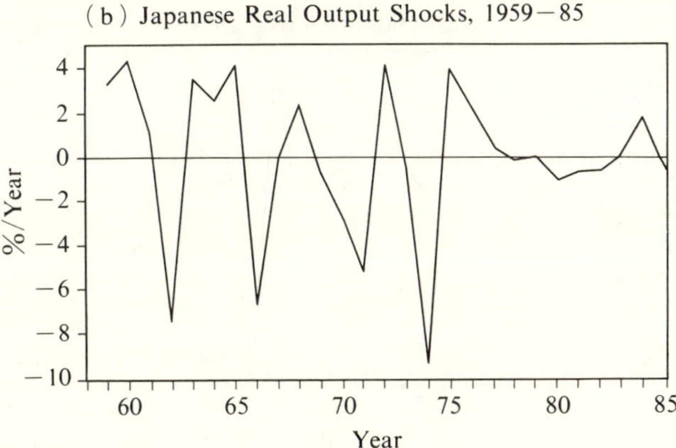

Figure 6.12
Japanese Real Output Growth (a); Japanese Real Output Shocks (b)

(a) U.K. Real Output Growth, 1958—85

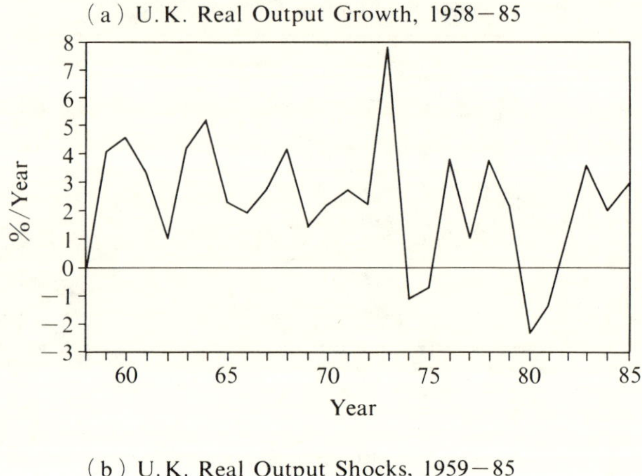

(b) U.K. Real Output Shocks, 1959—85

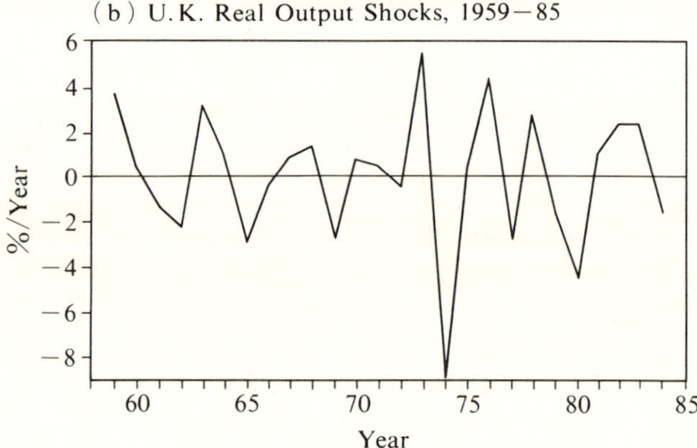

Figure 6.13
U.K. Real Output Growth (a); U.K. Real Output Shocks (b)

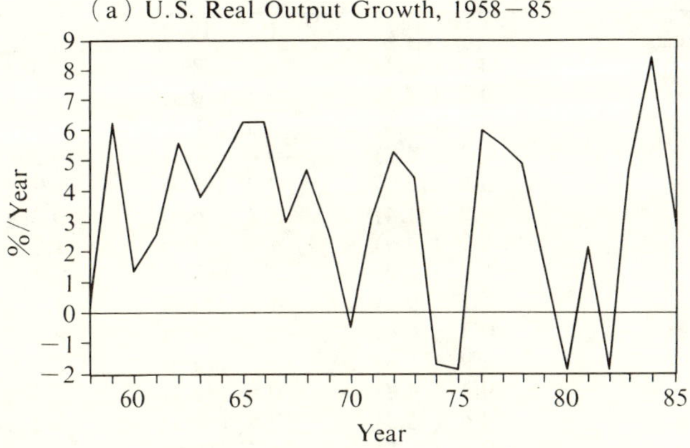

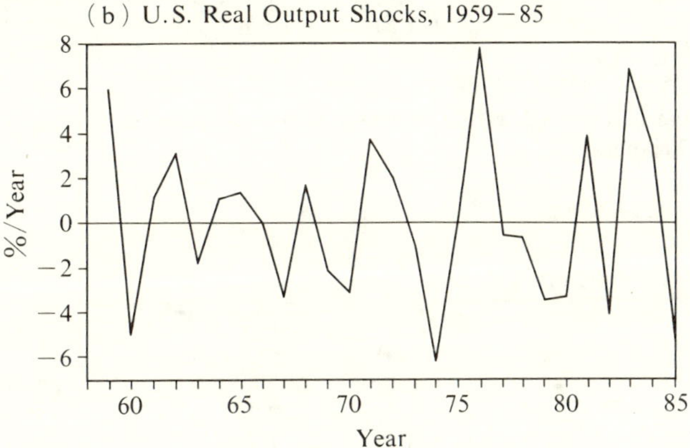

Figure 6.14
U.S. Real Output Growth (a); U.S. Real Output Shocks (b)

Table 6.4 Real G.D.P. Growth

	1958–1970	1971–1974	1975–1985
Canada	4.7 (3.1)	6.0 (2.9)	2.6 (7.6)
	0.1 (4.4)	0.2 (10.9)	0.1 (17.4)
France	5.7 (2.0)	5.0 (1.5)	2.0 (2.5)
	0.3 (4.2)	−0.6 (1.3)	−0.2 (4.9)
Germany	5.6 (16.0)	3.0 (3.9)	1.9 (4.3)
	0.2 (31.4)	−1.2 (6.8)	0.2 (7.5)
Italy[a]	6.2 (4.9)	4.0 (5.1)	1.8 (8.2)
	0 (5.9)	−0.3 (12.9)	−0.2 (21.7)
Japan	11.2 (9.8)	4.8 (20.7)	4.3 (0.9)
	0.3 (16.4)	−2.7 (33.9)	0.5 (2.4)
U.K.	2.9 (2.3)	2.9 (13.8)	1.5 (4.5)
	0.2 (4.8)	−0.8 (37.1)	0.4 (7.4)
U.S.A.	3.6 (5.3)	2.8 (9.7)	2.8 (12.7)
	−0.1 (9.5)	−0.3 (18.6)	0.4 (20.9)
World[a, b]	4.9 (0.8)	4.1 (3.7)	2.8 (3.2)
	−0.1 (1.5)	−0.5 (6.4)	0 (5.9)

Notes: [a] 1975–1984.

[b] 1960–1970.

Line 1 is growth rate and line 2 is change in growth rate, mean and (variance).

Table 6.5 Inflation

	1958–1970	1971–1974	1975–1985
Canada	2.7 (1.9)	8.2 (28.9)	8.0 (9.7)
	0.2 (0.6)	2.8 (9.7)	−1.1 (5.6)
France	4.6 (7.5)	7.7 (5.8)	10.1 (5.3)
	−0.6 (13.1)	1.4 (2.0)	−0.5 (3.8)
Germany	3.5 (2.6)	6.7 (1.3)	3.8 (1.3)
	0.3 (2.9)	−0.1 (3.0)	−0.4 (1.0)
Italy[a]	3.9 (5.9)	10.9 (31.0)	16.7 (8.3)
	0.4 (6.1)	2.9 (14.3)	−0.8 (9.0)
Japan	4.1 (10.9)	11.2 (52.6)	3.7 (5.6)
	0.8 (17.7)	3.3 (25.7)	−1.7 (14.9)
U.K.	3.7 (2.8)	9.9 (11.9)	12.4 (47.9)
	0.3 (2.6)	1.9 (17.8)	−0.8 (45.8)
U.S.A.	2.7 (2.4)	6.7 (6.5)	6.6 (10.6)
	0.4 (0.7)	1.1 (4.4)	−0.6 (6.7)
World[a, b]	4.2 (1.1)	9.8 (20.4)	12.2 (2.8)
	0.3 (0.6)	2.5 (7.5)	0.1 (7.4)

Notes: [a] 1975–1984.

[b] 1960–1970.

Line 1 is inflation rate and line 2 is change in inflation rate, mean and (variance).

Table 6.6 Reserve Money Growth

	1958–1970	1971–1974	1975–1985
Canada	5.7 (7.0)	13.8 (1.7)	7.9 (24.3)
	−0.1 (16.1)	1.9 (12.0)	−0.7 (9.6)
France	7.2 (19.0)	15.7 (40.3)	6.2 (68.4)
	−0.5 (15.5)	3.3 (156.6)	−0.4 (123.2)
Germany	8.2 (31.7)	14.8 (130.1)	4.6 (17.8)
	0 (64.7)	−3.5 (249.0)	0.5 (27.8)
Italy[a]	10.7 (28.3)	15.8 (23.9)	19.7 (44.8)
	0.4 (54.5)	1.2 (54.1)	−0.7 (37.5)
Japan	16.4 (25.3)	23.7 (67.7)	7.3 (12.6)
	1.2 (33.0)	1.4 (120.9)	−1.8 (37.2)
U.K.	4.5 (5.0)	13.0 (133.1)	6.7 (13.4)
	0.2 (11.2)	2.0 (284.1)	−0.8 (13.2)
U.S.A.	3.5 (8.6)	7.7 (2.3)	6.7 (3.1)
	0.5 (3.1)	0.9 (7.7)	−0.8 (4.9)
World[a, b]	7.3 (2.6)	14.1 (4.6)	13.2 (3.0)
	0.5 (1.1)	1.6 (6.1)	−0.2 (5.5)

Notes: [a] 1975–1984.

[b] 1960–1970.

Line 1 is growth rate and line 2 is change in growth rate, mean and (variance).

Table 6.7 Money Supply Growth

	1958–1970	1971–1974	1975–1985
Canada	6.3 (38.8)	9.8 (9.4)	9.2 (70.8)
	−1.2 (50.1)	2.5 (66.2)	2.4 (56.8)
France	9.3 (28.0)	12.4 (2.9)	10.7 (7.6)
	−0.6 (13.1)	3.5 (65.9)	−0.5 (16.9)
Germany	8.6 (8.4)	9.3 (19.0)	7.0 (20.8)
	−0.5 (8.7)	−0.2 (36.3)	−0.2 (28.2)
Italy[a]	14.1 (12.5)	19.6 (8.1)	16.2 (30.8)
	1.1 (16.2)	−1.3 (15.7)	−0.5 (38.5)
Japan	18.8 (63.9)	21.7 (36.0)	6.8 (17.3)
	0.9 (96.1)	−1.3 (80.5)	−0.8 (20.6)
U.K.	3.2 (6.2)	10.9 (31.7)	13.1 (18.4)
	0.6 (14.2)	−0.9 (44.6)	1.2 (37.1)
U.S.A.	3.4 (3.4)	6.6 (1.1)	7.4 (3.1)
	0.2 (2.3)	0.3 (4.5)	0.4 (5.3)
World[a, b]	7.5 (2.2)	12.8 (0.4)	13.7 (2.0)
	0.4 (2.1)	1.4 (4.2)	0.1 (2.8)

Notes: [a] 1975–1984.

[b] 1960–1970.

Line 1 is growth rate and line 2 is change in growth rate, mean and (variance).

Table 6.8 Money Plus Quasi-Money Growth

	1958–1970	1971–1974	1975–1985
Canada	8.5 (17.6)	15.9 (36.1)	11.7 (36.9)
	−0.3 (26.3)	4.7 (11.3)	−1.7 (33.8)
France	12.2 (14.9)	17.4 (3.8)	11.8 (7.6)
	−0.1 (10.1)	2.8 (47.3)	−0.9 (4.5)
Germany	12.6 (4.9)	10.9 (6.7)	7.0 (5.5)
	−0.8 (3.5)	−0.2 (11.4)	−0.2 (4.4)
Italy[a]	13.9 (4.6)	18.5 (5.8)	17.2 (21.6)
	0 (9.1)	2.0 (0.9)	−0.9 (10.9)
Japan	19.1 (12.0)	20.0 (23.4)	9.9 (7.4)
	0 (17.3)	−1.2 (37.3)	−0.5 (3.8)
U.K.	4.9 (4.6)	19.9 (39.1)	13.5 (14.5)
	0.3 (6.8)	3.0 (61.2)	−0.6 (20.6)
U.S.A.	6.5 (3.3)	10.0 (9.3)	9.5 (10.7)
	−0.3 (3.8)	0.5 (29.6)	0.3 (18.4)
World[a,b]	10.0 (2.0)	15.4 (1.0)	16.3 (2.3)
	0.2 (2.2)	1.7 (8.5)	0.2 (2.7)

Notes: [a] 1975–1984.
     [b] 1960–1970.
     Line 1 is growth rate and line 2 is change in growth rate, mean and
     (variance).

the seven countries. Tables 6.6, 6.7, and 6.8 set out the national variances of the growth rates of the three definitions of the money supply—
monetary base, narrow money, and broad money (money plus quasi-
money).

What can we learn from the cross-country variations in output,
inflation, and money growth?

A Country Model

Each country's aggregate fluctuations can be described by a model
similar to that for the world as a whole but one that recognizes the
openness of the individual economies. Each country has an aggregate
demand function given by:

$$y_{it}^d = m_{it} + v_{it} - p_{it} \qquad \text{(aggregate demand)} \qquad (14)$$

and an aggregate supply function given by:

$$y_{it}^s = y_{it}^* + \gamma(p_{it} - E_{t-1}p_{it}) + u_{it} \quad \text{(aggregate supply)} \qquad (15)$$

Equilibrium determines output as:

$$y_{it}^d = y_{it}^s = y_{it} \qquad \text{(equilibrium)} \qquad (16)$$

Purchasing power parity holds in each country so that:

$$p_{it} = p_t + s_{it} - \rho_{it} \qquad \text{(purchasing power parity)} \qquad (17)$$

where ρ is a stochastic process describing the real exchange rate, and s is the nominal exchange rate. Notice that I am not asserting that purchasing power parity is associated with constant international relative prices. I am suppressing all the detail of the determination of international relative prices such as that between traded and nontraded goods and capturing such features in the stochastic process ρ_{it}.

Financial technology evolves in accordance with:

$$\Delta v_{it} = \lambda \Delta m_{it-1} + x_{it} \qquad \text{(financial technology)} \qquad (18)$$

Monetary policy depends on the exchange rate regime. Under flexible exchange rates the money supply is controlled to achieve domestic objectives and is assumed to follow:

$$\Delta m_{it} = \alpha - \beta \Delta p_{it-1} + z_{it} \qquad \begin{array}{l}\text{(monetary policy} \\ \text{under flexible rates)}\end{array} \qquad (19a)$$

Under fixed exchange rates the change in the exchange rate is zero. That is,

$$\Delta s_{it} = 0 \qquad \text{(monetary policy under fixed rates)} \qquad (19b)$$

A reasonable assumption on the real exchange rate is that it follows a random walk so that:

$$\Delta \rho_t = \zeta_{it} \qquad (20)$$

The solution to the country model depends on the exchange rate regime. Under fixed exchange rates output, prices and the money supply evolve according to:

$$y_{it} = y_{it}^* + \gamma(p_t - E_{t-1}p_t + \zeta_{it}) + u_{it} \qquad (21)$$

$$\Delta p_{it} = \Delta p_t + \zeta_{it} \qquad (22)$$

$$\Delta m_{it} = \Delta p_t - \gamma \Delta m_{it-1} + (y_{it}^* - y_{it-1}) \\ + (1 + \gamma)\zeta_{it} + u_{it} - x_{it} \qquad (23)$$

Output is a random process and driven by real domestic supply shocks and world price shocks. The inflation rate is tied to world inflation and departs from it in a random fashion, and money supply growth is demand driven.

Under flexible exchange rates the solutions are:

$$y_{it} = y_{it}^* + \frac{\gamma}{1 + \gamma}(\varepsilon_{it} + \xi_{it}) + \frac{1}{1 + \gamma}u_{it} \qquad (24)$$

$$\Delta p_{it} = \alpha + \hat{x}_{it} + \hat{z}_{it} - \beta\Delta p_{it-1} + \lambda\Delta m_{it-1} + (y_{it-1} - y^*_{it-1})$$
$$+ \frac{1}{1+\gamma}(\varepsilon_{it} - u_{it}) \tag{25}$$

$$\Delta m_{it} = \alpha + \hat{z}_{it} - \beta\Delta p_{it-1} + \varepsilon_{it} \tag{26}$$

Again output is determined by domestic technology shocks and also by domestic money and velocity shocks. Inflation is now generated by domestic monetary policy and by the random shocks to the money supply, velocity, and technology. The money supply is determined by the monetary policy actions of the central bank.

The relative variability of output under the fixed and flexible exchange rate regimes depends on the relative magnitudes of the domestic supply shocks and also on the relative magnitudes of domestic money supply and velocity shocks under flexible rates compared with world price level shocks and fixed rates. Output could be more or less variable under flexible rates depending on how domestic monetary policy is conducted. If that policy is conducted in an erratic fashion it is likely that output will be more variable under flexible rates than under fixed rates, while if policy is highly stable, flexible rates make it possible to achieve greater stability in output.

Comparing price level fluctuations under fixed and flexible exchange rates is less clear-cut. Under fixed rates domestic price level fluctuations are independent of domestic supply shocks, unless those shocks affect the real exchange rate, while under flexible rates the price level is influenced by domestic supply shocks. Also, under flexible rates the domestic price level is independent of the real exchange rate, while under flexible rates the real exchange rate has a one-for-one effect on the domestic price level. As a result of this larger number of relevant shocks determining the price level, there is no clear prediction of how a country's price level variability should rank based on variability in monetary policy.

Money supply growth variability under fixed rates depends on the variability in the demand for money, while under flexible rates it depends on monetary policy.

The model set out above to describe an individual country is a good deal more complicated than that for the world aggregate economy. It has to take into account two exchange rate regimes as well as international linkages through prices in markets for goods. (The markets for assets, which also, of course, provide additional linkages, have been suppressed.)

With the number of observations available we clearly cannot hope to estimate country models that are comparable to the one that was estimated for the world aggregate. What we can do, however, is to examine the cross-section data for the countries and see whether there is any evidence that variability across countries is associated with monetary variability. The central prediction of the above model is that the variability of output is directly related to the variability of money supply growth. This proposition does not imply causality between money growth and output growth. The model predicts contemporaneous correlation rather than causality. It also predicts a contemporaneous correlation regardless of exchange rate regime. Under fixed exchange rates, the innovations that produce output fluctuations also produce demand-induced fluctuations in money growth. Under flexible exchange rates, policy-induced variability in money growth also produces variability in output growth.

To test the predictions concerning output variability and money supply growth I constructed a pooled cross-section and regime data set based on the numbers set out in Tables 6.4 (for real output growth) and 6.6, 6.7, and 6.8 (for money supply growth). I then examined the relationship between the variability of output and the variability of money supply growth (looking at both the growth rates and their changes), controlling for country and regime.

There is virtually no cross-country association between growth rates of reserve money or growth rates of narrow money and growth rates of output. (The same is true for the relation between the second differences among these variables.) There is, however, a significant relationship across countries between variability of real output growth and the variability of *broad* money growth. That relationship is summarized in the regressions set out in Table 6.9. Evidently the variance of output growth is reasonably well described as a constant plus 0.4 times the variance of money supply growth. Exactly that same coefficient (0.4) turns up when we look at changes in output growth and changes in money supply growth. The coefficient is quite well determined. The only country dummies that are significant are those for Canada and France in the growth rates. None of the country dummies is significant in the changes in the growth rates.

What do the cross-section correlations shown in Table 6.9 mean? Do they tell us that monetary variability is, in part, responsible for real output variability, or are they a reflection of the fact that broad money is essentially an endogenous variable determined by the demand for it?

A definitive answer to this question would require the formulation of some further detailed hypotheses concerning national monetary

Table 6.9   Cross-Section and Regime

(a) Growth Rates
$\text{Var}(\Delta y) = 7.55 + 0.41\ \text{Var}(\Delta m)$
$\phantom{\text{Var}(\Delta y) = }$ (4.50)   (0.14)
-13.95 (4.88) Canada
$-\ 7.68$ (3.68) France
$-\ 0.34$ (3.69) Germany
$-\ 4.35$ (3.70) Italy
$-\ 1.46$ (3.79) Japan
$-\ 7.16$ (4.04) U.K.
$-\ 1.64$ (2.72) (71–74)
$-\ 2.88$ (2.56) (75–85)
$R^2 = 0.60$

(b) Changes in Growth Rates
$\text{Var}(\Delta^2 y) = \ \ 9.66 + 0.41\ \text{Var}(\Delta^2 m)$
(10.47)   (0.20)
$-\ 8.11$ (8.65) Canada
-14.27 (8.58) France
$+\ 3.30$ (8.82) Germany
$+\ 1.34$ (8.80) Italy
$+\ 0.36$ (8.56) Japan
$-\ 4.93$ (8.90) U.K.
$-\ 0.69$ (6.60) (71–74)
$-\ 0.37$ (5.62) (75–85)
$R^2 = 0.47$

(Standard errors in parentheses.)

policies that would have to be tested on finer disaggregations of national data. It is clear, however, that most countries in this sample did regard the targeting of a broad money aggregate as the centerpiece of their monetary policies under floating exchange rates. In the case of Japan, M2 plus Certificates of Deposit was the monetary target. In the case of the United Kingdom sterling M3 was the target. Germany targeted central bank money, which is highly correlated with German broad money. Of these seven countries only Canada explicitly embraced a narrow monetary aggregate. The United States targeted broad and narrow aggregates, paying more attention to the broader aggregates at a time when financial innovation was making the interpretation of the narrower aggregates difficult.[4]

The fact that most countries did regard broad money as the relevant

---

[4] For a useful summary of official descriptions of monetary targeting in six of the countries studied here see Paul Meek (ed.), 1983; pp. 6–31 (Germany), pp. 32–50 (U.S.A.), pp. 51–71 (U.K.), pp. 80–85 (Japan), pp. 100–105 (Canada), pp. 105–114 (France).

target suggests that it is the monetary base that should be regarded as endogenous being manipulated by the authorities in order to achieve a target (exogenous) path for the broader aggregate. If this interpretation is correct—and it seems a good description of Japan, the United Kingdom, and Germany, the three countries whose output innovations fell—then the results generated here are consistent with the view that monetary policy contributes to output fluctuation—or, in the case of some countries, to its absence. The results are also consistent with the view that the business cycle is generated by a mechanism in which money does matter. The purest real business cycle theory is not consistent with this interpretation of the cross-section of data.

Conclusion

I have set out simple models of the world aggregate and national economies and used those models to interpret fluctuations in aggregate output, prices, and money; the conclusions reached are strong and clear.

The major source of output fluctuations in recent years has been real shocks to technology. Real shocks have not, though, been the only source of aggregate fluctuations. Money has also played an important role. Output fluctuations appear to have been independent of the forecastable component of money supply growth. Forecast errors in money supply growth have, though, generated fluctuations in output. Countries that have pursued highly stable targeting of a broad monetary aggregate have experienced lower output variability than countries that have paid little attention to the variability (and forecastability) of broad money growth.

Inflation has been generated by a mixture of monetary policy and supply shocks though mainly by monetary policy. The higher world aggregate inflation rate of the 1970s was the product of accelerating world money supply growth in the 1960s and early 1970s. Supply shocks, while raising the price level, do not produce ongoing inflation through monetary accommodation. Monetary policy was significantly counterinflationary in the world aggregate data.

References

Fischer, Stanley. 1977. Long-Term Contracts, Rational Expectations, and the

Optimal Money Supply Rule. *Journal of Political Economy* 85 (1): 191–206.

King, Robert G., and Charles I. Plosser. 1984. Money, Credit and Prices in a Real Business Cycle Model. *American Economic Review* 74 (3): 363–80.

Kydland, Finn E., and Edward C. Prescott. 1982. Time to Build and Aggregate Fluctuations. *Econometrica* 50 (6): 1345–70.

Long, John B., and Charles I. Plosser. 1983. Real Business Cycles. *Journal of Political Economy* 91 (1): 39–69.

Lucas, Robert E. Jr. 1972. Expectations and the Neutrality of Money. *Journal of Economic Theory* 4 (2): 103–24.

———. 1973. Some International Evidence on Output-Inflation Tradeoffs. *American Economic Review* 63 (3): 326–34.

Meek, Paul (ed.) 1983. *Central Bank Views on Monetary Targeting.* New York: Federal Reserve Bank of New York.

Phelps, Edmund S., and John B. Taylor. 1977. Stabilizing Powers of Monetary Policy under Rational Expectations. *Journal of Political Economy* 85 (1): 163–190.

Taylor, John B. 1979. Staggered Wage Setting in a Macro Model. *American Economic Review, Papers and Proceedings* 69 (2): 108–13.

———. 1980. Aggregate Dynamics and Staggered Contracts. *Journal of Political Economy* 88 (1): 1–23.

7

Monetary Policy and Performance in the U.S., Japan, and Europe, 1973–86

Stanley Fischer

In the period since 1973, each of the major economies has succeeded in reducing the inflation rate after suffering the inflationary impacts of the two oil shocks. In this paper, I analyze the policy choices—with the emphasis on monetary policy—and tradeoffs that resulted in lower inflation for the United States, Japan, Germany, and the United Kingdom.[1]

The extraordinary stability of inflation, output growth, and monetary growth in both Japan and Germany after the first oil shock appear to support the view that adherence to stable, preannounced money growth targets is the key to macroeconomic stability. The remarkable stability of U.S. growth, combined with low inflation in the period since 1984 in the face of unprecedented variability of monetary growth, casts some doubt on that presumption. The main aim of this paper is to draw lessons for monetary policy from the recent historical record.

I start with an overview of macroeconomic developments in the four countries in the period 1972 to 1986, from the collapse of the Bretton Woods system through the two oil shocks and into the disinflationary 1980s. Economic policy decisions in the four countries during the two oil shocks are examined more closely in Section II.[2] In Section III, I describe the different monetary targeting and, briefly, short-run operating procedures of policy in the four countries. The paper concludes with a discussion of the lessons of this period for mone-

[1] I am grateful to Phillip Cagan, Rudiger Dornbusch, Robert Feldman, Karen Johnson, Helmut Schlesinger, and Masahiko Takeda for helpful discussions; Takeo Hoshi for research assistance; Data Resources Inc. and Takashi Ōyama of the Bank of Japan for data; and the National Science Foundation for financial support.

[2] Meltzer (1985) examines shocks and policy decisions in Japan and the U.S. in the fixed and floating exchange-rate periods. His econometric emphasis is on policy reactions to all types of shocks, whereas this paper presents a less formal examination of policy responses of the four countries to the two oil shocks.

tary targeting and policy, the role of the credibility of policymakers, and the flexible exchange rate system.[3]

I. Shocks and Policy Responses

Basic macroeconomic developments in the four economies for the period 1972–86 are summarized in Figures 7.1, 7.2, and 7.3, which present information on real GNP growth, inflation (measured by the CPI[4]), and unemployment respectively, and in Table 7.1. The period has seen a slowing of real GNP growth in all four countries, a slowing

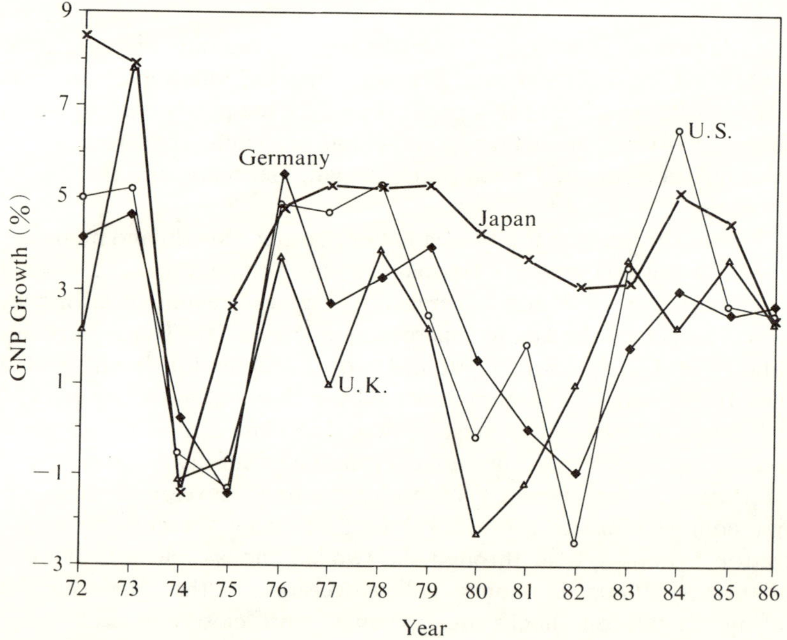

Figure 7.1
Annual Real GNP Growth Rates

[3] Meek (1983) contains several very informative papers on monetary policy procedures in major economies.

[4] Inflation rates of the GNP deflator and the CPI often differ significantly over this period. For instance, although CPI inflation for the United States exceeded 10% on a year-over-year basis four times, GNP deflator inflation never rose into double digits. In 1986, when CPI inflation rates in Germany and Japan were −0.2% and 0.6% respectively, GNP deflators rose by 3.0% and 2.3%.

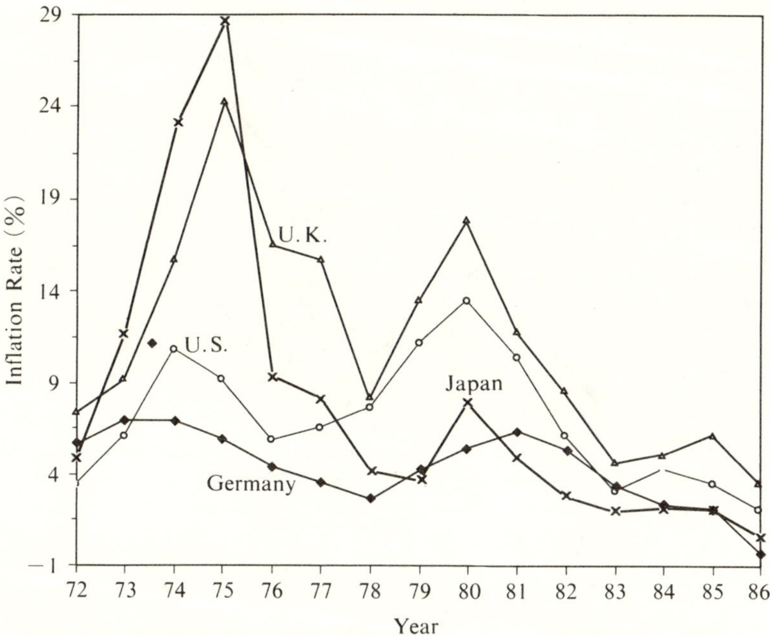

Figure 7.2
Annual CPI Inflation Rates

of inflation, and an increase in unemployment.[5] The increases in the
German and United Kingdom unemployment rates stand out. There
was in 1986 a remarkable convergence of GNP growth rates and, to a
lesser extent, inflation rates, though there were wide disparities in
unemployment rates among the four economies.

The oil shocks are clearly visible in the behavior of the inflation
rate in Figure 7.2. The first oil shock sharply raised the inflation rate
in the U.S., Japan, and the U.K., but caused barely a ripple in German
inflation. The second oil shock produced rapid increases in inflation
in the U.S. and the U.K., a 7.8% (CPI) inflation rate for 1980 in Japan,
and more than 6% per annum (CPI) inflation in Germany. In the second oil shock, CPI inflation rates for Germany, Japan, and the U.S.
were well above rates of increase of the GNP deflator:[6] in the case of

---

[5] These are OECD-standardized measures of unemployment. The German data
here are lower than the national statistics.

[6] A data appendix which contains all the data referred to in the paper and presented in the figures is available from the author on request.

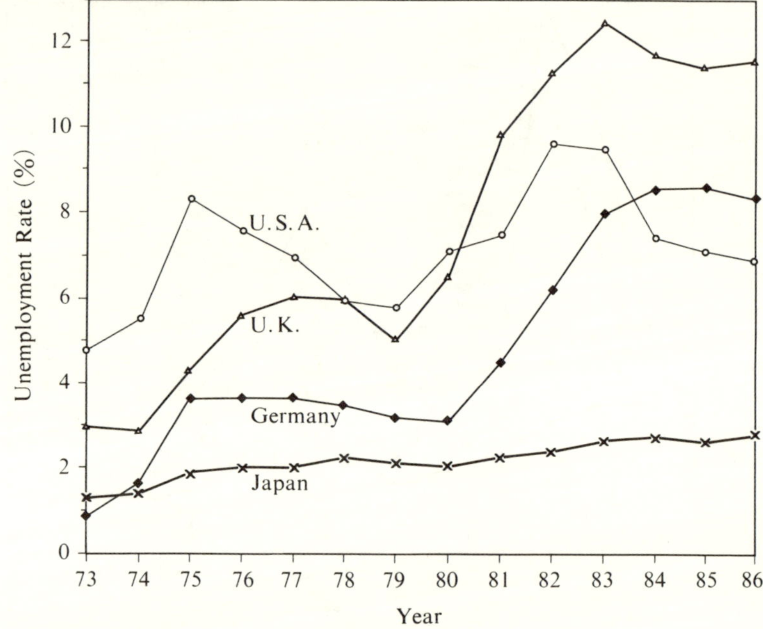

Figure 7.3
Unemployment Rates

Japan, the year-over-year CPI inflation rate for 1980 of 7.8% contrasts with just 3.8% on the GNP deflator.[7]

Each oil shock was followed by a significant slowdown in growth or by a recession, with one exception. Japan, which had grown at double-digit rates in the 1960s and at more than 8% per annum in 1972–73, suffered the trauma of a recession in 1974. Its year-over-year growth rate never reached 5.5% thereafter, though it remained the most rapidly growing of the major economies. Japanese growth slowed very little during the second oil shock; over the entire 10-year period starting in 1976, Japanese annual real GNP growth was remarkably stable, at rates between 3.1% and 5.3% per annum.

Germany suffered recessions during both oil shocks; unemployment rose to a new higher level after each, and has only recently shown

---

[7] Because of its inappropriate treatment of housing prices, the U.S. CPI significantly mismeasured inflation in the period before 1982. For instance, the 13.5% for 1980 seen in Figure 7.2 is less than 12% when calculated on the basis of the corrected CPI introduced after 1982.

Table 7.1   Macroeconomic trends, 1973–86

	1973–74	1985–86
Unemployment		
U.S.	5.3%	7.0%
Japan	1.4	2.7
Germany	1.2	8.5
U.K.	3.0	13.1
Inflation (CPI)		
U.S.	8.5%	2.7%
Japan	17.4	1.3
Germany	6.7	1.0
U.K.	12.5	4.8
Current Account/GNP		
U.S.	0.3%	−3.2%
Japan	−0.5	4.1
Germany	2.1	1.9
U.K.	−2.7	0.6

Source: *OECD Economic Outlook*, December 1986, and Data Resources, Inc.
Note: Unemployment data are OECD-standardized definition.

modest signs of reduction. The U.K. similarly experienced a recession with each oil shock and a steep increase in the level of unemployment to a new higher level with only very recent signs of improvement.

The pattern for the U.S. was different. The first oil shock recession was followed by a rapid recovery and decline in unemployment. The second oil shock produced two recessions,[8] the second with the highest unemployment rate of the post-World War II period. Rapid recovery again brought the unemployment rate down quite fast, but it nonetheless remains above 1973 estimates of the natural rate of about 5.5%.

Not so evident in the figures is the effects of the U.S. fiscal policy shock of 1981–83 and accompanying fiscal tightening in the other three countries. Some of the effects show up in rapid U.S. recovery from the 1981–82 recession and slower recovery in the other economies; others are reflected in the current account changes seen in Table 7.1.

I now review in more detail the policy choices made in each country during the two oil shocks.

---

[8] Because the 1980 recession lasted only six months and the recovery from that recession a year, it is sometimes argued that the entire period from the beginning of 1980 to the end of 1982 should be regarded as one long recession.

II. Dealing with the Oil Shocks

The first oil shock hit a booming world economy that had recently abandoned the Bretton Woods system. Raw material prices were already rising fast as domestic inflation rates rose. Free from the constraints of pegged exchange rates, countries believed they could pursue their own goals with little outside constraint. In the case of Germany, the goal was low inflation; in Britain it was the maintenance of high growth. Real growth in Britain, at 7.9% in 1973, for a short while matched the Japanese rate. In 1973, even before the oil price shock, inflation was high in the United States as a result of expansionary monetary and fiscal policy and the ending of wage and price controls. It was higher in Britain and much higher in Japan.

Monetary growth data for the period are shown in Figure 7.4.[9]

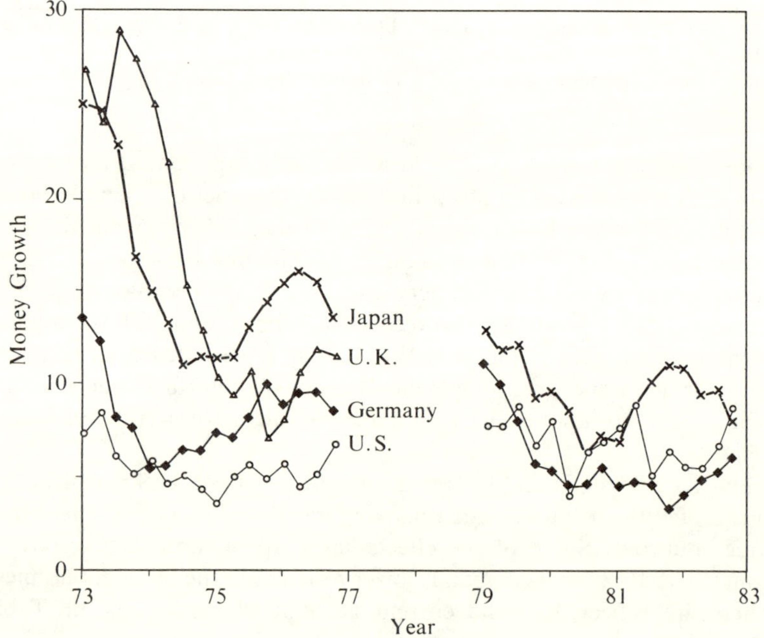

Figure 7.4
Money Growth, Two Oil Shocks

[9] Tables in the appendix provide the data underlying each figure. All growth rates are at annual rates for the quarter relative to the same quarter a year before. Figure 7.4 shows for each country that monetary variable which receives most attention from the monetary policymakers: M1 in the U.S., (M2 + CD's) in Japan; Central Bank Money in Germany; and sterling M3 in the U.K. Growth rates

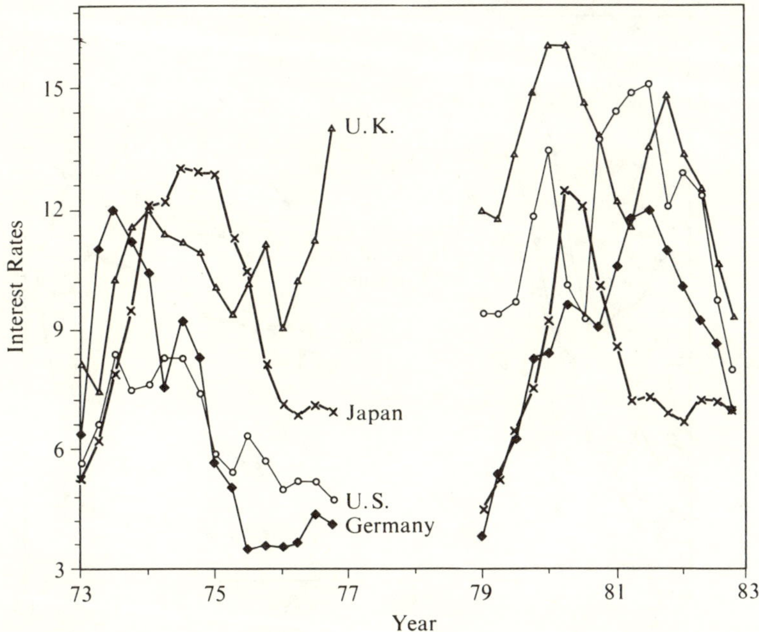

Figure 7.5
Interest Rates, Two Oil Shocks

Money growth in both the U.K. and Japan exceeded 20% per annum in 1972 and 1973.[10] Such growth rates of money had been common in Japan during its high-growth period, but not in Britain. The growth rate of both M1 and M2 was sharply reduced in Japan at the end of 1973, before the oil price shock hit, but money growth in the U.K. (M2) was still 27.5% (quarter over same quarter a year earlier) in the fourth quarter of 1973. U.S. M1 and M2 growth were reduced in 1973. With the shift to a floating exchange rate allowing Germany to pursue its domestic inflation goals, the growth rate of central bank money in Germany was cut drastically in the second quarter of 1973. Thus, by the time of the oil price increase, money growth rates were being reduced in three of the four countries. And if monetary policy is judged by the nominal interest rate (Figure 7.5), monetary policy had turned tight in Britain too in mid-1973.[11]

---

for a variety of monetary variables for each country are presented in Tables 7.3–7.6.

[10] This applies to both M1 and M2 growth rates in Japan, and M2 and sterling M3 in the U.K. U.K. M1 growth was 14% in 1972 but only 5% in 1973.

[11] In this period, money growth was not taken as a measure of the thrust of mone-

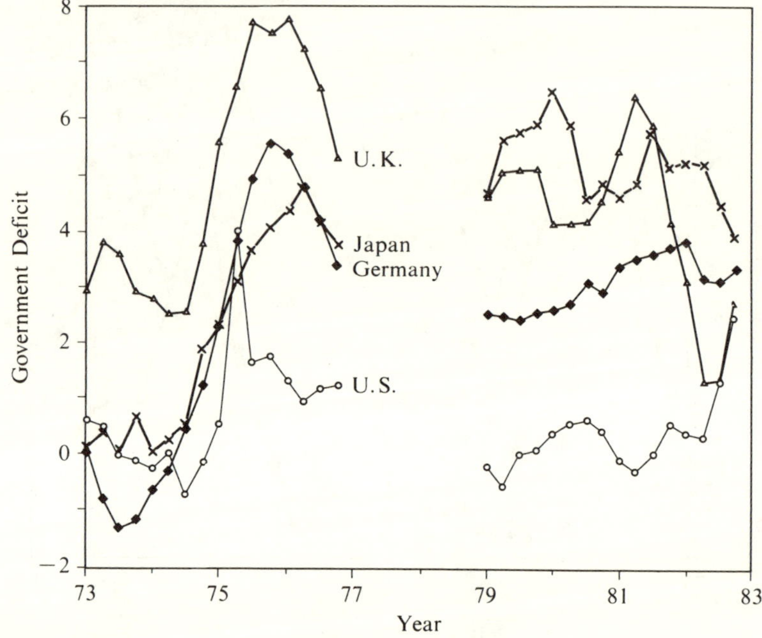

Figure 7.6
Government Deficits, Two Oil Shocks

In the next year, higher oil prices fed through into higher inflation in each country. Although there were deflationary forces in place already, the high inflation and continuing high wage growth reinforced the resolve of the monetary authorities in each country to keep money growth low.[12] With the oil shock adding to the rate of inflation, real balances in each country were falling, putting further pressure on interest rates and demand. Nominal interest rates stayed high through 1974, though they were falling rapidly in Germany.

Slowdowns or recessions began in each country in the first quarter of 1974. In part because the nature of cost shocks was not then well understood, and because the unemployment rate was slow to rise, the slowdowns did not cause any change in policy. Given the short lag between the oil price increase and the start of the recessions, the

tary policy in Britain. Even if it were, the differences between the growth of M1, which fell drastically after the middle of 1973, and the growth rates of M2 and M3 would have complicated the interpretation of policy. It was in large part the correlation between M3 growth in 1973 and 1974 with the subsequent inflation that led to its later use as a monetary target.

[12] U.K. money growth began to fall from the second quarter of 1974.

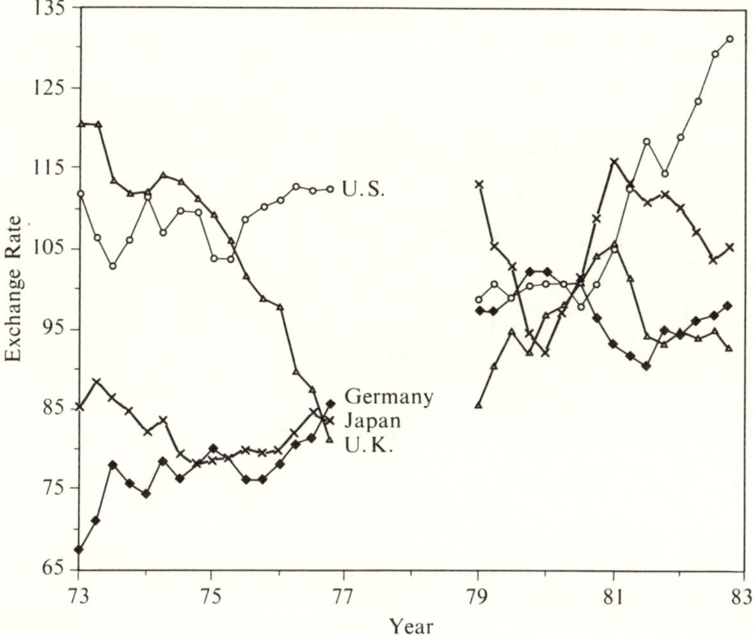

Figure 7.7
MERM Exchange Rates, Two Oil Shocks

recessions must already have been en route, and would have taken place as a result of the tightening of policies in mid-1973 even without the oil price increase.

The oil price rise served rather to intensify the recessions, as high inflation, continued low unemployment, and rapid wage growth kept monetary and fiscal policy tight through 1974. In the U.S., the main thrust of policy until almost the end of 1974 was to fight inflation. Both M1 and M2 money growth were kept low and the Treasury bill rate held high (Figure 7.5). There was a small full-employment surplus in 1974 (Figure 7.6), and proposals for a tax increase to deal with the inflation. Rates of wage increase (Figure 7.10) stayed high through 1974 as inflation accelerated.

In Japan, money growth was well below the 20% rate of inflation in 1974, with the result that real balances fell and interest rates increased. With the monetary squeeze, real GNP growth (Figure 7.9) turned negative at the beginning of 1974, and stayed negative (quarter over same quarter a year before) throughout the year. But rates of wage increase and inflation remained above 20% for another year.

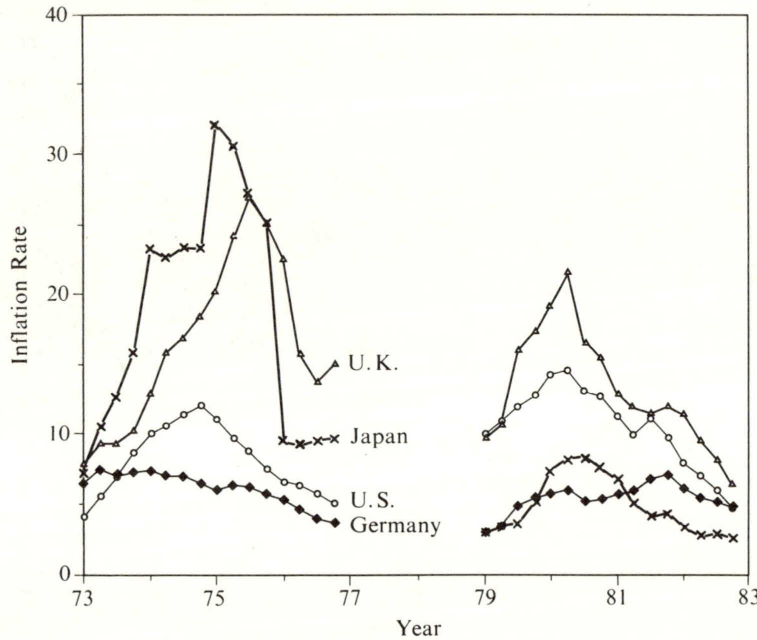

Figure 7.8
CPI Inflation, Two Oil Shocks

By the end of 1974, the inflation rate in Japan was beginning to fall, though wage increases were still rapid, and the government budget was moving into a larger deficit.

Money growth was kept low in Germany through 1974. Real GNP growth was low in 1974, turning negative at the end of that year and for most of 1975. High rates of wage increase continued through 1974, and inflation still stayed high, while unemployment remained below 2%. M2 and M3 growth were reduced in Britain in mid-1974 with interest rates and the government budget deficit remaining high. In Britain, the rate of wage increase was accelerating at the end of 1974.

Only at the end of 1974 did unemployment start rising in each country. At that point, interest rates in the U.S. and Germany were falling fast. The seriousness of the recession struck home in the U.S. at the end of 1974, leading in March 1975 to a fiscal stimulus in the form of a $50-per-taxpayer check, visible in Figure 7.6 in the sharp temporary increase in the full employment deficit. The recession, high rates of wage increase, and high inflation continued well into 1975, with the unemployment rate peaking in the second quarter. Monetary

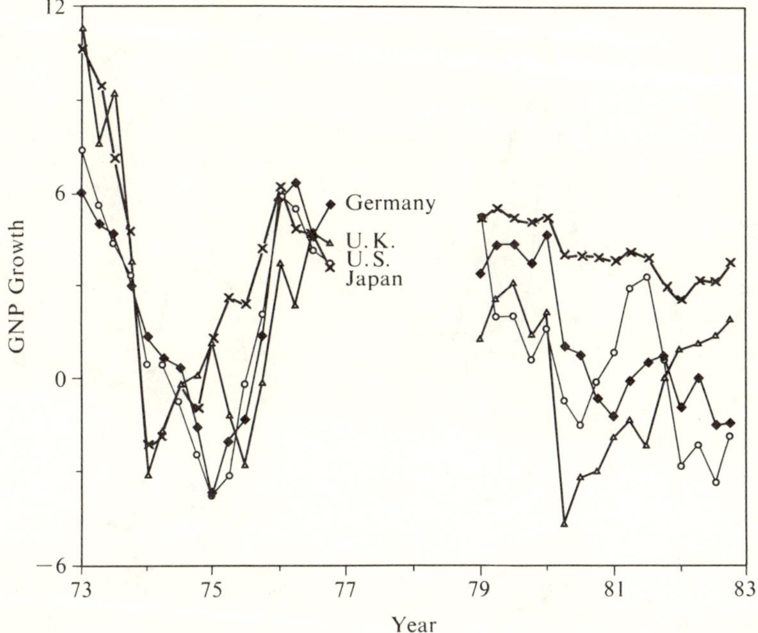

Figure 7.9
Real Growth, Two Oil Shocks

growth (M1) was procyclical in this recession, falling through the first quarter of 1975 and only then beginning to increase. Even so, the annual growth rate of M1 (quarter over the same quarter a year before) did not exceed 6% over the entire three years starting in 1973:4. M2 growth also fell sharply in the recession but then increased to more than 10% for the two years following the end of the recession. Inflation fell rapidly after the middle of 1975, and by the time of the election campaign at the end of 1976, CPI inflation was at less than 5%.[13] Wage increases were still at double-digit rates into 1975, and did not fall to much below 8% even after the recession.

The decisive change in Japanese inflation came at the end of 1974 and the beginning of 1975, with the new wage agreement in 1975 reducing wage inflation by more than 10%. At the same time, nominal interest rates began to decline, and money growth was raised. The central government budget deficit began to increase from 1975, and

[13] GNP deflator inflation never fell much below 6%, the difference again resulting in part from the incorrect treatment of the costs of housing.

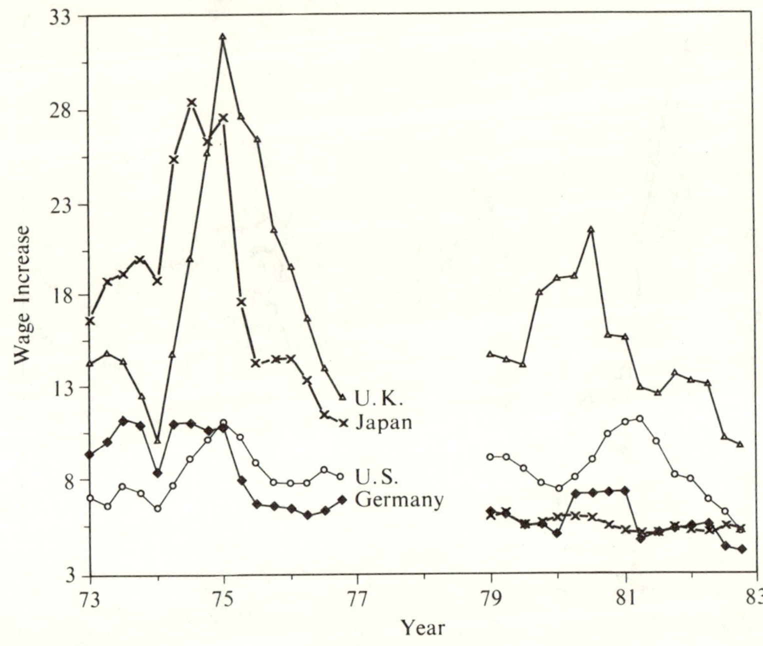

Figure 7.10
Rates of Wage Increases, Two Oil Shocks

continued rising until it reached more than 5.4% of GNP in 1978.[14] The recovery of real growth started early in 1975.

In Germany, central bank money growth was raised at the beginning of 1975. Inflation and rates of wage increase also declined from early 1975, and real GNP growth turned around at about the same time as in the United States, though unemployment peaked in the last quarter. The recession and inflation lasted longer in the U.K.; indeed, there were two separate periods of negative real GDP growth in 1974 and 1975. Wage inflation was sharply reduced during 1975, moving from a (quarter-over-same-quarter-a-year-earlier) peak of 32% in 1975:1 to 21.5% in 1975:4. Inflation moved into the low teens in 1976 as money growth continued well below the inflation rate through 1975 and nominal interest rates remained high. Despite a renewal of growth in 1976, the unemployment rate in the U.K. continued rising until the end of 1977, when it reached 6.3%, compared with 2.6% at the end of 1973.

Perhaps the most revealing contrast in this period is that between

[14] Data are from Hamada and Hayashi (1985), pp. 86–87.

the U.K. and Japan. Before the recession and oil price shock, both countries had high rates of money growth. In 1973, Britain had lower price and wage inflation, suggesting that inflationary pressures for 1974 were higher in Britain with her lower rate of growth of potential output. Japanese money growth was decisively reduced at the end of 1973; it took longer in Britain. Output growth turned negative at the same time in both countries in 1974 but recovered somewhat during that year. However, the Japanese recession represented a much larger reduction in growth below trend rates than the British recession. In both countries, rates of wage increase rose in 1974, though more so in Britain.

The decisive difference occurs at the beginning of 1975, when Japanese wage inflation fell sharply in the new wage agreement, but British wage inflation continued high through the end of the year. With money growth (broader definitions) kept down in Britain in 1975 and wage increases continuing at high rates, further recession occurred.[15] Inflation in the U.K. came down from the 20% range to the low teens at the end of 1976, but stayed in double digits virtually through the remainder of the decade.

What are the lessons of this episode? First, the fact that the oil shock hit overheated economies made dealing with the shock more difficult. But it is the nature of such shocks that they are more likely to occur when demand is booming than when economies are in recession. Second, it may be argued that the fact that an oil price increase is both inflationary and recessionary means that monetary policy was too restrictive for too long a time. Japan certainly brought about a big recession measured by the loss of potential output. Quite likely a more gradual reduction in the growth rate of money in Japan, and some accommodation of inflationary pressures in 1974 in the U.S. and Germany, would have moderated the recessions, at the cost of a less rapid reduction in inflation. Third, through the end of the recession exchange rates moved surprisingly little (Figure 7.7). The Deutsche mark appreciated in the first half of 1973, the yen and sterling depreciated during the recession as implied by their greater inflation, but exchange rate movements did not play a large part in the adjustment to the oil shock. Fourth, it is difficult not to give the behavior of wages an independent role in the story. Japanese inflation fell fast after rates of wage increase came down; U.K. inflation stayed high with high wage

---

[15] Once again, the different money stocks give different signals in Britain as M1 growth was relatively high in 1975. Nominal interest rates were held in the double digits, but real interest rates were still substantially negative.

inflation. Later in the paper I examine whether the credibility of the policymakers in the two countries explains the difference.

In both Germany and Japan, monetary policy was in part guided by the hope of establishing the credibility of the central bank's determination to maintain low inflation in the new floating-exchange rate world. The recessions could be viewed as investments in reputation, which paid off in the case of Japan in the second oil crisis. That leaves open the question of why there was not a similar payoff for Germany.

After the first oil shock, German and Japanese monetary policies were embarked on new anti-inflationary courses. Despite the introduction of monetary targeting in 1975, there appears to have been no significant change in the nature of U.S. monetary policy, and U.K. monetary policy was still difficult to understand (Fischer 1987).

In the years between the oil shocks, the U.S. economy showed rapid growth and declining unemployment from 1976 to 1978 while inflation increased; Japan grew rapidly, albeit slowly by its historical standards, with slowing inflation; German growth was moderate with slowly falling unemployment while inflation remained at around 4%; and the U.K. succeeded in reducing the unemployment rate slightly, while the inflation rate, except in 1978, remained in double digits.

In retrospect, it is clear that U.S. monetary policy in the period between the oil shocks was too expansionary, even though money growth rates did not rise much. Rather, the rapid growth and rising inflation were accompanied by an increasing velocity of circulation (the case of the missing money). In Japan, gradually slowing money growth was accompanied by a rising budget deficit until 1978. The possibility of countercyclical fiscal policy was neutralized by the existence of a massive budget deficit, a condition that is familiar in the U.S. Central bank money growth in Germany remained around 8–11% for the period until 1980. Money growth and budget deficits in the U.K. were high through the end of the decade.

A. The Second Oil Shock

The real price of oil fell from the end of 1976 until the beginning of 1979, then virtually doubled within the next year, continuing its increase until mid-1981. With unemployment continuing to fall in the United States and rates of wage increase rising, the second oil shock, like the first, hit an economy that was already operating close to full capacity and with high inflation. The other major countries too had grown rapidly in 1978.

In the U.S., the falling dollar during 1978 had led to a change in monetary policy at the end of that year. Both M1 and M2 growth were slightly lower in 1979 than in 1978, and interest rates were higher. Inflation nonetheless increased, with the CPI rising 13.3% during 1979. The GNP deflator grew 8.8%, year-over-year, in 1979, and at virtually the same rate during the year. Rising interest rates and oil prices account for the more than 4% difference between CPI and GNP deflator inflation.

Paul Volcker was appointed Chairman of the Fed in August 1979. Confronted with rising inflation and continued dollar weakness, the Fed in November 1979 made its decision to stem the inflation. Accompanying this decision, the Fed declared a change in its operating procedures to place far more weight on meeting its monetary targets and to reduce the emphasis put on interest rates.

CPI inflation rates exceeding 18% per annum in the first quarter of 1980 led to a panic imposition of credit controls in March 1980, intensifying an extraordinarily short, sharp recession that can now be seen to have started in January 1980. M1 growth was cut to negative rates in the second quarter of 1980, and then raised as the extent of the recession became clear. The recession ended in mid-1980 with CPI inflation down but GNP deflator inflation little reduced, and with inflation outpacing money growth and thereby reducing real balances. Interest rates had fallen rapidly in the recession but rebounded just as rapidly and moved to new highs at the start of the 1981–82 recession. It was during this period that the Fed maintained the monetary pressure that broke the inflationary momentum. Money growth was kept low into 1982.

The Fed kept up the pressure—visible both in low money growth and high nominal interest rates—through August 1982, by which time it was clear the inflation rate had fallen and that unemployment was rising rapidly. In August 1982, the start of the international debt crisis, the Fed announced the end of the monetary policy inaugurated three years earlier. Money growth was increased sharply and interest rates were driven down, fueling the recovery that began at the end of 1982. A second expansionary force came from the major tax cuts that went into effect in 1982; a third was the decline in the price of oil that began in 1982.

The U.S. took a long time to deal with the second oil shock, with the imposition of credit controls and the 1980 recession probably prolonging the adjustment period. Rates of wage increase started falling rapidly only after mid-1981, and by the end of 1982—with the unemployment rate above 10.5%—had fallen to less than half their 10.8% level of early 1981. They have continued falling since then, as disinflation has continued.

M1 growth since 1982 has been on average higher than over any other four-year period since World War II, and (except in 1984) well above its target ranges. M2 growth has continued relatively smoothly, within its target ranges. Nominal interest rates were actually higher in 1984 than in 1982 and 1983, but subsequently fell, reducing the real interest rate.

The great success of Japanese macroeconomic policy was the avoidance of a recession in the second oil shock. Money growth was cut at the end of 1979 and kept down into 1981. The nominal interest rate rose rapidly; growth slowed somewhat; inflation rose; real growth fell, especially in 1981; but still during 1981 real GNP grew 2.5%. Wage inflation was falling over this entire period, thereby avoiding the pass-through of higher prices into wages. Japan was thus spared the choice between accommodation and a wage-price spiral, or a recession, perhaps because that choice had already been made once before. Once it was clear that inflation was under control, the Bank of Japan permitted an increase in money growth in the latter half of 1981. The yen had depreciated between 1979 and 1980 but then appreciated into 1981, assisting the disinflation.[16]

Germany met the second oil price increase with a cut in the growth rate of central bank money from 10% per annum in the first half of 1979 to 5% in the first half of 1980, with interest rates moving in the opposite direction. Price and wage inflation rose into 1980 and unemployment was still falling. The Bundesbank evidently saw this as the time when control over inflation had to be asserted; it also attributed part of the tightness of monetary policy in 1981 to the necessity of stemming the depreciation of the currency; and it regarded the budget deficit as another reason to maintain monetary tightness.

Recession started in 1980, and unemployment began its ascent in the middle of that year. From 2.9% (standardized definition) in the second quarter of 1980, unemployment kept increasing until it reached more than 8% three years later. Low money growth (4%) and the recession continued for over two years, with recovery getting under way only in 1983, when central bank money growth was increased to

---

[16] In February 1980, the Bank of Japan demonstrated its independence and its intention of keeping inflation low by, for the first time, raising the official discount rate during the budget debate in the Diet.

near 8%. Wage and price inflation were surprisingly strong through 1982, with CPI inflation still above 5%, and wages and the GNP deflator rising more than 4% in 1982. The continuing wage increases and weakness of the Deutsche mark were the main factors ensuring the maintenance of monetary tightness through 1982. The Bundesbank was clearly determined to move the core inflation rate down from about 4%, the rate before the oil shock, closer to zero, and was willing to pay the price of a long recession and rising unemployment. It does not appear that the oil price shock itself played a large part in creating this recession in Germany.

The U.K. succeeded in bringing its inflation rate down in this same period, but here the oil price shock played only a small part. Sterling appreciated as the price of oil increased; wage inflation likewise increased from 1979 to 1980. Money growth (all definitions) was kept well below the inflation rate and nominal interest rates increased. A recession started in the second quarter of 1980; over six quarters from the end of 1979 the unemployment rate more than doubled to reach a level of 10.2%. Wage inflation came down but did not fall below 10% until mid-1983.

Under the Medium Term Financial Strategy announced in 1980, monetary growth (M3) was to be steadily reduced along with the public sector borrowing requirement (PSBR). Both money growth and the PSBR initially exceeded target levels but were reduced steadily, and, with the pressure of rising unemployment, wage and price inflation finally fell. By 1983 and 1984, U.K. inflation was close to U.S. levels. However, unemployment rates were well above those in the U.S. and were showing very little sign of recovery. The monetary situation was once again confused, this time because the demand function for sterling M3 appeared to be shifting.

During the period from 1979 to 1983, the U.S., Germany, and the U.K. each undertook a period of extremely restrictive policy designed to break inflationary momentum. Each created a major recession, and in Germany and the U.K., a long-term increase in unemployment. Each did succeed in bringing down inflation. The second oil price increase was more important in determining the timing of the U.S. policy measures than those in the other two countries. Even so, both the U.S. and the U.K. would in any event have had to deal with the high inflation they were suffering before the oil price shock.

The German disinflation of 1980–83 is in many respects puzzling. Relative to the U.S. and Britain, it accomplished little on the inflation front. Year over year, the CPI inflation rate peaked at 6.3%, compared with its minimum of 2.7% in 1978; the GNP deflator never rose more than 4.8%,[17] compared with its minimum of 3.6% in 1976. Wage inflation peaked in 1980 at a little over 7%. By the time monetary policy was relaxed in 1983, the GNP deflator was rising at 3%. During this period the unemployment rate increased from 2.9% to more than 8%. There are two puzzling questions. First, why did the relatively low inflation produce so much determination to maintain restrictive policies? The answer here starts from the Bundesbank's stern views on the dangers of inflation, and on its failure to hit its money targets (see Table 7.5 below) in 1976 through 1978. It was afraid that inflation would get out of hand. Second, why did those policies have so large an effect on unemployment and so little effect on inflation? It is not at all clear why the Phillips curve for Germany appears to be so flat during that period. Nor is it clear why the Bundesbank pressed so hard on money growth rather than trying to produce a more gradual disinflation, such as had been achieved by the Bank of Japan.

Here the contrast between Germany and Japan is most interesting. The Bank of Japan clearly had achieved credibility by 1980. It is hard, though, to credit the view that the Bundesbank lacked credibility. Up to 1979 it is difficult to tell the monetary policies of the two banks apart—including an increase in money growth at the end of 1978 and an increase in inflation in 1980. Once again, wage behavior seems to be the key: Japanese workers were willing to take a real wage cut; German workers obtained higher nominal wage increases as inflation rose in 1980, and rates of wage increase slackened only as unemployment rose (Bruno and Sachs 1986).

The two oil shock episodes tell less clear stories about the role of policy than might have been expected. The political lessons of the U.S. and U.K. cases are clear: eventually the pressure to deal with double-digit inflation becomes overwhelming. But the failure of the Bundesbank's restraint in the years following the first oil shock to pay off in the second oil shock raises important questions about both the role of monetary targets and credibility in monetary policy.

B. The Aftermath

The U.S. rebound from the 1982 recession contrasts with the failure of unemployment in Germany and the U.K. to recover significantly. In contrast to the accommodative monetary policy of the Fed, the

---

[17] At its quarter-over-same-quarter-a-year-before peak, GNP deflator inflation in 1980:2 was 5.7%.

Table 7.2 Fiscal Policy, 1980–86

	1980	1981	1982	1983	1984	1985	1986
General government							
(Surplus/GNP, as %)							
United States	−1.3	−1.0	−3.5	−3.8	−2.7	−3.4	−3.4
Japan	−4.4	−3.8	−3.6	−3.7	−2.2	−1.4	−1.5
Germany	−2.9	−3.7	−3.3	−2.5	−1.9	−1.1	−1.0
U.K.	−3.5	−2.8	−2.3	−3.6	−3.9	−2.6	−3.1
*Fiscal impulse**							
United States	0.5	−0.9	1.3	0.6	0.5	0.8	0.1
Japan	−0.2	−0.6	−0.7	−0.6	−1.0	−0.5	−0.3
Germany	0.2	−0.1	−1.5	−1.4	−0.2	−0.6	0.3
U.K.	−1.1	−2.9	−1.4	1.1	0.8	−0.5	0.7

Source: *OECD Economic Outlook*, Dec. 1984, Table 3 (for fiscal impulse, 1980–1983); Dec. 1986, Table 5 (for remaining data).

* Fiscal impulse is the increase in the structural budget deficit as a percentage of GNP.

Bundesbank kept central bank money growth at 5% or less until 1986. In the U.K., money growth, as measured by the broader aggregates, was highly expansionary, though interest rates were increased in 1985 as wage inflation resumed.

The major difference in policies was fiscal. Table 7.2 presents fiscal policy data for the period 1980–86. From 1982 on, U.S. fiscal policy was strongly expansionary; in 1982 and 1983 in particular, German fiscal policy was strongly contractionary. With both monetary and fiscal policy contractionary in Germany, there was little to propel a recovery from the recession. Although the dollar appreciation might suggest a depreciation of the Deutsche mark that would have allowed exports to serve as the engine of growth, as they did to some extent in Japan, the mark—tied to its major trading partners through the EMS—did not in fact depreciate much during this period.

Bundesbank annual reports note the policy tradeoff between inflation and more rapid growth, express satisfaction with the pace of the recovery, and regret the failure until the end of 1986 of more rapid real growth to have an effect on unemployment. The decision to expand more slowly than in the United States was a deliberate one, reflecting a greater weighting on low inflation than the U.S. political system imposes. The Bundesbank notes frequently that its prime task is to preserve the value of money, and it is clear that maintaining low or perhaps eventually even zero inflation is its chief long-run goal. This goal may reflect dissatisfaction with the outcome of policy between the oil shocks when concern over unemployment was more evident in Bundesbank reports but the inflation rate stayed around 4%.

III. Monetary Targeting

Between the oil shocks, each of the central banks either introduced monetary targeting, or shifted its procedures to focus more on the money stock as an intermediate objective of policy. How, if at all, did this change contribute to the secular reduction in inflation experienced by each country?

A. United States

Monetary targeting was introduced in the U.S. in March of 1975; target ranges were specified for M1, M2, and M3 growth rates. As shown in Table 7.3, M1 and M2 outcomes fell within their target ranges in the first year, M1 even toward the bottom of its range. But in a pattern that was to become quite standard, not all the money targets were achieved simultaneously.

Monetary targeting did not help prevent the inflationary buildup between 1976 and 1979, in part because of data difficulties. There are significant differences between money stock measures reported at the time and measures based on subsequent data revisions and redefinitions.[18] The period from 1976 saw rising M1 (new definition) growth and steadily declining target ranges for M1—part of the then widely espoused gradualist strategy for reducing the inflation rate. M1 growth (new definition) rose sharply at the beginning of 1977, succeeding in keeping nominal interest rates falling until late 1978 as the recovery proceeded rapidly. But by the then current definitions, M1 growth fell in 1978 and was even lower in 1979, suggesting at the time that monetary policy was not especially expansionary. Nonetheless, the inflation rate steadily increased, from less than 6% at the end of 1976 to near 9% at the end of 1979. Rapid output growth, propelled in part by a rising full employment deficit and a falling real price of oil, was possible with little rise in the money growth rate because of rising velocity, caused in part by higher interest rates and in part by a shift out of M1 (both the case of the missing money and the case of the creation of new forms of checkable deposits).

From the viewpoint of monetary control, the period from 1976 to

[18] In particular, the 5.5% M1 growth reported in Table 7.2 for 1979 was for the then current M1-A definition of money, which excluded non-bank checkable deposits. The growth rate for M1-B, which included the latter deposits and is close to current M1, was nearly 2% higher.

Table 7.3   U.S. Money Growth Targets and Outcomes, 1975–87

Year	M1		M2		M3	
	Target	Out-come	Target	Out-come	Target	Out-come
1975	5.0–7.5	5.3	8.5–10.5	9.7	10.0–12.0	12.3
1976	4.5–7.5	5.8	7.5–10.5	10.9	9.0–12.0	12.7
1977	4.5–6.5	7.9	7.0–10.0	3.8	8.5–11.5	11.7
1978	4.0–6.5	7.2	6.5– 9.0	8.7	7.5–10.0	9.5
1979	3.0–6.0	5.5	5.0– 8.0	8.3	6.0– 9.0	8.1
1980	4.0–6.5	7.3	6.0– 9.0	9.6	6.5– 9.5	10.2
1981	3.5–6.0	2.3[a]	6.0– 9.0	9.5	6.5– 9.5	11.4
1982	2.5–5.5	8.5	6.0– 9.0	9.2	6.5– 9.5	10.1
1983*	4.0–8.0	10.0	7.0–10.0	8.3	6.5– 9.5	9.7
1984	4.0–8.0	5.2	6.0– 9.0	7.7	6.0– 9.0	10.5
1985*	4.0–7.0	11.9	6.0– 9.0	8.6	6.0– 9.5	7.4
1986	3.0–8.0	15.2	6.0– 9.0	8.9	6.0– 9.0	8.8
1987			5.5– 8.5		5.5– 8.5	
Mean		7.7		9.1		10.2
Std. dev.[b]		3.3		0.8		1.6
Std. err[c]		2.6		0.7		0.9
Cum. excess[d]		29.6%		14.3%		20.0%

Source: Isard and Rojas-Suarez (1986), Table 35, p. 84, for data through 1985. Targets for 1987 and 1986 outcomes are from "Monetary Policy Report to the Congress", *Federal Reserve Bulletin*, April 1987: 239–254.
Note: Data for targets and outcomes are for then current definitions.

* These are target ranges announced at the start of the year. Targets were rebased in midyear.

[a] Both the target and reported outcome for M1 are for M1 adjusted for shifts into NOW accounts, i.e., numbers here are lower than in Figure 7.4.

[b] Standard deviation.

[c] Mean square difference between outcome and center of target range.

[d] Cumulative excess of final level of the actual money stock over level that would have been produced by growth at the midpoint of the target range each year, starting from initial level.

1979 is interesting because (1) the Fed clearly intended to move the inflation rate down through gradual reduction of the growth rate of the various money stocks, and (2) in terms of then available data the Fed seemed to be doing that from 1977 to 1979 (the growth rate of each of the M's falls in Table 7.3 during that period), but (3) it nonetheless turns out to have been feeding the inflation.

With the shift in monetary policy at the end of 1979, money targets were to receive more weight and interest rates were to be allowed to fluctuate more. But in its first two years, the new regime had to deal with the effects on the demand for money of financial deregulation.

The Fed declared targets for two measures of M1 that were then being used, and in 1980 came close to meeting them. In 1981, however, it was significantly below its M1 target,[19] and in any event had at that time declared targets for four different M1 measures, together with M2, M3, and bank credit. Aside from the undershooting of the M1 target in 1981, the Fed was above on all targets specified in Table 7.3 in the years (1980–82) that it was supposedly following monetary targets.

Nonetheless, it was during this period that the Fed broke the inflationary momentum of the previous 20 years—and the monetary targets assisted in that endeavor. The reason is that the unprecedentedly high nominal interest rates of 1980 and 1981 would not have been politically possible without money targets as the supposed guides for monetary policy. When, in August 1982, it became clear that the recession and disinflation were well underway, and with high interest rates exacerbating the developing international debt problem, the money targets gave way, with M1 money growth exceeding 12% in the next year and M2 money growth exceeding 17%.

The high rates of money growth are consistent with the increase in the demand for real balances that comes with the end of an inflationary period or, more prosaically, with a reduction in the nominal interest rate. As nominal interest rates decline and the quantity of real balances demanded increases, the central bank is faced with the choice of supplying money more rapidly than simple nominal GNP targeting would imply, or forcing the increase in real balances through further disinflation. So long as money growth targets are not sacrosanct, and provided the monetary authority can exercise self-control, the growth rate of money can indeed be temporarily increased. Even beyond the normal increase in the demand for real balances that comes from a reduction in interest rates, the U.S. disinflation seems to have seen a shift in the M1 demand function.[20]

Instability of the demand for M1 is in part a result of regulatory changes and innovations in the monetary system that have changed the nature of both M1 and M2. With most interest rate controls on bank liabilities removed, the pace of financial innovation that affects

---

[19] The target in Table 7.3 is for M1-B, close to current definitions of money.

[20] Rasche (1987) presents the results of a comprehensive re-examination of U.S. money demand functions, concluding that while the shift in the demand for money function cannot be adequately explained, it can be simply parameterized, and that money demand functions therefore continue to play a useful role in the setting of money targets.

M1 demand is likely to slow, but it is certainly the fate of central bankers to contend with shifts in the demand function for money in future as well.

The extraordinary feature of U.S. monetary policy in the 1980s has been its success at reducing the inflation rate despite extremely high rates of money growth. And, in the period since 1984, highly variable money growth has been fully compatible with steady real output growth—with 1987 likely to be another year of moderate growth and moderate inflation despite 15% M1 growth in 1986.

Despite its consistent failure to achieve money targets, the Fed is required by law to announce them. That requirement serves a useful purpose, which is to force the Fed in advance to explain its choice of targets, and to explain *ex post* its failure to achieve them. I examine below the question of whether it should be forced to adhere to them more closely.

B. Japan

We have already seen how Japan, immediately following the first oil shock, dealt with its inflation problem decisively and at high cost. Up to the end of the Bretton Woods system, Japanese macroeconomic policy, sheltered behind capital controls, had been driven by the current account of the balance of payments and the fixed exchange rate. Current account deficits produced contractionary policy and a growth slowdown; surpluses turned the Stop sign to Go. Money growth had been high and variable, and there was very little other than the exchange rate to guide policy. The domestic financial markets were repressed, with monetary policy operating to a large extent through rationing and moral suasion (Suzuki 1980, Feldman 1986).

With the exchange rate anchor for monetary policy gone in 1973, the Bank of Japan switched to domestic price stability as the main criterion for policy, with the strategic aim of gradually reducing the inflation rate, and with the money stock as an intermediate policy objective.[21] It took decisive action in 1974 by reducing the growth rate of (M2 + CDs) to 11%, less than half the value of the previous year.

So strong and sudden a contraction produced a serious recession. But by the middle of 1975, the inflation rate was below double digits,

---

[21] In the Translator's Note to Suzuki, Greenwood (1980), states that the Bank of Japan announced its intention to pursue monetary targets in July 1974. This probably refers to an internal Bank of Japan decision; money stock projections were first announced in 1978.

Table 7.4 (M2 + CD) Growth Projections and Outcomes, Japan

	Projection	Actual	(in %)
1978	12–13	12.6	
1979	11	10.3	
1980	8	7.6	
1981	10	10.4	
1982	8	8.3	
1983	7	6.8	
1984	8	7.9	
1985	8	9.0	
1986	8–9	9.2	
Mean	9.0	9.1	
Std.dev.[a]		1.7	
Std.err.[b]		1.2	

Source: For 1978 through 1983, BIS *Annual Report*, 1983: 71; for later years, BIS *Annual Report*; for 1986 actual, IFS.

Note: Data are for fourth quarter of each year.

[a] Standard deviation.

[b] (Mean square difference between actual and mean of projection) × 4, to transform error to an annual rate.

and it has stayed there; indeed, it continued falling virtually throughout, except for a small rise during the second oil crisis. Since the beginning of 1982, the inflation rate has not exceeded 2.5% on a year-over-year basis. Money growth has continued to fall with the inflation rate.

Although the Bank of Japan has annual money growth targets, it does not announce them (Suzuki 1985). Rather, the Bank each quarter publishes a projection of the growth rate of (M2 + CDs) for the four quarters ending at the close of that quarter. Data for fourth quarter targets for the years from 1978 are shown in Table 7.4.[22]

Suzuki (1985) explains the use of projections rather than targets as giving the central bank flexibility and freeing it from political pressures. In addition, this method of targeting has the benefit of largely describing what has already been done. It also means that divergences from target in the current quarter appear to be only one-quarter their actual size at an annual rate. Even so, the outcomes are reasonably close to the projections.[23] Note further that the general trend of both

[22] These data differ somewhat from those presented in Meltzer (1986), Table 1.

[23] It is not possible to infer from Table 7.4 how accurately the Bank of Japan meets its annual targets. One possibility is that the error would increase more than proportionately with time because the known initial conditions are further away;

projections and actuals is negative, which is consistent with the gradual decline of the inflation rate in Japan. The projected growth rates do change cyclically though. There was a nearly 3% per annum increase in the growth rate in 1981 (this can be seen also in Figure 7.4) and a more than 2% increase in the rate of growth between 1983 and 1986.

Remarkably, though, the standard errors in Tables 7.3 and 7.4 do not show the Fed doing a significantly worse job than the Bank of Japan in meeting the M2 target or projection. Using the "standard errors" in the two tables, the Fed appears to come closer to attaining its M2 target than the Bank of Japan does to its (M2+CD) projection.[24] Furthermore, the standard deviation of the M2 outcome is lower in the U.S. than in Japan.

C. Germany

The Bundesbank, the first central bank to announce money targets, has targeted "central bank money" since the end of 1974. Targets and outcomes are presented in Table 7.5.[25] Central bank money consists of non-bank currency plus 16.6% of demand deposits, 12.4% of time deposits and borrowed funds, and 8.1% of savings deposits. In origin it is equal to currency plus required reserves, a concept that could be called the "required base," except that the required reserves are calculated using reserve ratios of 1974. The Bundesbank describes it rather as a weighted sum of components of the broad money stock, with weights reflecting the liquidity of the components.

Until 1978 the target was quite high (relative to later years), and the outcome higher. From 1979 the targets were given as a range. The Bundesbank typically indicates where in the range it expects to come out, and why: accordingly, "it has not been possible for the announced target [range] to be interpreted arbitrarily by the general public or by the Bundesbank itself."[26] The target range was gradually reduced from 1979; although the actual growth rate of CBM did not fall steadily, it was lower after 1978 than before, and (except in 1986)

---

the other is that the Bank would have more time to correct any errors.

[24] The comparison is not straightforward because while the Japanese data are end-of-period, the U.S. data are quarterly averages, which biases the comparison against the Japanese results. See also the preceding footnote.

[25] A useful account through 1982 is contained in Schlesinger (1983). See also "The longer-term trend and control of the money stock," *Monthly Report of the Deutsche Bundesbank*, Vol. 37, 1 (Jan. 1985): 13–26.

[26] *Report of the Deutsche Bundesbank*, 1980, p. 30.

Table 7.5   Central Bank Money Targets, Germany

	Target	Actual	(in %)
1975	8.0	9.9	
1976	8.0	9.3	
1977	8.0	9.0	
1978	8.0	11.4	
1979	6.0–9.0	6.4	
1980	5.0–8.0	4.8	
1981	4.0–7.0	3.5	
1982	4.0–7.0	6.1	
1983	4.0–7.0	7.0	
1984	4.0–6.0	4.6	
1985	3.0–5.0	4.5	
1986	3.5–5.5	7.8	
1987	3.0–6.0		
Mean:	6.3	7.0	
Std.dev.		2.4	
Std.err.[a]		1.0	

Sources: Isard and Rojas-Suzarez (1986), Table 35, p. 84, through 1985; *Monthly Report of the Deutsche Bundesbank* (Jan. 1987), p. 2, for 1986 and 1987 data.

Note: For 1975, target is December-over-December; for 1976 to 1978, year-over-year; for remaining years, fourth-quarter-over-fourth-quarter.

[a] Mean square difference between outcome and mid-point of target range.

within or below the range. Typically, the Bundesbank was aiming for the lower part of its range.

Until 1980 the Bundesbank derived its target essentially by targeting nominal GNP.[27] There was an allowance for unavoidable inflation, plus growth of real GNP, typically at the growth rate of potential output, plus an estimate of velocity change. The real growth rate is that of potential output because the Bundesbank tries rigorously to limit the temptation to engage in countercylical policy. Since 1980 the Bundesbank has stopped allowing for velocity change, on the grounds that it is unpredictable. It adjusts for unemployment only within the target range: for instance, in 1982 and 1983 it aimed for the upper half of the target range explicitly because unemployment was high.[28] While it emphasizes that its primary responsibility is to maintain the value of money, it permits deviations in response to exchange rate movements— particularly in light of the Deutsche mark's role in the EMS—and

[27] I am grateful to Dr. Helmut Schlesinger for discussion on these procedures.
[28] *Report of the Deutsche Bundesbank*, 1983: 33.

also interest rate movements. Any deviation generates a detailed explanation.[29]

The Fed's justification of its targets is generally less precise, probably because it presents ranges for four variables and sometimes more. Nor do past failures receive a careful explanation such as that of the Bundesbank, again, probably for the above reason.

The targeting procedures and explanations provided by the Bundesbank appear fully serious. By comparison with the procedures of the Fed and the Bank of Japan, they raise the question of whether CBM is the optimal target, whether there should be only one target, and whether targets are preferable to projections. The outcome of the Bundesbank's policies also raises the question of whether a central bank should be directed to consider the impacts of its actions on unemployment as well as the value of money.

D. United Kingdom

The Bank of England adopted M3 targets for internal use in 1973, and began announcing the targets in 1976. The official explanation of their adoption stressed the fight against inflation and the need to anchor expectations.[30] The U.K. has continued to publish an M3 (since 1977, sterling M3) target since then, but since 1982 has added other targets, and in 1987 is tending to place more weight on MO, the monetary base. Table 7.6 presents U.K. targets and outcomes.

Table 7.6 should be read in conjunction with Figure 7.2 showing CPI inflation. The first few years of monetary targeting appeared successful, both in meeting targets (except for 1977) and in bringing down the inflation rate. But then in 1980, M3 grew far in excess of the target range as inflation returned to nearly 20%. The very high rate of growth of M3 in 1980 can be explained as a result of reintermediation following regulatory changes and the end of foreign exchange controls. The Bank of England's failure to control its growth may be attributed to its reluctance to push interest rates higher than they already were at a time of sterling strength.

Because the sterling M3 demand function appeared to be breaking down, the Bank of England added both an M1 and a broader monetary aggregate target in 1982 and 1983. Policy did not succeed in bringing those variables within the target range, either. Since it appears that M0, the monetary base, has a stable relationship with nominal GNP,

---

[29] For example, "The monetary target for 1987," *Monthly Report of the Deutsche Bundesbank*, (Jan. 1987): 1–2.

[30] I draw freely in this section on Fischer (1987).

Table 7.6   Money Targets, United Kingdom

(in %)	M3		M1		M0	
	Target	Out-come	Target	Out-come	Target	Out-come
1976	9.0–13.0	7.3				
1977	9.0–13.0	15.4				
1978	8.0–12.0	11.4				
1979	8.0–12.0	10.3				
1980	7.0–11.0	19.4				
1981	6.0–11.0	12.8				
1982	8.0–12.0	11.2	8.0–12.0	12.3		
1983	7.0–11.0	9.5	7.0–11.0	14.0		
1984	6.0–10.0	11.9			4.0–8.0	7.7
1985	5.0– 9.0	16.5			3.0–7.0	3.3
1986	11.0–15.0	18.2*			2.0–6.0	4.5*
Mean	9.6	13.1				
Std. dev.		3.6				
Std.err.		3.2				

Sources: Isard and Rojas-Suarez (1986), Table 35, p. 84, through 1985. 1986 data from *OECD Economic Outlook*, (December 1986), Table 1.

Note: Targets were also specified for two years for a broader liquidity aggregate.

* Data through September.

the Bank has more recently switched to announcing M0 targets. It has succeeded in hitting these at the same time as inflation has come down, though it emphasizes that it does not target M0 in order to control the money supply through the base. Rather, it targets M0 because of the apparent stability of its demand function, aiming to hit that target through adjustments of market interest rates.

The Bank of England has not been successful in achieving its monetary targets, and, in the period up to 1982, was not successful either at controlling the inflation rate. Since then inflation has come down, though M3 growth has remained high and unstable, and unemployment has been high and stable, finally showing signs of declining in 1987.

E. Operating Procedures

There has been much controversy in the United States over the Fed's operating procedures.[31] It was argued that the Fed, although specifying operating targets for monetary policy in terms of both reserves and

---

[31] For a Federal Reserve view of the issues, see Lindsey (1986); for a technical description of the operating procedures from 1979 to 1982, and references, see Goodfriend *et al.* (1986).

interest rates, was allowing the interest rate targets to dominate, and therefore losing sight of the quantity targets.

In Japan, Germany, and the U.K., monetary policy is operated in the short run largely through control of interest rates; and in Japan and Germany, also through control over the quantity of central-bank credit provided the banking system.[32] Open market operations are considered a means of influencing interest rates and thereby the quantity of money demanded, rather than controlling the money base and thus, through a stable money multiplier, the supply of money.

These procedures and their rationale would be severely criticized if the Fed were to espouse them explicitly. Nonetheless, they have not hampered the ability of the Bank of Japan and the Bundesbank to attain their monetary targets. Of course, both the Bank of Japan and the Bundesbank hope to develop more efficient money and capital markets in which to conduct open market operations, and the trend is clearly in that direction.[33] Still, it is difficult when examining German and Japanese monetary policy to believe that much of the blame for the Fed's failures to hit its monetary targets can derive from imperfections in the way it tries to control the money stock, as opposed to conscious decisions that the targets should not be met in a particular period.[34]

IV. Conclusions

The record of policy reviewed in this paper raises questions about the role of monetary targets, gradualism, and credibility. In the background there are also questions about the flexible exchange rate system.

---

[32] Feldman (1986) provides a detailed description of the Japanese financial system. Suzuki (1986) compares U.S. and Japanese financial innovations; Suzuki (1987) is an extremely accessible account of the liberalization and internationalization of Japanese financial markets, and the implications for monetary policy. Descriptions of Bundesbank operating procedures can be found from time to time in the *Monthly Report of the Deutsche Bundesbank*; "The Bundesbank's transactions in securities under repurchase agreements" (March 1983: 23–30) is useful. The Bank of England's *The Development and Operation of Monetary Policy, 1960–1983* describes the money supply process and decisions.

[33] In Japan the large government budget deficit and the consequent increase in the supply of bonds have been instrumental in the development of the money and bond markets.

[34] This argument is made, on the basis of Japanese operating procedures, by Dotsey (1986).

A. Monetary Targeting

Monetary targeting serves the valuable purpose of forcing the central bank to announce its intentions for the next year, and of explaining why it failed to meet them this year. Provided the targets are taken seriously, targeting lends a coherence to monetary policy that operating by the "touch and feel" of the market does not. Even where targeting has not been successful, as in the U.K., the failures suggest where to look for an explanation, and to some extent how to improve policy.

The adoption of monetary targeting does not necessarily imply inactive policies. None of the four countries, including Japan, has tried to keep money growth constant, and all have responded to the business cycle, to velocity shocks, and to the exchange rate.

(i) *Nominal GNP Targeting*: The activist procedure explicitly followed by the Bundesbank until 1980 is the right way of doing nominal GNP targeting (Taylor 1985). Each year a target is chosen for nominal GNP, based on the desired breakdown between inflation and real growth. The monetary target is then derived from target GNP and a forecast of velocity. Approval of targeting in that fashion does not, however, imply that the target real growth rate should always be the growth rate of potential output, or that the target rate of inflation need necessarily be zero.

(ii) *How Many Goals of Policy*? The Bundesbank and the Bank of Japan both have as their main task the preservation of the value of the currency. The Bank of Japan was able to reduce the inflation rate after 1975 without an apparent cost in terms of higher unemployment. The Bundesbank's policies from 1979, combined with tight fiscal policy, succeeded in wringing inflation out of the system at the expense of much higher unemployment. There was in Germany virtually none of the respite from monetary tightness that the Fed provided in the U.S. in 1982 as the recession worsened. By giving the central bank both real independence and as its primary responsibility the maintenance of price stability, which virtually absolves it from concern over unemployment, the legal system may produce a deflationary bias in the economy. If there is a significant probability that the central bank will be the main economic policymaker—and the growing immobilization of countercyclical fiscal policy makes that increasingly the case—there is good reason to require it to give weight to unemployment as well as inflation when making its decisions.[35]

---

[35] The question arises of whether central bank policy has any influence on real variables like the rate of unemployment. There is much evidence that expansionary

(iii) *Projections versus Targets*: The choice between "projections" and "targets" is a subtle one. The Bank of Japan has in the last few years maintained stable money growth and stable projections, and presumably it therefore has also been attaining its unpublished targets. At the same time, by projecting only for the current quarter, it leaves itself great flexibility for any longer period. Its credibility appears sufficient for the projections to be regarded as targets. It is unlikely that other central banks can rely on being able to achieve similar "targeting without targets" in the near future.

(iv) *How Many Money Targets*? The Bundesbank and the Bank of Japan have each elected to focus on just one monetary variable, the Fed on many, and the Bank of England sometimes one and sometimes more. There is a strong theoretical justification for the multi-target view, arising from the fact that the central bank in fact influences many monetary variables, each of which has a slightly different and uncertain effect on ultimate target variables—and feedback from which makes it easier for the monetary authority to decipher changes in the economy. By using several targets, including perhaps interest rates (and a rule for deciding how to compromise when they cannot all be attained), the central bank reduces the uncertainty about the effects of its actions on the economy. For instance, the failure of the Fed to meet its M1 targets on many occasions appears less serious when it does come close to achieving the other targets.

Nonetheless, the clarity of the one-variable approach is appealing, both in its impact as a signal, and for the consistency it might force on the central bank. If it could be shown empirically that there was little to be gained (in an expected utility sense) by having more than one money target—for instance, because the correlation between one of the monetary variables closely controllable by the central bank and nominal GNP was exceptionally strong—it might be worthwhile narrowing the list of targets to one.

In both Japan and Germany, the single targeted monetary variable has smaller variance of velocity than that of other money concepts.[36] In the U.K. M3 velocity has been highly unstable, which partly accounts for the shift to M0 targeting. In the U.S. M2 velocity is more

---

policy can in the short run lead to an expansion of output; if some hysteresis-like view of the economy is correct, then such short-run changes in output tend to be permanent.

[36] Data are presented in Isard and Rojas-Suarez (1986), Table 32; of course, the predictability of velocity over the next year rather than its variability is the more relevant measure of the suitability of a given target variable, but in practice predictability and variability are closely related.

stable than that of M1, though less stable than the velocity of M3. On the basis of the stability of its velocity and the Fed's success in hitting that target, M2 currently would appear to be a useful target variable—even though the collection of assets in M2 has little analytic coherence, and it would remain to be seen whether a switch to M2 targeting would put Goodhart's Law into effect and destroy the relative stability of M2 velocity.

B. Gradualism and Credibility

After a sharp change in money growth and a deep recession in 1974, the Bank of Japan succeeded in gradually reducing both money growth and inflation over the succeeding decade, with an interruption from the second oil shock. The short, sharp shock worked for the Bank of Japan. But it did not work for the Bundesbank. After bringing down inflation in 1973–74, the Bundesbank faced generally rising inflation until the second oil shock and then was only able to reduce inflation by creating and maintaining high unemployment. Similarly, both the Fed and the Bank of England had to create massive recessions in the early 1980s to get the inflation rate down, despite their successes at reducing inflation in the first oil shock.

It is easy to believe that the Bank of England lacked credibility, and that the Fed lacked credibility until 1982. But why should that have been true of the Bundesbank? Perhaps, though it is unlikely, it had tolerated too-high inflation in the late 1970s. Any analysis that stresses credibility has to explain why the inflation rate came down in Japan with only one recession, while it took two or three recessions for each of the other countries, and in two of them prolonged high unemployment.

The difference may lie much more with the work force than with the policymakers. Whereas nominal wage increases rose in each of the other three countries in the second oil shock, Japanese wage inflation did not. If it had, the Bank of Japan would have created another recession. That threat is not sufficient to stop wage increases—in evidence, note that the Bundesbank's implicit threat had to be carried out when wage inflation increased in Germany in 1981.

U.S. policy after 1982 also suggests that credibility is not a simple function of money growth performance (Blanchard 1987). M1 growth in the U.S. has been higher in the period since 1982 than over any comparable period. There has been no perceptible impact on sensitive asset-market variables, such as interest rates, let alone on wages or prices. Obviously, the markets believe that the M1 growth signifies nothing about future inflation. They are probably right.

The lesson is that someone with credibility can take and explain sensible actions that at other times would be viewed with the greatest suspicion. Further, I believe the lesson is also that credibility is earned by successful outcomes, rather than by holding rigorously to intermediate targets. This is the case for not attempting to force central banks to hold strictly to their money targets in the face of shifts in velocity or other relevant circumstances.

C. Exchange Rates

Exchange rates and current account imbalances have received little explicit attention in this paper. In the U.K. and Germany, monetary policy has at times been dominated by the behavior of the exchange rate. That was true in the United States in 1978, and may be about to happen in Japan now.

However, this does not suggest that the U.S., Japan, and Germany will anytime soon be willing to forego monetary independence in the interests of stabilizing exchange rates. Bundesbank reports make it clear, time and time again, that it views price stability as the overriding goal. European countries that want to accept or attain the German inflation rate can join the EMS, and Britain may do that. The U.S. is less concerned with inflation relative to unemployment than is Germany, which means that a newly fixed dollar–Deutsche mark exchange rate would suffer the same fate it did in the early 1970s—particularly given divergent fiscal policies. Since Japan's inflation preferences are different from those of the U.S., and its trading patterns are different from those of Europe, it is unlikely to fix exchange rates against either the dollar or the Deutsche mark.

References

Blanchard, Olivier J. 1987. "Reaganomics," forthcoming in *Economic Policy*.

Bruno, Michael, and Sachs, Jeffrey. 1986. *Economics of Worldwide Inflation*. Cambridge, Mass: Harvard University Press.

Dotsey, Michael. 1986. Japanese Monetary Policy, a Comparative Analysis. *Monetary and Economic Studies*, 4, 2: 105–28.

Feldman, Robert A. 1986. *Japanese Financial Markets*. Cambridge, Mass: MIT Press.

Fischer, Stanley. 1987. British Monetary Policy. Forthcoming in Layard, Richard, ed., *The British Economy*. London: Oxford University Press.

Goodfriend, Marvin *et al*. 1986. A Weekly Rational Expectations Model of the Nonborrowed Reserve Operating Procedure. Federal Reserve Bank of Richmond, *Economic Review*. 72, 1: 11–28.

Hamada, Koichi, and Hayashi, Fumio. 1985. Monetary Policy in Postwar Japan. in Ando, A., et al., eds., *Monetary Policy in Our Times*. Cambridge, Mass: MIT Press.

Isard, Peter, and Rojas-Suarez, Liliana. 1986. Velocity of Money and the Practice of Monetary Targeting: Experience, Theory, and the Policy Debate. *Staff Studies for the World Economic Outlook* (July). Washington, D.C.: IMF.

Lindsey, David E. 1986. The Monetary Regime of the Federal Reserve System. In Campbell, Colin, and Dougan, William, eds., *Alternative Monetary Regimes*. Baltimore, MD: Johns Hopkins Press.

Meek, Paul, ed. 1983. *Central Bank Views on Monetary Targeting*. New York: Federal Reserve Bank.

Meltzer, Allan H. 1985. Variability of Prices, Output and Money Under Fixed and Fluctuating Exchange Rates: An Empirical Study of Monetary Regimes in Japan and the United States. *Monetary and Economic Studies*, 3, 3: 1–46.

———. 1986. Lessons from the Experience of Japan and the United States under Fixed and Fluctuating Exchange Rates. *Monetary and Economic Studies*. 4, 2: 129–46.

Rasche, Robert H. 1986. M-1 Velocity and Money Demand Functions: Do Stable Relationships Exist? forthcoming in Carnegie-Rochester Conference Series on Public Policy, vol. 27.

Schlesinger, Helmut. 1983. The Setting of Monetary Objectives in Germany. In Meek, ed., *Central Bank Views*.

Suzuki, Yoshio. 1980. *Money and Banking in Contemporary Japan*. New Haven, Conn: Yale University Press.

———. 1985. Japan's Monetary Policy Over the Past 10 Years. *Monetary and Economic Studies*, 3, 2: 1–10.

———. 1986. A Comparative Study of Financial Innovation, Deregulation and Reform in Japan and the United States. *Monetary and Economic Studies*, 4, 2: 147–59.

———. 1987. Monetary Policy in Japan under Financial Liberalization and Internationalization. FAIR Fact Series, Japan's Financial Markets, Vol. 40, Foundation for Advanced Information and Reserach, Japan.

Taylor, John B. 1985. What Would Nominal GNP Targetting Do to the Business Cycle? In Brunner, Karl, and Meltzer, Allan, eds., *Understanding Monetary Regimes*. Carnegie-Rochester Conference Series on Public Policy, Vol 22. North-Holland.

Comments

Eduard J. Bomhoff

Parkin successfully describes the degree of variability of output and inflation in different countries, with conclusions quite similar to those of Allan Meltzer. His statistical procedures are less sophisticated than those used by Meltzer and by Suzuki and Naniwa at the Bank of Japan. In my opinion the Bayesian techniques used by the Bank of Japan and by Meltzer have some important advantages. For instance, a strict choice between the extreme alternatives of using rates of growth on the one hand and first differences of growth rates (accelerations) on the other hand is not necessary. The Kalman filter techniques allow us to let the data guide us towards an intermediate model if the two extremes are inappropriate, as they often are. Parkin's simplicity is achieved at a cost of implicitly adopting possibly inappropriate time series models for his variables. Kalman filter techniques (or Box-Jenkins models) deliver estimates of residual variances that are based upon the most appropriate time series model within its class.

Parkin's paper goes beyond statistical measurement, since he compares different macroeconomic structures. That part of the paper seems somewhat less convincing for two reasons. First, the regressions do not quite correspond to the theoretical model in the paper. Also, annual data are not ideal for testing hypotheses on causal mechanisms. This part of the paper, therefore, seems quite preliminary in its present form.

Fischer assesses the long-term success of monetary policy by looking at trends in inflation. This is correct, since central banks can and should react to persistent changes in the trends of the income velocity of money and the rate of growth of income or wealth. They should be able to set the medium-term rate of growth of the money supply considering the trend rates of growth of velocity and real income (or wealth) and thus be able to steer the medium-term trend in their domestic price level.

Fischer also evaluates the short-term appropriateness of monetary policy. He looks at the historical record for unemployment or economic growth and holds it against the Central Bank if the historical record for unemployment or economic growth is disappointing. This technique of assessing the success of short-term monetary policy seems very dangerous for three reasons:

1. All domestic factors that influence economic growth and unemployment in addition to short-term (unexpected) changes in monetary policy may be neglected if certain outcomes for economic growth or unemployment are blamed directly on domestic monetary policy.

2. All international influences on unemployment may also be neglected.

3. The indicator variable—unemployment or economic growth—that is used by Fischer to gauge the success of monetary policy may be non-stationary or subject to measurement error, so that the simple observation that unemployment is above its average for some historical period or that the rate of economic growth does not attain its historical level may be meaningless for causal inference.

Fischer criticizes monetary policy in Germany, for example, because German unemployment increased by a large margin for a protracted period. Lindbeck and Snower have pointed out, however, that the high unemployment in Europe since the 1970s is predominantly a labor market phenomenon and should be analyzed with the help of a model of a fragmented labor market. The natural rate of unemployment in Europe has increased as the result of institutional changes. Fischer does not mention this alternative hypothesis but instead puts blame on German monetary policy without embedding the effects of changes in the money supply in a model that also allows for other domestic or international influences as well as possible changes in institutions. As a simple illustration of the shortcomings of Fischer's informal approach, in Table 1 I have regressed the rate of growth of real income in the United Kingdom, Japan, and Germany on a constant, lagged dependent variable, the current and one-year lagged changes in the logarithm of the money stock, and the current and one-year lagged rates of growth of real world imports.

The simple specification does not pretend to adequately describe changes in economic growth, but it serves to show the importance of at least one important omitted variable in Fischer's analysis. The rate of growth of real world imports is highly significant both in the United Kingdom and in Germany. A simple calculation shows, for example,

Table 1

Dependent variable: rate of real growth, yr
Sample: 1960–1985
OLS estimates:

	U.K.	Japan	Germany
constant	0.004	0.009	0.016
	(0.346)	(0.622)	(0.985)
$yr_{(-1)}$	0.294	0.474	0.225
	(1.239)	(2.209)	(1.121)
m	0.017	0.119	0.033
	(0.252)	(1.322)	(0.240)
$m_{(-1)}$	0.086	0.021	0.245
	(1.322)	(0.260)	(1.609)
imp	0.379	0.212	0.416
	(3.951)	(1.104)	(2.602)
imp_{-1}	0.094	0.045	0.034
	(0.759)	(0.233)	(0.187)
S.E.	0.017	0.031	0.026
R^2	0.47	0.55	0.57
AR(1)	0.006	0.17	2.060
AR(2)	0.023	0.651	1.115

(t-values between parentheses)
AR(i): LM-test on i^{th} order autocorrelation
            (approximately $F(i, T-K-i)$)

yr: real GNP
m: money
imp: real world imports
All variables are first differences of natural logarithms.
Source of data: International Financial Statistics.

that the deceleration world trade contributes almost 1.5 percentage points to the decline in economic growth in Germany between the mid-1970s and the early 1980s.

Another remarkable example of Fischer's tactics of judging the appropriateness of short-term monetary policies by looking at another macroeconomic variable and deeming monetary policy successful if this other variable has been satisfactory and judging monetary policy a failure if the indicator variable has proved disappointing is his discussion of the U.S. stock market and the insights it provides about the monetary policy of the Federal Reserve. Fischer claims that U.S. monetary policy must have been appropriate because the asset markets show their approval. Do we really want U.S. economic policy to be judged by the daily change in the Dow-Jones Index? If so, then a big drop in that Index would be necessary before policy were changed. Again, this type of market orientation can only be justified if no other factors but changes in the money supply influence the stock market, or if a "good" monetary policy is a necessary condition for a rising stock market. It seems to me that no meaningful model of stock prices satisfies these conditions.

To conclude, one has to be very careful when using changes in real variables or in asset prices to judge short-term monetary policy. Other domestic variables may be important, international effects may have been dominant or the indicator variable may be inappropriate on grounds of principle because it is non-stationary.

References

Lindbeck, Assar, and Dennis Snow (1986a). Wage Setting, Unemployment, and Insider-Outsider Relations. AEA, Papers and Proceedings, Vol. 76, No. 2, pp. 235–239.

Lindbeck, Assar (1986c). Union Activity and Economic Resilience, CEPR, Discussion Paper no. 114, London.

Naniwa, Sadao. Nonstationary Covariance Structure of Detrended Economic Time Series: A Time Varying Model Approach. Chart Book as produced for the Third International Conference of the Bank of Japan.

Meltzer, A.H. On Monetary Stability and Monetary Reform. Paper in this volume.

Comments

Choi Yeon-Jong

This afternoon I would like to discuss two interesting and distinguished papers that analyze causes of domestic instability. The first paper, by Professor Parkin, investigates the sources of output and price fluctuations in the world aggregate economy and in the seven major industrial countries.

As I extensively agree with Professor Parkin's sensible analysis, I find it difficult to comment directly on the paper. Most economists would agree with his conclusion that the major source of output fluctuations in recent years has been real shocks rather than nominal ones. He also reaches the eminently reasonable conclusion that money has also played an important role in these fluctuations; countries that have pursued highly stable targeting of monetary aggregates have experienced lower output variability than countries that have allowed growth of money supply.

I have some reservations, however, about one of the conclusions in Section I, which states that vector autoregression results are consistent with equilibrium models of both the real and monetary varieties, while rejecting a Keynesian sticky-price model. There are two reasons for my reservation.

First, since this conclusion is based on data of the world aggregate economy, it needs to be examined using relevant national data. This he could not do because of the limited number of available observations.

Second, I think that vector autoregression results by themselves are not sufficient to discriminate between different theories.

The regression results show that a monetary disturbance one period earlier causes, in a "Granger sense," price innovations but not output innovations.

The results do not show, however, that monetary shocks have no significant effect on output growth, because some variables left out of the system may have strong correlations with output innovations or money and price innovations.

For example, if fiscal policy, which is not dealt with in the system, is strongly counter-cyclical and monetary policy counter-inflationary at the same time, output innovations may appear to be uncorrelated with earlier monetary and price innovations, whereas price innovations appear to be correlated with earlier monetary disturbances. This is because effects of money innovations on output, which could have been detected *ceteris paribus*, may have been obscured by effects of innovations in other variables.

Having noted this reservation about a minor point in the paper, I would now like to reiterate that I concur with Professor Parkin's conclusions concerning the causes of fluctuations in output and prices. Indeed, I think the careful empirical and theoretical analysis offered by Professor Parkin is clearly pertinent to other countries outside the seven major industrial economies.

I can only offer my personal view on causes of instability, or rather stability, and the role of monetary policy in recent years in Korea.

Table 1 presents Korean data for six variables—real output, price level, broad money, velocity of money, reserve money, and money multiplier—in terms of growth rates and organized according to the two identities used by Professor Parkin.

The only difference between this and Professor Parkin's analysis is that for the Korean data the time periods are broken down into the 1970s and 1980s.

There are two striking features of the data shown in Table 1.

First, the average inflation rate fell dramatically from 20% in the 1970s to 6% in the 1980s, while the average growth rate of output remained virtually unchanged at slightly above 8%.

The second is the decreased volatility of both output growth and inflation. The variance of output growth rate in the 1980s was 2.9%, down from 5.1% in the 1970s. Similarly, the variance of inflation in the 1970s was 6.5% while in the 1980s it decreased to 4.4%. Why has inflation gone down so rapidly in the 1980s, compared with the 1970s, in the Korean economy? Are the narrower fluctuations of output and prices, in amplitude, attributable to changes in money supply growth rate or to some other reasons?

Let us first consider the means of the variables. It is clear that the decline in inflation, from 20% in the 1970s to 6% in the 1980s, is closely associated with a decline in the growth rate of money supply,

Table 1   Means and Variances of Korean Data

	(a) *Income, Prices, Money, and Velocity*						
	Δy	+	Δp	=		Δm	+	Δv
1971–80	8.1		20.0	= 28.1	$\cong$	30.2	−	0.3
	(5.1)		(6.5)	(6.7)		(5.5)		(6.0)
1981–86	8.4	+	6.0	= 14.4	$\cong$	19.1	−	3.4
	(2.9)		(4.4)	(4.2)		(6.8)		(4.2)

	(b) *Money, Reserve Money, and the Money Multiplier*			
	Δmqm		= Δmb	+ Δmm
1971–80	30.2	$\cong$	29.9	+ 2.3
	(5.5)		(19.1)	(13.3)
1981–86	19.1	$\cong$	7.4	+ 11.4
	(6.8)		(6.6)	(10.0)

Notes: 1) All the variables are logarithms.
2) y is real output, p the GNP deflator, mqm the M2, v the velocity of M2, mb the reserve money and mm the multiplier.
3) Δ is the difference operator.
4) Identities do not hold exactly in the data because second-order interaction terms are ignored.
5) Numbers in parentheses are variances.

from 30.2% to 19.1%, and to a lesser degree, with a rise in the absolute negative-rate-of-change value of velocity.

The decline in the growth rate of money supply is associated with a more conspicuous decline in the growth rate of reserve money.

On the other hand, a rise in the rate of change of the money multiplier prevented the growth rate of money supply from further declining.

Now I would like to offer my interpretation of what happened in the Korean economy in the 1980s. Because the monetary authority in Korea adopted M2 as its principal target in 1979, it is reasonable to assume that reserve money was endogenously manipulated in order to keep M2 on its targeted path.

Indeed, this seems to be very evident in the case of Korea because it was the growth rate of reserve money that most dramatically declined, from 29.9% to 7.4%.

It should also be pointed out that the variance of the growth rate of reserve money decreased from 19.1% in the 1970s to 6.6% in the 1980s.

The decline in the growth rate of money supply, however, was not as great as the decline in the growth rate of reserve money would suggest, because the money multiplier rate of change increased from 2.3% to 11.4%. This was largely due to a reduction in the required reserve ratio to 11% in 1980, from 20%, and again to 5.5% in 1981 and finally to 4.5% in 1984. In addition, the decrease in the ratio of cash holdings to money by the private sector contributed to an increase in the money multiplier rate of change.

On the other hand, the increase, in absolute value, in the rate of growth of velocity in the 1980s, which implies that the rate of change of velocity was falling rapidly in the 1980s, seems to be associated with the decline in inflation that heightened the preference to hold broad money.

Also, financial innovations and the notable growth of nonmonetary financial institutions in the 1980s may also have contributed to the decline in the rate of change of velocity.

In short, inflation was brought down to an average of 6% in the 1980s, from an average of 20% in the 1970s, thanks to persistent counter-inflationary monetary policies, which relied on a tight control of reserve money. These policies cannot take all the credit, however. In fact, the drop in the price of oil, as well as that of other major raw materials, greatly benefited Korea since it depends completely on imported oil.

It would not have been possible, however, to bring inflation firmly under control in so short a period of time unless such a counter-inflationary monetary stance was pursued.

Let us now turn to the variances. It should be noted that the variance of aggregate nominal demand decreased more than changes in variances of growth rate of money supply and velocity would suggest. This was because the negative covariance between growth rate of money supply and velocity increased in absolute value.

I cannot argue with Professor Parkin's conclusion that stable money supply growth contributes to stable aggregate nominal demand. One of the aims of discretionary monetary policy is, however, to reduce the variance of aggregate nominal demand (Y) not only by shrinking the variance of money supply (m), but also by making the covariance between money supply and velocity (v) sufficiently negative to offset the otherwise higher value of the money supply variance.[1]

It appears that in Korea's case a negative covariance between the rate of change of money supply and velocity became sufficiently large to offset the higher variance of money supply. To claim that monetary policy alone was responsible for all these developments may be a bit

---

[1] $Y = m + v$. Thus, Var Y = Var m + Var v + 2cov (m, v), where Y is aggregate nominal demand, m the money supply, and v the velocity, and all variables are logarithmic growth rates.

impetuous. Nevertheless, it was fortunate for the Korean economy that the growth rate of money supply decreased and the negative covariance between money and velocity increased at the same time.

The second paper, by Professor Fischer, analyzed policy choices with emphasis on the monetary policies of the United States, Japan, Germany, and the United Kingdom. I applaud Professor Fischer's approach to comparative study of monetary policy among nations because I believe that a careful descriptive study can, after all, reveal more than a complex econometric analysis.

I strongly agree with Professor Fischer's conclusion that credibility is earned by successful outcomes, rather than by holding rigorously to intermediate targets.

I also agree that the behavior of wages, although it is not a policy variable per se, has played an important role in price movements.

Korea's experience from 1972 to 1986 bears out these conclusions. Domestic credit was supposed to be a guideline for monetary policy in the 1970s. It is questionable, however, whether domestic credit had ever been seriously intended as an intermediate target.

In fact, the monetary policy had been, in general, lenient after the first oil shock, resulting in two-digit inflation throughout the latter half of the 1970s, though economic growth rates quickly rose back to the 10% level thanks to favorable external conditions. It should also be noted that high wage inflation had fueled an inflation spiral in the 1970s. In response, the Bank of Korea adopted M2 as an intermediate target beginning in 1979, hitting target rates most of the time.

As Professor Fischer aptly put it, "The recessions could be viewed as investments in reputation." It took considerable time for the Bank of Korea to earn credibility in its resolve to fight inflation because of the lack of investments in reputation in the 1970s. It was not until 1982 that the inflation spiral was finally broken, thanks partly to drops in prices of raw materials such as oil.

Meanwhile, the wage increase rate quickly went down after 1980, in sharp contrast to the 1970s, contributing to disinflation. If it had not, it would have been more difficult for the Bank of Korea to maintain inflation below a 1% level for four consecutive years since 1983.

Comments

William R. White*

The Agenda states that the purpose of this session is to identify the causes of domestic economic instability in the major countries since 1973. It then goes on to suggest three generic reasons why the world has unfolded as badly as it has: (1) the inherent nature of the flexible exchange rate system, (2) policy mistakes, and (3) supply side shocks. Before turning to the Parkin and Fischer papers in detail, let me offer two comments on the question that was put to us.

First, I believe that the fundamental cause of instability since 1973 was the instability prior to 1973. That is, we had a positive nominal shock which pushed up inflation in the late 1960s and early 1970s. Since then, the principal objective of monetary policy in the G-7 has been the restoration of price stability—and in pursuit of this objective we have gone through two recessions, with perhaps further difficulties still to come.[1] Thus, I suggest that the question we should seek to answer in this session is why this initial nominal shock should have had such continuing real effects. Why has the adjustment back to price stability and attendant full employment not been much faster than it has proved to be?

Second, it is possible to contend that the three above-mentioned influences need not be mutually exclusive and are not even independent.

(1) The advent of *generalized floating* in the early 1970s, itself a product of the different policies being followed in different countries, may have encouraged inflation further. Policymakers in countries with appreciating currencies were inclined to ease, while policymakers in countries with depreciating currencies did not respond symmetrically.

---

* This paper was written jointly by W.R. White and Pierre Duguay.

[1] The principal cloud on the current horizon is the overhang of debt—sovereign, government, and sectoral—which has been one part of the legacy of relying principally on monetary policy to initiate the reduction of inflation.

(2) Had the U.S. and many other countries (including Canada) not been so expansionary in the latter part of the 1970s, the same could be said. In effect, *policy error* contributed to the inflationary upswing of the late 1970s and the subsequent recession, in spite of the fact that the original intention of policy was to effect a smooth deceleration of inflation over the whole period.

(3) As for *supply side shocks*, the major increases in oil and other commodity prices in the early and late 1970s were certainly not helpful in that they imposed real shocks on top of on-going nominal developments. However, we must also be careful not to overstate the exogeneity of these relative price changes. In large part, commodity prices (including oil) moved up as sharply as they did because of excessively rapid economic growth[2] and highly inelastic short-run demand and supply functions for such products. Moreover, the subsequent decline of real commodity prices in large part reflected the much larger price elasticities which prevail over the longer run. Neither the Parkin nor the Fischer paper gives enough attention to this important point.

"Monetary Policy and Aggregate Fluctuations"

Even for a person who likes small models, Professor Parkin's paper is a "tour de force." To paraphrase the American comedian Shelly Berman, Parkin says, "Let's take three equations and talk about the world." And what is even more impressive is that (1) his model appears to fit the data, and (2) this reviewer is very sympathetic with many of the conclusions to which he comes. Let me just note two such conclusions, which in fact are at the heart of this model and most models of this sort: (a) excessive monetary growth caused the inflation of the 1970s; and (b) supply side shocks and mistaken expectations about prices can have a major effect on output.

My belief in the former conclusion simply comes naturally to a central banker. As to the latter conclusion, Canada had by far the deepest recession in the G-7 in 1981–82. In large part, this outcome was a product of the earlier commodity price boom which encouraged heavy investment at what were then considered to be "low" real interest rates—assuming general inflation would persist. When the boom

---

[2] I say "excessively rapid" since, in fact, the rates of growth recorded in the second half of the 1970s by the G-7 countries were not high by traditional standards. However, given the unexpected downward shift of productivity growth and the level of potential, demand growth was nevertheless high enough to contribute to inflation.

burst, inflation dropped and real interest rates rose *ex post* to 10 and 20% per annum in some industries. Severe retrenchment with consequent job losses was the final effect. However, in the spirit of my introductory comment above—that *all* the hypotheses may be true—I would stress that this was not the only contributing factor to the last Canadian recession. I believe that sticky wages and prices (many of them regulated) also played a major role.

Having said I like some of the conclusions at which Professor Parkin arrives, I have substantial difficulties with the model that he has used to generate them. I will generally restrict attention to the world model.

1. Data

I have a problem with both the concept and measurement of world inflation. At the conceptual level, inflationary shocks can be expected to have quite different real side effects depending on the inflationary experience of the economy in question (think of Lucas's early work) and the degree of indexation. Does it make sense to aggregate very different inflation experiences? As to measurement, Parkin's graphs show inflation has been stuck at 12% since 1974, whereas we know that G-7 inflation has been declining. Would the substitution of one series for the other not have a major effect on the econometric results? Put another way, is not Parkin's world inflation series being increasingly dominated by hyper-inflating small countries whose effective weight in the index is constantly increasing? I would suggest that a more appealing measure of world inflation would be a chain-linked index (to avoid giving increasing weight to hyperinflating countries) and would use variable weights based on relative holdings of real money balances rather than real output.

2. Model Specification and Model Properties

Professor Parkin concludes that excessive monetary growth caused the inflation of the 1970s. This is a standard "monetarist" result. The odd thing is that his estimated model does not appear to be "monetarist" in the sense of exhibiting long-run monetary neutrality. Nor, in simulation, does it behave in a monetarist fashion. Consider the following:

Specification of velocity:

$$\Delta^2 v = \lambda \, \Delta^2 m_{-1}$$

This equation implies that the level of velocity is a function of the

the level of money supply. (Δ operator cancels on both sides of the equation). However, if increases in the money supply permanently increase velocity, how then can homogeneity between money and prices be assured?

Aggregate supply equation:

$$\Delta^2 y = \frac{\gamma}{1 + \gamma}\,\varepsilon$$

As I interpret this equation, an *innovation* in money growth (ε_t) has a *permanent* effect on output *growth*. At most, I would have expected a *transitory* effect of unexpected money growth on the *level* of output.

Aggregate output:

$$\Delta^2 y = f(\Delta r)$$

This reduced form equation seems to say that *growth* of output is a function of the *level* of relative prices.

We have carried out some simulations, with the model as estimated, and it does indeed seem to have odd properties consistent with the points made just above. Fuller details are provided in an Appendix to these Comments.

Random shock to Δr:

Raising real commodity prices by 50% (as in 1973) causes real growth to fall permanently by 5%, inflation to rise permanently by 3%, and money growth to fall. Thus, Parkin's model seems in simulation to lay most of the blame for inflation on supply side shocks rather than monetary expansion.

Random shock to $\Delta^2 m$:

In simulation, a large and lasting increase in money growth leads to a negligible increase in inflation. Thus, in Professor Parkin's model the homegeneity condition seems far from being accepted.

3. Estimation

Professor Parkin asserts from "eyeballing" the graphs of his data that the growth rates of y, p, and m are random walks. He thus feels justified in differencing the data prior to carrying out his econometric work. Unfortunately his assertion is not supported by a more careful examination of the evidence.

a) Professor Parkin provides statistics in his text for the variances

Δy, $\Delta^2 y$ (etc.). These data can be used to provide an estimation of parameter α in

$$\Delta y = \alpha \, \Delta y_{-1} + \varepsilon$$

where $\alpha \ (= 1\text{-Var} \, (\Delta^2 y)/2 \, \text{Var} \, (\Delta y))$ should *not* be significantly different from 1 under the maintained hypothesis. In fact, for output this hypothesis is rejected for each data period identified by Parkin, and for prices and money it is rejected for the last decade.

b) My colleague Pierre Duguay has also tried to replicate Parkin's data and has reestimated Tables 3.2 and 3.3 using these replicated data. He reestimated Tables 3.2 and 3.3 with Δm_{-1}, Δy_{-1}, and Δp_{-1} introduced in all three equations, and found that Parkin's hypothesis that the coefficients on these variables be jointly *zero* is definitely rejected for $\Delta^2 y$. He also found that the unrestricted model is more consistent with the "monetarist" model proposed by Stein than with Parkin's restrictions (*i.e.*, cointegration of Δp and Δm cannot be rejected). In particular, monetary innovations seem to have lagged effects on prices.

Parkin emphasizes the fact that there were major changes in the variance of his data between the 1960s and the 1970s. However, he made no effort to explain this increased variance other than by introducing Δr in his equations to capture supply shocks, and did not test for structural breaks or heteroscedasticity. While it has to be recognized that the data series provide only very limited degrees of freedom, this must nevertheless give some cause for concern.

Finally, how can Parkin maintain the hypothesis of a stable world money supply process while at the same time accepting that there were structural changes in the money supply process in individual countries after the adoption of generalized floating? How, too, does he explain the fact that inflation and money growth stopped behaving like random walks after the collapse of Bretton Woods? These are questions that could usefully have been pursued.

"Monetary Policy and Performance in the U.S., Japan, and Europe, 1973–1986"

I would like to begin with what may be more than a quibble. The first few lines of Professor Fischer's paper could be read to imply that inflation is down and out and equilibrium has been reestablished in the major countries. Whether or not that was his intention, I would first question whether inflation is indeed out in North America. As oil prices rebound and the effects of currency depreciation mount we will have to see whether what could be a once-and-for-all level shift in prices becomes a more generalized and ongoing inflation problem. In many other countries (including Canada), inflation may be well down but the rates of unemployment remain very high relative to historical norms. Of course, it is possible that the natural rate of unemployment has risen significantly in all these countries in recent years but, barring this, I would conclude that the economies in these countries are not yet back to equilibrium. Nor have we yet seen the full impact on real variables of the build-up of debt worldwide in recent years. The really interesting question for policymakers is to identify the factors which have contributed to this unsatisfactory outcome.

1. Main Body of Paper

Professor Fischer provides some information pertinent to this question by identifying countries which appear to have done better than others and looking for the secret to their success. Yet, looking at his data and charts, I find it hard to conclude anything other than that the Japanese have done better since the mid-1970s than everyone else. Was it, as some say, because they announced and met their monetary targets? I would give this some, but not undue, importance. Rather, I agree with Fischer's statement that the success of the Japanese has had most to do with the remarkable moderation of their wage increases in the face of real shocks. This in turn was likely a product of the relative severity (relative to previous growth experience) of the 1974–75 recession in Japan. In effect, Japanese wage earners came to recognize early what many of us in other countries are still having trouble accepting, that real shocks *will* force adjustments and that the only choice is between a less painful and a more painful adjustment process.

Moreover, I think the Japanese experience, as well as the body of the paper, also leads us to the further conclusion drawn by Professor Fischer: "I believe the lesson is also that credibility is earned by successful outcomes rather than by holding rigorously to intermediate targets."

This conclusion certainly conforms to Canadian experience. We had explicit monetary targets in Canada from 1975 to 1980, and we hit them each year *without* base drift. Yet this period was followed by a resurgence of wage and price inflation and the deepest recession in postwar history. A crucial problem was that economic agents did not believe the Bank of Canada when it said that increases in inflation would not be tolerated. Rather, credibility was established only when actions followed words.

Let me now turn to the other conclusions noted at the end of Professor Fischer's paper. While not very closely related to the body of the paper, nevertheless, they are interesting in themselves.

2. Conclusions

a) Monetary targeting. Professor Fischer says it is valuable to target monetary aggregates because it gives policymakers a framework in which to explain their activities and provides an incentive to do so. I agree with this, yet two further points should be noted. First, if the demand for money function shifts unexpectedly, then monetary targeting may lead to interest rate changes which are inappropriate under the circumstances. Second, the argument in support of targeting put forward by Professor Fischer is far less compelling than those used to support targeting in the mid-1970s; no long-run inflationary bias, automatic countercyclical movements in interest rates, clear guides for expectations, and so on. Clearly, practical experience with monetary targeting has moderated our enthusiasm significantly.

b) Nominal GNP targeting. Professor Fischer seems to support this approach to implementing monetary policy, and goes further by suggesting that the Bundesbank's "activist procedure" has a lot to commend it. I too have some sympathy with this approach, but must also note its shortfalls. As to nominal income targeting, an important practical problem is political. Surely governments as well as central banks will feel they should have some input here, and this raises some tricky questions about cooperation and the degree of independence of central banks. Further, the public may not believe that the central bank can control nominal income over any reasonably short period (say a year or two), and, given observed lags in the effects of monetary policy, they could well be right.

As to the "activist procedure" of the Bundesbank, it is in fact highly discretionary. If prices are not stable to begin with, then choosing a nominal income target for the year demands knowledge of the short-run trade-off between output and inflation. If the demand for money shifts, then a judgement must be made about how to respond. How are past errors in meeting growth targets to be dealt with? Should they be ignored or should compensation be made? All of this judgement stands in very sharp contrast to the original idea in the 1970s of a nominal "rule" which would strongly condition monetary growth over time and minimize any longer-term inflationary bias.

c) How many goals of policy? Professor Fischer feels central banks should worry more than they do about short-run growth and unemployment. In contrast, as a general rule I feel central banks should keep their eye firmly on their medium-term goal of price stability. It was the excessive concern with short-run growth in the 1970s that led central bankers to contribute to the inflationary surge whose by-products are still troubling us today.

He also notes the reduced room for manœuvre for countercyclical fiscal policy given large government deficits, particularly in North America. The normative inference I draw from his comments is that monetary policy should be eased significantly should the world economy slow significantly. I agree that interest rates would and should decline in such circumstances. Yet, recalling Keynesian arguments about liquidity traps and the merits of "pushing on a string," it may be that monetary policy would not be the policy best suited to ensure economic recovery were the turndown to be quite severe. It would be much more preferable and prudent to restore the room for fiscal manœuvre by cutting North American government deficits vigorously now when the economy is relatively strong.

d) How many monetary targets? Professor Fischer seems to conclude that monetary authorities should have multiple targets. I am not so sure. First, technically it may well be impossible to hit more than one target if the monetary aggregates under consideration have demand functions with different interest rate elasticities. Given a nominal income shock, an interest rate change which will put one aggregate just back on track will be either less or more than the change required to control the other aggregates. Second, as Professor Fischer suggests, multiple targets may well be politically useful in that central banks can switch between them to provide evidence that they are doing "a good job." Conversely, this very capacity can allow a central bank to avoid doing the hard things it often has to do in the process of behaving responsibly. The fact that multiple monetary targets may confuse the public's inflationary expectations must also be taken into account.

Finally, Professor Fischer raises the issue of choice between competing monetary aggregates in a given country, and suggests that the stability of velocity is the principal criterion in this regard. Stability of the chosen demand for money function is important in principle, but it is also a rather fuzzy concept in practice. For example, a badly fitting function is more likely to be statistically stable, but the relatively large error terms may make targeting on such an aggregate very difficult. In particular, close attention to hitting the target may lead to undesired interest rate fluctuations. This raises the broader question of other criteria for choice. I would contend that we cannot begin to provide such criteria until we have first identified clearly the objectives sought in trying to control a monetary aggregate in the first place.[3] This is too rarely done.

e) Exchange rates. Professor Fischer notes that exchange rates and current account balances receive little explicit attention in his paper. Yet, given the very high degree of substitutability between national financial instruments, exchange rate movements are in many countries the cutting edge of monetary policy since real interest rates are effectively set at world levels. This does create both possibilities and problems. Consider the case of a country working to reduce inflation, say the United States in 1980 and afterwards. A restrictive domestic monetary policy will cause the real exchange rate to appreciate with a direct effect on prices. This is the good news. The bad news is twofold. First, the policy will over time cause some deterioration in the current account and lead to the need for a subsequent depreciation whose magnitude will be affected by the size of the debt built up over the period. Second, since one country's appreciation is somebody else's depreciation, such a policy really amounts to exporting the inflation in the home country (say, the U.S.) to somebody else (say, Canada). Viewed from this perspective, the need for countries to consider the international implications of their actions seems to me to be very clear.

Appendix

(i) Innovation in $\Delta^2 p$ due to random shock to Δr:

	$\Delta^2 y$	$\Delta^2 p$	$\Delta^2 m$	Δy	Δp	Δm
1973	-5	$+5$	0	-5	$+5$	0
1974	0	$-2.$	-3.6	-5	3.0	-3.6
1975	0	-0.6	$+1.4$	-5	2.4	-2.2
1976	0	$+0.8$	$+.4$	-5	3.2	-1.8
1977	0	$+0.2$	$-.6$	-5	3.4	-2.4
1978	0	-0.3	$.1$	-5	3.1	-2.3

[3] See W.R. White, *Alternative Monetary Targets and Control Instruments in Canada: Criteria for Choice*, Canadian Journal of Economics, November 1979.

(ii) One percent orthogonal innovation in Δ^2m:

	Δ^2m	Δ^2p	Δm	Δp
t	1	0	1	0
$t+1$	0	.4	1	.4
$t+2$	$-.29$	$-.16$	.71	.24
$t+3$	.12	$-.05$	.83	.19
$t+4$	.04	.07	.87	.26
$t+5$	$-.05$	$-.01$	.82	.25

A large and lasting increase in money growth leads to a negligible increase in inflation.

(iii) One percent simultaneous innovations in Δ^2m and Δ^2p, on (extreme) monetarist assumption that innovation in Δ^2m (ε_t in Eq. 10) is fully reflected in Δ^2p ($\gamma = 0$ in Eq. 9):

	Δ^2m	Δ^2p	Δm	Δp
t	1	1	1	1
$t+1$	$-.72$	0	.26	1
$t+2$	0	$-.29$	.28	.71
$t+3$	.21	.12	.19	.83
$t+4$	$-.08$	.04	.41	.87
$t+5$	$-.03$	.05	.38	.92

Comments*

John L. Scadding

As described in the Conference abstract, the purpose of this session is one of "identifying the causes of domestic instability . . . that took hold in the major countries from 1973." As Governor Sumita noted in his opening remarks this morning, the questions are easier to pose than they are to answer. It in no way detracts from either Professor Parkin's or Professor Fischer's considerable contributions that their papers demonstrate the truth of this dictum.

Several reasons have been suggested for the greater instability after 1973. First is the international monetary regime, that is, the system of national fiat monies connected by floating exchange rates that succeeded the collapse of the Bretton Woods system. The second reason identified is, in the words of the Conference abstract, "inappropriate policy management," which, if it is to be distinguished from the first reason, must mean that the advantages of the floating rate system for domestic stabilization were not sufficiently exploited—what Alan Meltzer earlier described as the wrong amount of policy discretion. The third reason advanced for greater instability after 1973 is simply bad luck of the draw—exogenous shocks to the system, most notably the oil price increases of 1973 and 1979.

Both Parkin and Fischer concentrate primarily on the latter two causes. Both papers provide an incredible amount of detail about the economic performance of the major industrialized countries over the past 15 to 25 years, as well as a comprehensive survey by Professor Fischer of monetary policy practices in the U.S., Japan, Germany, and the U.K. It is a tribute to the organizational and expository talents of both authors that one is not overwhelmed by the wealth of information

* The views expressed here do not necessarily reflect those of the Federal Reserve Bank of San Francisco or the Federal Reserve System.

provided. By the same token, the sheer size of this narrative task doubtless explains why the papers generally are more successful in raising the questions than they are in answering them. However, both the Parkin and Fischer papers help to refine the issues and suggest some tantalizing questions of their own.

To make my task manageable, I will concentrate on Michael Parkin's examination of world economic performance of pre- and post-1973, and in discussing individual country performances, focus on one intriguing cross-country comparison pointed out by Stan Fischer. Parenthetically, I should note that I am not entirely convinced by Michael Parkin's characterization of the world economy as the analog of the single-country closed economy that is the standard paradigm of macroeconomics. Since 1973, at least, the world economy has lacked one of the distinguishing features of a closed economy, namely, a common currency.

In any event, Michael's examination of the behavior of money, prices, and output for the world economy pre- and post-1973 leads him to at least two important conclusions. The first is that the greater income and inflation variability observed after 1973 were not "generated by increased variability in money supply growth." It is important to understand that this conclusion is *not* necessarily the same as saying that monetary policy was as stable after 1973 as before. If velocity became more variable after 1973, as was in fact the case, the amount of variability in money necessary to produce the same degree of economic stabilization might have to increase. In that case, evidence of unchanging money variability across episodes could be evidence of less stabilization before.

Michael's second important conclusion, that rising world inflation over the whole period has its approximate source in rising trends in rates of money growth, does not, as he acknowledges, settle what the root cause of inflation is. Rising money growth may reflect, for example, monetary accommodation of the two oil price shocks, in which case the latter are more appropriately viewed as the "cause" of world inflation.

To address this issue more systematically, Michael estimates a small structural model of the world economy on annual data for a period of approximately the last 25 years. His estimation results indicate that *both* a monetary policy partially accommodative to aggregate supply shocks and an exogenous upward drift in money growth account for rising world inflation.

This conclusion, and others from Michael's model, might be more definitive if one were more confident about the methodology employed.

His approach appears to be in the spirit, at least, of Blanchard and Watson. However, Michael's implementation of this methodology is marred by his choosing to "interpret," as he puts it, the residuals from differencing a series to produce stationarity with the innovations in these series, in the sense of their unforecastable part using the model's full information set. In general, this correspondence will not be true, and consequently, whether the results in Michael's paper are reliable estimates either of the fundamental "primitive" shocks to the world economy or their propagation mechanism remains an open question. In turn, Michael's conclusion that the major source of instability after 1973 is aggregate supply shocks, and that his results reject the sticky-price theory of the cycle, still must remain conjectures at this point.

I am also dubious about Michael's specification of real output as a random walk in *growth rates*. This runs counter to the work of Nelson and Plosser and others, who find output is a random walk (with drift) in levels. Thus innovations displace the trend path of output; in contrast, Michael's formulation implies the growth rate of output is permanently affected by a shock, which seems unlikely.

In the short space remaining, I cannot hope to do justice to Stan Fischer's paper. Let me make two comments. First, I think it is worth reemphasizing the point in Stan's paper—which also has been pointed out by Dr. Suzuki and others—that the published monetary "targets" for Japan are not in fact targets in the sense normally meant by that term. It is regrettable that this point does not have greater currency in the U.S. popular press, where comparisons between the Japanese and U.S. numbers are common. The conclusion of these comparisons, that the Bank of Japan does a better job than the Fed in monetary targeting, may be correct, but as Stan points out, we cannot infer this from the published record.

Like Stan I am intrigued by the question of why Germany's output-price performance was relatively poor after 1979, looking more like that of the U.S. than the much more successful record of Japan. Better wage performance in Japan does not seem to me to be an adequate explanation, because it was more likely a symptom of credible Japanese anti-inflation policy than its cause. Perhaps a better explanation can be found in the superficially common growth recoveries of the U.S., Japan, and Germany after 1975, shown in Figure 9 of Stan's paper. For all countries, economic growth had jumped into the 6% range by 1977. However, relative to their respective potentials, these growth rates were in fact quite dissimilar. We know in retrospect that policy was too robust in the U.S. in the late 1970s, letting output grow too rapidly relative to potential, and setting off another inflationary surge.

This episode may account for the markets' apparent lack of confidence in the Fed's anti-inflation resolve, as evidenced by the severity of the recession necessary to break inflation in the U.S. Similarly, despite the apparent commitment of the Bundesbank to fighting inflation, exemplified in its successful monetary targeting procedure, the fact that in Germany output also grew in excess of the economy's potential in the late 1970s may account for that country's poor inflation-output tradeoff after 1979. In contrast, the failure of Japan's growth rate to return to the robust rates of the pre-1973 era may indicate that measured against potential, Japan's recovery after 1974 was relatively weak, and may explain therefore the ability of the Japanese economy to shrug off the second oil price shock with relative ease.

The Causes of International Imbalances in the 1980s

The Causes of International Imbalances in the 1980s

8

Generating International Disturbances

Jürg Niehans

I. Introduction

Since the collapse of the Bretton Woods system, international monetary arrangements among developed economies (except for the European Monetary System) can hardly be called a system. Every country is essentially free to do as it pleases. The basic question is whether the working of this non-system can be improved by again incorporating systematic elements like policy rules, international coordination of policies, or pegged exchange rates.

The search for such measures is usually motivated by the serious disturbances which have plagued the international economy. The main indicators of these disturbances are taken to be the large and persistent trade imbalances (and thus capital flows), and the wide fluctuations in exchange rates and the terms of trade. Even the widespread depression of the early 1980s is sometimes attributed to the malfunctioning of the international economy. It is not clear, though, to what extent it was actually transmitted internationally and to what extent it was rather caused by the parallel policy of disinflation followed by several countries simultaneously, but independently.

In the collapse of the Bretton Woods system one contributing factor was the deficient understanding of the economic mechanisms on which it was based; the creation of "paper gold" at a time when the system already labored under an excess supply of paper money illustrates that deficiency. To be successful, efforts to improve international arrangements must be based on an understanding of the mechanisms by which the disturbances are generated. To such an understanding, elusive as its exact logical nature may be, the present paper is intended to make a modest contribution. Since institutional improvements must be essentially long-term in nature, the paper concentrates on a few mechanisms which, in the author's judgement, may be regarded as fundamental features of present arrangements, while other aspects, because they seem to be more ephemeral, are disregarded.

The analysis will be limited, in particular, in the following respects:

(1) It focuses on economies with developed financial systems and largely convertible currencies.

(2) International debt crises are left out of account; debts are assumed to be paid.

(3) The world economy is assumed to be in a stationary state; the possible extension of the analysis to growing economies is only mentioned in passing.

(4) Long-run inflation is omitted on the ground that monetary policies have, in fact, succeeded in reducing it to relatively low levels.

(5) Exchange rates are assumed to be freely floating, but the implications of fixed rates are taken up in section X.

(6) While policy actions are assumed to be unexpected, people are supposed to be endowed with perfect foresight about their consequences. In the case of massive and historically "unique" uses of fairly familiar policy instruments this seems an appropriate assumption. Nobody will deny that foresight is, in reality, less than perfect, but economists have little specific knowledge about systematic biases in these imperfections, and it is advisable to remain silent about what one does not know.

The paper is based on the premise that, except for the oil price shocks, the principal (though not the only) source of serious international disturbances since 1973 (just as in the 15 years before 1973) were the monetary and fiscal policy shifts of the United States. These shifts included a relaxation of monetary policy in the years 1977–78, abrupt monetary restraint in the years 1979–80, and a tax reduction in 1981 followed by large and continuing budget deficits. Surely other countries shifted their policies too (the abrupt monetary contraction in the United Kingdom in 1979 is an example), but their smaller weight in the world economy made the international repercussions less serious. The nature of these repercussions is the subject of the following sections.

II. A Basic Two-Country Model

Once the principal mechanisms of international disturbances are clearly understood, they can be reduced to a theoretical model.[1] Such a model is presented in this section,[2] and further aspects will be added in subsequent sections. Most of the individual features of the model can be found in the literature, though not with the same sort of interaction. The principal novel elements are the dynamics of fiscal policy in the presence of investment lags (section IV) and the integration of monetary and real aspects, permitting a new interpretation of exchange overshooting and capital flows (sections V and VI).[3]

The model applies to two economies. The "domestic" economy, denoted by capital letters and unstarred parameters, plays the active part by varying its monetary or fiscal policy. The "foreign" economy, denoted by small letters and starred parameters, adjusts to these policy shifts. In the basic version these economies produce a uniform consumer good whose outputs, X and x, depend on the stocks of capital goods, K and k, according to

$$X = X(K), \qquad\qquad x = x(k), \qquad\qquad (1)$$

with positive, but declining, marginal products. The analysis is simplified by linearizing the marginal product curves around some base values indicated by barred symbols:

$$X' = X''(K - \bar{K}) + \bar{X}', \qquad x' = x''(k - \bar{k}) + \bar{x}', \qquad (2)$$

where X'' and x'' are negative constants.

Capital goods consist of uniform "machines," financed by homogeneous securities which are internationally traded and whose dividends correspond to machine rentals. The domestic government also has an outstanding public debt, F, consisting of the same type of securities (and thus having a coupon equal to the dividend on private securities). Some securities, S and s, are held in private portfolios, while the balance, B and b, is held by the two central banks, so that

$$K + k + F = S + s + B + b. \qquad\qquad (3)$$

The net foreign assets of the domestic economy, A, are defined as the excess of the securities it owns over those it has issued, namely

$$A = S + B - K - F = -(s + b - k) = -a. \qquad\qquad (4)$$

---

[1] It is symptomatic that adequate models of the Bretton Woods system only became available after it had collapsed.

[2] It is similar to that used in Niehans (1987).

[3] The basic analysis of monetary policy in interdependent economies is provided in Hamada (1985), but it excludes capital flows, which play the major role in the present paper.

By virtue of equation (3), net foreign assets of the domestic economy are negatively equal to those of the foreign economy, a.

The demand for securities depends positively (and linearly) on their yields, denoted by R and r, and domestic demand also depends on domestic debt:

$$S = S_0 + \sigma R + \phi F, \qquad s = s_0 + \sigma^* r. \qquad (5)$$

The appearance of ϕ reflects the assumption that government debt is used to finance tax reductions while government expenditures for goods and services remain unaffected and may thus be omitted from the model.[4] This assumption is intended to capture the main feature of the Reagan tax cut. From the present point of view it is equivalent to the assumption that government securities are distributed to domestic residents as transfers.

If the private sector, fully discounting its future tax liability, bases its behavior only on present values, ϕ is unity; government dissaving would be automatically matched by private saving, and the private sector would indifferently hold any amount of government debt. On the other hand, if, besides present value, the precise nature of claims and liabilities also matters, ϕ is different from unity. In particular, if private assets consisting of government securities are considered as more liquid than the corresponding tax liability, an increase in F (at a constant interest rate) induces the private sector to sell some private securities. The whole theory of money, banking, and finance is based on the conviction that asset transformation (at constant present value) is economically important. This notion implies that $0 < \phi < 1$. With $\phi = 1$, debt, as modeled here, has no effect, but in this case one would not expect to find a developed financial system in the first place.

In each economy, the yield on capital goods corresponds to the marginal product of capital,

$$R = X'(K), \qquad r = x'(k), \qquad (6)$$

and the perfect substitutability of securities implies $R = r$.

Equations (1)–(6) constitute the capital section of the model. It is self-contained in the sense that it determines output, capital stocks, security portfolios, foreign assets, and interest rates in both economies for given values of F, B, and b.

---

[4] This is in contrast to Frenkel and Razin (1985a, b). Treating fiscal policy as roughly equivalent to (useless) consumption may reveal a potentially interesting aspect, but this can be only one among many such aspects, and in the case of the 1981 tax cut, since this left government consumption largely unchanged, it cannot have been important.

Real incomes are determined by adding to output the interest receipts on foreign assets:

$$Y = X + RA, \qquad\qquad y = x + ra. \qquad\qquad (7)$$

The trade balance is negatively equal to the flow of interest payments:

$$T = -RA = ra = -t. \qquad\qquad (8)$$

The preceding parts of the model describe its "real" features. To determine prices, P and p, one has to introduce money. Money appears in the balance sheet of the central bank as a counterpart of its security portfolio:[5]

$$\frac{M}{P} = B \qquad\qquad \frac{m}{p} = b. \qquad\qquad (9)$$

The demand for real balances is assumed to depend linearly on the interest rate:

$$\frac{M}{P} = L_0 + \lambda R \qquad\qquad \frac{m}{p} = l_0 + \lambda^* r. \qquad\qquad (10)$$

Whatever happens in the capital sector thus has repercussions on prices, but shifts in the demand for money have no influence on the capital sector.

The exchange rate, finally, in this one-good world, is determined simply by the law of one price,

$$e = \frac{P}{p}. \qquad\qquad (11)$$

The present model, since it is stationary, has no room for budget deficits in a flow sense. To allow for equilibrium deficits one has to introduce economic growth. In the steady state of balanced noninflationary growth at rate w, the annual deficit is then equal to the growth in debt, wF. The present model can thus be transformed into a growth model, in which all propositions now relating to the stock of debt have a counterpart in similar propositions for the flow of the deficit. For given expenditures, the interpretation of fiscal policy as a change in the stock of debt is thus less restrictive than it might first seem. It should be noted that the transition from balanced growth with low deficits to balanced growth with high deficits may involve large increases in debt and may take a long time. Suppose the deficit is raised

---

[5] Central bank equity is omitted. It should be remembered that changes in prices are reflected in net worth and not in M or B, so that $dB = 1/P\,dM$.

from \$20 billion to \$100 billion. At a growth rate of 2%, this involves an increase in debt from \$1000 billion to \$5000 billion, and it would take 40 years of \$100 billion deficits to reach the new growth path.

III. Permanent Effects of Fiscal and Monetary Shifts

The subject of the present section is the permanent effects of policy shifts, which may be regarded as the primary disturbances generated by these policies. They can be determined by elementary comparative statics, whose details are not reproduced here.

A. Fiscal Policy

A shift in fiscal policy is represented by a change in F, while M and m remain unchanged.[6] This will be called a pure debt expansion. It has no macroeconomic effects if $\phi = 1$; all of its effects are proportional to $(1 - \phi)$. It is clearly of decisive importance whether or not a "gift" of securities, combined with the corresponding tax liability, induces the private sector to sell securities and, if so, in what amount. While this issue is, in general, not settled,[7] the international experiences of recent years suggest that ϕ is significantly different from unity for the United States.[8] The following discussion is based on this assumption, which represents Ricardo's non-equivalence proposition.

In this case, an increase in domestic debt inevitably raises the rate of interest both at home and abroad. The reason is that domestic residents wish to sell some of their additional securities. As a consequence, the stock of real capital goods is reduced in both countries; output declines. Floating exchange rates provide no insulation of the foreign economy against these repercussions.

Security portfolios rise in both countries. Combined with the decline in the foreign capital stock, this implies that net foreign assets of the domestic economy decline; it experiences a cumulative capital inflow. The model illustrates the fact that this inflow has nothing to do with interest differentials, which have been excluded by assumption. Nor has it anything to do with the terms of trade, which are fixed at unity,

---

[6] This is similar to Blanchard (1985).

[7] An excellent survey of this issue was recently provided by Brunner (1986).

[8] Empirical evidence on the effect of budget deficits on interest rates is provided in Makin (1983), Arndt, Sweeney, and Willett (1985), and Hoelscher (1986).

or with a deterioration in the competitiveness of the domestic economy.[9] The fundamental reason for the capital inflow is rather that the debt expansion induces domestic residents to finance a temporary spurt in consumption by security sales, even at a uniform interest rate. Such disturbances could conceivably be avoided by suppressing international indebtedness, but only at the price of a large loss in welfare for both economies.[10]

The steady-state effect of debt expansion on the trade balance is generally ambiguous. If foreign assets have initially been zero ($A = 0$), the trade balance of the domestic economy turns positive, because a new foreign debt now has to be serviced through exports. In the case of a debtor country ($A < 0$), the increase in the trade surplus is even larger, because the higher interest rate increases the burden of the service on the existing debt. In the case of a creditor country ($A > 0$), however, the loss of interest through the reduction of assets is counteracted by the higher interest receipt on the remaining assets, and the net result may actually be a higher trade deficit.

Real incomes change primarily through the changes in output, which are negative in both countries. A secondary effect arises from the international redistribution of assets. It is negative for the domestic economy, but positive for the foreign economy. On balance, the foreign economy is more than compensated for the output loss by the additional return on the foreign assets, and the domestic economy is, in effect, burdened with the output loss of *both* economies. In addition, there is a tertiary effect through the change in interest on the existing debt, whose sign depends, of course, on the sign of A. This is a rather complex picture, but the important point is that capital income tends to compensate the foreign economy for the output losses resulting from higher interest rates.

The price effects of debt expansion are linked to the interest effect. At a higher world interest rate, both economies wish to hold lower real balances, which is achieved through higher price levels. Debt expansion in one country results in higher prices everywhere. The more elastically a country's demand for money reacts to the rate of interest, the larger will be the increase in its prices.

---

[9] A close analogy is provided by the transfer problem, for which Samuelson (1952) has demonstrated that price differentials do not play an essential role in the explanation of specie flows.

[10] The unambiguous direction of the capital flow depends crucially on the assumption that securities are the only international asset. If cash balances are also internationally diversified and/or if direct investments are distinguished from securities, debt expansion may result in a capital outflow (Niehans 1986).

The permanent consequences for the exchange rate, finally, are ambiguous, depending simply on the relative increases in commodity prices and thus on the interest elasticities of cash balances. At this basic level of analysis there is no presumption in favor of either appreciation or depreciation of the domestic currency. In particular, there is no relationship between exchange-rate changes and asset flows or the trade balance.

B. Monetary Policy

Pure monetary expansion may be defined as an increase in M at unchanged B. It is most easily incorporated into the model as a downward shift in L_0. Alternatively, it can be visualized as resulting from open-market purchases by the central bank associated with an equal increase in government debt to keep private bond portfolios constant. It can easily be ascertained that such a purely monetary shift is neutral. Its only consequences are corresponding changes in domestic prices and in the exchange rate. There are, in particular, no repercussions on the capital sector, on foreign indebtedness, and on the foreign economy.

This means that under full-employment conditions, purely monetary shifts are relatively harmless internationally. The (important) qualification due to employment fluctuations is discussed in section VIII. While the adjustment of security portfolios can only take place through international capital and trade flows, the adjustment of real cash balances can be accomplished simply through domestic price changes.

An open-market sale by the central bank is a combination of pure debt expansion with pure monetary contraction. Its permanent effects, therefore, correspond to the difference between those of the policies considered before. Its real effects and its foreign effects are the same as for pure debt expansion, but domestic prices now decline and the domestic currency will most certainly appreciate. It appears, therefore, that from the point of view of the permanent effects, the disturbance potential of open-market operations arises not from their monetary side but from their security side.

This means that open-market operations are clearly non-neutral. In order to neutralize their real and foreign effects, open-market expansion would have to be combined with debt expansion, and open-market contraction with debt contraction. In U.S. policies in the early 1980s, however, debt expansion tended to be associated with monetary stringency. While the domestic price effects were thereby reduced, the real and international effects, working through the world interest rate, were aggravated.

IV. Gestation Lags

The preceding analysis was restricted to comparative statics. It will now be extended to the dynamics of the adjustment path. These dynamics will turn out to be a secondary source of disturbances by which the primary disturbances are often magnified.[11]

There are many possible reasons for non-instantaneous adjustment. The present section concentrates on just one of them, namely, gestation lags in the production of capital goods, which were early identified by Aftalion (1927) as one of the major sources of cyclical disturbances. With the growing impediments against almost any large-scale investment project, the planning periods have probably lengthened considerably. To the extent that international capital mobility is measured by the speed with which the capital stock can be increased in one country while being reduced in another, capital mobility is probably lower today than it was a century ago. It will turn out that such gestation lags are potential generators of international disturbances.[12]

For the present purpose it is sufficient to formalize the gestation lag by the crude assumption that the rates of change of the capital stocks are proportional to the deviations of the relative capital goods prices from their equilibrium values, normalized at unity. This can be written

$$\dot{K} = \beta(Q - 1), \qquad\qquad \dot{k} = \beta^*(q - 1), \tag{12}$$

where Q and q are Tobin's q's. Denoting the money prices of capital goods by Π and π, their relative prices are defined as $Q = \Pi/P$ and $q = \pi/p$.

The expected changes in relative capital-goods prices now become a component of capital yields, and with correct foresight they are equal to actual changes, so that

---

[11] An empirical effort to combine short-run and steady-state effects is made in Hutchison and Throop (1985).

[12] The international implications of gestation lags were explored in Niehans (1984). The consequences for monetary policy were analyzed in Niehans (1987) and econometrically investigated for Switzerland by Rotheli (1986). This section extends the analysis to fiscal policy.

$$R = \frac{X'}{Q} + \frac{\dot{Q}}{Q}, \qquad\qquad r = \frac{x'}{q} + \frac{\dot{q}}{q}, \qquad\qquad (13)$$

but costless arbitrage still equalizes yields, so that $R = r$. The remainder of the model is unchanged.

The question of this section concerns the influence of β and β^* on the international adjustment path. Ideally, both β and β^* should be varied from zero to infinity. However, the model, with four differential equations, is too complex for a general solution. A partial answer can be given by limiting the analysis to two polar cases, each characterized by an infinite adjustment speed in one of the countries. To simplify the exposition (without affecting the conclusion), the central-bank portfolios are left out of account ($B = b = 0$), and in the demand functions for securities the constant terms are suppressed ($S_0 = s_0 = 0$). A further simplification can be obtained by reckoning real cash balances in terms of machines instead of consumer goods,

$$\frac{M}{\Pi} = L_0 + \lambda R, \qquad\qquad \frac{m}{\pi} = l_0 + \lambda^* r. \qquad\qquad (14)$$

This modification only affects the details of the adjustment path.[13]

A. Domestic Gestation Lag

In the first case, there is a domestic gestation lag, but $\beta^* = \infty$. This implies that $\dot{q} = 0$, $q = 1$, $\pi = p$ and $r = x'$. The path of Q is then governed by

$$\dot{Q} = RQ - X' = RQ - X''(K - \bar{K}) - \bar{X}'. \qquad\qquad (15)$$

The demand functions for securities (equation 5) and the equilibrium condition (3) can be used to express R in terms of K and F, namely

$$R = \frac{1}{\sigma + \sigma^* - 1/x''} \left[K + (1 - \phi)F + \bar{k} - \frac{\bar{x}'}{x''} \right]. \qquad (16)$$

This can be substituted into (15) to give

$$\dot{Q} = \frac{1}{\sigma + \sigma^* - 1/x''} \left\{ KQ + \left[(1 - \phi)F + \bar{k} - \frac{\bar{x}'}{x''} \right]Q \right\}$$
$$- X''(K - \bar{K}) - \bar{X}'. \qquad\qquad (17)$$

---

[13] In this and the following section the influence of expected inflation on the demand for real balances is disregarded. It is shown in section VI that this is a minor simplification.

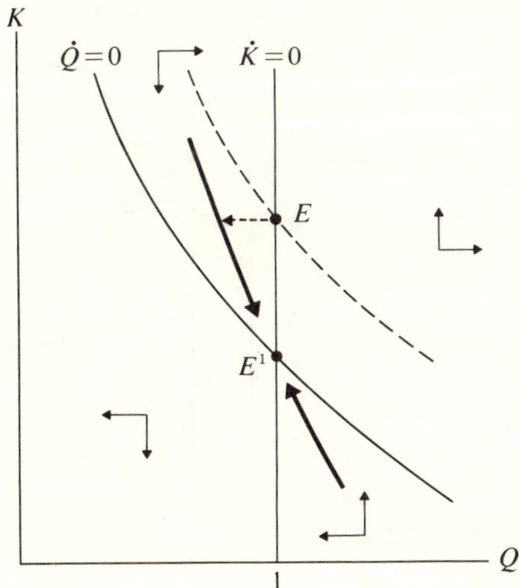

Figure 8.1
Domestic Gestation Lag

In the neighborhood of the equilibrium values $K = K^*$ and $Q = 1$, this nonlinear, nonhomogeneous differential equation in Q and K can be approximated by the linear, homogeneous differential equation in the deviations from equilibrium

$$\dot{Q} = G(Q - 1) + H(K - K^*) \tag{18}$$

with

$$G = \frac{1}{\sigma + \sigma^* - 1/x''}\left[K^* + (1 - \phi)F + \bar{k} - \frac{\bar{x}'}{x''}\right] > 0$$

and

$$H = \frac{1}{\sigma + \sigma^* - 1/x''} - X'' > 0.$$

The domestic investment function

$$\dot{K} = \beta(Q - 1) \tag{19}$$

may be repeated for convenience.

As so often for perfect myopic foresight, equations (18) and (19) constitute an unstable saddle-point system. The only path consistent with perfect long-term foresight is the stable arm. The salient features of the adjustment process are described in Figure 8.1. The domestic

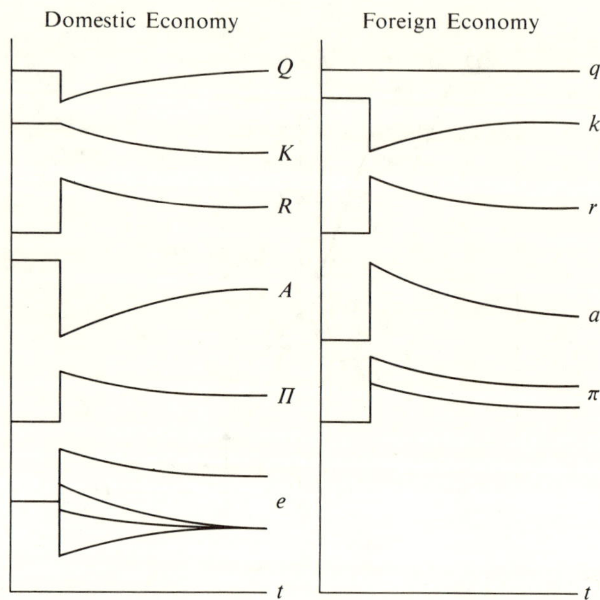

Figure 8.2
Domestic Gestation Lag

capital stock remains stationary if $\dot{K} = 0$ and thus $Q = 1$. The price of capital goods is stationary for $\dot{Q} = 0$, the locus of which is a falling curve. With perfect foresight, movements in the course of time can only take place along the stable arm, indicated by the heavy arrows.

Suppose the economy was so far in equilibrium at point E. Now a debt expansion raises F. As a consequence, the $\dot{Q} = 0$ curve shifts downward from the broken to the solid position. The new equilibrium E', however, in view of the domestic gestation lag, can only be approached along the heavy arrow. This will be reached by an instantaneous leftward "jump" in the price of domestic capital goods along the dotted arrow. Capital goods prices "overshoot" their (unchanged) equilibrium levels in a downward direction, which makes disinvestment profitable. The subsequent adjustment process is characterized by a monotonic decline in the domestic capital stock (i.e., negative investment) and a monotonic recovery in capital goods prices.

The associated adjustment paths of the other variables are described in Figure 8.2. It follows from equation (16) that, with F now fixed at the higher level, the rate of interest changes according to

$$\dot{R} = \frac{1}{\sigma + \sigma^* - 1/x''} \dot{K}, \tag{20}$$

which means that the world interest rate declines hand-in-hand with K. Since it was shown in section III to be higher in the long-run equilibrium, this implies that R (and thus r) initially overshoots.

The foreign capital stock, with its infinite adjustment speed, gradually rises as r declines. Since its terminal equilibrium is below the initial level, it first overshoots downward. Domestic debt expansion thus triggers a pronounced investment slump abroad, followed by gradual recovery.

The path of foreign assets depends on the difference between the domestic demand for securities and the supply of capital goods. The security demand can, in turn, be related to the change in R and thus (through equation 20) to that in K. This results in

$$\dot{A} = \dot{S} - \dot{K} = \sigma\dot{R} - \dot{K} = - \frac{\sigma^* - 1/x''}{\sigma + \sigma^* - 1/x''} \dot{K}. \tag{21}$$

It follows that foreign assets gradually rise as K declines. Capital flows are thus characterized by an instantaneous inflow followed by a gradual outflow. The initial inflow overshoots its equilibrium mark. The instantaneous capital flow should not be taken literally. In the model, it results from the assumption that security holdings adjust instantaneously to their new value, implying infinite rates of consumption and trade flows. In reality, the "jump" in foreign assets will look more like a "hump."

Since prices are determined by the demand for money, they decline parallel to the world interest rate. If fully flexible, they thus overshoot. Domestic and foreign prices will generally not be at the same level, though. In particular, the country with the higher interest elasticity of money demand will have higher prices, both during the adjustment process and in the new steady state.

The exchange rate, finally, may do almost anything. If the interest elasticity of the demand for cash balances is higher in the domestic economy, the price of foreign exchange rises in the steady state. In this case there is instantaneous overshooting followed by decline. In the opposite case there is a steady-state decline in the price of foreign exchange, but it may be preceded either by instantaneous depreciation or appreciation of the domestic currency, and the latter may either over- or undershoot the steady-state exchange rate. In conjunction with the clear-cut patterns of interest rates and capital flows, the ambiguous course of exchange rates implies that there is no clear-cut relationship between interest rates and capital flows on one hand and exchange rates on the other. As indicators of international disturbances, exchange rates are unreliable.

B. Foreign Gestation Lag

These adjustment paths can be compared to those resulting from a foreign gestation lag, where β^* is finite while β is infinite. In this case $\dot{Q} = 0$, $Q = 1$, $\Pi = P$, and $R = X'$. Reasoning analogous to the first case yields two differential equations in q and k, namely

$$\dot{q} = g(q - 1) + h(k - k^*) \tag{22}$$

and

$$\dot{k} = \beta(q - 1), \tag{23}$$

with

$$g = \frac{1}{\sigma + \sigma^* - 1/x''}\left[k^* + (1 + \phi)F + \bar{K} - \frac{\bar{x}'}{x''}\right] > 0$$

and

$$h = \frac{1}{\sigma + \sigma^* - 1/x''} - x'' > 0.$$

This is again a saddle-point system whose phase diagram looks qualitatively similar to Figure 8.1. The adjustment paths it implies are graphed in Figure 8.3.

The main differences compared to the first case can be summarized as follows. It is now the domestic economy which suffers an acute investment slump, while the foreign economy is at first protected by the gestation lag.[14] As a consequence, there is now no overshooting of foreign assets, but rather a monotonic capital inflow. Whether or not an expansion of debt, after the instantaneous effect, is followed by capital inflows or outflows is thus seen to depend crucially on the respective gestation lags. As a consequence, it is not clear whether fiscal expansion is followed by a period of trade deficits or surpluses. Neither interest differentials nor changes in relative prices have anything to do with the outcome, both being excluded from the model.

While fiscal policy in the presence of gestation lags thus generates

---

[14] We note that precisely the economy with the investment slump experiences unchanged relative prices of capital goods while monotonic adjustment of the capital stock is associated with depressed capital goods prices.

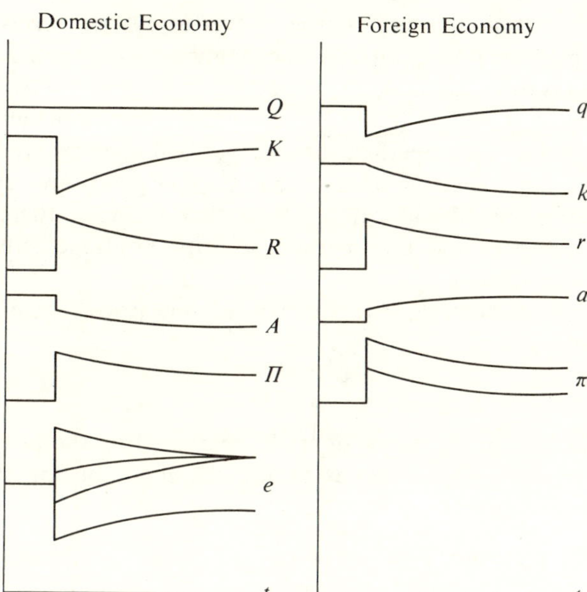

Figure 8.3
Foreign Gestation Lag

complicated international repercussions, pure monetary expansion results only in a shift in the domestic price level. Money is still neutral. It follows that an open-market contraction has the same effects as debt expansion except that domestic prices are shifted downward.[15]

In general, this analysis shows that the sequence of capital imports and exports by which, after a shift in fiscal or monetary policy, the international economy reaches its new equilibrium depends crucially on gestation lags. This is intuitively plausible. Capital imports reflect an excess of domestic investment over saving. Their path, therefore, should be expected to depend heavily on the behavior of investment in different countries.

V. Terms-of-Trade and Interest Parity

Shifts and distortions in the terms of trade are widely considered to be the basic source of international disturbances. The preceding

---

[15] The adjustment to monetary policy shifts is fully described in Niehans (1987).

sections show that this is not true. Nevertheless, the terms of trade may still play an important role. To analyze this role, the model of section II has to be extended to include heterogeneous goods.

The extension means that domestic goods, say cloth, and foreign goods, say wine, are imperfect substitutes. Real incomes are evaluated in terms of the respective home good. Capital goods are regarded as "frozen" home goods, as before. Note that R and r, therefore, still are pure numbers and that perfect security arbitrage still requires $R = r$ in equilibrium.

With heterogeneous goods, the law of one price (equation 11) is replaced by

$$ep/P = \theta, \tag{24}$$

where θ stands for the terms of trade, measured by the price of wine in terms of cloth. One also has to add the condition for balance-of-payments equilibrium

$$\theta I(\theta, Y) - i(\theta, y) - RA = 0, \tag{25}$$

where I is domestic imports (in units of foreign goods) and i is foreign imports (in units of domestic goods) with $I_\theta < 0, i_\theta > 0, I_Y > 0, i_y > 0$. Gestation lags are now disregarded.

It has sometimes been argued that fiscal expansion results in a permanent improvement in the terms of trade, in a "deterioration in the competitive position." This proposition can be checked by taking differentials of the modified model and solving for $d\theta/dF$. The result is a complex expression of ambiguous sign. In general, therefore, the effect of fiscal policy on the terms of trade is unclear.

One source of ambiguity is evidently the change in interest payments on the existing foreign assets. It can be removed by assuming that initially $A = 0$. In this case one obtains

$$\frac{d\theta}{dF} = \frac{(1 - \phi)R}{\chi(1 + \varepsilon + \varepsilon^*)I}\left[\frac{i_y}{x''} - \frac{I_Y}{X''} - (1 - I_Y - i_y)\right.$$
$$\left.\left(\sigma^* - \frac{1}{x''}\right)\right] \gtrless 0, \tag{26}$$

where $\chi = \sigma + \sigma^* - 1/X'' - 1/x'' > 0$, while ε and ε^* are the elasticities of imports with respect to the terms of trade. The sign of this expression turns out to be still ambiguous, even if the Marshall/Lerner term has the normal negative sign and if $1 - I_Y - i_y$ is certain to be positive. The only troublesome term in this case, however, is I_Y/X''. A large domestic propensity to import, since domestic income declines, calls forth a large decline in import demand, which counteracts the deterioration in the terms of trade resulting from the other factors. If the domestic propensity to import is small enough, fiscal expansion will normally result in a permanent deterioration in the terms of trade. As θ rises, the "competitiveness" of the domestic economy is improved so that interest payments on the foreign debt can be financed.

In determining the permanent effect of fiscal policy on the nominal exchange rate, the ambiguous price effects discussed in section III have to be supplemented by the terms-of-trade effect discussed in the preceding paragraph. Since the terms-of-trade changes are likely (though not certain) to push in the direction of a depreciation of the domestic currency, a depreciation is now more likely than with homogeneous goods.

The steady-state trade balance, perhaps surprisingly, is not affected by the heterogeneity of commodities and the terms of trade at all, depending solely on the interest rate and on initial foreign assets. On reflection this is plausible: Asset stocks and interest rates determine the required trade surplus. Foreign trade elasticities then determine the terms of trade required to produce this surplus. Causation runs clearly from capital assets to trade.

Overall, the permanent terms-of-trade effects of fiscal policy are unlikely to be dramatic. During the adjustment process, however, the terms of trade may generate major disturbances. The reason is that during the adjustment process, capital gains from expected changes in the terms of trade are an additional component of asset yields. If expectations are correct, arbitrage will see to it that they are equal to the interest differential,

$$\dot{\theta}/\theta = R - r. \tag{27}$$

This is the interest-parity condition; whenever it is satisfied for real yields, the rate of change of the nominal exchange rate is automatically equal to the difference in nominal interest rates.

Abstracting from income effects for simplicity ($I_Y = i_y = 0$), equations (1)–(5) can be used to express R in terms of A, namely

$$R = \frac{1}{\sigma - 1/X''}\left[A + (1 + \phi)F - \frac{\bar{X}'}{X''} + \bar{K}\right]. \tag{28}$$

At any moment, domestic interest rates must be such that individuals are willing to hold foreign assets, A. The higher is A, the higher must be R, because a high interest rate raises the domestic demand for securities, S, and reduces their supply, K. The higher is debt, F, the higher is R, because the demand for securities must be stimulated and the private supply reduced.

For the deviations from the equilibrium values R^* and A^*, equation (28) yields (with constant F),

$$R - R^* = \frac{1}{\sigma - 1/X''} (A - A^*). \tag{29}$$

For r there is the corresponding expression,

$$r - r^* = - \frac{1}{\sigma^* - 1/x''} (A - A^*). \tag{30}$$

This condition sees to it that the foreign country is willing to hold net foreign assets in the amount of $-A$.

The rate of change of the terms of trade can thus be expressed as a linear homogeneous function of the deviation of foreign assets from their equilibrium value, namely

$$\frac{\dot{\theta}}{\theta} = \frac{\chi}{(\sigma - 1/X'')(\sigma^* - 1/x'')} (A - A^*). \tag{31}$$

Whenever foreign assets stand above their equilibrium value, θ is rising; the terms of trade move against the domestic economy. Asset disequilibria again appear as the basic generator of dynamic disturbances.

Capital flows, defined as the rate of change of foreign assets, are determined by the current account, including both trade and debt service, according to

$$\dot{A} = i(\theta) - \theta I(\theta) + RA = T(\theta) + RA, \tag{32}$$

where T' is assumed to be positive. The equilibrium solution is

$$0 = T(\theta^*) + R^*A^*. \tag{33}$$

In the neighborhood of equilibrium, $\dot{A}$ can be approximated by a function which is linear in the deviations from equilibrium, namely

$$\dot{A} = T'(\theta - \theta^*) + A^*(R - R^*) + R^*(A - A^*)$$

$$= T'(\theta - \theta^*) + \left(\frac{A^*}{\sigma - 1/x''} + R^* \right)(A - A^*). \tag{34}$$

The simultaneous linear differential equations (31) and (34) can be used to determine the path of θ and A during the adjustment process, provided the deviations from equilibrium are relatively small.

Equations (31) and (34) constitute another saddle-point system. Its

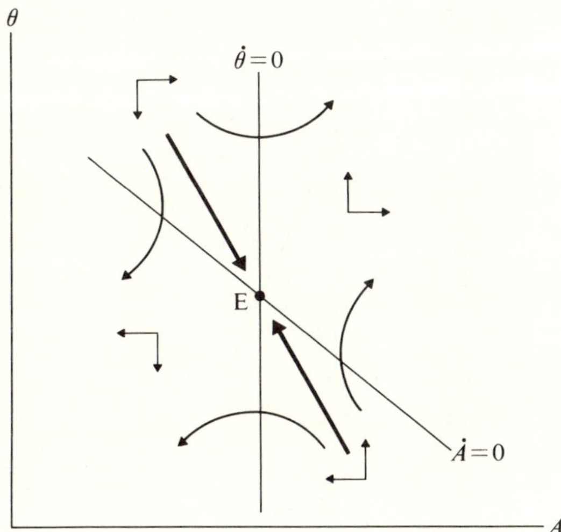

Figure 8.4
Terms-of-Trade Adjustment

properties are summarized in Figure 8.4. Paths with myopically correct foresight are generally unstable, as usual, but only a movement along one of the stable arms, drawn as heavy arrows, is consistent with long-run perfect foresight.

The dynamic consequences of debt expansion are described in Figure 8.5. Suppose the initial equilibrium was at E. An increase in F shifts both equilibrium curves to the left. In the new equilibrium E', foreign assets will certainly be lower, but θ may, as was shown above, either rise or fall. The graph depicts the case, more frequent on average, of a permanent rise in θ. The new equilibrium can only be reached, however, along the rising arrow. This requires an instantaneous drop in the terms of trade along the dotted arrow, followed by a gradual rise. During the adjustment process, after the initial decline in the relative price of foreign goods, the capital inflow is associated with a gradual improvement in the competitive position of the domestic economy.

The overshooting of the terms of trade described in Figure 8.5 is the counterpart, for the present model, of the interest-parity overshooting familiar from the Dornbusch (1976) model. In contrast to Dornbusch's analysis, however, overshooting appears here as a "real" phenomenon; neither money nor price rigidity play a role. The contrary impression one gains from Dornbusch seems to arise from the incomplete specification of the capital-goods and security sector.

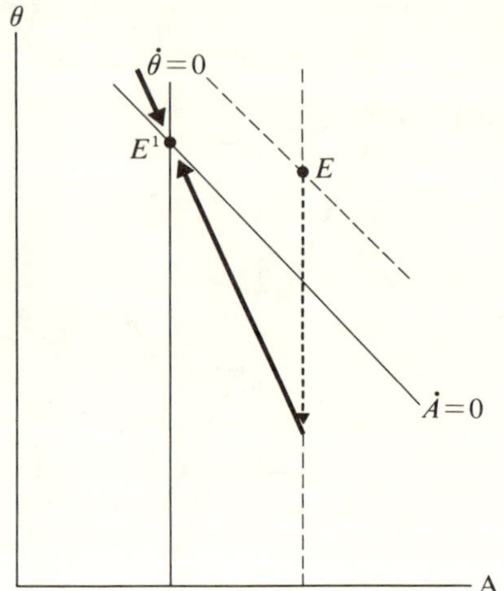

Figure 8.5
Terms-of-Trade Overshooting

In an important sense, overshooting in the terms of trade may be said to be basically due to foreign assets. It would be incorrect, however, to attribute it to capital *flows*, which are, in fact, determined by the terms of trade. The basic generator of disturbances is rather the shift in the desired asset *stocks*. The terms of trade change in the course of the adjustment process because people must be made willing to hold the off-equilibrium stock by interest rates which are different at home and abroad. Overshooting occurs, not because capital is mobile, but rather because it is not mobile enough. The more promptly capital flows occur, the smaller is the overshooting.[16] This suggests the policy conclusion that impediments to trade and capital flows accentuate the disturbances in the terms of trade rather than reducing them.

The adjustment paths of interest rates, trade, prices, and the exchange rate associated with the just-described paths of A and θ are plotted in Figure 8.6. The increase in debt is accompanied by a sharp rise in domestic interest rates, followed by a decline at home and a rise abroad. The initial divergence of interest rates is thus gradually reduced. It would be wrong to say, however, that the interest differential causes

---

[16] In Figure 8.5, a higher mobility of capital would be reflected in a flatter inclination of the $\dot A = 0$ curve.

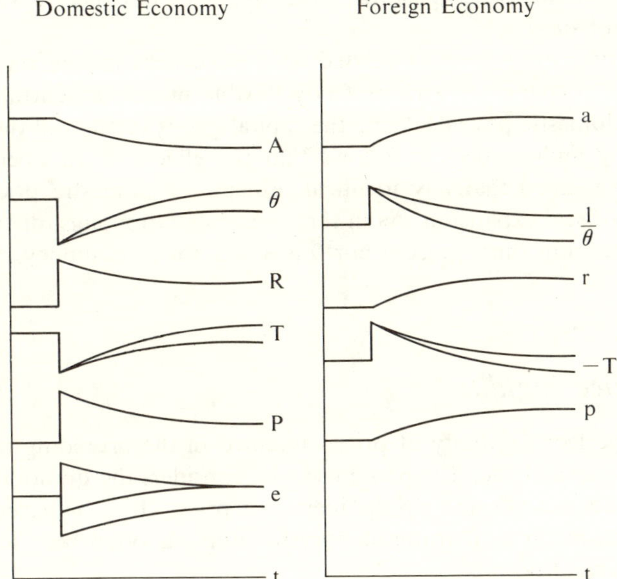

Figure 8.6
Terms-of-Trade Overshooting

the capital inflow, because the differential is continually neutralized by the expected capital gain.

The development of the trade balance, of course, reflects that of the terms of trade, thus beginning with a large deficit that is gradually reduced and may even turn into a surplus.

Domestic prices, still assumed to be perfectly flexible, initially respond to the debt expansion, in view of the higher interest rates, with an instantaneous increase followed by a gradual decline. The gradual rise in foreign prices reflects the decline in desired real balances caused by the rising interest rates.

The exchange rate, depending on the terms of trade and prices, may conceivably do almost anything. There is, in particular, no straightforward relationship between the course of capital flows and the exchange rate. It is also not clear that the nominal exchange rate overshoots downward at all; if the interest elasticities of cash balances are high enough, an instantaneous depreciation is followed by gradual appreciation. In any case, the monetary sector, far from causing overshooting of exchange rates, rather tends to dampen it. A policy that focuses on the exchange rate, therefore, does not have a very good chance of success.[17]

The preceding analysis related to a pure debt expansion. A pure monetary expansion, with perfectly flexible prices, is neutral. It only affects domestic prices, leaving the capital goods sector and the foreign economy undisturbed. It follows that the effects of an open-market expansion are negatively identical, except for domestic prices, with those of fiscal expansion. As in the case of gestation lags, disturbances originate from shifts in asset portfolios and not from money.

VI. Price Rigidity

The perfect flexibility of prices assumed in the preceding models is probably unrealistic. The present section considers the question of how the results are affected by the inertia of prices. It is of particular interest inasmuch as Dornbusch-overshooting has often been attributed to price rigidity.

Imperfect price flexibility is introduced by assuming that real cash balances adjust with a lag. At the same time, desired real balances are made to depend on the nominal interest rate, thus dropping the ad hoc simplification used in sections IV and V. For the domestic economy, the adjustment in real balances can be written as

$$\frac{d}{dt}\left(\frac{M}{P}\right) = \mu\left[\left(\frac{M}{P}\right)^D - \frac{M}{P}\right], \tag{35}$$

with desired balances

$$\left(\frac{M}{P}\right)^D = L_0 + \lambda\left(R + \frac{\dot{P}}{P}\right).$$

This expression can be solved for the inflation rate

$$\frac{\dot{P}}{P} = -\left(\frac{1}{1/\mu + \eta}\right)\left(\frac{L_0}{M}P + \eta R - 1\right), \tag{36}$$

where η is the interest elasticity of domestic cash balances. If desired real balances depend on the real rate of interest, as initially assumed, the only modification is the disappearance of η in the first parenthesis.

---

[17] The adjustment path described in Figure 8.6 corresponds in important respects to the analysis in the excellent paper by Hutchison and Pigott (1984), though capital flows are interpreted somewhat differently.

The following exposition is again based on this simplified case. An analogous expression can be derived for foreign prices,

$$\frac{\dot{p}}{p} = -\mu^*\left(\frac{l_0}{m}p + \eta^*r - 1\right). \tag{37}$$

The implications of sticky prices for international disturbances depend on the remainder of the model. With homogeneous goods and in the absence of gestation lags (section III), interest rates are equalized, moving instantaneously to their new equilibrium level, R^*. Inflation rates can thus be written as linear homogeneous functions of the deviation of prices from their equilibrium values, P^* and p^*, namely

$$\frac{\dot{P}}{P} = -\mu\frac{L_0}{M}(P - P^*), \qquad \frac{\dot{p}}{p} = -\mu^*\frac{l_0}{m}(p - p^*). \tag{38}$$

Following an expansion of debt, sticky prices are seen to rise gradually toward their higher equilibrium levels. The same applies to the exchange rate, since its rate of change is simply the difference between the two inflation rates. While instantaneous adjustment is thus replaced by asymptotic adjustment, the stickiness of prices has no further consequences.

In the presence of gestation lags, the homogeneity of goods still keeps real interest rates equal, but the world interest rate now follows the adjustment path described in section IV. The important point is that there is no feedback from the monetary sector to the rate of interest and the remainder of the real sector. Again using capital goods prices as deflators of cash balances, the inflation rates can be written

$$\frac{\dot{\Pi}}{\Pi} = -\mu\left[\frac{L_0}{M}(\Pi - \Pi^*) + \eta(R - R^*)\right]$$

$$\frac{\dot{\pi}}{\pi} = -\mu^*\left[\frac{l_0}{m}(\pi - \pi^*) + \eta^*(r - r^*)\right]. \tag{39}$$

The instantaneous overshooting is thus replaced by gradual price rises, driven both by the low level of actual prices compared to their equilibrium values and the initial overshooting of the world interest rate. The adjustment path of the exchange rate is of similar type. Far from generating overshooting, price rigidity tends to prevent it.

If the gestation lag is replaced by imperfect commodity substitution, the domestic inflation rate becomes

$$\frac{\dot{P}}{P} = -\mu\left[\frac{L_0}{M}(P - P^*) + \frac{\eta}{\sigma - 1/x''}(A - A^*)\right]. \tag{40}$$

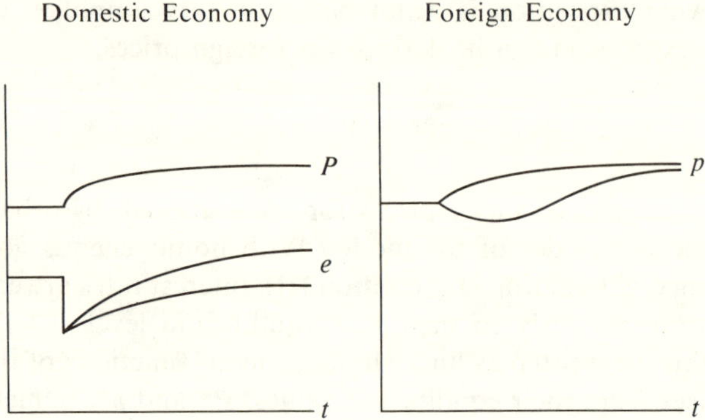

Figure 8.7
Sticky Prices

It thus depends negatively on the deviation of the price level, and (since $\eta < 0$) positively on the deviations of foreign assets, from their respective equilibrium values. Through foreign assets, the real sector influences prices, but there is still no feedback from prices to the real sector. Fiscal policy affects the course of inflation both through the path of A and through the equilibrium values A^* and P^*.

What are the characteristics of the resulting price path? Imagine first that $A - A^* = 0$. In this case, debt expansion simply raises P^*, thus initiating a period of rising prices with declining inflation rates. In fact, of course, $A - A^*$ cannot be zero, beginning with a positive value followed by a gradual decline. This adds a further impulse to domestic inflation. The path of P thus looks as drawn in Figure 8.7. The positive, but declining, inflation rates are in sharp contrast to the case of flexible prices with its initial overshooting followed by deflation.

By analogous reasoning, foreign inflation can be shown to be

$$\frac{\dot{p}}{p} = -\mu^*\left[\frac{l_0}{m}(p - p^*) - \frac{\eta^*}{\sigma^* - 1/x''}(A - A^*)\right]. \tag{41}$$

Again the negative $p - p^*$ provides an inflationary impulse, but $A - A^*$ now appears with a negative coefficient, which reduces the inflation rate. Foreign prices thus tend to approach their higher equilibrium levels more slowly than domestic prices and in the early phases they may even decline.

The path of the exchange rate, finally, is again implied in the paths of national prices and the terms of trade. Since prices cannot react instantaneously, the instantaneous (downward) overshooting of the exchange rate corresponds to that of the terms of trade. The final equilibrium is, of course, the same as for flexible prices, in many cases above the initial level. The intervening adjustment path is governed by the differential equation

$$\frac{\dot{e}}{e} = \frac{\dot{\theta}}{\theta} - \mu\left(\frac{\eta}{\sigma - 1/x''} + \frac{\eta^*}{\sigma^* - 1/x''}\right)$$

$$(A - A^*) - \mu\frac{L_0}{M}(P - P^*) + \mu^*\frac{l_0}{m}(p - p^*). \tag{42}$$

It is difficult to describe the qualitative characteristics of this path. The fact that $A - A^* > 0$ and $P - P^* < 0$ contributes to the appreciation of the foreign currency, but $p - p^* < 0$ pulls in the opposite direction. The result is a curve of the general type shown in Figure 8.7.

In contrast to the Dornbusch model, price rigidity in the present model far from explains the downward overshooting of the exchange rate following an expansion of debt. Its function is rather to counteract the upward (or "perverse") overshooting that may occur under perfectly flexible prices. With imperfect price flexibility, exchange rates show qualitatively about the same behavior as the terms of trade, while the behavior of perfectly flexible prices may be very different.

Overall, price rigidity plays a far less important role in the present model than in much of recent literature. The decisive factor is rather the international redistribution of financial assets, which can only take place through capital flows. The function of the demand and supply of money is the determination of national prices and of the deviations of the nominal exchange rate from the terms of trade, which can take place without international disturbances.

Suppose, for example, all cash balances were doubled overnight, without any change in financial assets, as if by magic. In Dornbusch's model, with imperfect price flexibility, this produces a temporary decline in domestic interest rates and thus an overshooting in the terms of trade. In the present model it only produces a lagged adjustment in domestic prices and the nominal exchange rate, but the terms of trade and real interest rates are not affected. No international capital flows and no changes in trade are required. This is, essentially, because real balances can be adjusted simply by an adjustment in national prices.

It is different for shifts in financial assets. These require an international redistribution of assets through trade balances and capital

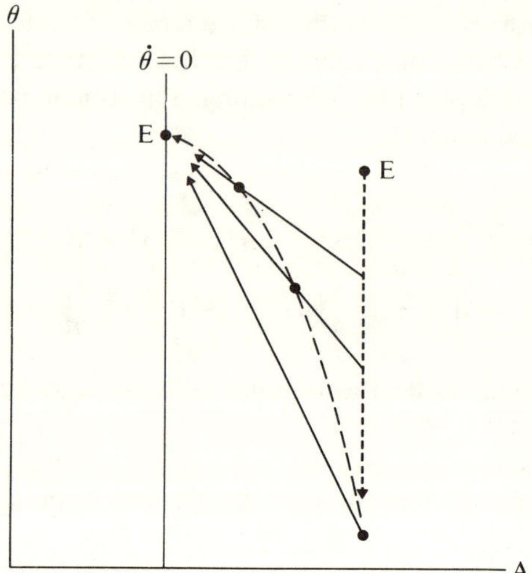

Figure 8.8
The J-Effect

flows. The present model thus puts more weight on international assets and capital flows than the Dornbusch model.

VII. The J-curve

In the analysis of section V, the degree of terms-of-trade overshooting depends decisively on the foreign trade elasticities, ε and ε^*, as summarized in the parameter T' of equation (34). Higher (absolute) elasticities make the $\dot{A} = 0$-curve in Figure 8.4 flatter, and thus reduce the overshooting depicted in Figure 8.5. With homogeneous goods, the elasticities would be infinite and there would be no overshooting. In this sense, overshooting is due to the finite price elasticities of international trade. (A very different reason is the gestation lags of section IV.)

The analysis of section V was based on the assumption that the foreign-trade elasticities, and thus T', are constant. This assumption is clearly unrealistic. It has long been known that foreign trade reacts to changes in the terms of trade with a lag, beginning with very low values and gradually rising towards their steady-state levels in the course of several years.

In the context of the present analysis, this "J-effect" means that the curve for $\dot{A} = 0$ in Figure 8.4 has initially a steep slope and then turns counterclockwise to become gradually flatter. The same is true for the stable arm as indicated by the solid arrows in Figure 8.8. With perfect foresight, the system would thus approach the new equilibrium E along the broken trajectory. It follows that the J-effect accentuates the initial overshooting. In fact, with high steady-state substitutability of traded goods, the J-effect (in the absence of gestation lags) may be the major generator of terms-of-trade disturbances. The more promptly the flows of goods and services react to fluctuations in the terms of trade, the smaller these fluctuations will be.

VIII. Employment Fluctuations

The preceding analysis was based on the assumption of "normal" employment of resources. For steady states, this assumption requires no modification. In particular, trade deficits, be they ever so large, involve no permanent deviations from normal employment, and trade surpluses promise no permanent employment gains. The widespread notion that large trade deficits and surpluses indicate serious international "imbalances" is clearly erroneous. It is a remnant of mercantilist thinking kept alive by interested pressure groups and lobbies.

This verdict applies not only to the overall trade balance of a country but also, and even more strongly, to its separate accounts with individual trade partners. It is sad for an economist to observe that policy-makers are using bilateral trade statistics to justify trade restrictions. In fact, even a country's overall balance of trade is not revealing. Large and persistent deficits and surpluses may be perfectly compatible with a healthy state of affairs.

During the adjustment process this may be different, since employment may deviate from its normal level. The resulting employment fluctuations will now have to be taken into account. There are two important sources of adverse employment fluctuations, namely (1) excess supply of commodities relative to money, and (2) excess supply of domestic commodities relative to foreign commodities. Correspondingly, excess demand for domestic commodities, both relative to cash balances and to foreign commodities, results in above-normal employment and output.

Recent macroeconomic theory offers different ways to model such employment fluctuations. In the tradition of classical, neoclassical, and Keynesian economics, the stickiness of money wages would be assigned an important role. In recent years, alternative approaches placed the emphasis on the difficulty (already mentioned by Pigou) of distinguishing between changes in absolute and relative prices, and the intertemporal shifts in the labor supply caused by relative price changes. For the present purpose the choice between such approaches can be left in abeyance. The essential point is that the adjustment path to a higher, steady-state price level includes a stage of temporary employment gains, while the reverse adjustment is associated with temporary unemployment. Temporary unemployment may also be caused by a downward shift in the steady-state terms of trade, probably sharply aggravated by (downward) overshooting.

The employment disturbances thus resulting from different policies can be summarized as follows. In the presence of gestation lags, debt expansion, since it leads to higher interest rates and thus higher prices, will stimulate employment both at home and abroad. The effort to reduce real balances causes people to go, so to say, on a spending spree. The main new element is that even pure monetary expansion now has real effects. Their main component is the temporary stimulation of domestic employment, but through the income effects on import demand there will also be some stimulation abroad. In any case, domestic monetary impulses are transmitted in a parallel sense. For open-market expansion, being the difference between monetary and fiscal expansion, this ceases to be true. A steady-state increase in domestic prices is in this case accompanied by deflationary pressure abroad. Domestic prosperity will thus tend to be associated with foreign stagnation. It should be noted that these employment effects occur even with perfectly homogeneous goods, where the terms of trade are fixed by assumption.

To these price-level effects one now has to add the terms-of-trade effects. The initial fall in the terms of trade through overshooting exerts a depressive influence on the domestic economy associated with a positive stimulus abroad. In the course of the adjustment process, these impulses will often not only vanish, but actually reverse themselves. This seems to be the component that has provoked most of the international controversies in recent years. With high foreign-trade elasticities, and thus small overshooting, these disturbances are much reduced. Prompt reactions of foreign trade to terms-of-trade changes thus seem to be an important contribution to the mitigation of employment disturbances.

It is instructive to compare these conclusions with those from Mundell's familiar model (1963). Monetary expansion, so Mundell argued, leads to a capital outflow and thus a trade surplus, which has its counterpart in a trade deficit in the rest of the world. Prosperity at home is thus associated with recession abroad. In the present model the causal chain is different. In the case of pure monetary expansion, the domestic employment impulse is transmitted in a parallel fashion through the income effects. In the case of open-market expansion, there is indeed inverse transmission, but this is not due to capital flows triggered by interest differentials. In fact, the interest sensitivity of capital flows is not a meaningful concept in the present context.

Overall, the employment effects tend to enhance the significance of the monetary sector relative to the capital sector as a generator of disturbances. On the assumption of full employment, money seems relatively harmless internationally; disturbances largely originate from shifts in desired security portfolios. Once it is taken into account that money, though neutral in the long run, has short-run employment effects, the disturbances from monetary expansion may easily dominate those from debt expansion. The transitory effects of open-market operations may now originate more from the side of money than from the side of securities.

IX. Capital Mobility and Asset Preferences

The literature on international disturbances tends to assign a major role to what is called the international mobility of capital. This is often said to be dangerously high, and there are colorful descriptions of the immense capital flows triggered by a few telephone calls, with the consequent disturbances in foreign exchange markets and trade. These notions will now be considered in the analytical framework of the present model. It will turn out that in the discussion of international disturbances, capital mobility is largely a red herring.

It is convenient to begin with the conceptual distinction between asset arbitrage and net capital flows. Asset arbitrage consists in a change in the composition of assets within the same total portfolio value; assets are reshuffled by exchanging one against another at current market prices. Net capital flows consist in a net change in foreign asset portfolios, which requires (or rather, implies) a shift in saving relative to investment. Arbitrage relates to different assets, regardless of their owners. Capital flows relate to the wealth of the residents of different countries, regardless of the assets which this wealth consists of.

This distinction is economically important because there is no direct link between asset arbitrage and capital flows. In particular, asset arbitrage does not usually involve capital flows. What takes place in forward-exchange markets, for example, is mere asset arbitrage; the net foreign assets of individual countries are not affected; no capital flows take place. Whatever a financier can do on the telephone is sure to be limited to asset arbitrage; capital flows take more than a telephone. On the other hand, capital flows do not require arbitrage between different assets; one homogeneous asset like gold or a standard security is enough. In an important sense, arbitrage is even the antithesis of capital flows because its function is to equalize the yields of different assets in the absence of any adjustment in their total stock and thus of capital flows.

What has been observed to be very high in recent years is the promptness of arbitrage; even minute yield differentials are rapidly eliminated. In the model of this paper, this observation has been formalized in the assumption that arbitrage is perfect. The mobility of international capital flows, on the other hand, is measured by the speed with which, after a disturbance, net foreign assets are approaching their new equilibrium; it depends, in principle, on all parameters in the dynamic system, including the foreign-trade elasticities and gestation lags. Since foreign-trade elasticities may well be lower, and gestation lags longer, than in earlier periods, it is quite possible that the true mobility of capital flows has been declining. In fact, this would offer a plausible explanation for the persistence of international adjustment problems.[18]

While this paper focuses on capital flows, there is still the question whether arbitrage may generate major international disturbances. In the framework of the present model, it can be discussed by introducing asset substitution caused by shifts in asset preferences.

At the level of cash balances, this opens the door to currency substitution. This subject has been widely discussed, often with the conclusion that currency substitution may result in serious disturbances.[19] This conclusion is open to doubt. It may first be noted that non-interest-bearing cash balances are not highly diversified internationally. They are usually restricted to transactions balances, and most participants in foreign-exchange markets try to keep them at a minimum by switching into interest-bearing money-market assets even over-

---

[18] Feldstein (1983) has provided empirical evidence for the view that the international mobility of capital is relatively low.

[19] For a recent survey, see Putnam and Wilford (1986, part 3).

night. In a discussion of basic factors it seems justified, therefore, to abstract from currency substitution altogether, as has been done so far in this paper.

It is nevertheless instructive to inquire what the consequences of currency substitution would be. They can be investigated in the present model by assuming that the domestic demand for cash balances spontaneously declines ($dL_0 < 0$) while the foreign demand increases ($dl_0 > 0$). The result is simply that domestic prices rise while foreign prices decline. In most cases, these price adjustments would be associated with high employment at home and some unemployment abroad. This is the basic consequence of currency substitution. In fact, currency substitution acts like pure monetary expansion in one country associated with pure monetary contraction in the other. If it occurs to a significant extent, it is relatively easy to counteract it by foreign exchange transactions of central banks.

It should be noted that currency substitution requires neither capital flows nor changes in interest rates and the terms of trade, except for the income effects of employment changes. Real cash balances have the property of being adjustable by domestic inflation or deflation without international asset shifts.

For security substitution this is different. Suppose, first, that assets are still homogeneous, but the domestic demand for securities declines ($dS_0 < 0$) while foreign demand rises by the same amount ($ds_0 = -dS_0$). In the new steady state the world interest rate is the same as before, since the aggregate demand for securities is unchanged. Prices, therefore, are also unchanged. The net foreign assets of the domestic economy are reduced, of course. Since it thus earns less interest abroad, the trade surplus is increased and in the case of heterogeneous goods the terms of trade deteriorate. These static consequences will hardly create serious problems, though.

The dynamic adjustments are potentially more important. Except for the scale factors ϕ and ϕ^*, they are the same as those of a fiscal expansion at home combined with fiscal contraction abroad. They can thus be derived from the results of sections IV and V. In the presence of a domestic gestation lag, the adjustment path resulting from security substitution (except for e) can be determined as follows. (1) Exchange the left side and the right side in Figure 8.3 to obtain the adjustment to foreign fiscal expansion in the presence of a domestic gestation lag. (2) Turn the individual curves upside down to obtain the effect of foreign fiscal contraction. (3) Add the results to those of Figure 8.2. If there is a foreign gestation lag, Figure 8.2 and Figure 8.3 are reversed. It turns out that the world interest rate and prices remain constant throughout. The required trade flows can be achieved without dynamic disturbances. With homogeneous goods, security substitution is harmless.

With heterogeneous goods this is different. To obtain the relevant adjustment from Figure 8.6 (again except for *e*), (1) exchange sides, (2) turn the curves upside down, and (3) add the result to the curves of Figure 8.6. Domestic interest rates are seen to shoot up, followed by a gradual decline, while foreign interest rates begin with an instantaneous decline followed by a gradual recovery. The associated adjustments in trade, capital flows, and the terms of trade are qualitatively similar to those in Figure 8.6, but roughly twice as large. With imperfect commodity substitution, security substitution turns out to be a potential source of major international disturbances.

In fact, the mental experiment of the preceding paragraph did not adequately capture what is usually meant by asset substitution. To capture the common meaning, one has to make domestic and foreign securities imperfect substitutes, so that wealth owners in each country have reason to diversify their portfolios depending on relative yields and risks. Asset substitution would then be expressed as a change in asset preferences by the same wealth holders, be they domestic or foreign.

An analysis of this problem would require a considerable extension of this model, and it goes far beyond the scope of this paper. The main points are relatively straightforward, though. First, the principal consequence of a shift in asset preferences is a change in the international interest differential. Second, this interest differential, since it is continually matched by a risk differential, has no tendency to initiate capital flows. Third, there will, in general, be repercussions on desired foreign asset stocks and thus on capital flows, but their nature is entirely unclear. In particular, it is not necessarily true that a stronger preference for domestic assets relative to foreign assets will produce a capital inflow. Fourth, lower domestic interest rates will often be associated with a capital inflow. Fortunately, the international repercussions from shifts in asset preferences are not only intricate and ambiguous, but probably also minor overall. The main effect is simply an instantaneous twist in interest differentials.

X. Policy Implications

This paper is intended as a theoretical background to policy discussion, not as a policy discussion itself. The final section will thus be limited to a number of policy conclusions implied in the preceding analysis. A few others have already been mentioned in the preceding sections.

The first consideration concerns the economic function of floating rates. The preceding analysis confirms that floating rates insulate the foreign economy against most repercussions from pure monetary policy of the domestic country. This is their main virtue. At the same time, the effects of one's own monetary policy are bottled up at home. The income effects from the associated output fluctuations still remain, though; they are internationally transmitted in a parallel sense.

Floating rates do not insulate an economy against repercussions from fiscal policy abroad. Could the foreign country devise any policy that would provide such insulation? The general answer, unfortunately, is No. There is no general antidote against fiscal policy; there are only partial antidotes against specific effects, and they tend to make other repercussions even worse.

Suppose the foreign country seeks to offset the long-run interest and price effects of domestic debt expansion. It can achieve this objective by engaging in debt contraction. It was noted in section IX that the total effect, given the appropriate levels of df relative to dF, is equivalent to security substitution as there defined. This was shown to leave interest rates and prices in the steady state unchanged. At the same time, the required shifts in foreign assets are magnified. With homogeneous goods (as in section IV), these asset shifts can be achieved without temporary disturbances in interest rates and terms of trade. However, to the extent that traded commodities are imperfect substitutes (as in section V), the associated disturbances in interest rates and terms of trade would be massive.

Suppose, on the other hand, the foreign country undertakes to offset the temporary disturbances in trade and capital flows. In this case, it has to react to domestic debt expansion with a debt expansion of its own. This is the sort of "cooperation" which the United States has at times suggested to its trade partners. Since shifts in international assets are effectively prevented in this case, there are indeed no disturbances in trade, but now the effects on interest rates, capital stocks, and prices (and thus the temporary employment effects) are magnified. This would clearly be a very shortsighted sort of international co-operation.

If monetary policy is conducted by open-market operations, floating rates insulate against the repercussions from the monetary component, but those from the security component remain. Again, there is no general antidote.

It may plausibly be argued that, by and large, the employment fluctuations associated with price adjustments, though relatively uncomplicated, are the most virulent type of international disturbances. If this argument is accepted, floating rates would still offer an economy valuable protection against policy shifts abroad. It is by no means certain, however, that the disturbances resulting from fiscal policy shifts are generally more manageable. Furthermore, protection against monetary shifts can also be obtained by avoiding such shifts in the first place.

A second consideration concerns the implications of fixed rates. With fiat currencies, one country can conduct an autonomous monetary policy while the others adjust passively by exchanging foreign money against domestic money at the fixed rate. Suppose the domestic economy is the dominant economy. What are the implications of fixed rates in this case?

In the case of pure monetary policy the answer is clear. The foreign country is compelled to engage in currency substitution, thus reducing the supply of domestic (dominant) money while expanding the supply of foreign money (its own). Domestic inflation thereby becomes world inflation, and the temporary employment effects, while diluted domestically, are transmitted abroad. This was the experience of the 1960s. If the foreign country happens to agree with the conduct of domestic monetary policy, the fixed-rate system will be viable. If there is no such consensus, the fixed-rate system will break down. The necessity of policy coordination is the curse of fixed exchange rates between fiat currencies. It can only be exorcised by an enlightened and steady policy of the dominant country.

The case of fiscal policy is much less clear. The basic reason is that the nature of the required central-bank operations is ambiguous. Consider, for example, the case of heterogeneous goods without gestation lags. Figure 8.6 shows that under flexible prices a floating exchange rate may do almost anything. With sticky prices, as Figure 8.7 shows, the picture is somewhat simplified, but still complicated enough. The exchange rate is simply not a reliable indicator of international disturbances.

Special cases permit more specific answers. Suppose domestic debt expansion happens to have no long-run effect on the exchange rate, but there is an instantaneous appreciation of the domestic currency followed by a gradual decline. In this case the foreign central bank would have to begin by selling a large amount of the domestic currency, thus contracting the supply of its own money. Inflation in the domestic economy would be accelerated while in the foreign economy the approach to the higher, steady-state price level would be retarded. The disturbances in trade and capital flows, since they depend on real factors, would remain unaffected. In particular, the pegging of the exchange rate does not eliminate overshooting of the terms of trade, as is often believed. Instead of being reflected in the exchange rate, changes in the terms of trade are now simply reflected in larger international differences in inflation rates. It follows that fixed exchange rates do not insulate the foreign economy against the repercussions from domestic fiscal policy. On the other hand, neither do they make these repercussions significantly worse.

In the final case of a domestic open-market expansion, the required exchange operations of the foreign central bank again correspond to the difference between those under pure monetary expansion and pure debt expansion. The monetary impulse is thereby transmitted to the foreign economy, while the consequences of the fiscal impulse are ambiguous.

My personal conclusion is that in the presence of frequent and abrupt shifts in monetary and fiscal policies, the task of international coordination is virtually hopeless. This skepticism has both an economic and a political root. From an economic point of view, it is difficult to conceive of any rules that can be confidently relied upon to reduce international disturbances. The recent papers by Miller and Salmon, by Currie and Levine, and by Oudiz and Sachs in the NBER conference volume on international policy coordination (Buiter and Marston 1985) strongly suggest that the only beneficiary of the search for such rules will be the technology of differential games. From a political point of view, it is hard to see how governments, in particular the government of the United States, should be able to submit to any sort of international coordination as long as they are domestically too weak to avoid abrupt shifts in their monetary and fiscal policies. The first, and most promising, step to reducing international disturbances must surely be the avoidance of the policy shifts that produce them. Especially for the dominant economy, the United States, the most important part of cooperation is steadiness.

Skepticism about international coordination does not necessarily entail pessimism. Complaints about international "imbalances" have been with us as far as memory reaches, and they are not likely to disappear under the best of circumstances. It is not clear that they are more serious today than, say, 20 years ago. In fact, it may be argued that, given the enormous shifts in U.S. policies, the international monetary non-system has proved to be remarkably resilient. Over the last seven years, in particular, there was, on balance, a clear improvement. World inflation has been much reduced, unemployment has been largely (though not completely) normalized, and there has not been a significant recession for more than five years. If the United States succeeds in steadying the course of its fiscal and monetary policies, the international prospects are indeed quite bright. If they do not succeed, no international cooperation will help.

References

Aftalion, Albert. 1927. The Theory of Economic Cycles Based on the Capitalistic Technique of Production. *Review of Economics and Statistics* 9: 165–70.

Arndt, Sven W., Sweeney, Richard J., and Willett, Thomas D., eds. 1985. *Exchange Rates, Trade, and the U.S. Economy*. Washington, D.C.: American Enterprise Institute.

Blanchard, Olivier J. 1985. Debt, Deficits, and Finite Horizons. *Journal of Political Economy* 93: 223–47.

Brunner, Karl 1986. Fiscal Policy in Macro Theory: A Survey and Evaluation. In Hafer, R.W., ed., *The Monetary Versus Fiscal Policy Debate: Lessons from Two Decades*. Totowa, N.J.: Rowman and Allanheld.

Buiter, Willem H., and Marston, Richard C., eds. 1985. *International Economic Policy Coordination*. Cambridge: Cambridge University Press.

Dornbusch, Rudiger. 1976. Expectations and Exchange Rate Dynamics. *Journal of Political Economy* 84: 1161–76.

Feldstein, Martin. 1983. Domestic Saving and International Capital Movements in the Long Run and the Short Run. *European Economic Review* 21: 129–51.

Frenkel, Jacob A., and Razin, Assaf. 1985(a). Government Spending, Debt, and International Economic Interdependence. *Economic Journal* 95: 619–36.

————, 1985(b). Fiscal Expenditures and International Economic Interdependence. In Buiter, Willem H., and Marston, Richard C., eds. *International Economic Policy Coordination*. Cambridge: Cambridge University Press.

Hamada, Koichi. 1985. *The Political Economy of International Monetary Interdependence*. Cambridge, Mass.: MIT Press.

Hoelscher, Gregory. 1986. New Evidence on Deficits and Interest Rates. *Journal of Money, Credit, and Banking* 18: 1–17.

Hutchison, Michael M., and Pigott, Charles. 1984. Budget Deficits, Exchange Rates and the Current Account: Theory and U.S. Evidence. *Federal Reserve Bank of San Francisco Economic Review* 4: 5–25.

————, and Throop, Adrian W. 1985. U.S. Budget Deficits and the Real Value of the Dollar. *Federal Reserve Bank of San Francisco Economic Review* 4: 26–43.

Makin, John H. 1983. Real Interest, Money Surprises, Anticipated Inflation and Fiscal Deficits. *Review of Economics and Statistics* 65: 374–84.

Mundell, Robert A. 1963. Capital Mobility and Stabilization Policy under Fixed and Flexible Exchange Rates. *Canadian Journal of Economics and Political Science* 29: 475–85.

Niehans, Jürg 1984. *International Monetary Economics*. Baltimore: Johns Hopkins University Press.

———. 1986. A General-Equilibrium Analysis of International Capital Flows. In Neumann, M.J.M., ed. *Monetary Policy and Uncertainty: Collected Papers from the 1982–1984 Konstanz Seminars*. Baden-Baden: Nomos.

———. 1987. Monetary Policy and Investment Dynamics in Interdependent Economics. *Journal of Money, Credit, and Banking* 19: (forthcoming).

Putnam, Bluford H., and Wilford, D. Sykes, eds. 1986. *The Monetary Approach to International Adjustment*, revised edition. New York: Praeger.

Rotheli, Tobias F. 1986. *Das Volkseinkommen und die internationalen Kapitalbewegungen*. Berner Beitrage zur Nationalökonomie, 50. Bern: Haupt.

Samuelson, Paul A. 1952. The Transfer Problem and Transport Costs: The Terms of Trade when Impediments are Absent. *Economic Journal* 62: 278–304.

9

Sources of Macroeconomic Imbalances in the World Economy: A Simulation Approach

Jeffrey D. Sachs and Nouriel Roubini*

This paper uses a global macroeconomic simulation model to identify the factors that have contributed to global trade and financial imbalances in the 1980s. After investigating the properties of monetary and fiscal policies in the model, we examine whether the budgetary shifts in the OECD economies in the 1980s can account for the bulk of trade and exchange rate movements. Our conclusions are mixed. The combination of sharply higher fiscal deficits in the United States and sharply reduced deficits in Japan goes far to explain the movements of the trade balances and exchange rates of the two economies. However, the drop in the dollar vis-à-vis the yen since late 1985 is not well explained by the model. We also investigate the prospects for a reduction of the U.S. trade deficits if U.S. budget deficits are in fact reduced, as well as the possible role for Japanese monetary and fiscal policies in reducing the trade imbalances of the two countries.

I. Introduction

During the 1980s there have been several striking developments in world trade and financial patterns. As shown in Table 9.1, the United States shifted from a trade deficit of about 1% of GNP at the end of the 1970s to a trade deficit of over 3% of GNP in 1985. Japan, on the other hand, shifted from a small surplus to a surplus in excess of 4% of GNP in the same period. The non-oil developing countries

* Jeffrey Sachs would like to thank Dr. Yoshio Suzuki and other staff members of the Institute for Monetary and Economic Studies of the Bank of Japan, for helpful discussions and warm hospitality during his visit to the Bank of Japan, November 1986 to January 1987.

Table 9.1   Changes in Trade Balances

	Average Trade Balance (% of GNP), 1978–80	Trade Balance (% of GNP), 1985	Change
United States	−1.2	−3.1	−1.9
Japan	1.0	4.2	2.2
Canada	2.3	3.8	3.2
Rest of OECD,[a] of which:	−0.6	0.4	1.0
Germany	2.4	4.6	1.8
France	−0.9	−0.9	0.0
United Kingdom	−0.7	−0.5	0.2
10 smaller countries[b]	−2.2	−0.3	1.9
Non-oil LDC's[c]	−2.2	−0.3	1.9

Notes: [a] 1982 weights.

  [b] Australia, Austria, Belgium, Denmark, Finland, Greece, Netherlands, Norway, Spain, Sweden.

  [c] Percent of U.S. GNP.

Source: International Financial Statistics, IMF.

also experienced a dramatic change, with their large trade deficits at the end of the 1970s being virtually eliminated by 1985.

The financial counterparts of these trade changes are well known and equally dramatic. The U.S., which in 1980 was the world's large net creditor country, is now the largest net debtor country, while Japan has replaced the U.S. as the world's preeminent creditor country. At the same time, most non-oil developing countries virtually lost their access to market borrowing in the early 1980s, and many of the largest borrowers in the late 1970s became net repayers of debt in the mid-1980s.

The trade and financial imbalances in recent years have generated enormous political pressures in the United States for measures to "restore balance." Different interpretations of the reasons for the imbalances have led to differing emphases in the policy proposals. Many U.S. politicians, for example, ascribe the Japanese trade surpluses to unfair Japanese trading practices. The policy proposal most closely identified with this interpretation is the Gephardt Amendment, which calls for U.S. tariff increases against foreign countries that have large bilateral trade surpluses vis-à-vis the U.S., and are certified by the U.S. International Trade Commission to be engaging in unfair trade practices against U.S. goods.[1]

---

[1] At the time of this writing, the Gephardt Amendment has been included in the Omnibus Trade Bill passed by the U.S. House of Representatives. The trade legis-

Table 9.2 Changes in General Government Financial Balances, percent of GNP, 1979–1985

	Actual Balance	Inflation-Adjusted Structural Balance
United States	−4.3	−4.4
Japan	3.6	3.7
Canada	−3.6	−2.2
Rest of OECD,[a]	−1.3	0.5
of which:		
Germany	1.3	3.3
France	−3.1	0.5
United Kingdom	0.5	1.9
10 smaller countries[b]	−2.0	−0.8

Notes: [a] 1982 GDP weights.

[b] Australia, Austria, Belgium, Denmark, Finland, Greece, Netherlands, Norway, Spain, Sweden.

Source: Atkinson, P. and Chauraqui, J-C., "The Origins of High Real Interest Rates," OECD Economic Studies, Autumn 1985, Table 3, p. 16.

Many business analysts and some economists see the U.S. trade deficits as resulting from a long-term decline in U.S. "competitiveness," resulting from poor management practices, old-fashioned labor-relations procedures, a lack of entrepreneurship, or other factors that have contributed to slow productivity growth. Advocates of this point of view have urged a new industrial policy in the United States, usually with some variant of labor-management-government cooperation to overcome structural problems in the U.S. economy.

Most economists, however, regard the trade imbalances as deriving from macroeconomic causes, and therefore look to macroeconomic solutions.[2] The most common interpretations of the U.S. and Japanese imbalances stress the role of expansionary U.S. fiscal policies and contractionary Japanese fiscal policies. The differing movements in the budgets of the two countries, as measured by changes in the structural inflation-adjusted (full-employment) budget deficit, can be seen in Table 9.2. Between 1979 and 1985, the U.S. structural budget deficit widened by 4.4% of potential GNP in the U.S., while the Japanese deficit was reduced by 3.7%. In the rest of the OECD, Germany also reduced its structural deficit, by 3.3% of GNP, while

---

lation is now under consideration by the U.S. Senate. The President has stated that he will veto a trade bill that includes the Gephardt Amendment in its current form.

[2] It is possible, of course, to agree with the diagnosis that there has been an important productivity slowdown in the U.S. economy, while at the same time interpreting the trade balance developments as resulting from other macroeconomic factors rather the productivity slowdown itself.

Table 9.3　Real Bilateral Exchange Rate vis-à-vis $ U.S.

| | Real Exchange Rate vis-à-vis $ U.S.
(1978–1980 = 100) | | | |
	1985	1986	Change 1978–80/ 1985	Change 1985/ 1986
Japan	76	106	−24	30
Canada	91	91	−9	0
Rest of OECD, 　of which:	61	77	−39	16
Germany	55	73	−45	18
France	58	76	−42	18
United Kingdom	78	78	−32	10

Source: The real exchange rate is defined as $P/E\,P^u$, where P is the CPI of the country or region, E is in units of currency per dollar, and P^u is the CPI of the United States. A rise in the index signifies a real depreciation of the dollar.

the smaller economies generally had a small increase in their deficits. In the most common interpretation of the trade imbalances (and one that is largely supported in this paper), the U.S. fiscal expansion cum Japanese fiscal contraction raised U.S. interest rates relative to Japanese rates, induced a capital inflow from Japan, and caused a dollar appreciation and a worsening of the U.S. trade imbalance.

Other economists put less weight on fiscal policy, and argue that the dollar exchange rate had a "life of its own" in the 1980s, with much of the appreciation of the dollar between 1980 and 1985 resulting from speculative movements that pushed the dollar well above "fundamental" levels, and thereby inducing a U.S. trade deficit. Movements in the real exchange rate of the U.S. vis-à-vis other countries are shown in Table 9.3 (real exchange rates are measured there as the nominal exchange rate adjusted for relative consumer price level changes). Whether the 24% real appreciation of the dollar vis-à-vis the yen between 1978–80 and 1985, and the 39% appreciation vis-à-vis the rest of the OECD, are explained by budget deficits or by a speculative bubble, there is little doubt that the exchange rate movements played an important role in generating the trade imbalances of the early 1980s. Note that the model ideally should explain both the appreciation of the dollar up to 1985 and the sharp depreciation afterwards.

Other economists suggest that the U.S. experienced an investment boom in the 1980s due to a favorable economic climate and high level of business confidence. They argue that the trade deficits in the U.S. are a sign of investment strength and economic *vigor* rather than economic weakness. Some go so far as to aver that the apparent relationship of the budget deficit and the trade deficit is purely coincidental, and that the real story of the U.S. trade imbalance is not a fall in national savings (coming from larger public sector deficits), but rather a rise in national investment.

Each of these differing macroeconomic interpretations leads to a distinct policy recommendation. Those who stress the fiscal sources of the trade imbalances usually stress the need for fiscal action in the major industrial countries as the way to reduce the trade imbalances. A standard view is that the U.S. should have a fiscal contraction, while Japan and Europe should engineer an offsetting fiscal expansion. Economists emphasizing the *independent* role of the exchange rate stress the need for coordinated management of the exchange rate, in addition to any fiscal actions which may be warranted. The dollar should be "talked down," or pushed down if necessary by foreign exchange intervention policies or relatively expansionary U.S. monetary policies. Finally, those who see evidence of an investment boom in the data argue that nothing particular needs to be done. International capital is simply flowing to the economy with the most exceptional investment opportunities.

The goal of this paper is to present a simulation model of the world economy to examine the fiscal policy interpretation of the trade imbalance. The argument for such an approach is that the issue at hand requires quantitative evidence that can best be adduced in the context of a structural macroeconomic model. We can be confident, for example, that the fiscal actions in the U.S., Europe, and Japan have contributed to the trade imbalances in recent years. But is it reasonable to attribute most or all of the observed imbalances to this factor? Do we have to invoke additional factors, such as speculative exchange rate movements or declining U.S. productivity, to account for the large shifts that have occurred in recent years? The simulation model presented in this paper can provide a quantitative assessment of such issues.

The simulation results suggest that the combination of fiscal policies in the OECD and the cutoff in lending to the LDCs in the early 1980s can account for most of the trade balance movements of the U.S. and Japan, and *some* (though not all) of the exchange rate movements since 1980. However, there remain major areas of uncertainty, especially in explaining the extraordinary drop in the dollar in the past year. The model also suggests several interesting points regarding the international transmission of policy changes. Most importantly, the international linkages among the major economies are probably not strong enough to justify the recent intense pressures from the U.S. for "international policy coordination." U.S. economic growth and trade imbalances, for example, will be little affected by the fiscal policy choices made by Japan and Europe. Even the direction of effect of one country's monetary and fiscal policies on other countries is often contrary to the conventional view. Perhaps most important, the use of monetary policies in the U.S. and abroad to induce a further depreciation of the dollar would, by itself, do little to reduce the U.S. trade deficits.

The model is described briefly in Section II. (The model equations are listed in Appendix A to the paper.) A more detailed description of the model will soon be available in McKibbin and Sachs (1987). The basic policy simulation results are described in Section III, where a comparison is made with the standard Mundell-Fleming two-country model. In Section IV, the model is used to track several of the developments in the period since 1980, and is used to make some forecasts of the next few years. In Section V, we underscore several limitations of the model and describe some extensions that are now under way.

II. The MSG2 Model of the World Economy

The model in this paper, which we term the MSG2 model, is a further development of the McKibbin-Sachs Global (MSG) model, which has been decribed elsewhere (see especially McKibbin and Sachs (1986) and Ishii, McKibbin, and Sachs (1986) for discussion of the earlier version). The new model extends the earlier version by including a more satisfactory treatment of aggregate supply and investment behavior. The new model, however, is still very much in a developmental stage, and we are indeed dissatisfied with the specification of some of the key relations in the present version.

A. An Overview of the Model

The MSG2 is a dynamic general equilibrium model of a six-region world economy, divided into the United States, Japan, Canada, the rest of the OECD economies (denoted ROECD, and constituted mainly by OECD Europe), the non-oil developing countries (LDCs), and OPEC. The model is of moderate size (about three dozen behavioral equations per industrial region). It is distinctive relative to most other global models in that it solves for a full intertemporal equilibrium in which agents have rational expectations of future variables. In theoretical conception, therefore, the model is close in design to intertemporal dynamic models of fiscal policy in Lipton and Sachs (1983) and Frenkel and Razin (1986). Those studies, like the present simulation model, examine fiscal policy in an intertemporal perfect-foresight environment, with considerable attention given to intertemporal optimization and intertemporal budget constraints. Frenkel and Razin are noteworthy in being able to derive analytical results from their model, rather than relying on simulations, as in the current study.

The model has a mix of Keynesian and classical properties by virtue of a maintained assumption of slow adjustment of nominal wages in the labor markets of the U.S., Canada, and the ROECD. (Japan is treated somewhat differently, as described below.)

The model is solved in a linearized form, to facilitate policy optimization exercises with the model, and especially to use linear-quadratic dynamic game theory and dynamic programming solution techniques.[3] The global stability of the linearized model can be readily confirmed by an analysis of the model's eigenvalues. At this point, the model is parameterized by choosing parameters based on existing econometric research in the literature, rather than by undertaking our own econometric estimation of the model parameters. The procedure of relying on other research estimates for key parameters represents, in our opinion, a healthy division of labor between those who focus on general equilibrium modeling and those who focus on the econometric study of particular aspects of the macroeconomy.

Speaking broadly, the model has several attractive features. First, all stock-flow relationships are carefully observed. Budget deficits cumulate into stocks of public debt; current account deficits cumulate into net foreign investment positions; and physical investment cumulates into the capital stock. Underlying growth of Harrod-neutral productivity plus labor force growth is assumed to be 4% per region. Given the long-run properties of the model, the world economy settles down to the 4% steady-state growth path following any set of initial disturbances.

A second attractive feature is that the asset markets are efficient in the sense that asset prices are determined by a combination of intertemporal arbitrage conditions and rational expectations. By virtue of the rational expectations assumption and the forward-looking behavior of households and firms, the model can be used to examine the effects of anticipated future policy changes, such as the sequence

---

[3] In general, quantity variables are linearized around their levels relative to potential GDP, while price variables are linearized in log form.

of future budget deficit cuts called for by the Gramm-Rudman legislation in the U.S. Indeed, one of the difficulties of using the MSG2 model is that every simulation requires that the "entire" future sequence of anticipated policies be specified. In practice, 40-year paths of policy variables, or endogenous policy rules, must be specified.

A third attractive feature of the model is the specification of the supply side. There are several noteworthy points here. First, factor input decisions are based (with a few exceptions) on intertemporal profit maximation by firms. Labor and intermediate inputs are selected to maximize short-run profits given a stock of capital which is fixed within each period. The capital stock is adjusted according to a "Tobin's q" model of investment, derived along the lines in Hayashi (1984). Tobin's q is the shadow value of capital, and evolves according to a rational expectations forecast of future post-tax profitability.

Another point of interest regarding the supply side is the specification of the wage-price dynamics in each of the industrial regions. Extensive macroeconomic research has demonstrated important differences in the wage-price processes in the U.S., Europe, and Japan, and these differences are incorporated in the model. In particular, the U.S. and Canada are characterized by nominal wage rigidities arising from long-term nominal wage contracts. In Japan, on the contrary, nominal wages are assumed to be renegotiated on an annual, synchronized cycle, with nominal wages selected for the following year to clear the labor market on average. In the ROECD, nominal wages are assumed to be more forward looking than in the U.S. and Canada, though real wages adjust slowly to clear the labor market.

A third feature of the supply side of some interest is the assumption regarding trade prices. Many observers have recently pointed out the fairly significant lag in the pass-through of exchange rate changes into import price changes in the U.S. economy (and probably in the other economies as well, which have been less extensively examined). The appreciation of the dollar during 1981–85 did not bring about an instantaneous and equivalent fall in U.S. import prices, and the recent depreciation of the dollar has not brought about an equivalent rise in prices. To capture part of this effect, we assume that exporters into the U.S. market set their prices in dollars one period in advance, in order to equate the export price with the *expected* home market price in the following period. If the dollar then unexpectedly appreciates, the importers into the U.S. reap an unanticipated windfall, in that the price they receive in the U.S. market, expressed in local currency at the spot market exchange rate, exceeds the domestic price of output. This divergence will be eliminated, on average, in the following period, when the trade prices are reset. There are of course other reasons for the failure of exchange rate movements to pass through into prices, most of which involve imperfect competition in trade (see Dornbusch [1986] or Krugman [1986] for details). We plan to incorporate such imperfect competition features into a later version of the model.

B. A More Detailed Look at MSG2

The complete MSG2 model is presented in Appendix A, and a complete technical description will be found in McKibbin and Sachs (1987). Here we will merely sketch out some of the key structural features of the model.

Each of the regions in the model produces a good which is an imperfect substitute in the production and spending decisions of the other regions. Each industrialized region produces one final good which is used for investment and consumption purposes in that region and in all of the other regions. LDC and OPEC each produce one good which is a primary input in the production processes of the industrial regions. Demands for the outputs of LDC and OPEC are therefore derived demands for the production inputs. The U.S., Europe, and Canada are also each assumed to produce an exogenous amount of domestic oil, which is a perfect substitute for imports from OPEC.

In the model version in this paper, only the four industrial country regions are fully modeled with an internal macroeconomic structure. In LDC and OPEC, only the foreign trade and external financial aspects are modeled (we are now upgrading the model to include an internal macroeconomic structure for LDC). Note that in referring to variables of the various regions, we will use the following notation: U.S. (U); ROECD (R); Japan (J); OPEC (O); and LDC (L). The currency of the ROECD will be termed "ECU," though in fact the countries included in the ROECD and in the actual ECU are not exactly the same.

To understand the model, it is best to consider one bloc of the model, that of the U.S., and to indicate where necessary any differences in the modeling of the other OECD regions. The cornerstone of aggregate supply in the model is a representative firm which maximizes income by producing a single output Q at price P, subject to a two-input production function (for simplicity, potential growth is ignored in the equations that follow, even though a constant underlying potential growth rate of 4% is included in the model). Thus, aggregate production is given as:

$$Q = Q(V, N). \tag{1}$$

Gross output Q is a produced with value-added V, and primary inputs N. In turn, V is produced with capital K and labor L, while N is produced with the imports from OPEC (net of domestic oil production) N_0 and the LDCs N_L:

$$V = V(K, L) \tag{2}$$

$$N = N(N_0, N_L). \tag{3}$$

The capital stock changes according to the rate of fixed capital formation J and the rate of geometric depreciation δ:

$$K_{t+1} = J_t + (1 - \delta)K_t. \tag{4}$$

J is itself a composite good, produced with a Cobb-Douglas technology that has as inputs the domestic goods and the final goods of Canada, Europe, and Japan. The price of J is simply a weighted sum of the prices of the home goods P (P^U for the U.S.) and the dollar import prices (P_W^i, i = R, J, C) of goods from the other OECD regions:

$$J = (J^U)^{\theta}1 \ (J^R)^{\theta}2 \ (J^J)^{\theta}3 \ (J^C)^{\theta}4 \tag{5}$$

$$p^J = \theta_1 p^U + \theta_2 p_W^R + \theta_3 p_W^J + \theta_4 p_W^C \tag{6}$$

As is customary in modern models of investment, it is assumed that the investment process is subject to rising marginal costs of installation, with total nominal investment expenditures $P^J I$ equal to the value of direct purchases of investment $P^J{*}J$, plus the per-unit costs of installation. These per-unit costs, in turn, are assumed to be a linear function of the rate of investment J/K, so that adjustment costs are $P^J{*}J[(\phi_0/2) \ (J/K)]$. Total investment expenditure is therefore

$$P^J I = [P^J + P^J(\phi_0/2) \ (J/K)] \ J. \tag{7}$$

The goal of the firm is to choose inputs of L, N, and J to maximize intertemporal net-of-tax profits. In fact, the firm faces a stochastic problem, a point which is ignored in the derivation of the firm's behavior (in other word's, the firm is assumed to hold its estimates of future variables with subjective certainty). The firm's deterministic problem, formally stated, is

$$\max \sum_{\tau=t}^{\infty} (1 + R_\tau)^{-1}[Q - (W/P)L - (P_N/P)N - (P^J/P)I] \qquad (8)$$

where $(1 + R_\tau)^{-1}$ is a discount factor equal to:

$$\prod_{i=t}^{\tau} (1 + r_i)^{-1}$$

and r_i is the period i short-term real interest rate.

The solution to this problem is now well known (see Bruno and Sachs, 1985, as an example). There are three key points. First, inputs of L and N are hired to the point where marginal productivities of these factors equal their factor prices. This leads to equations for the derived demand for L and N of the form

$$L = L(W/P, P_N/P)K \qquad (9)$$

$$N = N(W/P, P_N/P)K \qquad (10)$$

Gross fixed capital formation can be written in terms of Tobin's "marginal" q, in the following manner:

$$J = [(q - 1)/\phi_0]K \qquad (11)$$

Third, q (the shadow value of new investment) equals the discounted value of future profits, with q given by:

$$q/(P^J/P) = \sum_{\tau=t}^{\infty} (1 + R_\tau)^{-1}(F_K + \Phi_K) \qquad (12)$$

Here F_k is the marginal product of capital in the production function, and Φ_K is the marginal product of capital in reducing adjustment costs in investment.

In the specific application in the model, the gross output production function is taken to be a two-level CES function in V and N, with V a Cobb-Douglas function of L and K, and N a CES function of oil and non-oil primary inputs. The investment function derived in (11) is also modified, for empirical realism, by writing J as a function not only of q, but also of the level of flow capital income at time t, and the change in the level of gross output, along standard investment accelerator lines. The modified investment equation is of the form

$$J_t = \theta[(q - 1)/\phi_0]K + (1 - \theta)[Q - (W/P)L - (P_N/P)N]$$
$$+ \epsilon(Q_t - Q_{t-1}) \qquad (11')$$

Total private consumption spending is written as a function of labor income net of labor taxes (γ_L is the labor income tax rate) and total nominal financial wealth $P*F$, as in:

$$P^C C = C_L[WL(1 - \gamma_L)] + C_K(P * F) \tag{13}$$

This equation is certainly the most problematic of the model. The equation is an *ad hoc* compromise between alternative conceptions of aggregate consumption, in line with the empirical evidence that consumption is partly determined along life-cycle lines, with considerable intertemporal consumption smoothing, and partly along simpler Keynesian lines (perhaps because of liquidity constrained households). Thus, we specify that spending is a fixed proportion of current net-of-tax labor income (with no consumption smoothing of the labor income flow), as in standard Keynesian models, and a fixed proportion of wealth, as in standard life-cycle models with infinite-lived individuals. We are now experimenting with other variants of the consumption function that include at least some degree of consumption smoothing of post-tax labor income.

Once $P^C * C$ is determined, it is divided into purchases of the domestic good and imported final goods from Canada, ROECD, and Japan. The division of $P^C * C$ is made to maximize an instantaneous utility function of CES form. The result is demands for home goods and imported goods of the form

$$C^i = C^i(P_W^J/P^U, P_W^C/P^U, P_W^R/P^U) * (P_C * C) \tag{14}$$

with $\quad P^C * C = P_W^J * C^J + P_W^C * C^C + P^U * C^U + P_W^R * C^R$

where $\quad i = \text{J, C, R, U.}$

Note that P_W^i signifies the import price paid by U.S. consumers for imports from country i.

We assume that the government divides spending G among the final goods in the same proportion as does the private sector (this assumption is for convenience only), so that:

$$G^i/G^U = C^i/C^U \quad \text{for } i = \text{C, R, J} \tag{15}$$

The price of imports is derived as follows. U.S. imports from ROECD, Canada, and Japan are invoiced in dollars, according to an equation which makes the invoice price in period $t + 1$ equal to the (rationally) expected dollar price of the output of country i in period $t + 1$:

$$_t(p_W^i)_{t+1} = {}_t p_{t+1}^i + {}_t e_{t+1}^i \tag{16}$$

where $_t X_{t+1}$ signifies the period t rational expectations of variable X at time $t + 1$. Equation (16) holds that the (log) price in period $t + 1$ of a U.S. import from country i is determined in period t, as the sum of the (log) expected exchange rate and the (log) price of output in country i in period $t + 1$. On average, the import price will equal the U.S. dollar price of output in country i. However, if the actual exchange rate of the dollar in period $t + 1$ turns out to be stronger (weaker) than expected, the import price in the U.S. market will be higher (lower) than the price of country i output converted at the actual exchange rate.

The U.S. is in fact the only major market in which import prices are invoiced in the *importer's* currency. In most other markets, the imports are invoiced in the exporter's currency, so that exchange rate changes of the importing country are quickly passed through into import prices. Thus for all exports of final goods by country i to country k other than the U.S. ($k = $ R, J, C), the price of imports in country k is given by the contemporaneous P^i multiplied by E_k^i, the contemporaneous exchange rate between currency i and k.

For the primary goods of OPEC and the LDCs, there is a single uniform world price of goods which applies in all markets at all times (i.e., the law of one price holds). Letting P^0 be the *dollar* price of OPEC goods, we assume that P^0 is a variable markup over a basket of OECD goods, so that

$$P^0 = P^0(P^U, E_U^J * P^J, E_U^R * P^R, E_U^C * P^C) * h(X^0) \qquad (17)$$

with $h' > 0$.

Note that E_U^i is units of dollars per unit of currency i. The function $P^0 (. , . , . , . , .)$ is linear homogeneous and increasing in the prices of the OECD goods. The function $h(X^0)$ makes the OPEC markup an increasing function of the total demand for OPEC exports X^0 to the other regions. A similar equation governs the price of LDC commodities. The local currency price of OPEC goods in a non-U.S. region j is then given by $P_j^0 = E_j^U * P^0$, according to the law of one price. A similar equation applies for the LDC commodity export.

The supply side of the U.S. block of the model is completed with the wage equation, which makes the nominal wage change a function of past consumer price (p^c) changes, rationally expected future price changes, and the level of unemployment in the economy, according to a standard Phillips curve mechanism:

$$(w_{t+1} - w_t) = \alpha \, (p_t^c - p_{t-1}^c) + (1 - \alpha) \, ({}_t p_{t+1}^c - p_t^c)$$
$$+ \, \beta(L_t/L^f) \qquad (18)$$

where L^f represents the inelastically supplied full-employment stock of labor. The parameter α in (18) determines how much weight is given to backward-looking versus forward-looking price expectations.

As already noted, we allow for differences in the wage dynamics of the different regions. In Japan, we specify that wages are set one period ahead at their expected *market clearing* levels. Thus, let $({}_tw_{t+1})^f$ be the wage expected to clear the labor market at time $t + 1$, in the sense that ${}_tL_{t+1} = L^f$. Then:

$$w^J_{t+1} = ({}_tw^J_{t+1})^f \tag{19}$$

The rest of the model can be quickly stated. Prices in the U.S. (and the other OECD regions) are fully flexible within each period, so that demand for U.S. output (domestic demand plus export demand) equals output supply. Money demand equations are specified for each OECD region in a standard Goldfeld-type transactions demand equation. Asset markets are assumed to be perfectly integrated across the OECD regions. Expected returns of loans denominated in the currencies of the various regions are equalized period to period, according to the following interest arbitrage relations:

$$i^i_t = i^j_t + {}_t(e^i_j)_{t+1} - e^i_{jt} \tag{20}$$

Thus, we do not allow for risk premia on the assets of alternative currencies. We choose the assumption of perfect capital mobility and zero risk premia in light of the failure of the empirical exchange rate literature to demonstrate the existence of stable risk premia across international currencies.

For the U.S., Canada, Japan, ROECD, and OPEC, the current account is determined under the assumption that domestic agents have free unrationed access to international borrowing and lending at the international interest rate. It is assumed for simplicity that all international borrowing and lending takes place in dollar denominated assets. For the LDCs, in distinction, the scale of borrowing is set *exogenously*, under the assumption that the amount of loans available to the LDCs is rationed by country risk considerations. One of the experiments that we study later is an exogenous shift in the amount of lending made available to the LDCs.

The model is parameterized using estimates of behavioral and technological parameters from the econometrics literature. Thus, elasticities of demand for home and foreign goods, the elasticities of demand for money balances, the factor shares in the production function, etc., are taken from other studies. The only real calibration that takes place using actual data is in the trade bloc, where the free parameters of the utility function are selected to reproduce the patterns of trade among the various industrial regions as of 1986. Thus, by choice of utility function parameters, the baseline of the model exactly reproduces the direction of trade among the various regions in the first half of 1986. Choosing 1986 as the basis for linearization is of course a bit problematic for simulations of the 1981–86 period, but we chose to use the 1986 base to give a better picture here of the *current* policy multipliers.

III. Simulation Results for Monetary and Fiscal Policies

We now employ the model to try to understand the reasons for the shifts in global trade and financial imbalances in recent years, and to understand better the nature of the international transmission of macro-economic policies. We begin with standard simulations of the effects of monetary and fiscal policy, and then turn to the policy changes of the period 1980–85.

A. Fiscal Policy in the U.S. and Japan

Various simulation results for fiscal policies are shown in the next few tables. Before these results are discussed, however, it is important to understand the precise experiment that is being undertaken. In line with rational expectations modeling, policy experiments must define an entire future path of policies, and not just a change during the simulation period. In the case of fiscal policy, it is important that tax and spending policies be consistent with the intertemporal budget constraint of the public sector. In particular, starting from any initial stock of public debt, the discounted value of current and future taxes must equal the discounted value of government spending plus the initial value of outstanding public debt.

In our case, a permanent fiscal expansion, as shown in Table 9.4, is treated in the following way. The basic experiment is a sustained rise in government spending (later we consider a cut in taxes). Government final expenditure rises permanently by 1% of potential GDP. Initially, the tax schedule remains unchanged, with taxes increasing only to the extent that the fiscal expansion raises output and thereby induces an endogenous tax increase (in other words, the cyclically adjusted budget deficit rises by one percent of GDP, the full amount of the spending increase). The actual fiscal deficit rises by about 0.85 of 1% of GDP following the 1% of GDP rise in government spending, because of the induced increase in taxes of 0.15% of GDP. The deficit

Table 9.4 Effect of Permanent U.S. Fiscal Expansion (1% GNP)

Year		1	2	3	4	5
U.S. Economy						
Output	%	0.37	0.23	0.37	0.34	0.27
Priv Consumption	% GNP	−0.22	−0.07	−0.04	−0.05	−0.10
Priv Investment	% GNP	0.00	−0.16	−0.07	−0.12	−0.15
Govt Consumption	% GNP	1.00	1.00	1.00	1.00	1.00
Exports	% GNP	−0.18	−0.16	−0.15	−0.15	−0.15
Imports	% GNP	0.16	0.13	0.14	0.13	0.12
Imports (quant.)	% GNP	0.23	0.37	0.36	0.34	0.33
Trade Balance	% GNP	−0.34	−0.29	−0.29	−0.28	−0.28
Labor Demand	%	0.52	0.32	0.57	0.54	0.48
Inflation	D	−0.04	−0.26	0.06	0.03	0.09
Int Rate (sh)	D	0.86	0.44	0.54	0.50	0.52
Int Rate (lg)	D	0.59	0.53	0.50	0.46	0.44
Tobin's q	%	−3.15	−2.61	−2.62	−2.68	−2.86
Real Exchange Rate						
$/ECU	%	−3.85	−3.15	−2.80	−2.54	−2.42
$/yen	%	−4.20	−3.58	−3.36	−3.27	−3.32
$/Can.	%	−2.66	−2.23	−2.02	−1.80	−1.67
ROECD Economies						
Output	%	0.07	−0.07	−0.20	−0.33	−0.44
Priv Consumption	% GNP	−0.16	−0.23	−0.30	−0.36	−0.42
Priv Investment	% GNP	−0.13	−0.23	−0.23	−0.26	−0.28
Govt Consumption	% GNP	0.00	0.00	0.00	0.00	0.00
Exports	% GNP	0.14	0.19	0.15	0.12	0.08
Imports	% GNP	−0.04	−0.06	−0.07	−0.08	−0.09
Imports (quant.)	% GNP	−0.23	−0.20	−0.19	−0.18	−0.17
Trade Balance	% GNP	0.27	0.24	0.22	0.19	0.18
Labor Demand	%	0.25	−0.04	−0.14	−0.25	−0.33
Inflation	D	0.29	0.14	0.15	0.13	0.13
Int Rate (sh)	D	0.41	0.33	0.40	0.42	0.48
Japanese Economy						
Output	%	0.03	−0.04	−0.10	−0.15	−0.20
Priv Consumption	% GNP	−0.20	−0.31	−0.38	−0.41	−0.46
Priv Investment	% GNP	−0.14	−0.27	−0.24	−0.25	−0.27
Govt Consumption	% GNP	0.00	0.00	0.00	0.00	0.00
Exports	% GNP	0.17	0.34	0.32	0.31	0.30
Imports	% GNP	−0.02	−0.04	−0.05	−0.05	−0.06
Imports (quant.)	% GNP	−0.20	−0.20	−0.20	−0.21	−0.22
Trade Balance	% GNP	0.39	0.38	0.37	0.36	0.36
Labor Demand	%	0.31	−0.00	−0.00	−0.00	−0.00
Inflation	D	0.28	0.18	0.12	0.07	0.08
Int Rate (sh)	D	0.51	0.41	0.51	0.53	0.58

is financed entirely by the issuance of public debt, with the money stock held constant.

If the tax schedule were not subsequently altered, the stock of public debt would eventually rise without bound, at an explosive geometric rate. To prevent this, we assume that labor income taxes are increased each year by enough to cover the increasing interest costs on the rising stock of public debt. Letting B_0 be the pre-expansion stock of debt, the tax rule is therefore:

$$T_t = T_0 + \gamma_L(W/P)\,L$$
$$+ \gamma_K[Q - (W/P)L - (P_N/P)N] + T_s. \tag{21}$$

Here, γ_L is the average tax rate on labor income, and γ_K is the average tax rate (corporate and personal) on capital income. T_s is a shift term in the tax schedule that rises along with the increase in interest payments on the public debt, $r_t B_t - r_0 B_0$. It is assumed that T_s falls entirely on labor income (this assumption is made for convenience only, and will be modified in a later version of the model). T_0 is an exogenous tax shift parameter.

In this way, the overall deficit remains fairly constant at about 1% of GNP following a rise in government spending (it fluctuates slightly due to fluctuations in real economic activity). The primary deficit (government spending net of interest payments, minus total taxes), given as $(G_t - T_t)$, eventually turns to a surplus, as is necessary to prevent an explosive growth in debt. Since the *level* of debt eventually stabilizes given the way that we have conducted this experiment, while the real economy grows at its potential rate of 4% in the long run, the debt to GNP ratio in fact eventually falls to zero after an initial increase following the rise in government spending.

Consider now the effects of a permanent rise in U.S. government spending shown in Table 9.4. All variables are expressed as deviations from an initial baseline. Output is recorded as a percentage deviation from the initial baseline, while consumption, investment, exports, imports, and the trade balance are all reported as deviations from the baseline in percent of potential GDP. Thus, in 1986, private consumption falls relative to the baseline by 0.22 of 1% of U.S. GDP. Labor input (total manhours in the economy), is measured as a percentage deviation from the baseline. Inflation and interest rates are measured as percentage point deviations from the baseline. Thus, inflation in the first year of the fiscal expansion falls by 0.04 percentage points, while short-term interest rates increase by 0.86 percentage points. The three bilateral *real* exchange rates are reported as percent changes from baseline values. Note that a negative value for the exchange rate indicates an *appreciation* of the dollar, since the exchange rates are measured as dollars per unit of foreign exchange.

How do the simulation results compare with our expectations from the simple Mundell-Fleming model of policy transmission under flexible exchange rates? According to the standard model, we should expect a bond-financed fiscal expansion, in the presence of perfect substitutability of home and foreign financial assets, to result in a rise in domestic income, an appreciation of the exchange rate, a rise in short- and long-term interest rates, and a worsening of the trade balance. Tobin's q might rise or fall. On the one hand higher interest rates will tend to depress q, while on the other hand, higher output (and greater profits) will tend to raise q, with the overall effect being ambiguous. We see from Table 9.4 that the model behaves in line with these expectations. Output rises, though with a multiplier considerably less than 1. The dollar appreciates in real terms by 3.85 % vis-à-vis the ECU, 4.20 percent vis-à-vis the yen, and 2.66 % vis-à-vis the Canadian dollar. Short-term interest rates rise by 0.86 percentage points, and long-term rates rise by 0.59 percentage points. The trade balance deteriorates by 0.34% of potential GDP in the first year, and that deterioration persists for the next several years. Note that Tobin's q in fact falls, by 3.15%. Investment nonetheless does not fall in the first year of the fiscal expansion because of the accelerator effect (which operates in addition to q), while investment is depressed relative to baseline in the later years.

Let us next turn to the international transmission effects. Importantly, the Mundell-Fleming model, when extended to allow for endogenous wages and prices, teaches that the international transmission effect of a fiscal expansion on foreign output is *ambiguous*. On the one hand, the U.S. expansion raises world interest rates, which tends to depress investment abroad. On the other hand, the expansion causes an appreciation of the dollar, which tends to raise net exports abroad. Europe, Japan, and Canada benefit from a trade boom, but suffer a drop in domestic investment. The net effect on output is therefore ambiguous, despite a tendency of many commentators to assume that foreign fiscal expansions are necessarily stimulative of the domestic economy.

As described in Bruno and Sachs (1985, Chapter 5) and in Oudiz and Sachs (1984), the transmission is more likely to be negative if

Table 9.5   Permanent Japanese Fiscal Expansion (1% GNP)

Year		1	2	3	4	5
U.S. Economy						
Output	%	0.01	−0.02	−0.13	−0.22	−0.29
Priv Consumption	% GNP	−0.02	−0.09	−0.16	−0.22	−0.27
Priv Investment	% GNP	−0.06	−0.08	−0.12	−0.14	−0.15
Govt Consumption	% GNP	0.00	0.00	0.00	0.00	0.00
Exports	% GNP	0.04	0.03	0.02	0.02	0.01
Imports	% GNP	−0.03	−0.03	−0.04	−0.05	−0.05
Imports (quant.)	% GNP	−0.05	−0.12	−0.13	−0.13	−0.13
Trade Balance	% GNP	0.07	0.06	0.06	0.06	0.06
Labor Demand	%	0.01	−0.01	−0.14	−0.22	−0.28
Inflation	D	0.05	0.15	0.12	0.11	0.09
Int Rate (sh)	D	0.01	0.11	0.13	0.19	0.23
Int Rate (lg)	D	0.21	0.21	0.21	0.20	0.19
Tobin's q	%	−0.76	−1.03	−1.22	−1.38	−1.53
Real Exchange Rate						
$/ECU	%	0.08	0.03	0.02	−0.02	−0.04
$/yen	%	3.93	3.56	3.43	3.22	3.03
$/Can.	%	0.07	0.06	0.07	0.05	0.03
ROECD Economies						
Output	%	0.04	−0.06	−0.13	−0.19	−0.26
Priv Consumption	% GNP	−0.07	−0.12	−0.17	−0.22	−0.26
Priv Investment	% GNP	−0.06	−0.10	−0.11	−0.13	−0.14
Govt Consumption	% GNP	0.00	0.00	0.00	0.00	0.00
Exports	% GNP	0.05	0.04	0.03	0.03	0.02
Imports	% GNP	−0.02	−0.03	−0.04	−0.04	−0.05
Imports (quant.)	% GNP	−0.12	−0.12	−0.12	−0.13	−0.13
Trade Balance	% GNP	0.07	0.07	0.07	0.07	0.07
Labor Demand	%	0.05	−0.06	−0.12	−0.18	−0.23
Inflation	D	0.13	0.09	0.09	0.09	0.08
Int Rate (sh)	D	0.08	0.09	0.15	0.19	0.23
Japanese Economy						
Output	%	0.38	0.02	−0.00	−0.02	−0.05
Priv Consumption	% GNP	0.08	0.03	−0.04	−0.08	−0.13
Priv Investment	% GNP	0.06	−0.11	−0.09	−0.09	−0.10
Govt Consumption	% GNP	1.00	1.00	1.00	1.00	1.00
Exports	% GNP	−0.35	−0.53	−0.52	−0.51	−0.49
Imports	% GNP	0.09	0.07	0.07	0.06	0.06
Imports (quant.)	% GNP	0.42	0.37	0.36	0.34	0.32
Trade Balance	% GNP	−0.63	−0.60	−0.59	−0.57	−0.55
Labor Demand	%	2.44	0.00	0.00	0.00	0.00
Inflation	D	0.33	0.09	0.09	0.06	0.05
Int Rate (sh)	D	0.38	0.20	0.28	0.32	0.35

foreign wages and prices rise rapidly in response to the depreciation of the foreign currencies vis-à-vis the dollar. If foreign nominal wages are perfectly fixed, as in the original Mundell-Fleming model, then the U.S. fiscal expansion must raise output abroad. The simple version of the Mundell-Fleming model is probably the source of the misconception that fiscal expansions are always transmitted positively.

As can be seen in Table 9.4, for Japan and the rest of the OECD, the transmission is positive in the first year but then negative in later years.[4] Note that net exports indeed expand everywhere abroad as expected, but that both foreign consumption and investment tend to get crowded out by the U.S. expansion. The negative effect on foreign consumption derives from the adverse effect of the fiscal expansion on the value of foreign Tobin's q. As q falls abroad, not only does investment decline, but so too does consumption, due to a negative wealth effect. Since Canada is so dependent on U.S. trade, the expansionary trade effects dominate the contractionary effects on C and I. In the ROECD and Japan, however, the negative effects on domestic spending dominate the export stimulus.

Table 9.5 records the dynamic adjustments to a permanent fiscal expansion in Japan. Note that by the assumption of wage setting in Japan, the rise in Japanese employment following the fiscal expansion can last just one period. By the second period, Japanese wages exactly enough to restore exact full employment in the labor market. As in the U.S., the Japanese fiscal expansion raises output, depresses Tobin's q at home and abroad, appreciates the yen vis-à-vis the other currencies, and worsens the Japanese trade balance. Indeed, the adverse effect on the trade balance is even larger than in the U.S. as a percent of own GDP, with the trade balance falling by 0.63% of GDP.

The Japanese fiscal expansion has a contractionary effect on the U.S. economy after the first year. Inflation rises, and output goes down. It is true that the trade balance improves, but by a minuscule $3–4 billion (in 1987 $ US) for each 1% of GNP Japanese fiscal expansion. This improvement in the trade balance is more than crowded out by a drop in investment and consumption. Many observers have stressed the need for a Japanese fiscal expansion to help stabilize growth in the United States. Table 9.5 should give them pause.

The result that a Japanese fiscal expansion appreciates the yen and causes a very large trade deficit may be surprising to Japanese observers whose assessments of policy were formed during the pre-1980

[4] Only for Canada, whose results are not shown in the tables, is there an uninterrupted positive transmission from the U.S.

Table 9.6 Permanent Japanese Fiscal Expansion (1% GNP) with no Capital Mobility in Japan

Year		1	2	3	4	5
U.S. Economy						
Output	%	−0.01	−0.00	−0.01	−0.03	−0.04
Priv Consumption	% GNP	−0.00	−0.01	−0.01	−0.03	−0.04
Priv Investment	% GNP	−0.01	−0.01	−0.01	−0.02	−0.02
Govt Consumption	% GNP	0.00	0.00	0.00	0.00	0.00
Exports	% GNP	0.00	−0.00	−0.00	−0.00	−0.00
Imports	% GNP	−0.00	−0.00	−0.00	−0.01	−0.01
Imports (quant.)	% GNP	−0.00	−0.01	−0.02	−0.02	−0.02
Trade Balance	% GNP	0.00	0.00	0.00	0.00	0.00
Labor Demand	%	−0.01	−0.00	−0.01	−0.03	−0.04
Inflation	D	−0.00	0.01	0.02	0.02	0.02
Int Rate (sh)	D	−0.01	−0.00	0.00	0.01	0.02
Int Rate (lg)	D	0.03	0.03	0.03	0.03	0.03
Tobin's q	%	−0.06	−0.09	−0.13	−0.17	−0.21
Real Exchange Rate						
$/ECU	%	−0.02	−0.02	−0.01	−0.01	−0.01
$/yen	%	−0.15	0.32	0.58	0.67	0.75
$/Can.	%	0.01	0.01	0.01	0.02	0.02
ROECD Economies						
Output	%	−0.01	−0.01	−0.03	−0.04	−0.06
Priv Consumption	% GNP	0.00	−0.01	−0.02	−0.04	−0.05
Priv Investment	% GNP	−0.01	−0.01	−0.02	−0.02	−0.03
Govt Consumption	% GNP	0.00	0.00	0.00	0.00	0.00
Exports	% GNP	−0.00	−0.00	−0.01	−0.01	−0.01
Imports	% GNP	−0.00	−0.00	−0.01	−0.01	−0.01
Imports (quant.)	% GNP	−0.00	−0.01	−0.02	−0.02	−0.03
Trade Balance	% GNP	0.00	0.00	0.00	−0.00	−0.00
Labor Demand	%	−0.01	−0.01	−0.03	−0.05	−0.06
Inflation	D	−0.00	0.02	0.03	0.02	0.02
Int Rate (sh)	D	−0.01	0.00	0.01	0.02	0.02
Japanese Economy						
Output	%	0.57	−0.03	−0.16	−0.24	−0.33
Priv Consumption	% GNP	−0.24	−0.44	−0.60	−0.66	−0.72
Priv Investment	% GNP	−0.14	−0.50	−0.41	−0.42	−0.43
Govt Consumption	% GNP	1.00	1.00	1.00	1.00	1.00
Exports	% GNP	0.01	−0.06	−0.10	−0.11	−0.13
Imports	% GNP	0.06	0.00	−0.00	−0.01	−0.02
Imports (quant.)	% GNP	0.05	0.03	0.05	0.05	0.05
Trade Balance	% GNP	−0.05	−0.06	−0.09	−0.10	−0.11
Labor Demand	%	0.78	−0.00	−0.00	−0.00	−0.00
Inflation	D	0.19	0.35	0.23	0.11	0.10
Int Rate (sh)	D	1.28	0.90	1.12	1.17	1.22

period of low international capital mobility and strong capital controls. As a counterfactual experiment it is useful to consider a permanent Japanese fiscal expansion under the assumption of complete *immobility* of capital, as an approximation to the Japanese policy environment before the liberalization of portfolio investment flows in 1980. The results are shown in Table 9.6. The importance of capital mobility to the earlier results is immediately evident. With capital immobility, the fiscal expansion crowds out a much larger share of investment and consumption, rather than net exports. Japanese short-term interest rates rise by 1.28 percentage points, much more that the rise of 0.38 percentage points observed in Table 9.5. The yen now *depreciates* after the first year, as is required to maintain current account balance in the face of a fiscal expansion. The results of Table 9.6 will be noted again when we consider the sources of the trade imbalances in the 1980s. The large Japanese trade surpluses of recent years would have been virtually impossible without the liberalization of Japanese capital outflows in the 1980s.

B. Monetary Policy in the U.S. and Japan

As with fiscal policy, the international transmission of monetary policy to foreign output has a theoretically ambiguous sign. A domestic monetary expansion almost surely raises home output temporarily, but it may raise or lower output abroad, depending on the strength of two competing channels. On the one hand, the monetary expansion tends to depreciate the domestic currency, thus shifting demand away from foreign goods and towards home goods. On the other hand, the monetary expansion lowers real interest rates and raises Tobin's q abroad as well as at home, and thereby spurs investment and consumption spending. In the simple Mundell-Fleming model with nominal wage rigidity, the (adverse) exchange rate effect dominates, so that foreign output falls when the home country expands the money supply. In more general models, with more flexible wages, the direction of effect can readily be reversed.

Monetary policy also has an ambiguous effect on the domestic trade and current account balances. Higher domestic money improves international competitiveness by depreciating the exchange rate. Assuming that the usual Marshall-Lerner conditions hold (as is true in MSG2), the exchange rate effect tends to raise output, national savings, and the trade and current account balances. On the other hand, the fall in real interest rates and the rise in Tobin's q tend to

Table 9.7   Permanent U.S. Monetary Expansion (1%)

Years		1	2	3	4	5
U.S. Economy						
Output	%	0.73	0.45	0.34	0.24	0.17
Priv Consumption	% GNP	0.41	0.33	0.23	0.17	0.12
Priv Investment	% GNP	0.31	0.03	0.04	0.02	0.01
Govt Consumption	% GNP	0.00	0.00	0.00	0.00	0.00
Exports	% GNP	0.06	0.05	0.04	0.03	0.02
Imports	% GNP	0.06	0.03	0.02	0.02	0.01
Imports (quant.)	% GNP	0.05	−0.05	−0.03	−0.02	−0.01
Trade Balance	% GNP	−0.00	0.02	0.01	0.01	0.01
Labor Demand	%	1.00	0.52	0.36	0.22	0.12
Inflation	D	0.28	0.20	0.15	0.10	0.08
Int Rate (sh)	D	−0.00	−0.25	−0.15	−0.12	−0.08
Int Rate (lg)	D	−0.04	−0.04	−0.03	−0.02	−0.01
Tobin's q	%	0.95	0.78	0.47	0.28	0.15
Real Exchange Rate						
$/ECU	%	1.01	0.89	0.57	0.37	0.24
$/yen	%	1.06	0.95	0.64	0.45	0.31
$/Can.	%	1.00	0.83	0.55	0.35	0.21
ROECD Economies						
Output	%	0.00	−0.00	0.03	0.04	0.03
Priv Consumption	% GNP	0.02	0.04	0.04	0.04	0.02
Priv Investment	% GNP	0.01	0.02	0.02	0.01	0.01
Govt Consumption	% GNP	0.00	0.00	0.00	0.00	0.00
Exports	% GNP	0.02	−0.03	−0.01	0.00	0.01
Imports	% GNP	0.00	0.01	0.01	0.01	0.00
Imports (quant.)	% GNP	0.04	0.04	0.03	0.02	0.01
Trade Balance	% GNP	−0.01	−0.03	−0.01	−0.00	0.01
Labor Demand	%	−0.04	−0.01	0.03	0.03	0.02
Inflation	D	−0.05	−0.04	0.00	0.01	0.02
Int Rate (sh)	D	−0.06	−0.10	−0.07	−0.05	−0.04
Japanese Economy						
Output	%	0.03	0.00	0.01	0.01	0.01
Priv Consumption	% GNP	0.02	0.05	0.04	0.03	0.03
Priv Investment	% GNP	0.01	0.02	0.01	0.01	0.00
Govt Consumption	% GNP	0.00	0.00	0.00	0.00	0.00
Exports	% GNP	0.04	−0.04	−0.02	−0.01	−0.00
Imports	% GNP	0.00	0.01	0.00	0.00	0.00
Imports (quant.)	% GNP	0.03	0.04	0.02	0.02	0.01
Trade Balance	% GNP	−0.02	−0.05	−0.03	−0.02	−0.01
Labor Demand	%	−0.04	0.00	0.00	0.00	0.00
Inflation	D	−0.04	−0.05	0.02	0.02	0.01
Int Rate (sh)	D	−0.07	−0.09	−0.07	−0.05	−0.03

spur investment demand, thereby worsening the current account and trade balances. Since both savings and investment tend to rise, the effect on the balance of savings minus investment (i.e., the external balance) is ambiguous theoretically.

Let us now examine these issues in the model. Table 9.7 reports the results of a permanent increase in the U.S. nominal money stock of 1%. The monetary expansion in the U.S. causes output to rise by 0.73% in the first year, and causes the nominal exchange rate vis-a-vis the yen to depreciate by 1.33% on impact while the real exchange rate depreciates by 1.06%. U.S. inflation increases by 0.28 percentage points in the first year, and 0.20 percentage points in the second. Note that there is far more inflation per unit of output increase than was found with the fiscal expansion in Table 9.4. A 2.7% of GDP increase in G raises U.S. GDP by 1.0% in the first year, and *lowers* inflation by 0.11 percentage points. A 1.37% monetary expansion also raises first period output by 1%, but *raises* inflation by 0.38%. The differential effects on inflation of monetary and fiscal policy of course result from their opposite effects on the dollar exchange rate: fiscal policy induces a currency appreciation, which reduces import prices, while monetary policy induces a depreciation, which raises import prices.

Remarkably, there is almost no effect of the dollar expansion on the U.S. trade balance, or on output and the trade balances in the other regions. *This is a striking and seemingly robust result of this model: monetary policy can be pursued by each region independently, without spillovers on the trade balances or level of economic activity in other regions.* The reason for the absence of spillovers has already been noted. Monetary expansion in the U.S. depreciates the dollar, which tends to reduce aggregate demand abroad, but it also lowers real interest rates abroad (and raises Tobin's q), thereby spurring aggregate demand abroad. Moreover, while the dollar depreciation spurs U.S. exports, the fall in U.S. real interest rates spurs U.S. spending and U.S. imports, keeping the trade balance almost exactly unchanged.

As can be seen from Table 9.8, the results on U.S. monetary policy also apply to a Japanese monetary expansion. Once again, the monetary expansion raises output, depreciates the currency, lowers real interest rates, and has little effect on the trade balance or the rest of the world. Because of the rapid labor market clearing in the case of Japan, the domestic effects of the monetary expansion on the real economy are dissipated by the second period. According to these results, the U.S. stands to benefit little or lose little from an easier monetary policy in Japan (or in the ROECD).

Table 9.8   Permanent Japanese Monetary Expansion (1%)

Year		1	2	3	4	5
U.S. Economy						
Output	%	0.00	−0.00	0.01	0.01	0.01
Priv Consumption	%GNP	−0.00	0.01	0.01	0.01	0.01
Priv Investment	%GNP	0.00	0.00	0.01	0.00	0.00
Govt Consumption	%GNP	0.00	0.00	0.00	0.00	0.00
Exports	%GNP	0.00	−0.00	0.00	0.00	0.00
Imports	%GNP	0.00	0.00	0.00	0.00	0.00
Imports (quant.)	%GNP	0.00	0.01	0.00	0.00	0.00
Trade Balance	%GNP	0.00	−0.00	−0.00	0.00	0.00
Labor Demand	%	0.00	−0.00	0.02	0.01	0.01
Inflation	D	−0.00	−0.00	0.00	0.00	0.00
Int Rate (sh)	D	0.00	−0.02	−0.00	−0.01	−0.00
Int Rate (lg)	D	−0.00	−0.00	−0.00	−0.00	−0.00
Tobin's q	%	0.02	0.04	0.02	0.02	0.01
Real Exchange Rate						
$/ECU	%	0.01	0.01	0.01	0.02	0.02
$/yen	%	−0.71	−0.45	−0.07	−0.05	−0.05
$/Can.	%	−0.01	−0.00	−0.00	0.01	0.01
ROECD Economies						
Output	%	−0.00	0.00	0.01	0.00	−0.00
Priv Consumption	%GNP	0.01	0.01	0.01	0.01	0.00
Priv Investment	%GNP	0.00	0.01	0.00	−0.00	−0.00
Govt Consumption	%GNP	0.00	0.00	0.00	0.00	0.00
Exports	%GNP	0.01	−0.00	0.00	−0.00	−0.00
Imports	%GNP	0.00	0.00	0.00	0.00	0.00
Imports (quant.)	%GNP	0.02	0.01	0.00	0.00	0.00
Trade Balance	%GNP	0.01	−0.00	−0.00	−0.00	−0.00
Labor Demand	%	−0.00	0.00	0.01	−0.00	−0.01
Inflation	D	−0.02	−0.01	0.01	0.01	0.00
Int Rate (sh)	D	−0.00	−0.01	−0.01	−0.01	−0.00
Japanese Economy						
Output	%	0.83	0.08	0.03	0.03	0.03
Priv Consumption	%GNP	0.44	0.14	0.02	0.02	0.01
Priv Investment	%GNP	0.33	−0.17	−0.00	0.00	0.00
Govt Consumption	%GNP	0.00	0.00	0.00	0.00	0.00
Exports	%GNP	0.07	0.07	0.01	0.01	0.01
Imports	%GNP	0.08	0.00	0.00	0.00	0.00
Imports (quant.)	%GNP	0.02	−0.04	−0.00	−0.00	−0.00
Trade Balance	%GNP	0.02	0.07	0.01	0.01	0.01
Labor Demand	%	1.16	0.00	0.00	0.00	0.00
Inflation	D	0.34	0.48	0.14	0.01	0.00
Int Rate (sh)	D	0.23	−0.24	−0.01	−0.01	−0.01

C. Policy Mix Effects and Miscellaneous Simulations

The simulation experiments in parts A and B of this section are often not the most useful way to consider fiscal or monetary policy changes. In present discussions in the United States, for example, it is widely recognized that cuts in the deficit will make it possible (and desirable) for the Fed to ease monetary policy. A plausible policy goal might be to tighten fiscal policy and ease monetary policies in tandem in order to hold employment constant. Table 9.9 and 9.10 report the results of such a policy mix in the United States and Japan.

Since the model is linear, the effects of a policy mix are simply the sum of the effects of the underlying component policies. However, modeling an employment-neutral fiscal expansion cum monetary contraction is not quite as easy as combining the results of Tables 9.4 and 9.7, or Tables 9.5 and 9.8. The reason is that with a permanent change in government spending, the whole path of monetary policy must be altered in order to stabilize employment. Of course, the maintained assumption is that from the beginning of the policy shift, the economic agents take into account the change in the entire path of the future money supply in making their production, spending, and portfolio decisions.

Comparing Table 9.4 with 9.9, and Table 9.5 with 9.10, we have the intuitive result that a fiscal expansion with monetary offset leads to a larger appreciation of the currency, a greater rise in long-term interest rates, and a greater crowding out of consumption and investment than does a fiscal expansion alone. The trade balance effect of the fiscal expansion is basically the same whether or not the monetary authorities lean against the expansion. This is a reflection of the earlier finding that monetary policy changes have little effect on the trade balance.

Before proceeding to the analysis of the policy shifts in the early 1980s, it is useful to study two more cases. First, we consider in Table 9.11 the implications of an exogenous decline in the availability of financing for the non-oil LDCs. When country risk considerations lead to a drying up of new capital for the LDCs, as occurred in 1982, the current account position of the LDCs must *per force* improve. Table 9.11 shows the effects of a sustained 10-year drop in new financing equal to 1% of U.S. potential GDP. For each OECD region, the effect of this shock is like a contraction of bond-financed fiscal spending in the rest of the world.

Thus, the effect on the U.S. of the cut in financiug for the LDCs is akin to a reduction in government spending in Japan (the effects of

Table 9.9 Permanent U.S. Fiscal Expansion (1% GNP) with Money Stabilizing Employment

Year		1	2	3	4	5
U.S. Economy						
Output	%	0.00	−0.04	−0.08	−0.13	−0.17
Priv Consumption	% GNP	−0.41	−0.22	−0.28	−0.34	−0.40
Priv Investment	% GNP	−0.16	−0.21	−0.22	−0.23	−0.24
Govt Consumption	% GNP	1.00	1.00	1.00	1.00	1.00
Exports	% GNP	−0.22	−0.19	−0.19	−0.19	−0.19
Imports	% GNP	0.13	0.12	0.11	0.10	0.09
Imports (quant.)	% GNP	0.21	0.41	0.39	0.37	0.34
Trade Balance	% GNP	−0.35	−0.31	−0.30	−0.29	−0.28
Labor Demand	%	0.01	0.00	0.00	0.00	0.00
Inflation	D	−0.18	−0.40	−0.31	−0.22	−0.14
Int Rate (sh)	D	0.73	0.22	0.36	0.48	0.59
Int Rate (lg)	D	0.70	0.65	0.63	0.61	0.58
Tobin's q	%	−3.80	−3.32	−3.42	−3.51	−3.60
Real Exchange Rate						
$/ECU	%	−4.45	−3.79	−3.47	−3.20	−2.96
$/yen	%	−4.80	−4.23	−4.06	−3.99	−3.93
$/Can.	%	−3.24	−2.82	−2.68	−2.46	−2.20
ROECD Economies						
Output	%	0.07	−0.07	−0.22	−0.37	−0.49
Priv Consumption	% GNP	−0.17	−0.26	−0.34	−0.42	−0.48
Priv Investment	% GNP	−0.14	−0.25	−0.26	−0.28	−0.30
Govt Consumption	% GNP	0.00	0.00	0.00	0.00	0.00
Exports	% GNP	0.13	0.21	0.16	0.12	0.09
Imports	% GNP	−0.04	−0.06	−0.07	−0.09	−0.09
Imports (quant.)	% GNP	−0.25	−0.23	−0.22	−0.21	−0.20
Trade Balance	% GNP	0.29	0.27	0.23	0.21	0.18
Labor Demand	%	0.27	−0.03	−0.16	−0.29	−0.38
Inflation	D	0.32	0.19	0.17	0.15	0.13
Int Rate (sh)	D	0.45	0.41	0.48	0.53	0.57
Japanese Economy						
Output	%	0.02	−0.04	−0.11	−0.16	−0.21
Priv Consumption	% GNP	−0.21	−0.35	−0.42	−0.46	−0.49
Priv Investment	% GNP	−0.15	−0.29	−0.25	−0.26	−0.27
Govt Consumption	% GNP	0.00	0.00	0.00	0.00	0.00
Exports	% GNP	0.15	0.38	0.34	0.33	0.31
Imports	% GNP	−0.02	−0.05	−0.05	−0.06	−0.06
Imports (quant.)	% GNP	−0.22	−0.22	−0.22	−0.23	−0.24
Trade Balance	% GNP	0.41	0.42	0.39	0.38	0.37
Labor Demand	%	0.34	−0.00	−0.00	−0.00	−0.00
Inflation	D	0.30	0.23	0.12	0.08	0.07
Int Rate (sh)	D	0.56	0.50	0.60	0.63	0.66

Table 9.10   Permanent Japanese Fiscal Expansion (1% GNP) with Money Stabilizing Employment

		1986	1987	1988	1989	1990
U.S. Economy						
Output	%	0.01	−0.02	−0.14	−0.22	−0.29
Priv Consumption	% GNP	−0.02	−0.10	−0.16	−0.22	−0.28
Priv Investment	% GNP	−0.06	−0.08	−0.13	−0.14	−0.15
Govt Consumption	% GNP	0.00	0.00	0.00	0.00	0.00
Exports	% GNP	0.04	0.03	0.02	0.02	0.01
Imports	% GNP	−0.03	−0.03	−0.04	−0.05	−0.05
Imports (quant.)	% GNP	−0.05	−0.12	−0.13	−0.13	−0.13
Trade Balance	% GNP	0.07	0.06	0.06	0.06	0.06
Labor Demand	%	0.01	−0.01	−0.14	−0.22	−0.28
Inflation	D	0.05	0.12	0.12	0.11	0.09
Int Rate (sh)	D	0.01	0.11	0.13	0.19	0.23
Int Rate (lg)	D	0.21	0.21	0.21	0.20	0.19
Tobin's q	%	−0.77	−1.04	−1.22	−1.40	−1.53
Real Exchange Rate						
$/ECU	%	0.08	0.03	0.02	−0.02	−0.04
$/yen	%	4.08	3.65	3.44	3.23	3.04
$/Can.	%	0.07	0.06	0.07	0.05	0.03
ROECD Economies						
Output	%	0.04	−0.06	−0.13	−0.20	−0.26
Priv Consumption	% GNP	−0.07	−0.12	−0.17	−0.22	−0.26
Priv Investment	% GNP	−0.06	−0.10	−0.11	−0.13	−0.14
Govt Consumption	% GNP	0.00	0.00	0.00	0.00	0.00
Exports	% GNP	0.05	0.04	0.03	0.03	0.02
Imports	% GNP	−0.02	−0.03	−0.04	−0.04	−0.05
Imports (quant.)	% GNP	−0.12	−0.12	−0.13	−0.13	−0.13
Trade Balance	% GNP	0.07	0.07	0.07	0.07	0.07
Labor Demand	%	0.05	−0.06	−0.12	−0.18	−0.13
Inflation	D	0.13	0.10	0.09	0.09	0.08
Int Rate (sh)	D	0.08	0.10	0.15	0.19	0.23
Japanese Economy						
Output	%	0.21	0.01	−0.01	−0.03	−0.05
Priv Consumption	% GNP	−0.00	0.01	−0.04	−0.09	−0.13
Priv Investment	% GNP	−0.01	−0.08	−0.08	−0.09	−0.10
Govt Consumption	% GNP	1.00	1.00	1.00	1.00	1.00
Exports	% GNP	−0.36	−0.54	−0.53	−0.51	−0.49
Imports	% GNP	0.08	0.07	0.07	0.06	0.06
Imports (quant.)	% GNP	0.42	0.38	0.36	0.34	0.32
Trade Balance	% GNP	−0.63	−0.62	−0.59	−0.57	−0.55
Labor Demand	%	0.01	0.00	0.00	0.00	0.00
Inflation	D	−0.40	−0.03	−0.03	−0.02	−0.02
Int Rate (sh)	D	0.32	0.16	0.20	0.24	0.28

Table 9.11 Cut in LDC's Current Account Financing (1% U.S. GNP) lasting 10 years

Year		1	2	3	4	5
U.S. Economy						
Output	%	−0.14	−0.00	0.16	0.32	0.48
Priv Consumption	% GNP	0.06	0.16	0.27	0.38	0.50
Priv Investment	% GNP	0.15	0.22	0.27	0.30	0.33
Govt Consumption	% GNP	0.00	0.00	0.00	0.00	0.00
Exports	% GNP	−0.23	−0.20	−0.19	−0.18	−0.16
Imports	% GNP	0.07	0.08	0.10	0.11	0.13
Imports (quant.)	% GNP	0.12	0.17	0.18	0.19	0.19
Trade Balance	% GNP	−0.30	−0.28	−0.29	0.29	−0.28
Labor Demand	%	−0.15	−0.01	0.14	0.28	0.41
Inflation	D	−0.15	−0.22	−0.22	0.23	−0.22
Int Rate (sh)	D	−0.25	−0.32	−0.43	0.55	−0.68
Int Rate (lg)	D	−0.50	−0.48	−0.46	0.43	−0.40
Tobin's q	%	2.33	2.70	3.07	3.39	3.65
Real Exchange Rate						
$/ECU	%	−1.34	−1.15	−1.09	−1.04	−1.01
$/yen	%	−0.84	−0.68	−0.54	−0.31	−0.08
$/Can.	%	−0.18	−0.19	−0.24	−0.23	−0.22
ROECD Economies						
Output	%	−0.22	−0.06	0.03	0.17	0.33
Priv Consumption	% GNP	0.10	0.12	0.20	0.29	0.39
Priv Investment	% GNP	0.13	0.21	0.24	0.29	0.33
Govt Consumption	% GNP	0.00	0.00	0.00	0.00	0.00
Exports	% GNP	−0.45	−0.38	−0.38	−0.37	−0.35
Imports	% GNP	0.02	0.03	0.04	0.06	0.08
Imports (quant.)	% GNP	−0.00	0.01	0.02	0.03	0.04
Trade Balance	% GNP	−0.43	−0.42	−0.43	−0.43	−0.42
Labor Demand	%	−0.22	−0.11	−0.05	0.07	0.21
Inflation	D	−0.05	−0.10	−0.18	−0.21	−0.24
Int Rate (sh)	D	−0.37	−0.32	−0.46	−0.60	−0.74
Japanese Economy						
Output	%	−0.25	0.04	0.11	0.17	0.22
Priv Consumption	% GNP	0.24	0.33	0.33	0.39	0.45
Priv Investment	% GNP	0.15	0.28	0.27	0.29	0.31
Govt Consumption	% GNP	0.00	0.00	0.00	0.00	0.00
Exports	% GNP	−0.46	−0.38	−0.37	−0.38	−0.37
Imports	% GNP	0.02	0.04	0.05	0.06	0.06
Imports (quant.)	% GNP	0.08	0.11	0.12	0.14	0.16
Trade Balance	% GNP	−0.43	−0.42	−0.42	−0.43	−0.44
Labor Demand	%	−0.28	0.00	0.00	0.00	0.00
Inflation	D	−0.15	−0.21	−0.18	−0.15	−0.15
Int Rate (sh)	D	−0.46	−0.40	−0.57	−0.70	−0.83

a fiscal *reduction* in Japan can be read from Table 9.5, simply by reversing the signs of all variables). U.S. interest rates go down, the trade balance deteriorates, and U.S. investment and consumption are "crowded in," while net exports are "crowded out." Indeed the cutoff in lending to the LDCs is even more contractionary to the U.S. than an equal-sized reduction in Japanese government spending, since the LDCs have a higher marginal propensity to spend on U.S. goods than does the Japanese government.

One argument sometimes made concerning the rise of the dollar in the early 1980s is that the cutoff in finance to the LDCs induced a net capital inflow into the U.S. that caused a large dollar appreciation. This argument is fallacious, as shown by the results of the simulation. The cutoff in lending induced a reversal of capital outflows from the OECD as a whole to the LDCs, but there is no reason why such a cutoff should be of first-order importance for exchange rates within the OECD. Nor is it important that most of the LDC lending was coming from U.S. banks, if in fact the OECD capital markets are indeed highly integrated. As we see from the Tables, a cutoff of lending of 1 % of U.S. GDP induces a dollar appreciation of a mere 1 to 2%. The cutoff that actually occurred was on the order of 1.4% of U.S. GDP, so that the resulting dollar appreciation from this effect was probably under 3%.

IV. A Simulation Analysis of the Trade and Financial Imbalances of the 1980s

We are now ready to ask whether the model can help us to understand the sources of the trade and international financial patterns noted at the beginning of the paper: the large U.S. trade deficits and Japanese trade surpluses, the sharp appreciation of the dollar during 1981–85, the rise in real interest rates, and the subsequent sharp fall in the dollar beginning in 1985 and accelerating in 1986. We divide the analysis into two stages, 1980–85, and 1986 onward (with forecasts until 1992). This division marks off two policy phases in both the U.S. and Japan. During the first period, the U.S. fiscal deficit widened significantly, while in Japan there was a steady reduction in the structural deficit. In the second period, the U.S. deficit is projected to decline, while the Japanese deficit is expected to stabilize, or even increase slightly.

In approaching the simulation exercise, we are more ambitious in some ways and less ambitious in others than other simulation studies that have been made. On the one hand, we go far beyond the common partial equilibrium approach of tracking trade balance developments for exogenously given paths of growth, exchange rates, etc. (For approaches along these lines, see for example Richardson [1987] of the OECD, and the Brookings Project summarized by Bryant and Holtham [1987].) We seek to explain the movements in growth, exchange rates, and so on, according to more fundamental shifts in policies.

On the less ambitious side, we do not propose at this point to track the year-to-year historical experience during 1981 to 1985, but rather to examine the overall *changes* between 1980 and 1985. Our reason for this more modest approach relates in part to the nature of rational expectations modeling. In order to understand year-to-year changes, it is necessary to model the expectations of future policies as of each year. This is a worthwhile exercise, but is beyond the scope of the present paper. Also, in modeling year-to-year changes, the timing of particular policy actions also becomes extremely important: when does a tax cut go into effect?; what is "old" versus "new" capital investment from the point of a corporate tax change?; what are the short-run lags on monetary policy? A third reason for avoiding a year-to-year analysis is the added difficulty of modeling the recession of 1981–82, which came in the wake of the anti-inflation policies of the OECD monetary authorities. By comparing 1980 and 1985, we can abstract from cyclical movements in economic activity. It is a separate, and interesting, question as to whether the model could in fact track the recession period, but one that we leave for a later date.

A. The Period 1980–85

Our strategy is to consider the shifts in the trade balance, exchange rates, etc., as resulting from five distinct factors, and to see whether the combined effect of these changes can explain the observed phenomena. The five shifts are as follows (see Table 9.2):

— A rise in the U.S. structural deficit of approximately 4.4% of U.S. GNP;

— A reduction in the Japanese structural budget deficit of approximately 3.4% of GNP;

— An increase in the structural deficit in Canada of approximately 2.2% of GNP, and an increase in the structural budget surplus in the ROECD of approximately 0.5% of GNP;

Table 9.12 1981–1985 Global Scenario with Money Stabilizing Employment

		1981	1982	1983	1984	1985
U.S. Economy						
Output	%	−0.00	0.07	0.08	0.05	0.01
Priv Consumption	% GNP	1.50	2.89	2.38	3.66	3.59
Priv Investment	% GNP	0.27	0.08	−0.04	−0.14	−0.17
Govt Consumption	% GNP	0.00	0.00	0.00	0.00	0.00
Exports	% GNP	−0.91	−0.96	−1.08	−1.15	−1.13
Imports	% GNP	0.55	0.61	0.69	0.73	0.71
Imports (quant.)	% GNP	0.86	1.93	2.19	2.33	2.27
Trade Balance	% GNP	−1.46	−1.57	−1.77	−1.88	−1.84
Labor Demand	%	0.05	0.05	0.05	0.04	0.03
Inflation	D	−0.75	−2.19	−2.52	−2.68	−2.56
Int Rate (sh)	D	−2.45	−3.98	−3.09	−1.50	−1.50
Int Rate (lg)	D	−0.83	−0.64	−0.37	−0.17	−0.09
Tobin's q	%	−0.49	−1.10	−3.16	−4.49	−4.49
Real Exchange Rate						
$/ECU	%	−14.52	−15.65	−17.65	−18.63	−18.11
$/yen	%	−20.98	−23.74	−27.40	−29.63	−28.96
$/Can.	%	−5.94	−5.75	−6.44	−6.60	−6.40
ROECD Economies						
Output	%	−0.42	−0.11	−0.17	−0.22	−0.26
Priv Consumption	% GNP	−0.45	−0.69	−0.85	−0.94	−0.89
Priv Investment	% GNP	−0.24	−0.24	−0.25	−0.24	−0.23
Govt Consumption	% GNP	0.00	0.00	0.00	0.00	0.00
Exports	% GNP	−0.32	0.18	0.22	0.23	0.16
Imports	% GNP	−0.10	−0.12	−0.15	−0.16	−0.15
Imports (quant.)	% GNP	−0.59	−0.63	−0.70	−0.73	−0.70
Trade Balance	% GNP	0.14	0.30	0.37	0.39	0.31
Labor Demand	%	−0.01	−0.01	−0.01	−0.00	−0.00
Inflation	D	0.56	0.73	0.96	1.10	1.13
Int Rate (sh)	D	0.64	1.30	1.63	1.71	1.63
Japanese Economy						
Output	%	−1.09	−0.16	−0.28	−0.37	−0.43
Priv Consumption	% GNP	−1.58	−2.15	−2.47	−2.34	−2.30
Priv Investment	% GNP	−0.62	−0.49	−0.44	−0.36	−0.33
Govt Consumption	% GNP	−0.50	−1.00	−1.50	−2.20	−2.20
Exports	% GNP	0.38	2.00	2.38	2.61	2.52
Imports	% GNP	−0.20	−0.27	−0.33	−0.36	−0.36
Imports (quant.)	% GNP	−1.22	−1.48	−1.75	−1.92	−1.89
Trade Balance	% GNP	1.62	2.27	2.71	2.97	2.88
Labor Demand	%	−0.07	−0.00	−0.00	−0.00	−0.00
Inflation	D	1.13	0.01	0.03	0.05	0.04
Int Rate (sh)	D	1.47	2.01	1.72	0.48	0.44

Table 9.13 Actual and Predicted Changes in Trade Balances and Real
Exchange Rates (1985 compared with average of 1978–1980)

	Actual	Predicted
Trade Balance Change (percent of GDP)		
U.S.	1.9	1.8
Japan	3.2	2.8
Rest of OECD	1.0	0.3
Real Exchange Rate Change of the U.S. relative to:		
Japan	24	28
Rest of OECD	41	18

Source: "Actual" from Tables 9.1, 9.3; "Predicted" from 1985 data in
Table 9.12.

— An exogenous reduction in the net flow of new borrowing (i.e.,
the current account deficit) of the LDCs in the magnitude of 1.4%
of U.S. GNP;[5]

— An assumed offset of monetary policy in Canada, Japan, the
United States and the rest of the OECD to maintain an unchanged
level of employment.

The combined effect of these changes (as a deviation from a baseline) is shown in Table 9.12, where we see that the effect of the package
is that the dollar appreciates sharply and the U.S. trade balance worsens
significantly as a percentage of GNP. In Table 9.13, we compare the
predictions on the trade balance, the dollar exchange rate, and the short-
term real interest rate with the actual effects observed in comparing the
1978–80 period with the year 1985. As noted earlier, the model does quite
well in explaining the shifts in the U.S. and Japanese trade balances
and the yen-dollar exchange rate. It does much more poorly with the
ROECD. In Table 9.14, we apportion the overall predicted shift in the
U.S. trade balance and real bilateral exchange rates to the various
underlying disturbances. Not surprisingly, the largest factor in explaining the U.S. and Japanese trade balance changes is the fiscal policy
in own country. Cross-country effects play a small role for the U.S.,
but a fairly important role for Japan. In both cases, the cutoff in lending
to LDCs accounts for about 20% of the trade balance shift in the
evolution of each country's trade imbalances.

[5] The current account balance of the non-oil LDCs was as follows (as percent of
U.S. GNP in parentheses): 1978, $33.2b (1.5); 1979, $49.7b (2.0); 1980, 74.4b
(2.8); and 1985 $28.7b (0.7). The average deficit during 1978–80 was 2.1 percent of
U.S. GNP, so that the shift from 1978–80 to 1985 was on the order of 1.4 percent
of U.S. GNP.

Table 9.14 Decomposition of Changes in Trade and Exchange Rates

| | Total Predicted Effect | Fiscal Policies in | | | Cutoff in LDC Lending | Offsetting Monetary Policy |
		U	J	$R+C$		
Effect on:						
U.S. Trade Balance	−1.84	−1.01	−0.23	−0.03	−0.40	−0.17
Japan Trade Balance	2.88	1.36	1.91	−0.06	−0.61	0.28
U.S.-Japan Real Exchange Rate	28.9	11.8	10.6	−0.03	−0.11	6.64

There are several puzzles not explained by the simulation model. Most importantly, while the model tracks the appreciation of the dollar vis-à-vis the yen during the period, it *fails* to track the larger appreciation of the dollar vis-à-vis the ROECD. We fear that part of the problem here is one of aggregation. The ROECD is a varied mix of countries with a quite varied mix of policies during this period. At the center of the ROECD we have West Germany, which pursued highly contractionary fiscal policies (see Table 9.2), and thus should be expected to have a large real depreciation vis-à-vis the dollar, as in fact occurred. On the other hand, most of the little OECD countries included in ROECD pursued mildly expansionary fiscal policies, and thus should not have experienced as large a real depreciation vis-à-vis the dollar as in fact occurred. The dollar rate vis-à-vis the overall ROECD, however, seems to behave in line with what would be predicted from *German* fiscal policy, rather than overall ROECD policy. This might be explained by the fact that many non-German ROECD countries peg their currencies to the Deutsche mark, and by the fact that much of the non-German ROECD has relatively closed capital markets (in which case a fiscal expansion leads to a depreciation).

One of the ironies in the 1980–85 period is that Japan liberalized its capital account in 1980 just as it started to tighten fiscal policy, and just as the United States started to run large budget deficits. Without the capital market liberalization, Japan would not have generated such enormous trade surpluses in response to the fiscal shifts in the United States and Japan, because the yen would have appreciated in response to the trade surpluses. Presumably, the political pressures now being felt by Japan would thereby have been largely avoided.

To examine this conclusion, the package of fiscal and financial

Table 9.15 1981–1985 Global Scenario with Stabilizing Money and No Capital Mobility in Japan

		1981	1982	1983	1984	1985
U.S. Economy						
Output	%	0.00	0.04	0.01	−0.06	−0.14
Priv Consumption	% GNP	1.49	2.64	3.05	3.28	3.19
Priv Investment	% GNP	0.15	−0.10	−0.24	−0.35	−0.39
Govt Consumption	% GNP	0.00	0.00	0.00	0.00	0.00
Exports	% GNP	−0.85	−0.88	0.98	−1.04	−1.02
Imports	% GNP	0.50	0.53	0.59	0.62	0.61
Imports (quant.)	% GNP	0.78	1.62	1.82	1.95	1.91
Trade Balance	% GNP	−1.35	−1.41	−1.57	−1.66	−1.63
Labor Demand	%	0.05	0.06	0.06	0.05	0.04
Inflation	D	−0.68	−1.78	−2.00	−2.08	−1.93
Int Rate (sh)	D	−2.50	−3.37	−2.22	−0.48	−0.43
Int Rate (lg)	D	0.17	0.35	0.58	0.72	0.75
Tobin's q	%	−2.07	−3.42	−5.76	−7.23	−7.29
Real Exchange Rate						
$/ECU	%	−14.13	−15.29	−17.17	−18.15	−17.61
$/yen	%	−15.27	−15.06	−17.47	−19.55	−19.60
$/Can.	%	−5.75	−5.64	−6.33	−6.49	−6.30
ROECD Economies						
Output	%	−0.41	−0.15	−0.24	−0.34	−0.42
Priv Consumption	% GNP	−0.52	−0.91	−1.16	−1.31	−1.27
Priv Investment	% GNP	−0.36	−0.40	−0.44	−0.44	−0.43
Govt Consumption	% GNP	0.00	0.00	0.00	0.00	0.00
Exports	% GNP	−0.27	0.27	0.35	0.37	0.29
Imports	% GNP	−0.13	−0.18	−0.21	−0.23	−0.23
Imports (quant.)	% GNP	−0.74	−0.89	−1.01	−1.04	−0.99
Trade Balance	% GNP	0.21	0.45	0.56	0.60	0.52
Labor Demand	%	−0.01	−0.01	−0.01	−0.01	−0.01
Inflation	D	0.70	1.13	1.50	1.73	1.79
Int Rate (sh)	D	0.74	1.87	2.50	2.74	2.71
Japanese Economy						
Output	%	−0.78	0.06	0.18	0.34	0.52
Priv Consumption	% GNP	−1.01	−0.79	−0.66	−0.27	−0.18
Priv Investment	% GNP	0.19	0.53	0.69	0.82	0.87
Govt Consumption	% GNP	−0.50	−1.00	−1.50	−2.20	−2.20
Exports	% GNP	−0.11	0.74	0.95	1.16	1.18
Imports	% GNP	−0.09	−0.08	−0.09	−0.10	−0.09
Imports (quant.)	% GNP	−0.65	−0.57	−0.70	−0.83	−0.85
Trade Balance	% GNP	0.75	0.82	1.04	1.26	1.26
Labor Demand	%	−0.04	−0.00	−0.00	−0.00	0.00
Inflation	D	0.59	0.00	0.00	−0.00	−0.00
Int Rate (sh)	D	2.44	1.02	−0.36	−2.17	−2.18

changes just discussed can be simulated under the counterfactual assumption of *zero* international capital mobility in Japan, as is done in Table 9.15. With zero capital mobility and freely floating exchange rates in Japan, the Japanese economy must be in current account equilibrium at all times. We see from Table 9.15 that if Japan had not liberalized its capital account, the result would have been a smaller yen depreciation in the period, and a much smaller trade surplus. The surplus would have risen by 1.26 % of GDP, instead of the 2.88% reported in Table 9.12 and the 3.2% that actually occurred.

Note, also, the effects on the U.S. Without the benefit of Japanese savings, the U.S. interest rates (both short and long term) would naturally have been higher, and investment would have been reduced, but the effect found by the simulation is smaller than is often supposed. The reason is that Japan provides only a modest share of OECD savings, despite the fact that Japan's current account surplus is by far the largest in the OECD. Under the maintained assumption of this model that *all* OECD savings are potentially available for international capital flows, the contribution from Japan is simply not overwhelming. To the extent that the bilateral trade surplus of Japan is reduced, the trade surpluses of Canada and the ROECD are increased. As the financial counterpart, of course, the U.S. gets more of its net international investment flows from the other two areas. It is possible that this simulation result understates the consequences of eliminating Japan's capital outflow, if on average Japan allows more international capital outflow than do the other countries in the OECD. To the extent that much of the ROECD is cut off from world capital markets (as is true of France, Italy, and much of Scandinavia), then Japanese savings would represent a larger fraction of the pool of

Table 9.16   U.S. Savings and Investment Rates. 1980–1985 (percent of GNP)

	Gross Private Savings	Gross Private Investment	Total Government Deficit	Current Account
1980	17.5	16.0	−1.3	0.5
1981	18.0	16.9	−1.0	0.3
1982	18.3	14.7	−3.6	0.0
1983	17.4	14.7	−3.8	−1.0
1984	17.9	17.6	−2.7	−2.4
1985	17.2	16.5	−3.4	−2.9
Change:				
1985–1980	−0.3	0.5	−2.1	−2.4

Source: *Economic Report of the President*, January 1987, Table B-27.

total savings available to finance U.S. current account deficits, even though Japanese savings represent a modest fraction of total OECD savings.

There is other direct evidence in support of the proposition that fiscal policies, rather than an investment boom, lie behind the U.S. trade deficits in recent years. Table 9.16 shows the evolution of the private savings and investment rates in the United States during 1980–85. As predicted by the model, the rise in the U.S. current account deficit is accounted for by the deterioration in the budget deficit, rather than a rise in the investment rate. There is no evidence in the data for the proposition that households in the U.S. have raised their private savings in anticipation of higher future taxes resulting from the large current U.S. budget deficits.[6]

B. The Period 1986–1992

Since 1985, there have been some significant changes in the economic outlook as well as large swings in exchange rates. Most importantly, there are increased prospects for a significant improvement in the U.S. fiscal situation. Those prospects are reflected in the legislative commitment in the Gramm-Rudman-Hollings (hereafter, GRH) law to a balanced budget by 1992. The questions in this section are twofold. First, can the shift in the fiscal outlook account for the dramatic decline in the dollar since mid-1985? Second, would implementation of the GRH targets be sufficient to restore trade balance in the United States?

The real depreciation of the dollar between 1985 and 1986 was shown in Table 9.3. For the cases of the European currencies, the dollar decline began in early 1985, and has continued apace since then. For the yen, most of the dollar decline has occurred since the Plaza meeting of finance ministers of the G-5 in September 1985. There are at least three interpretations of the recent exchange rate movements. The first is that the decline has come from a shift in macroeconomic policies, both current and anticipated. The second is that decline reflected a bursting of a speculative bubble that had been building since 1981. The third is that private portfolio holders have begun to demand

---

[6] Recently Robert Barro has suggested that the decline in U.S. national savings may be overstated since household purchases of consumer durables, which have risen as a share of GNP in the U.S., should be classified as investment spending rather than consumption spending. Even when that correction is made, however, the decline in the overall U.S. national savings rate and slight change in the U.S. investment rate is still found in the data. See Poterba and Summers (1986) for evidence on this point.

a larger risk premium for holding dollar assets, following a saturation of private portfolios with dollar claims in recent years. If the third interpretation is correct, the shift in required risk premium must have been unanticipated to explain the fact that the dollar first rose sharply then fell.

Unfortunately, the simplest interpretation, of a pure policy shift, is hard to reconcile with the magnitude of the recent dollar decline. In Table 9.17, we simulate the effects of a 1986 shift in public expectations about the future course of U.S. budget deficits. Specifically, we assume that the time path of deficit reductions called for in GRH is taken as the public's new expectation of U.S. fiscal policies.[7] It is further assumed that the Federal Reserve Board will accommodate the fiscal contraction with easier monetary policy, as necessary, in order to stabilize employment.

The results are interesting for several reasons. First, the dollar depreciates, as expected, but only by about 10% in real terms on impact. The long-term interest rate falls by more than 2 percentage points, though the short-term nominal interest rate rises. Inflation increases because of the dollar depreciation. The U.S. is forced to give up some of the low-inflation dividend that it enjoyed during the period of dollar appreciation though the inflation effect is modest.

The problem with the second interpretation of the exchange rate, i.e., a bursting of a speculative bubble, is that the dollar appreciation during 1981–85 seems to be well explained, at least vis-à-vis the yen, by the fiscal policy shifts studied earlier. There was some evidence of a speculative excess in the appreciation of the dollar vis-à-vis the ROECD currencies, but not against the yen.

The third interpretation, of a shifting risk premium, is the most problematic, and is difficult either to refute or accept. A portfolio balance effect is surely plausible, but should have been enough to limit the appreciation of the dollar in the first place, since portfolio holders could have foreseen the enormous buildup of U.S. dollar liabilities that would result from the projected U.S. current account deficits. It is possible that part of the story of the exchange rate is that the liberalization of the Japanese capital market led to a one-time stock shift in demand for dollars during 1981–86, which is now over because Japanese portfolio holders are saturated with U.S. assets. However, this story does not explain very well the movements of the dollar-DM

---

[7] Actually, since the fiscal year 1986 target was already missed by 1986, we look at a modified GRH schedule, which catches up with the legislative schedule by fiscal year 1988.

Table 9.17 1986–1990 Scenario: Gramm-Rudman and Oil Price Fall with Money Stabilizing Employment

		1986	1987	1988	1989	1990
U.S. Economy						
Output	%	−0.71	−0.62	−0.49	−0.33	−0.12
Priv Consumption	% GNP	−1.27	−1.56	−1.52	−1.47	−1.31
Priv Investment	% GNP	0.36	0.50	0.74	0.95	1.13
Govt Consumption	% GNP	0.00	−0.65	−1.35	−1.80	−2.25
Exports	% GNP	0.50	0.67	0.87	1.02	1.15
Imports	% GNP	0.15	0.07	−0.03	−0.08	−0.12
Imports (quant.)	% GNP	0.30	−0.42	−0.76	−0.98	−1.16
Trade Balance	% GNP	0.35	0.60	0.90	1.10	1.27
Labor Demand	%	−0.05	−0.05	−0.05	−0.05	−0.05
Inflation	D	−0.37	0.43	0.70	0.77	0.74
Int Rate (sh)	D	3.47	2.95	1.25	0.35	−1.03
Int Rate (lg)	D	−2.06	−2.31	−2.52	−2.60	−2.62
Tobin's q	%	3.71	7.65	11.56	14.36	16.84
Real Exchange Rate						
$/ECU	%	9.05	11.76	14.87	16.92	18.62
$/yen	%	8.47	11.12	14.34	16.51	18.38
$/Can.	%	4.58	6.38	8.54	9.95	11.20
ROECD Economies						
Output	%	−0.11	−0.00	0.26	0.53	0.81
Priv Consumption	% GNP	0.38	1.11	1.53	1.85	2.13
Priv Investment	% GNP	1.21	1.15	1.27	1.26	1.44
Govt Consumption	% GNP	0.00	0.00	0.00	0.00	0.00
Exports	% GNP	0.11	−0.24	−0.33	−0.33	−0.32
Imports	% GNP	0.59	0.67	0.73	0.78	0.83
Imports (quant.)	% GNP	1.81	2.01	2.21	2.34	2.45
Trade Balance	% GNP	−0.69	−0.91	−1.06	−1.12	−1.15
Labor Demand	%	0.02	0.02	0.02	0.02	0.02
Inflation	D	−1.74	−2.64	−3.48	−4.20	−4.89
Int Rate (sh)	D	−1.66	−4.08	−5.60	−6.83	−8.00
Japanese Economy						
Output	%	0.43	0.29	0.56	0.84	1.12
Priv Consumption	% GNP	0.90	1.65	2.11	2.48	2.84
Priv Investment	% GNP	1.32	1.18	1.32	1.42	1.51
Govt Consumption	% GNP	0.00	0.00	0.00	0.00	0.00
Exports	% GNP	0.05	−0.56	−0.74	−0.83	−0.89
Imports	% GNP	0.40	0.44	0.49	0.53	0.57
Imports (quant.)	% GNP	1.85	1.98	2.13	2.25	2.34
Trade Balance	% GNP	−0.73	−1.01	−1.23	−1.36	−1.46
Labor Demand	%	0.11	0.00	0.00	0.00	0.00
Inflation	D	−1.76	−0.02	−0.04	−0.05	−0.06
Int Rate (sh)	D	0.97	−0.78	−1.58	−2.19	−2.81

Table 9.18   1986–1990 Scenario: Permanent Rise in the Risk Premium on Dollar Assets (of 3%) and Money Stabilizing Employment

		1986	1987	1988	1989	1990
U.S. Economy						
Output	%	−0.01	−0.14	−0.26	−0.36	−0.46
Priv Consumption	% GNP	−0.41	−0.91	−0.94	−0.97	−0.99
Priv Investment	% GNP	−0.54	−0.52	−0.53	−0.53	−0.53
Govt Consumption	% GNP	0.00	0.00	0.00	0.00	0.00
Exports	% GNP	0.47	0.40	0.37	0.35	0.32
Imports	% GNP	−0.30	−0.28	−0.27	−0.27	−0.26
Imports (quant.)	% GNP	−0.47	−0.89	−0.84	−0.78	−0.73
Trade Balance	% GNP	0.77	0.67	0.65	0.62	0.59
Labor Demand	%	−0.01	−0.01	−0.01	−0.00	−0.00
Inflation	D	0.42	1.12	1.20	1.26	1.32
Int Rate (sh)	D	1.12	2.40	2.51	2.62	2.71
Int Rate (lg)	D	2.06	1.98	1.81	1.65	1.50
Tobin's q	%	−6.11	−7.07	−6.95	−6.84	−6.72
Real Exchange Rate						
$/ECU	%	9.96	8.41	7.73	7.07	6.44
$/yen	%	9.70	8.16	7.53	6.91	6.32
$/Can.	%	6.70	5.23	4.64	4.08	3.56
ROECD Economies						
Output	%	0.27	0.14	0.23	0.31	0.39
Priv Consumption	% GNP	0.70	0.74	0.74	0.74	0.74
Priv Investment	% GNP	0.49	0.43	0.43	0.42	0.41
Govt Consumption	% GNP	0.00	0.00	0.00	0.00	0.00
Exports	% GNP	−0.27	−0.47	−0.41	−0.35	−0.30
Imports	% GNP	0.16	1.15	0.15	0.15	0.15
Imports (quant.)	% GNP	0.65	0.57	0.53	0.50	0.46
Trade Balance	% GNP	−0.67	−0.62	−0.55	−0.50	−0.45
Labor Demand	%	0.00	0.00	0.00	−0.00	−0.00
Inflation	D	−0.59	−0.66	−0.77	−0.87	−0.95
Int Rate (sh)	D	−1.70	−1.95	−2.02	−2.08	−2.14
Japanese Economy						
Output	%	0.49	0.11	0.21	0.29	0.37
Priv Consumption	% GNP	0.71	0.77	0.78	0.79	0.81
Priv Investment	% GNP	0.47	0.42	0.42	0.41	0.41
Govt Consumption	% GNP	0.00	0.00	0.00	0.00	0.00
Exports	% GNP	−0.23	−0.69	−0.62	−0.56	−0.51
Imports	% GNP	0.08	0.09	0.09	0.09	1.10
Imports (quant.)	% GNP	0.45	0.39	0.37	0.35	0.33
Trade Balance	% GNP	−0.80	−0.77	−0.71	−0.65	−0.60
Labor Demand	%	0.02	0.00	0.00	0.00	0.00
Inflation	D	−0.39	−0.02	−0.02	−0.02	−0.02
Int Rate (sh)	D	−1.05	−1.23	−1.19	−1.17	−1.16

rate, since the German capital market has been open during the past 15 years.

Supposing that the recent depreciation of the dollar in fact reflects a portfolio shift against the dollar, we can introduce that into the simulation model by assuming that portfolio holders now demand a positive risk premium to hold dollar assets. In Table 9.18, we assume that the risk premium required to hold dollars rises permanently from zero in 1985 to 3 percentage points in 1986 and after. The result is a dollar depreciation of 7 to 10%, and a rise in the U.S. long-term interest rate of 2 percentage points. Somewhat surprisingly, even a large shift in the risk premium (too large, no doubt!) seems to produce a modest movement of the dollar, which does not well explain the 30–40% depreciation in 1986.

Using these results, let us now turn to the second question, the prospective evolution of the trade deficit of the United States. Would Gramm-Rudman-Hollings, by itself or together with the portfolio balance shift, be enough to restore trade balance in the United States by the early 1990s? The answer is that by itself GRH is unlikely to restore trade balance, at least not along a full-employment path for the U.S. economy. According to the results underlying Table 9.17, even if there is a complete elimination of the budget deficit by 1992, the improvement in the trade balance (at full employment) reaches 1.27% of GDP, leaving a trade deficit on the order of 1.8% of potential GDP (the equivalent of $70 b in 1987). Thus, GRH would have to be combined with a significant rise in the risk premium on the dollar, a further shift to budget surpluses, or some other unaccounted for shifts in savings and investment in the United States to restore trade balance. A recession might be another way to restore the trade balance.

Why is it that a complete elimination of the U.S. budget deficit would be insufficient by itself to restore trade balance at full employment? There are three main reasons. First, even before the buildup of the U.S. fiscal deficit after 1980, the U.S. was running a trade deficit on the order of 1–1.5% of GDP. Second, part of the worsening in the U.S. trade balance resulted from the cutoff in LDC financing, an event which is not likely to be reversed in the near term. And third, about 0.25% of GDP of the trade deficit resulted from the contraction of Japanese fiscal policies, which is also not likely to be reversed entirely (if at all).

Note finally that the simulation model is emphatic on two major points. First, monetary policies alone can do little, if anything, to rectify trade imbalances. Remembering the results in Tables 9.7 and

9.8, monetary policy shifts may depreciate or appreciate currencies, but will not by themselves contribute to major changes in the external balance. Second, fiscal or monetary expansion in Japan and the ROECD will do little or nothing for U.S. economic growth rates. A major Japanese fiscal expansion would raise world interest rates at the same time that it spurred U.S. export growth. The net effect on U.S. aggregate demand would be small and of uncertain sign.

VI. Conclusions and Some Possible Extensions

The simulation model reported in this paper was able to account for most of the observed movements in the trade balances of the U.S. and Japan during 1980–85 according to shifts in fiscal policies, and the decline in lending to the developing countries. The model did well in tracking the trade balance movements of the U.S. and Japan, as well as the yen-dollar rate through 1985. The model does much less well in accounting for the recent decline in the dollar vis-à-vis the yen and European currencies. The shift in expectations regarding U.S. budget deficits seems to be insufficient to account for the decline in the dollar of more than 30% since 1985. Other possible explanations for the dollar depreciation, such as a rise in the required risk premium on the dollar, can be examined in the model, but cannot be explained by the model, especially in view of the maintained assumption of perfect asset substitutability among the OECD financial assets.

The model is deficient in several important ways, so that the conclusions must allow for a considerable margin of error. Let us mention some of the key areas where the model needs strengthening. First, the private-sector consumption function should be respecified, to allow for some partial smoothing of labor income and labor-income taxes. Second, the ROECD should be disaggregated, most usefully between areas with and without capital controls. Third, imperfect competition in international trade should be introduced explicitly, to allow for the slow and incomplete pass-through of exchange rate changes into import and export prices.

Fourth, and perhaps most important, the assumption of perfect capital mobility should be reassessed. It will probably be wise to allow for some degree of imperfect asset substitutability, even though the empirical evidence on stable risk premia is virtually nonexistent. Surely portfolio holders these days must care about the buildup of dollar-denominated claims in their portfolios, even if the expected returns on dollars and other currencies are equalized.

Fifth, we should pay closer attention to the long-term trend decline in U.S. productivity growth. As Krugman and Baldwin (1987) have stressed, this long-term decline probably helps to explain the secular decline in the U.S. real exchange rate that is consistent with U.S. external balance. In our model, there is an implicit assumption that long-term U.S. balance is consistent with a stable, not depreciating, real exchange rate.

Sixth, we should give more attention to the apparent secular decline in the private Japanese savings rate, which should have important implications for the Japanese current account deficit in the next decades. If in fact the Japanese private savings rate is in steady decline, then the appearance of unrelenting Japanese external surpluses may be exaggerated.

Seventh, and finally, it will be useful to provide some disaggregation of the supply side in the U.S. and Japan, particularly since both economies will soon have to undergo important structural changes to adapt to the large swing in the exchange rate. The Maekawa Commission recommendations in Japan, for example, note that domestic-led growth in Japan can best be facilitated through the deregulation of land, and the liberalization of agricultural trade. A multisectoral model of the Japanese economy will be necessary to give adequate attention to such issues.

APPENDIX A: Six-Region World Model

U.S. Equations

Households

i. Utility Function

$$U^U = \log C^U$$

$$C^U = [\beta_2(C^{dU})^{\beta_3} + (1 - \beta_2)\,(C^{mU})^{\beta_3}]^{(1/\beta_3)}$$

$$C^{mU} = [\beta_4(C^U_R)^{\beta_5} + \beta_1(C^U_J)^{\beta_5} + (1 - \beta_1 - \beta_4)\,(C^U_C)^{\beta_5}]^{(1/\beta_5)}$$

$$\sigma^U_1 = \frac{1}{1 - \beta_3}\;;\;\; \sigma^U_2 = \frac{1}{1 - \beta_5}$$

ii. Demand Functions

$$P^{cU}C^U = \beta_{28}P^U F^U + \beta_{31}[W^U L^U(1 - \gamma_1) - TAX^U + P^O OIL^U]$$

$$C^{dU} = C^U \frac{P^{cU}}{P^U}\left[\frac{1}{1 + \Omega_1\beta_6}\right] \qquad \beta_6 = \left[\frac{1 - \beta_2}{\beta_2}\right]^{\sigma_1^U}$$

$$C^{mU} = C^U \frac{P^{cU}}{P^{mU}}\left[\frac{\Omega_1\beta_6}{1 + \Omega_1\beta_6}\right]$$

$$\Omega_1 = \left[\frac{P^{mU}}{P^U}\right]^{(1-\sigma_1^U)}$$

$$C_R^U = C^{mU} \frac{P^{mU}}{E^R P^R}\left[\frac{1}{1 + \beta_7\Omega_2 + \beta_{27}\Omega_3}\right]$$

$$C_J^U = C^{mU} \frac{P^{mU}}{E^J P^J}\left[\frac{\beta_7\Omega_2}{1 + \beta_7\Omega_2 + \beta_{27}\Omega_3}\right]$$

$$C_C^U = C^{mU} \frac{P^{mU}}{E^C P^C}\left[\frac{\beta_{27}\Omega_3}{1 + \beta_7\Omega_2 + \beta_{27}\Omega_3}\right]$$

$$\beta_7 = \left[\frac{\beta_1}{\beta_4}\right]^{\sigma_2^U} \qquad \beta_{27} = \left[\frac{1 - \beta_1 - \beta_4}{\beta_4}\right]^{\sigma_2^U}$$

$$\Omega_2 = \left[\frac{E^J P^J}{E^R P^R}\right]^{(1-\sigma_2^U)}; \quad \Omega_3 = \left[\frac{E^C P^C}{E^R P^R}\right]^{(1-\sigma_2^U)}$$

$$P^{cU} = \left[\beta_2^{\sigma_1^U} P^{U(1-\sigma_1^U)} + (1 - \beta_2)^{\sigma_1^U} P^{mU(1-\sigma_1^U)}\right]^{1/(1-\sigma_1^U)}$$

$$\text{or} \qquad P^{cU} = P^{U\beta_2} P^{mU(1-\beta_2)} \qquad \text{if } \sigma_1^U = 1$$

$$P^{mU} = \left[\beta_4^{\sigma_2^U} (E^R P^R)^{(1-\sigma_2^U)} + \beta_1^{\sigma_2^U} (E^J P^J)^{(1-\sigma_2^U)}\right.$$

$$\left. + (1 - \beta_1 - \beta_4)^{\sigma_2^U} (E^C P^C)^{(1-\sigma_2^U)}\right]^{(\sigma_2^U-1)}$$

$$\text{or} \qquad P^{mU} = (E^R P^R)^{\beta_4}(E^J P^J)^{\beta_1}(E^C P^C)^{(1-\beta_1-\beta_4)} \qquad \text{if } \sigma_2^U = 1$$

$$Y^U = Q^U - P^{nU}N^U + P^O OIL^U + r^U(B^U + A_L^U - A_U^R - A_U^J - A_U^O - A_U^C)$$

$$F^U = B^U + A_L^U - A_U^R - A_U^O - A_U^J - A_U^C + q^U K^U + (M^U/P^U)$$

Firms

i. Production Function

$$Q^U = \beta_{19}(L^U)^{\beta_8} (K^U)^{\beta_9} (N^U)^{\beta_{10}}$$

$$N^U = [\beta_{12}(N_0^U)^{\beta_{13}} + (1 - \beta_{12}) (N_L^U)^{\beta_{13}}]^{(1/\beta_{13})} \qquad \sigma_4^U = \frac{1}{1 - \beta_{13}}$$

ii. Factor Demands

$$L^U = \beta_8 \left[\frac{P^U Q^U}{W^U} \right]$$

$$N^U = \beta_{10} \left[\frac{P^U Q^U}{P^{nU}} \right]$$

$$N_0^U = \left[\beta_{12} \frac{P^{nU} N^U}{P^O} \right]^{\sigma_4^U} - OIL^U$$

$$N_L^U = \left[(1 - \beta_{12}) \frac{P^{nU} N^U}{P^L} \right]^{\sigma_4^U}$$

$$K_{t+1}^U = J_t^U + (1 + \beta_{14} + \alpha) K_t^U$$

$$J^U = \beta_{29} (q^U - 1) \frac{1}{\beta_{15}} K^U + (1 - \beta_{29}) \{ Q^U - W^U L^U / P^U - P^{nU} / P^U N^U \}$$
$$\qquad + \beta_{32} (Q_t - Q_{t-1})$$

$$P^{JU} I^U = P^{JU} J^U [1 + (\beta_{15}/2) J^U / K^U]$$

$$q_{t+1}^U = (1 + r_t^U + \beta_{14}) q_t^U - \frac{\partial Q^U}{\partial K^U} (1 - \gamma_2) - \frac{P^{JU}}{P^U} (0.5\beta_{15}) (J_t^U / K_t^U)^2$$

$$\frac{\partial Q^U}{\partial K^U} = \beta_9 \left[\frac{Q^U}{K^U} \right]$$

$$P^{JU} = P^{U\beta_{16}} (E^J P^J)^{\beta_{17}} (E^R E^R)^{\beta_{18}} (E^C P^C)^{(1-\beta_{16}-\beta_{17}-\beta_{18})}$$

$$I_R^U = \beta_{18} I^U / \wedge^R$$

$$I_J^U = \beta_{17} I^U / \wedge^J$$

$$I_C^U = (1 - \beta_{16} - \beta_{17} - \beta_{18}) I^U / \wedge^C$$

$$P^{nU} = \left[\beta_{12}^{\sigma_4^U} (P^O)^{(1-\sigma_4^U)} + (1 - \beta_{12})^{\sigma_4^U} (P^L)^{(1-\sigma_4^U)} \right]^{1/(1-\sigma_4^U)}$$

$$\text{or} \qquad P^{nU} = (P^O)^{\beta_{12}} (P^L)^{(1-\beta_{12})} \qquad \text{if } \sigma_4^U = 1$$

Asset Markets

$$\frac{M^U}{p^U} = \sigma_6 Q^U - \sigma_7 i^U$$

$$\wedge^R = P^R E^R / P^U$$

$$\wedge^J = P^J E^J / P^U$$

$$\wedge^C = P^C E^C / P^U$$

$$\wedge^L = P^L / P^U$$

$$\wedge^O = P^O / P^U$$

$$i_t^U = r_t^U + \Pi_t^U$$

$$r_t^U = R_t^U - ({}_tR_{t+1}^U - R_t^U)/R_t^U$$

$$\pi_t^U = (P_{t+1}^U - P_t^U)/P_t^U$$

$$\pi_t^{cU} = (P_{t+1}^{cU} - P_t^{cU})/P_t^{cU}$$

Balance of Payments

$$TB^U = C_U^R + C_U^J + C_U^L + C_U^O + C_U^C + I_U^R + I_U^J + I_U^C - \wedge^R(C_R^U + I_R^U)$$
$$- \wedge^J(C_J^U + I_J^U) - \wedge^C(C_C^U + I_C^U) - \wedge^O N_O^U - \wedge^L N_L^U$$

$$CA^U = TB^U + r^U(A_L^U - A_U^P - A_U^R - A_U^J - A_U^C)$$

Government Sector

$$DEF^U = G^U + r^U B^U - T^U$$

$$T^U = TAX^U + \gamma_1 \frac{W^U L^U}{P^U} + \gamma_2\left(Q^U - \frac{W^U L^U}{P^U} - \frac{P^{nU} N^U}{P^U}\right)$$

$$TAX^U = r^U B^U + TAXE^U$$

$$B_{t+1}^U = B_t^U(1 - \alpha) + DEF_t^U$$

Wage Contracts

$$w_{t+1}^U = w_t^U + \beta_{25}({}_tp_{t+1}^{cU} - p_t^{cU}) + (1 - \beta_{25})(p_t^{cU} - p_{t-1}^{cU}) + 1(L_t^U - \bar{L})$$

where $w = \log W$; $p^c = \log P^c$;

Market Equilibrium

$$Q^U = P^{cU}(C^U + G^U)/P^U + P^{JU}I^U/P^U + TB^U + (P^{nU}N^U - P^O OIL^U)/P^U$$

$$M^U = \bar{M}^U$$

LDC Equations

$$P^L = (P^U)^{\mu_1}(P^R E^R)^{\mu_2}(P^J E^J)^{\mu_3}(P^C E^C)^{\mu_4}(P^O)^{(1-\mu_1-\mu_2-\mu_3-\mu_4)}$$
$$(C_L^U + C_L^R + C_L^O + C_L^J + C_L^C)^{\mu_5}$$

$$C_U^L = \mu_1(C_U^L + \wedge^R C_R^L + \wedge^O C_O^L + \wedge^J C_J^L + \wedge^C C_C^L)$$

$$C_R^L = \mu_2(C_U^L + \wedge^R C_R^L + \wedge^O C_O^L + \wedge^J C_J^L + \wedge^C C_C^L)/\wedge^R$$

$$C_J^L = \mu_3(C_U^L + \wedge^R C_R^L + \wedge^O C_O^L + \wedge^J C_J^L + \wedge^C C_C^L)/\wedge^J$$

$$C_C^L = \mu_4(C_U^L + \wedge^R C_R^L + \wedge^O C_O^L + \wedge^J C_J^L + \wedge^C C_C^L)\Lambda^C$$

$$C_O^L = (1 - \mu_1 - \mu_2 - \mu_3 - \mu_4)(C_U^L + \Lambda^R C_R^L + \wedge^O C_O^L + \wedge^J C_J^L + \wedge^C C_C^L)/\wedge^O$$

$$TB^L = \wedge^L(C_L^U + C_L^R + C_L^O + C_L^J + C_L^C) - C_U^L - \wedge^R C_R^L - \wedge^O C_O^L - \wedge^J C_J^L - \Lambda^C C_C^L$$

$$CA_t^L = \bar{C}\bar{A}$$

$$DEBT = A_L^U + A_L^R \wedge^R + A_L^O + \wedge_L^I \Lambda^J + A_L^C \wedge^C$$

$$A_{Lt+1}^R \wedge_t^R = \mu_8[(A_{Lt+1}^U + A_{Lt+1}^R \wedge_t^R + A_{Lt+1}^O + A_{Lt+1}^J \wedge_t^J + A_{Lt+1}^C \wedge_t^C$$
$$- (A_{Lt}^U + A_{Lt}^R \wedge_t^R + A_{Lt}^O + A_{Jt}^J \wedge_t^J + A_{Lt}^C \wedge_t^C)(1-\alpha)] + A_{Lt}^R \wedge_t^R(1-\alpha)$$

$$A_{Lt+1}^O = \mu_9[(A_{Lt+1}^U + A_{Lt+1}^R \wedge_t^R + A_{Lt+1}^O + A_{Lt+1}^J \wedge_t^J + A_{Lt+1}^C \wedge_t^C)$$
$$- (A_{Lt}^U + A_{Lt}^R \wedge_t^R + A_{Lt}^O + A_{Lt}^J \wedge_t^J + A_{Lt}^C \wedge_t^C)(1-\alpha)] + A_{Lt}^O(1-\alpha)$$

$$A_{Lt+1}^J \wedge_t^J = \mu_{10}[(A_{Lt+1}^U + A_{Lt+1}^R \wedge_t^R + A_{Lt+1}^O + A_{Lt+1}^J \wedge_t^J + A_{Lt+1}^C \wedge_t^C)$$
$$- (A_{Lt}^U + A_{Lt}^R \wedge_t^R + A_{Lt}^O + A_{Lt}^J \wedge_t^J + A_{Lt}^C \wedge_t^C)(1-\alpha)] + A_{Lt}^J \wedge_t^J(1-\alpha)$$

$$A_{Lt+1}^C \Lambda_t^C = \mu_{11}[(A_{Lt+1}^U + A_{Lt+1}^R \wedge_t^R + A_{Lt+1}^O + A_{Lt+1}^J \wedge_t^J + A_{Lt+1}^C \wedge_t^C)$$
$$- (A_{Lt}^U + A_{Lt}^R \wedge_t^R + A_{Lt}^O + A_L^J \wedge_{tt}^J + A_{Lt}^C \wedge_t^C)(1-\alpha)] + A_{Lt}^C \wedge_t^C(1-\alpha)$$

$$A_{Lt+1}^U = -CA_t^L - [(A_{Lt+1}^J \wedge_t^J + A_{Lt+1}^C \wedge_t^C + A_{Lt+1}^R \wedge_t^R + A_{Lt+1}^O]$$
$$+ (A_{Lt}^U + A_{Jt}^J \wedge_t^J + A_{Lt}^C \wedge_t^C + A_{Lt}^R \wedge_t^R + A_{Lt}^O)(1-\alpha)$$

OPEC Equations

$$P^O = (P^U)^{\gamma_1}(P^R E^R)^{\gamma_2}(P^J E^J)^{\gamma_3}(P^C E^C)^{\gamma_4}(P^L)^{(1-\gamma_1-\gamma_2-\gamma_3-\gamma_4)}$$
$$(C_O^U + C_O^R + C_O^O + C_O^J + C_O^C)^{\gamma_5}$$

$$C_U^O = \gamma_1(C_U^O + \wedge^R C_R^O + \wedge^L C_L^O + \wedge^J C_J^O + \wedge^C C_C^O)$$

$$C_R^O = \gamma_2(C_U^O + \wedge^R C_R^O + \wedge^L C_L^O + \wedge^J C_J^O + \wedge^C C_C^O)/\wedge^R$$

$$C_J^O = \gamma_3(C_U^O + \wedge^R C_R^O + \wedge^L C_L^O + \wedge^J C_J^O + \wedge^C C_C^O)/\wedge^J$$

$$C_C^O = \gamma_4(C_U^O + \wedge^R C_R^O + \wedge^L C_L^O + \wedge^J C_J^O + \wedge^C C_C^O)/\wedge^C$$

$$C_L^O = (1 - \gamma_1 - \gamma_2 - \gamma_3 - \gamma_4)(C_U^O + \wedge^R C_R^O + \wedge^L C_L^O + \wedge^J C_J^O + \wedge^C C_C^O)/\wedge^L$$

$$TB^O = \wedge^O(C_O^U + C_O^R + C_O^L + C_O^J + C_O^C) - C_U^O - \wedge^R C_R^O - \wedge^L C_L^O - \wedge^J C_J^O - \wedge^C C_C^O$$

$$H^O = A_U^O + A_R^O + A_L^O + A_J^O \wedge^J$$

$$CA_t^O = \gamma_3[\gamma_6(C_{Ot}^U + C_{Ot}^R + C_{Ot}^L + C_{Ot}^J + C_{Ot}^C)(P_t^O/P_t^U) - H_{t-1}^O] + \alpha H_{t-1}^O$$

$$A^O_{Ut+1} = CA^O_t - (A^O_{Rt+1}\wedge^R_t + A^O_{Lt+1} + A^O_{Jt+1}\wedge^J_t + A^O_{Ct+1}\wedge^C_t)$$
$$+ (A^O_U + A^O_{Rt}\wedge^R_t + A^O_{Lt} + A^O_{Jt}\wedge^J_t + A^O_{Ct}\wedge^C_t)$$

$$A^O_{Rt+1}\wedge^R_t = \gamma_7[A^O_{Ut+1} + A^O_{Rt+1}\wedge^R_t + A^O_{Lt+1} + A^O_{Jt+1}\wedge^J_t + A^O_{Ct+1}\wedge^C_t)$$
$$- (A^O_{Ut} + A^O_{Rt}\wedge^R_t + A^O_{Lt} + A^O_{Jt}\wedge^O_t + A^O_{Ct}\wedge^C_t)(1-\alpha)] + A^O_{Rt}\wedge^R_t(1-\alpha)$$

$$A^O_{Jt+1}\wedge^J_t = \gamma_8[A^O_{Ut+1} + A^O_{Rt+1}\wedge^R_t + A^O_{Lt+1} + A^O_{Jt+1}\wedge^J_t + A^O_{Ct+1}\wedge^C_t)$$
$$- (A^O_{Ut} + A^O_{Rt}\wedge^R_t + A^O_{Lt} + A^O_{Jt}\wedge^O_t + A^O_{Ct}\wedge^C_t)(1-\alpha)] + A^O_{Jt}\wedge^J_t(1-\alpha)$$

$$A^O_{Ct+1}\wedge^C_t = \gamma_9[A^O_{Ut+1} + A^O_{Rt+1}\wedge^R_t + A^O_{Lt+1} + A^O_{Jt+1}\wedge^J_t + A^O_{Ct+1}\wedge^C_t)$$
$$- (A^O_{Ut} + A^O_{Rt}\wedge^R_t + A^O_{Lt} + A^O_{Jt}\wedge^O_t + A^O_{Ct}\wedge^C_t)(1-\alpha)] + A^O_{Ct}\wedge^C_t(1-\alpha)$$

Variable Definitions – World Model

A^j_i	real claims by country j against country i
B	real government debt
B^j_i	real concessional claims by country j against country i
C	real consumption of goods
C^d	real consumption of domestic goods
C^m	real consumption of imported goods
C^i_j	consumption by country i of country j goods
CA	current account balance
$DEBT$	LDC debt
DEF	real budget deficit
E	nominal exchange rate (\$/unit of foreign currency)
F	real financial wealth
G	real government expenditure on goods
$HOPEC$	net asset position of OPEC
i	short nominal interest rate
I	real investment expenditure inclusive of adjustment costs
I^i_j	demand for country j goods for investment in country j
J	gross fixed capital formation
K	capital stock
L	demand for labor
M	nominal money supply
N	basket of intermediate inputs used in production
N^i_j	import of country j goods used as intermediate input in i
P	price of domestic goods
P^m	price of imported goods
P^c	price of a basket of imported and domestic goods
P^I	price of investment goods
P^n	price of intermediate goods
π	product price inflation

π	consumer price inflation
Q	real gross output
q	Tobin's q
R	long real interest rate
r	short real interest rate
T	total nominal tax receipts
TAX	lump sum tax on households
$TAXE$	exogenous tax
TB	trade balance
v	short real concessional interest rate on LDC debt
W	nominal wage
α	growth rate of population plus labor-augmenting technical change
γ_1	tax rate on household income
γ_2	tax rate on corporate profits
σ_1	elasticity of substitution between domestic and imported goods
σ_3	elasticity of substitution between capital and labor
$\wedge^R$	real exchange rate (relative price of ROECD goods)
$\wedge^J$	real exchange rate (relative price of Japanese goods)
$\wedge^L$	real exchange rate (relative price of LDC goods)
$\wedge^O$	real exchange rate (relative price of OPEC goods)

Parameters

$$\alpha = 0.040$$

U.S.

$\beta1 = 0.332$	$\beta11 = -9.000$	$\beta21 = 0$
$\beta2 = 0.931$	$\beta12 = 0.202$	$\beta22 = 1.000$
$\beta3 = 0.000$	$\beta13 = 0.000$	$\beta23 = 0.089$
$\beta4 = 0.355$	$\beta14 = 0.083$	$\beta24 = 0.000$
$\beta5 = 0.471$	$\beta15 = 8.000$	$\beta25 = 0.250$
$\beta6 = 0.074$	$\beta16 = 0.933$	$\beta26 = 0$
$\beta7 = 0.881$	$\beta17 = 0.022$	$\beta27 = 0.785$
$\beta8 = 0.706$	$\beta18 = 0.025$	$\beta28 = 0.050$
$\beta9 = 0.263$	$\beta19 = 1.429$	$\beta29 = 0.200$
$\beta10 = 0.031$	$\beta20 = 1.000$	$\beta30 = 0$
	$\beta31 = 0.85$	$\beta32 = 0.25$
$\gamma1 = 0.350$	$\gamma2 = 0.000$	$\gamma3 = 0.000$
$\sigma1 = 1.000$	$\sigma2 = 1.891$	$\sigma3 = 0.100$
$\sigma4 = 1.000$	$\sigma5 = 1.000$	$\theta = 0.080$
$\sigma6 = 1.000$	$\sigma7 = 0.60$	

ROECD

$\beta 1 = 0.354$	$\beta 11 = -9.000$	$\beta 21 = 0$
$\beta 2 = 0.936$	$\beta 12 = 0.318$	$\beta 22 = 1.000$
$\beta 3 = 0.000$	$\beta 13 = 0.000$	$\beta 23 = 0.070$
$\beta 4 = 0.463$	$\beta 14 = 0.077$	$\beta 24 = 0.000$
$\beta 5 = 0.285$	$\beta 15 = 8.000$	$\beta 25 = 0.500$
$\beta 6 = 0.069$	$\beta 16 = 0.934$	$\beta 26 = 0$
$\beta 7 = 0.688$	$\beta 17 = 0.023$	$\beta 27 = 0.274$
$\beta 8 = 0.697$	$\beta 18 = 0.034$	$\beta 28 = 0.050$
$\beta 9 = 0.251$	$\beta 19 = 1.506$	$\beta 29 = 0.200$
$\beta 10 = 0.052$	$\beta 20 = 1.000$	$\beta 30 = 0$
	$\beta 31 = 0.85$	$\beta 32 = 0.25$
$\gamma 1 = 0.350$	$\gamma 2 = 0.000$	$\gamma 3 = 0.000$
$\sigma 1 = 1.000$	$\sigma 2 = 1.399$	$\sigma 3 = 0.100$
$\sigma 4 = 1.000$	$\sigma 5 = 1.000$	$\theta = 0.080$
$\sigma 6 = 1.000$	$\sigma 7 = 0.60$	

Japan

$\beta 1 = 0.473$	$\beta 11 = -9.000$	$\beta 21 = 0$
$\beta 2 = 0.950$	$\beta 12 = 0.546$	$\beta 22 = 1.000$
$\beta 3 = 0.000$	$\beta 13 = 0.000$	$\beta 23 = 0.031$
$\beta 4 = 0.423$	$\beta 14 = 0.095$	$\beta 24 = 0.000$
$\beta 5 = 0.146$	$\beta 15 = 8.000$	$\beta 25 = 0.500$
$\beta 6 = 0.052$	$\beta 16 = 0.950$	$\beta 26 = 0$
$\beta 7 = 1.139$	$\beta 17 = 0.023$	$\beta 27 = 0.195$
$\beta 8 = 0.652$	$\beta 18 = 0.027$	$\beta 28 = 0.050$
$\beta 9 = 0.292$	$\beta 19 = 1.558$	$\beta 29 = 0.200$
$\beta 10 = 0.055$	$\beta 20 = 1.000$	$\beta 30 = 0$
	$\beta 31 = 0.85$	$\beta 32 = 0.25$
$\gamma 1 = 0.350$	$\gamma 2 = 0.000$	$\gamma 3 = 0.000$
$\sigma 1 = 1.000$	$\sigma 2 = 1.171$	$\sigma 3 = 0.100$
$\sigma 4 = 1.000$	$\sigma 5 = 1.000$	$\theta = 0.080$
$\sigma 6 = 1.000$	$\sigma 7 = 0.60$	

Canada

$\beta 1 = 0.303$	$\beta 11 = -9.000$	$\beta 21 = 0$
$\beta 2 = 0.760$	$\beta 12 = 0.229$	$\beta 22 = 1.000$
$\beta 3 = 0$	$\beta 13 = 0.000$	$\beta 23 = 0.008$
$\beta 4 = 0.324$	$\beta 14 = 0.055$	$\beta 24 = 0.000$
$\beta 5 = 0.912$	$\beta 15 = 8.000$	$\beta 25 = 0.500$
$\beta 6 = 0.316$	$\beta 16 = 0.644$	$\beta 26 = 0$
$\beta 7 = 0.461$	$\beta 17 = 0.273$	$\beta 27 = 4.800$

$$\beta 8 = 0.776 \qquad \beta 18 = 0.057 \qquad \beta 28 = 0.050$$
$$\beta 9 = 0.203 \qquad \beta 19 = 1.329 \qquad \beta 29 = 0.200$$
$$\beta 10 = 0.022 \qquad \beta 20 = 1.000 \qquad \beta 30 = 0$$
$$\beta 31 = 0.85 \qquad \beta 32 = 0.25$$

$$\gamma 1 = 0.350 \qquad \gamma 2 = 0.000 \qquad \gamma 3 = 0.000$$
$$\sigma 1 = 1.000 \qquad \sigma 2 = 11.410 \qquad \sigma 3 = 0.100$$
$$\sigma 4 = 1.000 \qquad \sigma 5 = 1.000 \qquad \theta = 0.080$$
$$\sigma 6 = 1.000 \qquad \sigma 7 = 0.60$$

References

Atkinson, Paul, and Chouraqui, Jean-Claude. 1985. "The Origins of High Real Interest Rates," *OECD Economic Studies*, Autumn, pp. 7–56.

Baldwin, Robert, and Krugman, Paul. 1987. *BPEA*, 1.

Bruno, Michael, and Sachs, Jeffrey. 1985. *Economics of Worldwide Stagflation*. Cambridge: Harvard University Press.

Bryant, Ralph, and Holtham, Gerald. 1986. "The U.S. External Deficit: Diagnosis, Prognosis, and Cure," Brookings Discussion Papers in International Economics, The Brookings Institution, March.

Dornbusch, Rudiger. 1987. "Exchange Rates and Prices," *AER*.

Frenkel, Jacob, and Razin, Assaf. 1986. "Fiscal Policies and Real Exchange Rates in the World Economy," NBER Working Paper No. 2065, November.

Hayashi, Fumio. 1983. "Tobins Marginal q and Average q: A Neoclassical Interpretation," *Econometrica* 50, pp. 213–22.

Ishii, Naoko, McKibbin, Warwick, and Sachs, Jeffrey. 1986. "The Economic Policy Mix, Policy Cooperation and Protectionism: Some Aspects of Macroeconomic Interdependence Among the United States, Japan and Other OECD Countries," *Journal of Policy Modelling* 7(4), pp. 533–572.

Krugman, Paul. 1985. "Pricing to Market when Exchange Rates Change." NBER Working Paper No. 1927.

Lipton, David, and Sachs, Jeffrey. 1983, "Accumulation and Growth in a Two-Country Model," *Journal of International Economics* 15, pp. 135–159.

McKibbin, Warwick, and Sachs, Jeffrey. 1986. "Coordination of Monetary and Fiscal Policies in the OECD," National Bureau of Economic Research Working Paper No. 1800, Forthcoming in Jacob Frenkel (ed.), *International Aspects of Fiscal Policy*. Chicago: University of Chicago Press.

McKibbin, Warwick, and Sachs, Jeffrey. 1987. "An Introduction to the MSG2 Model," unpublished mimeo, Harvard University, forthcoming.

Poterba, James, and Summers, Lawrence. 1987. "Recent U.S. Evidence on Budget Deficits and National Savings," NBER Working Paper No. 2144, February.

Richardson, Pete. 1987. "Tracking the U.S. External Deficit, 1980–1985: Experience with the OECD Interlink Model," *OECD Working Papers*, February.

Sachs, Jeffrey, and McKibbin, Warwick. 1986. "Macroeconomic Policies in the OECD and LDC External Adjustment." Forthcoming in Van Wijnbergen Sweder, and Francis Colaco (eds.), *International Capital Flows and the Developing Countries*.

Comments

Ryūtarō Komiya

I believe the papers by Professors Niehans and Sachs are most valuable contributions to this kind of conference, where policymakers, practitioner economists, and academic economists gather, because nowadays there seems to exist between practioners and academics a divergence of opinions or a gap in understanding with respect to the current "international imbalances." These two papers show convincingly that some politicians' and practioners' perceptions are based upon misunderstanding.

A large gap in understanding seems to exist (1) with respect to the causes of U.S. current account deficits, and Japan's and Germany's surpluses, especially Japan's surplus, and (2) with respect to the means to correct current account imbalances.

(1) According to politicians and policymakers, the major cause of the U.S. trade deficit is tariff and non-tariff barriers and some other unfair practices on the part of Japan and other surplus countries, whereas according to academic economists the large trade imbalance is a macroeconomic phenomenon, which results from underlying macroeconomic forces in and fiscal and monetary policies of countries concerned, especially the United States. Niehans explicitly states in his paper that the principal source of serious international disturbances since 1973 was the monetary and fiscal policy shifts of the United States. His model shows clearly that fiscal expansion in a country induces its residents to finance a spurt of spending, turning its current accounts into deficits. Also, simulation analysis by Sachs shows that the major cause of U.S. current account deterioration in recent years is the rise in the U.S. budget deficit, although the cutoff of lending to developing countries as a result of the debt crisis also contributed to it substantially. Moreover, Sachs makes it clear that, even if the U.S. bilateral trade deficit vis-à-vis Japan is somehow

reduced, without a fundamental change in U.S. macroeconomic conditions the trade surpluses of Canada and Europe will be increased, leaving the U.S. overall deficit largely unchanged. This is because Japan provides only a modest share of the total OECD savings.

(2) Policymakers emphasize the need for international coordination of macroeconomic policies, but many academic economists are skeptical of its usefulness and workability.

Sachs' simulation results show that monetary policy can be pursued by each country more or less independently, without spillover affecting the trade balance or level of economic activity in other countries or regions, and that Japanese fiscal expansion has only a modest effect on the U.S. economy or on its trade balance. To my knowledge, more or less similar conclusions have been reached by other simulation studies.

Niehans raises a doubt on the workability of international coordination of macroeconomic policies from a political point of view as well, saying that it is hard to see how governments, in particular the U.S. government, should be able to submit to any sort of international coordination as long as they are domestically too weak to avoid abrupt shifts in their monetary and fiscal policies.

From Japan's point of view, the United States is a peculiar country with regard to the area of international economic cooperation. Its government or president generally tries to take leadership in the IMF-GATT regime of free, multilateral world trade, but its Congress almost entirely disregards GATT. The U.S. is the only member country of GATT in which many bills that would violate GATT if put into effect are presented to its legislature. Some of them have been legislated, and unilateral actions violating GATT and detrimental to the world trading system have been taken.

I have some questions and comments on both papers, but they are more or less technical ones, better taken up in the university seminar room than in this kind of meeting. Therefore, I will skip them and instead take up two broad policy-oriented issues related to the title of this session. The two questions are, first, are the existing current account imbalances something to be worried about and corrected within a short time?, and second, what is the corrective mechanism, and is it missing or not?

The present level of the U.S. current account deficit is by no means a very large one relative to its GNP. European countries sometimes run much larger deficits, and some of the smaller OECD countries such as Finland, Ireland, Iceland, and New Zealand have run much larger current account deficits relative to their respective GNP, up to 7, 8, or 10% over extended periods.

Apart from much political ado in the U.S. and politicization internationally, what are the purely economic reasons why one should be concerned about U.S. deficits? I understand that the present U.S. unemployment rate has declined substantially in recent years, and is now fairly close to the natural rate. In any case, it has been consistently lower than most major European countries. Also, what are the purely economic reasons why one should be concerned about Japanese or German surpluses? They are only a very small part of total OECD savings, as pointed out by Sachs.

From around 1860 to the First World War, Britain ran an annual current account surplus of about 4% of its GNP on the average, continuously over 50 years. Britain thus provided capital funds for developing countries at that time. Economically there is nothing disturbing or unusual in such a situation, where net saving countries provide capital funds to net investment countries.

No one can deny that exchange rate variability under the floating system has been excessive, but how can economists assert that current account deficits and surpluses have been excessive?

If a country has integrated, well-developed national financial markets, capital funds move from net saving regions to net investment regions within the country. OECD countries have been more and more integrated financially in recent years, so that capital funds now move from net saving countries to net investment countries more and more rapidly than before. As Sachs points out, it is inconsistent on the part of the U.S. to request liberalization of capital movement on the one hand, and complain about other countries' trade surpluses on the other.

In the United States, corporations, households, and federal and local governments individually are on the average willing to borrow in order to invest more than they save. Foreign borrowing is financing only a part of domestic capital formation, so that U.S. citizens' per capita net wealth is still increasing steadily.

I hope some of the American participants here will enlighten me on the reasons why U.S. trade deficits are worrisome from a purely economic point of view.

Finally, concerning an adjustment mechanism to correct balance of payments imbalances, or a lack of it, here again the United States is a peculiar country in the world. Since it is a key-currency country, its imports are invoiced in its national currency. In order to finance trade deficits, short-term or long-term funds denominated in its own currency abundantly flow into the country, as the U.S. has the most developed financial markets.

Whether under the old Bretton Woods or the floating system, if a country other than the U.S. experiences large current account deficits, it inevitably runs into payments difficulties, so that it has to take measures to improve the balance of payments. Some such countries go to the IMF, and the IMF responds with what is called conditionality; that is, the IMF provides short-term financing on the condition that the deficit country take restrictive monetary and fiscal policies. This has been the adjustment mechanism, at least since the end of World War II. Thus the United States, which has the largest voting power in the IMF, has always requested, through the IMF, deficit countries to take restrictive monetary and fiscal policies in order to improve their balance of payments positions.

The adjustment process has often been painful, but many deficit countries have somehow undergone such a process, and overcome the payment imbalances. Whether fortunately or unfortunately, the United States, being the key-currency country, does not have to go to the IMF for financing of its deficits.

I still do not know whether the U.S. trade deficit is worrisome from an economic point of view or whether there is an urgent need to correct it. If the answer is no, then there should not be much ado about it. American politicians should be educated not to make a fuss over it. If the answer is yes, the United States itself should take appropriate macroeconomic policies to correct its own imbalance. Niehans's and Sachs's papers together have shown us convincingly that other countries can do little by way of helping the U.S. to reduce its current account imbalance.

Comments

Edwin M. Truman

The central banker expecting to learn something useful about the causes of international imbalances in the 1980s and lessons about automatic adjustment mechanisms or the international transmission of policies from these papers is likely to be somewhat disappointed. He is left in the position of the President of the United States presented with two analyses of the issue of strategic defense. The Niehans presentation elegantly demonstrates that when the analysis is performed in an area brightly illuminated by the particular street lamp constructed by this analyst, the world is essentially unidimensional and frictionless. The lesson for the policymaker—at least one from a large Western country—is not to change his policies under any circumstances. In other words, the best strategic defense is no offense.

The Sachs presentation is subtler: it assumes a largely hypothetical, but also internally consistent, structure of the world economy. This hypothetical world is simulated and various inferences are drawn from the results. The policymaker is encouraged to construct his strategic defense based on those inferences, except that there are two or three loopholes that might prove to be fatal under real world conditions.

The policymaker is further perplexed because he is uncertain whether the two analysts are concerned with the same world. This problem is most clearly illustrated in the area of capital mobility. In the Niehans analysis, which implicitly associates capital mobility with the transfer of net claims on physical assets, it is asserted that capital mobility has declined because international trade elasticities are now lower (in absolute value) and gestation lags on investment projects are longer. Moreover, whatever capital mobility there is today (and there is none in equilibrium in Niehans's paper) has nothing to do with differentials in interest rates. A suggested "policy conclusion" is that impediments to capital flows accentuate disturbances in terms of trade.

In the Sachs analysis, it is asserted that the mobility of Japanese capital, implicitly defined as gross financial claims or liabilities, has increased since 1980. It is argued that this phenomenon has facilitated the development of large Japanese trade surpluses, benefited the United States, and probably disadvantaged Japan.

My major criticism of both papers is that they fail to recognize that the policies and problems of the 1980s are the legacy of the problems and policy failures of the 1970s. From my perspective, any analysis that does not connect the international imbalances of the 1980s with the domestic instabilities of the 1970s is fundamentally incomplete. Although the Niehans paper mentions in passing "the parallel policy of disinflation" followed by several countries simultaneously in the early 1980s, that observation plays no role, as far as I can tell, in his subsequent analysis. The Sachs paper does not appear to recognize this phenomenon at all. In the simulation presented, it is assumed, contrary to fact, that monetary policy held unemployment in the industrial countries unchanged from 1980 to 1985, and no mention is made of the disinflationary process that prevailed in these years as suggested by sustained declines in the prices of oil and other commodities.

Turning to specific comments on the two papers, I can be very brief on the Niehans paper. First, it beongs in the section of this conference on optimal policy management, not in the section on the causes of the so-called international imbalances of the 1980s.

Second, as far as I can tell, Niehans is not convinced that the 1980s present a problem worth analyzing. He appears to regard large and persistent trade deficits and surpluses as not very revealing or troublesome, and I am not sure I disagree with him on the first apsect. He also says that, on balance, there has been an improving trend during the 1980s.

Nevertheless, and third, Niehans's paper has a villain, and he identifies it clearly at the start qf the paper: "the principal. . .source of serious international disturbances since 1973 (just as in the 15 years before 1973) were the monetary and fiscal policy shifts of the United States." Never mind that his subsequent analysis only loosely illustrates, but does not prove, this assertion; his policy prescription is clear: In this year of the two-hundredth anniversary of the U.S. Constitution, Niehans is an advocate of breaking up the United States—I assume into units no larger than Switzerland—so it can't do any more damage.

Niehans's second-best approach is that the United States should have no policy or, more precisely, no changes in policies. This is what one might call the nihilistic policy solution. This view has a long tradition in political theory and in certain religions that stress the frailty and fallibility of men and women. I have never found such assumptions about human nature either convincing or attractive and, as a consequence, I may fail to appreciate the utility of the economic calisthenics Niehans puts the reader through.

As for the Sachs-Roubini paper, it provides somewhat more to think about. However, before one takes the analysis too seriously, one has to decide what one thinks about an approach that is based upon a simulation model that relies on assumed coefficients. On the one hand, the model (MSG2) is theoretically elegant, but the researcher by taking coefficients off the shelf releases himself from a critical constraint; his model does not have to be consistent with the data. Along the same lines, when one buys into Sachs's results, one buys into his framework, which he describes as solving "for a full intertemporal equilibrium in which agents have rational expectations of future variables." I recognize that such a framework has a certain appeal, but as applied it necessarily influences his results in ways that I believe are not entirely consistent with the real world.

My second point (or set of points) on the Sachs paper involves drawing upon the Multi-Country Model (MCM) the Federal Reserve staff uses to examine these kinds of issues. The MCM differs from the MSG2 in three important respects: (1) the MCM is not solved with forward-looking expectations; (2) the parameters in the MCM are estimated and not imposed; and (3) the MCM is more highly disaggregated. I want to comment on the MCM's results not because they are necessarily closer to the truth, but because they are different and, I would submit, equally plausible as a basis for policy. As a consequence, I would be inclined to caution policymakers from relying heavily on some of Sachs's rather dogmatic conclusions—no matter how comforting they may be to our Japanese hosts.

(1) In the MCM, the effects of a U.S. fiscal expansion are larger and more persistent than in MSG2, both at home and abroad. (Moreover, in the MCM the effects of a U.S. fiscal expansion on real GNPs abroad are generally positive, not negative, contrary to the MSG2 result!)

(2) In the MCM, the effects on the United States of a Japanese fiscal expansion are small and relatively transient, but they are an order of magnitude larger than in MSG2. (I would also note that the MSG2 apparently produces a rather large impact of a fiscal expansion on

Japanese trade with developing countries, and it is a bit mysterious why this does not feed back to improve the external account of the United States.)

(3) MCM simulations do not confirm the MSG2 result that the spillover effects of monetary policy are trivial; this is especially true for the case of U.S. monetary policy.

I have already noted my uneasiness about Sachs's treatment of monetary policy and commodity prices in his simulation of the period 1980–85. My third and last comment on the Sachs paper involves the simulation for the period up to 1992 under the influence of Gramm-Rudman-Hollings (GRH). I may well be mistaken, but the specification of this simulation seems a bit odd. If I understand correctly the structure of the model, it is assumed in effect that the long-run government budget constraint holds, and private agents know this fact. Therefore, I wonder what it means to simulate GRH by itself, especially when agents must have assumed all along that something like GRH would occur.

In conclusion, I regret to say that these two papers do not provide much guidance on how to protect ourselves from international imbalances in the future. The Niehans paper starts with the premise that U.S. fiscal policy is the culprit, and although I have a great deal of sympathy with that bias, it is merely a bias. The Sachs-Roubini paper, on the other hand, appears to assume that any temporary gyrations in U.S. fiscal policy are self-correcting. I wish it were so!

Comments

R. S. Masera

1. First, let me express my admiration for Professor Niehans's theoretical analysis. His basic two-country model and its subsequent modifications to examine the dynamics of the adjustment path to international disturbances are of considerable interest. By adopting a small set of simplifying assumptions, he is able to address in a compact and powerful way some key mechanisms of international economic adjustment.

A number of features in Niehans's model merit specific reference, and warrant detailed discussion. The treatment of gestation lags in investment and the non-traditional approach to exchange-rate and terms-of-trade overshooting deserve special attention. In my assigned ten minutes today, however, I could not even begin to do justice to these important but complex technical questions. Instead, I shall concentrate on one relatively simple and yet highly relevant issue, the analysis of the effect of a shift in fiscal policy in terms of his basic model. I believe this is also an important point with a view to addressing some of the current policy questions considered by Professor Niehans in the final part of his paper, to which I shall come later.

2. As will be recalled, the traditional conclusion reached via the Mundell-Fleming approach is that under floating exchange rates and with perfect substitutability of domestic and foreign assets, a bond-financed fiscal expansion has a positive impact on domestic income, the domestic real interest rate, and the real exchange rate, as well as a negative effect on the domestic current account.

The effect on foreign output is dependent upon two countervailing forces: a positive impulse from net exports, as a result of the real exchange rate depreciation; and a negative impulse on investment, because interest rates are driven up both domestically and abroad. The classic Mundell scheme indicated an overall *positive* response of foreign output. However, as has been subsequently shown, if foreign wages are flexible, thereby rising following the depreciation of the currency, fiscal expansion might result in a *negative* international output transmission.

3. Let us contrast these conclusions with Niehans's results. I take his prototype model where, in particular, the following simplifying assumptions are made: perfect substitutability of home and foreign securities; freely floating exchange rates, but fixed terms of trade; and Ricardo's nonequivalence between debt and expected tax liabilities. In these circumstances, fiscal expansion entailing a pure debt expansion domestically, with the money supply unchanged, raises the rate of interest at home as well as abroad. Residents finance an increase in consumption by selling securities. This drives up interest rates and reduces the stock of real capital both domestically and abroad. The net foreign assets of the domestic economy decline, as it experiences a capital inflow. The fundamental result is that (1) real output declines in both countries, while (2) real income in the foreign economy is positively affected by the additional returns on its foreign assets. It is the domestic economy which is therefore ultimately and definitively burdened with the loss of output of both economies. However, the steady-state effects of the debt expansion on the trade balance are generally ambiguous.

4. As Professor Niehans readily concedes, his paper is a theoretical background to policy discussion, and does not directly address current policy issues. In the concluding section, however, he does offer some considerations on topical points and policy prescriptions; it is in this area that I find it hard to agree with him.

His analytical conclusions on the negative output effect of fiscal action are, I believe, at the root of his policy conclusions. I do not necessarily wish to dispute the steady-state propositions derived from his model, but I am convinced that his generalized (crowding out) pessimism on the effects of fiscal impulses does not provide a satisfactory answer to our present predicament.

There are, in particular, three policy contentions with which I do not find myself at ease:

(i) First, there is the argument that international coordination of economic policies is a virtually hopeless task in the presence of frequent and abrupt shifts in the fiscal and monetary courses actually pursued by the various countries.

(ii) This skepticism on coordination does not entail pessimism: it is in fact argued that international imbalances are no more serious today than in the past; world inflation has indeed been beaten, and unemployment largely "normalized."

(iii) The final conclusion is that the only important element of cooperation now is that the United States should maintain a steady monetary course, while adjusting the budget.

5. As to the first point, I see a broader scope for international cooperation, and I have greater confidence that it can support and sustain the process of international adjustment by facilitating the pursuit of mutually compatible objectives among sovereign countries. These beliefs are not—I hope—merely the result of a distortion of my *a priori* probabilities, stemming from my work in contributing to the G10 Deputies' report (the "Dini Report") on the functioning of the international monetary system—which was endorsed by Ministers and Governors here in Tokyo exactly two years ago. As was noted by Governor Sumita in his opening address, in a world of growing interdependence, where there are only a few main actors, while the role of the key character is declining, spillover effects of domestic policies must be explicitly taken into account. The failure to do so will inevitably result in nonoptimal decisions. International economic stability is a public good whose externalities should be adequately recognized. These considerations clearly extend beyond the narrowly defined domain of monetary and fiscal policies to include the questions of the flow of funds to developing countries and of protectionism. I have no special enthusiasm for the booming game-theory literature, but I believe that some of its fundamental insights are correct.

We are indeed dealing with a problem that is not confined to the realm of economics: As the importance of the leader declines, while there is no immediate challenger, the only viable solution is harmonization of overall policies.

I should therefore turn Professor Niehans's argument around and point out that precisely because we witness such frequent and disruptive shifts in national economic policies and incompatible policy mixes, there is a role for international coordination and multilateral surveillance, through peers' and international organizations' pressure.

6. If I am less skeptical on surveillance and cooperation, I am more seriously concerned about the existing international imbalances. Coming to Niehans's second contention, I should like to make the following points.

To start with, the developing countries debt problem has become even more acute in 1986. The relevant summary ratios have all deteriorated, in spite of the decline of the dollar and of interest rates. The Baker initiative faces increasing challenges; personally, I have come to the conclusion that major innovative financial changes have to be devised to ensure the viability of the system. Above all, the world economic growth scenario envisaged in the Baker framework must be realized. But this is a problematic issue to which I shall presently return.

Next, there is of course the international debt problem of the United States. This is the first time that the reserve currency country has a *large net* international debtor position—is, indeed, the world's largest debtor. There is a very serious stock-flow problem here. As long as the rate of interest is higher than the domestic rate of growth, in order to stabilize the ratio of foreign debt to domestic income, the trade *surplus* as a proportion of domestic income will have to cover the interest rate burden on foreign debt. Accordingly, the higher the accumulated debt, the lower the equilibrium real exchange rate. The risk is that at some point surprise inflation may appear as a politically expedient way to "adjust," as is the case for protectionism today. There is, in this respect, an international "moral hazard" problem: it is clear in principle that the reserve currency center should not be a *very large* international debtor.

7. I come therefore to the final policy suggestion by Niehans: the only important element of cooperation is to ensure a steady course in U.S. economic policy. This indeed is the only action that now offers bright prospects for the world economy.

I agree wholeheartedly that a steadier course of economic policies in the United States since the beginning of the 1970s would certainly have been a prime factor in preventing international imbalances. And in the future, too, the world could not but benefit from a steadier course of U.S. policy impulses. We should not forget, however, that it was the U.S. expansion that pulled the world out of the stagflation of 1980–82.

In any event, the relevant issue now is what concrete "steady" policy the United States should adopt under present circumstances and whether this can be expected to cure today's imbalances. Broad consensus exists on the need for a steady reduction of the U.S. federal deficit; the true question, however, is how rapid the adjustment should be, and whether it should be accompanied by an offsetting *relaxation* of the fiscal stance in Japan, and in those European countries where budget consolidation has produced structural balances that are in broad equilibrium, if not in surplus.

As I have suggested elsewhere,[1] to a large extent the shifts between 1981 and 1986 in the current accounts of the United States on the one side and Japan and Germany on the other can be explained by the opposite changes in their *budget deficits*, account being taken of the fact that the U.S. fiscal expansion was accompanied by restrictive monetary policy, which assured confidence in control of inflation and high real yields on U.S. financial assets. In this aspect I agree with Professor Niehans that there has been a general understatement of the importance of fiscal policy shifts as generators of international disturbances.

I am therefore among those who believe that the necessary reversal of budget policy in the United States should be accompanied by some offsetting changes in the domestic saving-investment balances in Japan and Germany. Given the strength and relative stability of households' propensity to save in the latter two countries, and the significant negative impact of exchange rate appreciation on investment, some relaxation of the fiscal stance in Japan and in Germany is required. Otherwise, we run the risk that desired saving will exceed investment worldwide, unleashing recessionary forces, or that excessive pressure will be put on monetary relaxation. The recent slowdown in economic activity in Germany and in Japan, and the fact that during the first five months of 1987 the U.S. current account deficit was more than financed by increases in U.S. official monetary liabilities, are evidence of the twin dangers I am referring to.

What about exchange rates? I tend to disagree with the view expressed at this conference by Professor Tobin, that a hard landing of the dollar would now be desirable. The emphasis should rather be on domestic policy adaptations that enhance the effectiveness of the sizable exchange rate adjustments that have taken place since February 1985. By this I do not imply that *current* exchange rate levels are appropriate for a long and probably painful adjustment period. But current long-term interest-rate differentials of over 5% between the U.S. and Japan and some 3% between Germany and Japan are already consistent with gradual, but not disruptive, further adjustment of exchange rates over a relatively long period.

---

[1] See Masera, R.S., "Europe's Economic Problems in an International Perspective," *Banca Nazionale del Lavoro Quarterly Review*, No. 159, December 1986.

Optimal Monetary Regime and Policy Management for Economic Stability in the Future

10

Monetary Policy under Interest-Rate Targeting and Other Arrangements

Robert J. Barro

I. Introduction

Over the last decade and a half, the international monetary system has featured fiat currencies that are connected primarily by flexible exchange rates. The fiat nature of money means that individual countries do not face the constraints that would be imposed by a commodity-based currency. Similarly, flexibility of exchange rates means that countries do not have the external discipline that would be implied by fixed rates. Hence this system allows the various monetary authorities to carry out more or less independent monetary policies.

Some recent research, begun by Kydland and Prescott (1977) and carried forward by David Gordon and I (1983a, b), among others, provides positive theoretical analyses of monetary developments in this type of setting. With fiat currencies and flexible exchange rates, monetary authorities are free to pursue discretionary policies—that is, policies that further an objective from today onward without regard to prior commitments. Such commitments arise naturally within a commodity-based system, such as the gold standard, since monetary policy is constrained to maintain the pegged nominal price of the selected commodity or commodities. For a single country, the pegging of an exchange rate can serve a similar function. Even within a regime of fiat money and flexible exchange rates, it is possible for governments to establish rules for monetary aggregates or other nominal variables. Then these rules could provide the discipline that would arise automatically under a commodity standard or a regime with fixed exchange rates. But such rules tend to lack firm legal status, and seem often to degenerate into arrangements that are best described as discretionary.

The problem with a discretionary regime is that it creates incentives for the intelligent, well-meaning policymaker to generate surprise movements in money and the general price level. Such surprises help to expand the real economy in theoretical models that include some version of the Phillips curve. But even without the Phillips curve, nominal surprises look desirable from the standpoint of public finance. That is, if the government is a nominal debtor, surprise increases in money and prices effectively generate revenue (corresponding, as in explicit partial defaults, to reductions in the real value of outstanding debts). Moreover, since surprise inflation works like a capital levy on people's nominal assets, the revenue may be obtained without creating important economic distortions. At least, this tends to occur if—as may be true in a discretionary setting—the inflation surprises have little impact on the government's reputation for monetary stability.

Since people understand the government's constraints and incentives in a discretionary regime, inflation surprises would not have a positive bias in equilibrium. That is, rational expectations of inflation would take into account the tendency of governments to choose "high" rates of monetary growth and inflation. Because of this adjustment in expectations, the theory predicts that capital levies cannot occur systematically—that is, unexpected inflation must have a zero mean. However, the average rate of inflation ends up being higher than otherwise; in particular, higher than the value that would optimally be chosen under a monetary rule. Moreover, since the incentive to create nominal shocks depends on varying economic circumstances, the theory also predicts that inflation and monetary growth will be volatile. Correspondingly, the model predicts a great deal of variability in nominal interest rates. In a general way these kinds of predictions match up with the international economic performance since the advent of fiat currencies with flexible exchange rates in the early 1970s. The set of nominal variables—nominal interest rates, inflation rates, growth rates of money, and exchange rates—have all become substantially more volatile than at earlier times.

On the other hand, many economists and other observers have an unreasonable tendency to ascribe almost all of the world's economic ills since the early 1970s to flexible exchange rates. I know of no evidence that ties the fluctuations over the last decade and a half in real variables—such as real exchange rates, current-account balances, and real national products—to flexible exchange rates, per se. In fact, it seems likely that monetary policies had little to do with the recent performance of the real variables.

Consider, as an example, the experiences of Germany and Italy over the period from 1970 to 1985. These countries exhibited vastly different monetary policies, as demonstrated by the average annual inflation rates of 4.6% for Germany and 12.9% for Italy. Nevertheless, the average depreciation of the Italian lira and the average appreciation of the German mark were such as to generate similar patterns in the two real exchange rates with the U.S. dollar. The suggestion from these data is that the movements in the real exchange rates were governed primarily by real forces—which were similar for Germany and Italy in comparisons with the United States—and the very different monetary policies could not significantly alter these patterns. Instead, the monetary policies resulted primarily in differing paths of prices and nominal exchange rates. Of course, nothing in this analysis argues that the real exchange rates between either currency and the U.S. dollar would (counterfactually) be close to a fixed number, as suggested by some P.P.P. theories. But the idea is that the movements in the real exchange rates—which have been dramatic over the last decade and a half—represent real phenomena, which have little to do with monetary policies or with the flexibility of exchange rates, per se.

It seems that the high variance of real variables in recent years reflects mainly the greater incidence of real disturbances, such as oil shocks, technological advances, shifting patterns of comparative advantage across countries, and tax policies. It is probably preferable that the international economic system allowed the shocks to show up readily as movements in exchange rates and current-account balances. Without flexibility in these items, the same disturbances would have had to show up elsewhere, for example in greater fluctuations of domestic price levels or in increased restrictions on international trade in commodities and assets.

Although monetary policies probably have only second-order significance for the evolution of real variables, it is still important to consider the optimal design of these policies. Within a regime of flexible exchange rates and fiat currencies, each monetary authority can make an independent choice of monetary arrangements. I shall think about these choices in terms of alternative monetary rules, where a purely discretionary policy would appear as a polar case of a "rule" that involves no commitments. Hence I am assuming that the institutional structure allows for choices among different rules—that is, that legal or other enforcement mechanisms can be implemented to make the various rules credible.

Rules expressed in terms of monetary aggregates, such as Milton Friedman's (1960) proposals for expanding a particular concept of money at a constant rate, do not allow for reactions to disturbances. For example, shifts in the demand for money lead to changes in prices or nominal incomes or other variables, if the quantity of money does not respond. If the monetary authority's objective includes stability or predictability of the price level, then it may be preferable to allow for feedback from observed variables to the money supply. For instance, an increase in the real demand for money would call forth an expansion of the nominal quantity of money and thereby avoid an adjustment of the price level. The problem, however, is to generate the "correct" response of money to various shocks, and, in particular, to avoid a general tendency for excessive monetary growth.

Some economists have proposed a monetary policy that targets either an index of the general price level or another nominal variable, such as nominal GNP. Then, if an increase in money demand causes a decline in the price level or in nominal GNP, the rule calls for an increase in the money stock (accomplished perhaps by an open-market purchase of bonds). Some difficulties here include the lag in observing price indices and GNP, and the possibility that the "wrong" monetary reactions occur when there are changes in real GNP. (The results depend on whether systematic reactions of money to real GNP can help to stabilize the real economy. I am assuming that this type of countercyclical policy is not useful, but I do not analyze this issue in this paper.)

Most central bankers and some economists have focused on nominal interest rates as prime targets of monetary policy. One clear attraction of interest rates is that, unlike price indices and GNP, they are observable rapidly and with great accuracy. However, economists of the monetarist persuasion (such as Friedman 1968; and Brunner 1968) have generally viewed interest-rate targeting as inferior to rules expressed in terms of monetary aggregates. On one level, the sometimes vehement opposition to interest-rate targeting is surprising—after all, the nominal interest rate appears to be a perfectly fine nominal variable, which the monetary authority ought to be able to control, at least if it does not try simultaneously to peg some other nominal variable, such as the growth rate of money or the inflation rate or the rate of change of the exchange rate. Some arguments that have been offered in opposition to interest-rate targeting are first, too low an interest-rate target is thought to be inflationary, second, the pegging of a nominal interest rate may allow for substantial variability of the price level or of other variables that the policymaker cares about, and third, a particular nominal interest rate is consistent with any level of prices and money. The last point is sometimes expressed in terms of price-level determinism—pinning down the nominal interest rate seems to allow the price level and other nominal variables to take on arbitrary values.

II. Monetary Policy as Interest-Rate Targeting

In recent research I have changed my outlook on the desirability of interest-rate rules, and I now think that such rules can have desirable operating characteristics. The results can be illustrated by a simple stochastic model of money supply and demand, which is detailed in Barro (1987). Some related models were developed earlier by Goodfriend (1987) and McCallum (1986). The private economy is described by two equations, the first pertaining to interest-rate determination, and the second to the real demand for money:

$$R_t = E_t p_{t+1} - p_t + r + v_t \tag{1}$$

$$m_t - p_t = \alpha_t - \beta R_t + \eta_t \tag{2}$$

where the variables are

R_t: nominal interest rate,

p_t: log of price level,

$E_t p_{t+1}$: expectation of next period's log of price level, based on information available at date t,

m_t: log of quantity of money (measured empirically as the monetary base),

r: "permanent" part of the expected real interest rate, treated for simplicity as a constant,

v_t: temporary shock to the expected real interest rate, distributed independently as white noise, (mean 0, variance σ_v^2),

α_t: permanent part of level of real demand for money,

η_t: temporary shock to real demand for money, distributed independently as white noise, $(0, \sigma_\eta^2)$,

$\beta > 0$: coefficient of the nominal interest rate in the money-demand function.

The permanent component of money demand is generated from a random walk,

$$\alpha_t = \alpha_{t-1} + a_t \tag{3}$$

where a_t is distributed independently as white noise (mean 0, variance σ_a^2). In the present model, the shifts to money demand, a_t and η_t, include the effects from changes in output (permanent and temporary, respectively), which are treated as exogenous. Also, with m_t interpreted as the monetary base, the money-demand shocks would include changes in reserve requirements. In the model, the important assumptions are that the shocks to money demand (a_t and η_t) and to the expected real interest rate (v_t) are exogenous with respect to monetary movements.

I reluctantly treat the expected real interest rate as exogenous with respect to monetary variables because I lack an alternative specification that I regard as theoretically or empirically superior. However, even if this assumption is wrong, it may still be satisfactory in the present context if the connection between money and the expected real interest rate is much less important than that between money and expected inflation, and hence the nominal interest rate.

The monetary authority has the target, $\bar{R}_t$, for the nominal interest rate at date t. It turns out in this model that the authority has the ability and incentive to keep the actual rate, R_t, close to $\bar{R}_t$ in each period. Therefore, if $\bar{R}_t$ were constant, the model would predict little variations in nominal interest rates. But it is well known that, at least in recent years, nominal rates move around a good deal and in a largely unpredictable manner. In fact, even for short-term rates, a random walk turns out to be a fairly good description of the U.S. data. In order to accord with this observation, the model incorporates a target for the nominal interest rate that moves in a random-walk-like fashion,

$$\bar{R}_t = \bar{R}_{t-1} + u_t, \tag{4}$$

where u_t is an independent, white-noise process with moments, (0, σ_u^2). Mankiw (1986) provides a theoretical and empirical rationale for equation (4) from the standpoint of optimal public finance in an intertemporal context.

The monetary authority has control over the quantity of money (the monetary base), m_t, in each period. I consider here the interplay between interest rates and money in the form[1]

$$m_t - m_{t-1} = \mu_t + \lambda_1(R_t - \bar{R}_t) - \lambda_2(R_{t-1} - \bar{R}_{t-1}). \tag{5}$$

The term, μ_t, represents the permanent component of monetary growth. (A temporary part of monetary growth—possibly representing control

---

[1] More generally, the authority would react also to contemporaneous variables, such as a_t and $\bar{R}_t$. The price level is assumed to be observable with a one-period lag. Reactions to lagged values, such as p_{t-1}, turn out not to be useful.

errors—could also be added.) Consistency with the nominal interest rate target, $\bar{R}_t$, and the permanent part of the expected real interest rate, r, requires

$$\mu_t = \bar{R}_t - r. \tag{6}$$

Since $\bar{R}_t$ follows a random walk, the monetary growth rate in equation (5) includes the random-walk component, μ_t. Hence, if the nominal-interest-rate target is non-stationary, the monetary growth rate must also be non-stationary (see Goodfriend 1987).

Monetary growth in equation (5) depends on the current and lagged gap between the actual and target nominal interest rate. The term, $\lambda_1(R_t - \bar{R}_t)$ with $\lambda_1 >$ (which turns out to be the optimal sign), allows for the standard positive response of current monetary growth to an excess of the nominal interest rate above target. But, in the present model, the expected real interest rate is exogenous. Therefore, a positive reaction of $m_t - m_{t-1}$ to $R_t - \bar{R}_t$ can work to reduce R_t only if it lowers expected inflation, $E_t p_{t+1} - p_t$.[2] This reduction in expected inflation tends to occur if expected future monetary growth, $E_t m_{t+1} - m_t$, declines. In other words, an excess of R_t over $\bar{R}_t$ must create a tendency for some of today's infusion of money to be taken back in the future; for example, in the next period. This effect follows from the term, $-\lambda_2(R_{t-1} - \bar{R}_{t-1})$ with $\lambda_2 > 0$, in equation (5). In fact, to get a negative relation between $R_t - \bar{R}_t$ and $E_t m_{t+1} - m_t$ (and hence, $E_t p_{t+1} - p_t$), it will only be necessary to have $\lambda_2 > 0$. The value of λ_1 is irrelevant in this context because it affects equally the levels of money for periods t and $t + 1$. However, the choice of λ_1 turns out to matter if the monetary authority cares not only about targeting nominal interest rates, but also about the predictability of the price level. This last consideration pins down the desired response of the level of money to an interest-rate gap, which then determines the value of λ_1 (and thereby makes determinate the level of prices at each date).

The linear model described by equations (1)–(6) can be solved in the usual way by the method of undetermined coefficients (see Lucas 1973; Barro 1976; McCallum 1983, 1986; and Goodfriend 1987). The main issue is the specification of the information set used to compute

---

[2] Shiller (1980, p. 130) recognizes this possibility but regards it as implausible. "We usually think that increasing high-powered money is, if anything, a signal of higher inflation. It would seem implausible, then, that these lower interest rates are due to lower inflationary expectations. It is conceivable that exogenous increases in the money stock might be a sign of lower inflation over a certain time horizon if the parameters of our model were just right." In the present model the parameters turn out "just right" as a consequence of the monetary authority's own optimal behavior.

the expectation, $E_t p_{t+1}$. I assume that this information set includes R_t, m_t, $\bar{R}_t$, α_t, and all lagged variables. Given this specification, the analysis is straightforward (although lengthy), and I present only the final form of the solution:[3]

$$R_t = \bar{R}_t + \left[\frac{1}{1 + \beta + \lambda_2}\right](\eta_t + v_t) \tag{7}$$

$$p_t = -\alpha_t + m_{t-1} + (1 + \beta)\bar{R}_t - r - \lambda_2(R_{t-1} - \bar{R}_{t-1})$$

$$+ \left[\frac{\beta + \lambda_1}{1 + \beta + \lambda_2}\right]v_t - \left[\frac{1 + \lambda_2 - \lambda_1}{1 + \beta + \lambda_2}\right]\eta_t \tag{8}$$

$$m_t = m_{t-1} + \bar{R}_t - r - \lambda_2(R_{t-1} - \bar{R}_{t-1})$$

$$+ \left[\frac{\lambda_1}{1 + \beta + \lambda_2}\right](\eta_t + v_t). \tag{9}$$

Equation (7) shows that R_t depends on $\eta_t + v_t$, which combines the temporary shocks to money demand and the expected real interest rate. In the absence of any reaction of money supply, these terms would add to R_t. (An increase in η_t raises R_t by lowering today's price level relative to the next period's; an increase in v_t raises R_t directly by the increase in the expected real interest rate.) The reaction of future monetary growth, $m_{t+1} - m_t$, to the term, $-\lambda_2(R_t - \bar{R}_t)$, offsets these forces. In particular, equation (7) shows that a higher value of λ_2 reduces the effect on R_t from the temporary shocks, $\eta_t + v_t$.

I assume that the monetary authority seeks to minimize the magnitude of departures of R_t from $\bar{R}_t$, but also desires to hold down the (one-period-ahead) forecast variance of the price level, $E_t (p_{t+1} - E_t p_{t+1})^2$. Specifically, the objective is

$$\text{MIN. } J \equiv A \cdot VAR(R - \bar{R}) + B \cdot VAR(p) \tag{10}$$

where A and B are positive coefficients, and the variances are based on information from the previous period. Using equations (7) and (8), the two variances are

$$VAR(R - \bar{R}) = \left[\frac{1}{1 + \beta + \lambda_2}\right]^2 (\sigma_\eta^2 + \sigma_v^2). \tag{11}$$

$$VAR(p) = \sigma_\alpha^2 + (1 + \beta)^2 \sigma_u^2$$

$$+ \left[\frac{\lambda_1 + \beta}{1 + \beta + \lambda_2}\right]^2 \sigma_v^2 + \left[\frac{1 + \lambda_2 - \lambda_1}{1 + \beta + \lambda_2}\right]^2 \sigma_\eta^2. \tag{12}$$

---

[3] The derivation uses McCallum's (1983, 1986) procedure for selecting the unique, bubble-free solution.

I assume that the monetary authority chooses the interest-rate reaction parameters, λ_1 and λ_2, to minimize J in equation (10). Note that $VAR(R - \bar{R})$ in equation (11) is independent of λ_1. (The contemporaneous reaction of money to the interest rate, which depends on λ_1, affects the levels of money and prices, but not the rates of change that matter for the nominal interest rate.) Hence, λ_1 can be chosen to minimize $VAR(p)$ for a given value of λ_2. In particular, the solution for λ_1 as a function of λ_2 does not depend on the weights, A and B, in equation (10). The resulting condition is

$$\lambda_1 = \frac{(1 + \lambda_2)\sigma_\eta^2 - \beta\sigma_v^2}{\sigma_\eta^2 + \sigma_v^2}. \tag{13}$$

Given this choice for λ_1 as a function of λ_2, $VAR(p)$ in equation (12) becomes

$$VAR(p) = \sigma_a^2 + (1 + \beta)^2\sigma_u^2 + \sigma_\eta^2\sigma_v^2/(\sigma_\eta^2 + \sigma_v^2) \tag{14}$$

which is independent of λ_2. Therefore, as long as λ_1 varies along with λ_2 to satisfy equation (13), λ_2 can be chosen (independently of the weights A and B) to minimize $VAR(R - \bar{R})$. It follows immediately from equation (11) that the best choice is $\lambda_2 \to \infty$.[4] Equation (13) then implies $\lambda_1 \to \infty$, but the ratio, λ_1/λ_2, remains finite and is given by

$$\frac{\lambda_1}{\lambda_2} = \frac{\sigma_\eta^2}{\sigma_\eta^2 + \sigma_v^2}. \tag{15}$$

Hence $0 \leq \lambda_1/\lambda_2 \leq 1$—the lagged reaction of money to the nominal interest rate is greater in magnitude (and opposite in sign) to the contemporaneous reaction. However, in the limit, each reaction becomes infinite in order to keep the nominal interest rate, R_t, arbitrarily close to its target, $\bar{R}_t$, in each period.

Using the form of the monetary rule from equation (5) and the optimal choices for λ_1 and λ_2, the equilibrium solutions for R_t, p_t, and m_t in equations (7)–(9) become[5]

$$R_t = \bar{R}_t = R_{t-1} + u_t \tag{16}$$

---

[4] The choice $\lambda_2 \to -\infty$ seems also to work. However, $\lambda_2 \leq -(1 + \beta)$ can be ruled out on grounds discussed by McCallum (1986, p. 140, n.7). In particular, if $\lambda_2 \leq -(1 + \beta)$, then the realization of a shock—say η_t—causes an unstable dynamic response of the price level.

[5] The terms, $-(\eta_{t-1} + v_{t-1})$, in equations (17) and (18) are the limit of the expression, $-\lambda_2(R_{t-1} - \bar{R}_{t-1})$, as $\lambda_2 \to \infty$. Note that $R_{t-1} - \bar{R}_{t-1} = (\eta_{t-1} + v_{t-1})/(1 + \beta + \lambda_2)$ from equation (7).

$$p_t = -\alpha_t + m_{t-1} + (1 + \beta)\bar{R}_t - r - (\eta_{t-1} + v_{t-1})$$

$$- \left[\frac{\sigma_v^2}{\sigma_\eta^2 + \sigma_v^2}\right]\eta_t + \left[\frac{\sigma_\eta^2}{\sigma_\eta^2 + \sigma_v^2}\right]v_t \qquad (17)$$

$$m_t = m_{t-1} + \bar{R}_t - r - (\eta_{t-1} + v_{t-1})$$

$$+ \left[\frac{\sigma_\eta^2}{\sigma_\eta^2 + \sigma_v^2}\right](\eta_t + v_t). \qquad (18)$$

Equation (18) shows that monetary growth partially accommodates the current temporary shocks to money demand and the real interest rate, $\eta_t + v_t$; that is, the coefficient is $\sigma_\eta^2/(\sigma_\eta^2 + \sigma_v^2)$. Since σ_η^2 is the variance of temporary shocks to money demand, and σ_v^2 is the variance of temporary shocks to the expected real interest rate, the result says that contemporaneous monetary accommodation is greater the larger the variance of money demand relative to that of the expected real interest rate. Interpreting σ_η^2 as the variance of the LM curve and σ_v^2 as the variance of the IS curve, the results are reminiscent of those found by Poole (1970). However, in the present model, the tradeoff is not between targeting nominal interest rates and targeting monetary aggregates. The targeting of the nominal interest rate is complete here independently of the values of σ_η^2 and σ_v^2 (that is, of the relative volatility of the LM and IS curves). In the present model, the tradeoff that determines the extent of current accommodation comes, in equation (17), from the negative response of p_t to the money-demand shock, η_t, and the positive response to the real-interest-rate shock, v_t. (The former reflects the negative effect on prices from an increase in money demand less the positive effect from the monetary response. The latter reflects only the monetary reaction.) The extent of monetary accommodation is determined to make the overall variance of p_t from these two sources of disturbances as small as possible.

With a one-period lag, monetary growth has an inverse, one-to-one reaction to the temporary shocks ($\eta_{t-1} + v_{t-1}$ in equation [18]). This response generates the reduction in expected inflation (see equation [17]) that allows the monetary authority to offset an incipient excess of R_t over $\bar{R}_t$. In particular, although the temporary shock, $\eta_t + v_t$, induces an increase in today's monetary growth, it also generates the promise of an even greater reduction in next period's monetary growth.

One of the prime sources of temporary shifts to money demand, η_t, would be temporary fluctuations in output. The results in equations (17) and (18) imply (for a given expected real interest rate) that these temporary (exogenous) shifts in output would be contemporaneously negatively correlated with the price level and contemporaneously positively correlated with the money supply. (The same results obtain for permanent shifts in output, as reflected in a_t.) Thus the results are consistent with Fair's (1979) findings about the relation between shocks to output and prices for the United States in the post–World War II period. Also, the results accord with many analyses that report a positive correlation between money and output, although the relation reflects here the endogenous response of the money supply (which has been stressed by King and Plosser 1984). On the other hand, lagged output (that is, η_{t-1}) would be negatively correlated with current money (and prices). This result means that monetary growth would exhibit a countercyclical reaction to lagged output. This type of relation has been found for M1 growth in the post–World War II United States (Barro 1981).

III. Implications of the Theory for Monetary Base Growth and Inflation

Let $\Delta R_t = R_t - R_{t-1}$, $\Delta m_t = m_t - m_{t-1}$ (the growth rate of the monetary base), and $\Delta p_t = p_t - p_{t-1}$ (the inflation rate). Equation (16) implies that ΔR_t is white noise. (If $\bar{R}_t$ were not a random walk, but instead had a mean-reverting tendency in the long run, then the process for R_t would change accordingly.) Equations (17) and (18) prescribe the patterns for Δp_t and Δm_t that are consistent with this process for ΔR_t, given the underlying model in equations (1)–(6). These predictions about inflation and monetary base growth are the principal empirical content of the theory.

Taking first differences of equation (18) leads to

$$\Delta m_t = \Delta m_{t-1} + u_t + \left[\frac{\sigma_\eta^2}{\sigma^2 + \sigma_v^2}\right](\eta_t + v_t)$$

$$- \left[\frac{2\sigma_\eta^2 + \sigma_v^2}{\sigma_\eta^2 + \sigma_v^2}\right](\eta_{t-1} + v_{t-1}) + (\eta_{t-2} + v_{t-2})$$

$$= \Delta m_{t-1} + E_t = \Delta m_{t-1} + e_t + a_1 e_{t-1} + a_2 e_{t-1} \tag{19}$$

where E_t is a composite error term and e_t is a white-noise disturbance. In other words, the model implies that Δm_t is an ARMA (1, 2) process. Furthermore, the theory imposes restrictions on the coefficients of this process. The AR (1) coefficient is unity, which reflects the nonstationarity in monetary growth that is induced by the (assumed) nonstationarity of the nominal-interest-rate target (equation [4]). The two MA coefficients must be such as to satisfy the conditions,

$$a_1(1 + a_2)\sigma_e^2 = COV(E_t, E_{t-1})$$

$$= -(2\sigma_\eta^2 + \sigma_v^2)^2/(\sigma_\eta^2 + \sigma_v^2) < 0 \tag{20}$$

$$a_2\sigma_e^2 = COV(E_t, E_{t-2}) = \sigma_\eta^2 > 0 \tag{21}$$

$$\sigma_e^2[1 + (a_1)^2 + (a_2)^2] = VAR(E_t)$$

$$= \text{(terms involving } \sigma_u^2, \sigma_\eta^2, \sigma_v^2) \tag{22}$$

where σ_e^2 is the variance of e_t. Equations (20) and (21) imply $a_1 \leq 0$ and $a_2 \geq 0$. Moreover, the magnitude of a_1 is much greater than that of a_2—one inequality that holds is $|a_1| \geq 4a_2/(1 + a_2)$. As σ_u^2 becomes small, the solution approaches stationarity for $\bar{R}_t$, and hence for monetary growth and inflation. In particular, as σ_u^2 approaches zero, the solution tends toward $a_1 + a_2 = -1$.

The equation for the inflation rate comes from first differencing of equation (17). After substituting for Δm_{t-1} on the right side (using equation [18]) and simplifying, the results are

$$\Delta p_t = \Delta p_{t-1} - a_t + (1 + \beta)u_t - \left[\frac{\sigma_v^2}{\sigma_\eta^2 + \sigma_v^2}\right]\eta_t + \left[\frac{\sigma_\eta^2}{\sigma_\eta^2 + \sigma_v^2}\right]v_t$$

$$+ a_{t-1} - \beta u_{t-1} + \left[\frac{\sigma_v^2}{\sigma_\eta^2 + \sigma_v^2}\right]\eta_{t-1} - \left[\frac{2\sigma_\eta^2 + \sigma_v^2}{\sigma_\eta^2 + \sigma_v^2}\right]v_{t-1} + v_{t-2}$$

$$= \Delta p_{t-1} + F_t = \Delta p_{t-1} + f_t + b_1 f_{t-1} + b_2 f_{t-2} \tag{23}$$

where F_t is a composite error term and f_t is a white-noise disturbance (which is not generally independent of e_t). As before, Δp_t is an ARMA (1, 2) process with an AR (1) coefficient of unity. The two MA coefficients satisfy

$$b_1(1 + b_2)\sigma_f^2 = COV(F_t, F_{t-1})$$

$$= -\sigma_a^2 + \beta(1 + \beta)\sigma_u^2 - \left[\frac{\sigma_v^2}{\sigma_\eta^2 + \sigma_v^2}\right](4\sigma_\eta^2 + \sigma_v^2) \tag{24}$$

$$b_2\sigma_f^2 = COV(F_t, F_{t-2}) = \sigma_\eta^2\sigma_v^2/(\sigma_\eta^2 + \sigma_v^2) > 0 \tag{25}$$

$$\sigma_f^2[1 + (b_1)^2 + (b_2)^2] = VAR(F_t)$$

$$= \text{(terms involving } \sigma_a^2, \sigma_u^2, \sigma_\eta^2, \sigma_v^2). \tag{26}$$

If $\beta(1 + \beta)\sigma_u^2 < \sigma_a^2$, the coefficients satisfy $b_1 \leq 0$ and $b_2 \geq 0$. The magnitude of b_1 tends again to be much greater than that of b_2. Also, $\sigma_u^2 = 0$ implies $b_1 + b_2 = -1$.

IV. Empirical Findings

The main empirical results involve seasonally unadjusted U.S. data since 1890 on nominal interest rates (4- to 6-month prime commercial paper), the monetary base (unadjusted for changes in reserve requirements), the consumer price index (CPI-U, available since 1913, except that the index without the shelter component was used since 1970), and the producer price index (PPI, all commodities).[6] All variables are monthly but observed at the quarterly intervals of January, April, July, and October. The identification of the period in the theory with quarters is, of course, somewhat arbitrary.

The underlying data are averages of daily figures for interest rates and the monetary base (except that before August 1917 the available figures on the monetary base are at the end of each month). The price indices are some kind of average of observations during each month, although for the CPI some of the components are sampled only quarterly. The 3-month spacing between each monthly observation should minimize some of the problems related to time-averaged data.

Table 10.1 contains regression results for the recent period, 1954.1 to 1986.4. Starting in 1954 avoids the extremely low nominal interest rates through the early 1950s, for which the lower bound of zero would be significant (so that nominal interest rates could not be approximated as a random walk). Also, this sample excludes the effects on the price indices from the controls during World War II and the Korean War.

The basic format of the empirical results consists of estimated equations within a fairly general ARMA representation,

$$Y_t = c_1 S_{1t} + c_2 S_{2t} + c_3 S_{3t} + c_4 S_{4t} + c_5 Y_{t-1}$$
$$+ e_t + c_6 e_{t-1} + c_7 e_{t-2} + c_8 e_{t-3} + c_9 e_{t-4} \tag{27}$$

[6] The nominal interest rate applies to 4- to 6-month commercial paper (6-month paper in recent years), as reported since 1890 in U.S. Board of Governors of the Federal Reserve System, *Banking and Monetary Statistics, 1941–1970, Annual Statistical Digest, 1970–1979*, and later issues, and the *Federal Reserve Bulletin.* Earlier data, from Macaulay (1938, Appendix Table 10), refer to 60–90 day commercial paper. (These were adjusted upward by .014 to merge with the other series in 1890.) The monetary base since 1914 comes from the Federal Reserve sources noted above. Earlier data come from the National Bureau of Economic Research. The CPI since 1913 is from the Bureau of Labor Statistics (CPI-U, with the CPI less shelter used since 1970 to avoid problems with mortgage interest costs). The PPI (all commodities) since 1913 comes from the Bureau of Labor Statistics. Data from 1890 to 1912 are from U.S. Department of Labor, *Index Numbers of Wholesale Prices on Pre-War Basis*, U.S. Government Printing Office, 1928 (kindly provided by Jeff Miron). Data before 1890 are from Warren and Pearson 1933, Table 1.

Table 10.1   Regression Results for 1954: 1–1986: 4

Dep. Y_t	Var.	C	S1	S2	S3	S4	Y_{t-1}	MA (1)	MA (2)	MA (3)	MA (4)	$\hat{\sigma}$	$Q(10)$ (degrees of freedom, significance level)	Likelihood-Ratio Tests I	II
R	(1)	.000 (.001)					1					.0116	13.9 (10, .18)	1.6 (3, .67)	8.2 (8, .42)
	(2)	.004 (.002)					.934 (.030)					.0115	12.2 (9, .20)	1.5 (3, .68)	3.5 (7, .83)
Δm	(3)	.000 (.007)										.0849	601 (10, .000)	190 (3, .000)	268 (8, .000)
	(4)		.044 (.006)	−.081 (.006)	.099 (.006)	−.059 (.006)	1	−.799 (.089)	−.054 (.089)			.0326	9.7 (8, .29)	105 (3, .000)	1.80 (3, .62)
	(5)		.045 (.006)	−.079 (.010)	.099 (.006)	−.056 (.012)	.963 (.115)	−.787 (.148)	−.001 (.092)			.0325	9.5 (7, .22)	127 (3, .000)	.00 (2, .99)
Δp	(6)	.000 (.003)					1					.0300	39 (10, .000)	18.0 (3, .001)	86 (8, .000)
	(7)		−.006 (.004)	.015 (.004)	.005 (.004)	−.013 (.004)	1	−.676 (.089)	.063 (.090)			.0237	16.6 (8, .04)	23 (3, .000)	18.8 (3, .001)
	(8)		−.007 (.004)	.015 (.004)	.005 (.004)	−.013 (.004)	1	−.721 (.090)	.077 (.090)	.355 (.097)		.0228	7.2 (7, .42)	15.2 (3, .003)	7.0 (2, .03)
	(9)		−.003 (.005)	.019 (.004)	.010 (.005)	−.008 (.005)	.886 (.070)	−.657 (.114)	.087 (.092)	.361 (.101)		.0223	4.8 (6, .57)	14.0 (3, .005)	6.0* (5, .30)

Δ(PPI) (10)	.000				1					.0453	46	12.0	58
	(.004)										(10, .000)	(3, .009)	(8, .000)
(11)	.020	$-.008$	.001	$-.014$	1	$-.484$	$-.129$			.0396	20.1	8.0	17.5
	(.007)	(.007)	(.007)	(.007)		(.089)	(.090)				(8, .01)	(3, .05)	(3, .001)
(12)	.026	$-.002$	.011	$-.004$	.760	$-.325$	$-.048$	.250	.262	.0375	6.8	7.9	3.9*
	(.007)	(.008)	(.008)	(.008)	(.098)	(.134)	(.100)	(.102)	(.109)		(5, .24)	(3, .05)	(4, .43)

* Test versus model with 8 MA terms and unrestricted AR(1).

I: test for inclusion of seasonals, S1-S4

II: test versus inclusion of seasonals plus MA(1)-MA(4) plus unrestricted AR(1)

—that is, an ARMA (1, 4) process with deterministic seasonals, where e_t is a white-noise error and Y_t represents R_t, ΔM_t, ΔP_t, or $\Delta(\text{PPI})_t$. (R is the commercial paper rate, ΔM is the growth rate of the monetary base, ΔP is the growth rate of the CPI, and $\Delta[\text{PPI}]$ is the growth rate of the producer price index.) The variable S_{1t} is a seasonal dummy for the first quarter (1 for January, 0 otherwise), and similarly for S_{2t} (for April), S_{3t} (for July), and S_{4t} (for October). For R_t as the dependent variable, the hypothesis (under a regime of interest-rate smoothing) is $c_1 = c_2 = c_3 = c_4 = 0$ (or possibly a constant), $c_5 = 1$, $c_6 = c_7 = c_8 = c_9 = 0$. For ΔM_t, ΔP_t, and $\Delta(\text{PPI})_t$, the model under interest-rate smoothing suggests nonzero values for c_1, c_2, c_3, and c_4, $c_5 = 1$, $c_6 \leq 0$, $c_7 \geq 0$ (with $|c_6|$ much greater than c_7 and $c_6 + c_7 \geq -1$), and $c_8 = c_9 = 0$. (However, some of these restrictions depend somewhat on identifying the "period" in the theory with quarters in the data.)

Aside from the estimated coefficients and (asymptotic) standard errors, the table reports the following statistics:

$Q(10)$: Q-statistic for serial correlation of residuals with 10 lags, with degrees of freedom and asymptotic significance level (based on the χ^2 distribution) shown in parentheses,

I: likelihood-ratio statistic (equal to $-2 \cdot \log$ of likelihood ratio) for the equation with seasonals against the null hypothesis of the same equation except for no seasonality ($c_1 = c_2 = c_3 = c_4$), with degrees of freedom (three) and asymptotic significance level (based on the χ^2 distribution) shown in parentheses,

II: likelihood-ratio statistic for the estimated model as the null hypothesis against the alternative of unrestricted coefficients in the form of equation (27) (an ARMA [1, 4] with deterministic seasonals). Degrees of freedom and significance level (based on the χ^2 distribution) are shown in parentheses. Part of the null hypothesis tested here involves a unit AR(1) coefficient, but I have not corrected for unit-root problems of the sort explored by Fuller (1976) because I do not know how to make the appropriate adjustment within an ARMA model. Presumably the true significance levels are higher than those shown in the table (that is, the null hypothesis is actually more difficult to reject in each case).

The simple random-walk model, $R_t = R_{t-1} + \text{constant}$ (where the constant could be set to zero here), is satisfactory for the nominal interest rate in the post-1954 period. Notably, $Q(10)$ from line 1 of Table 10.1 has a significance level of .18, while the likelihood-ratio statistics *I* and *II* have significance levels of .67 and .42, respectively. Given this behavior of the nominal interest rate, the theoretical model's other predictions should apply to monetary base growth and inflation.

The estimated equation for the growth rate of the monetary base, shown in line 4 of Table 10.1 exhibits remarkably strong seasonality, with a likelihood-ratio statistic *I* of 105. The estimated MA(1) coefficient is highly significant, $-.80$, s.e. $= .09$, and conforms in sign and rough magnitude with the model's predictions. The estimated MA(2) coefficient, $-.05$, s.e. $= .09$, differs insignificantly from zero, but also differs insignificantly from the small positive values suggested by the theory. The ARMA (1, 2) model with the AR(1) coefficient restricted to unity appears satisfactory according to the Q-statistic and likelihood-ratio statistic *II*. Moreover, the unrestricted estimate of DM_{t-1}, shown in line 5, is .96, s.e. $= .12$.

For the CPI inflation rate, shown on line 7, the restricted ARMA (1, 2) model has significant seasonals, but at levels much smaller than those for the growth rate of the monetary base. The pattern of the two MA coefficients ($-.68$, s.e. $= .09$, and .06, s.e. $= .09$) also accords with the theory. However, the Q-statistic and likelihood-ratio statistic *II* indicate problems that are mostly eliminated by the addition of an MA(3) term (line 8 of Table 10.1) with estimated coefficient, .36, s.e. $=$ .10. (If the AR[1] coefficient is unrestricted, as in line 9 of the table, its estimated coefficient is .89, s.e. $= .07$, which probably differs insignificantly from one.) Overall, the CPI inflation rate shows somewhat greater "persistence" than predicted by the theory. This outcome may be explicable from a model that includes gradual adjustment of prices or in money demand. However, to fit the data, the model would have to generate extra persistence in prices without simultaneously generating this persistence in the monetary base or the nominal interest rate. It is also possible that the results can be explained on purely mechanical grounds, which include the infrequent sampling of some components of the CPI and the departure between reported and transactions prices.

The producer price inflation rate, considered in lines 11 and 12 of Table 10.1, also shows extra persistence. In this case (on line 12) the estimated MA(3) and MA(4) coefficients are each positive and significant (.25, s.e. $= .10$, and .26, s.e. $= .11$, respectively). Also, the freely estimated AR(1) coefficient, .76, s.e. $= .10$, may differ significantly from one. A possible interpretation of these results is that the producer price index amounts to a bad proxy for the price level that

Table 10.2　Regression Results for 1922: 1–1940: 4

Dep. Var, Y_t		C	S1	S2	S3	S4	Y_{t-1}	MA (1)	MA (2)	MA (3)	MA (4)	$\hat{\sigma}$	$Q(10)$ (degrees of freedom, significance level)	Likelihood-Ratio Tests I	II
R	(1)	−.0007 (.0005)					1					.0047	16.6 (10, .09)	6.0 (3, .12)	15.1 (8, .06)
	(2)		−.0014 (.0010)	.0001 (.0010)	−.0024 (.0010)	.0009 (.0010)	1	.235 (.119)				.0045	10.7 (9, .30)	8.7 (3, .04)	4.9 (4, .30)
	(3)		.0001 (.0014)	.0016 (.0013)	−.0010 (.0013)	.0022 (.0013)	.949 (.029)	.259 (.123)				.0045	9.3 (8, .32)	8.7 (3, .04)	2.5 (3, .48)
Δm	(4)	.003 (.015)					1					.1346	21.3 (10, .02)	19.4 (3, .000)	59 (8, .000)
	(5)		−.090 (.022)	−.011 (.022)	.075 (.022)	.039 (.022)	1	−.659 (.122)	−.276 (.122)			.0957	10.4 (8, .25)	16.4 (3, .001)	1.5 (3, .68)
	(6)		−.086 (.038)	−.010 (.023)	.076 (.022)	.045 (.032)	.946 (.250)	−.740 (.282)	−.125 (.132)			.0959	10.1 (7, .19)	23 (3, .000)	0.7 (2, .70)
Δp	(7)	.000 (.008)					1					.0669	18.8 (10, .04)	12.1 (3, .009)	49 (8, .000)
	(8)		−.036 (.012)	.007 (.012)	.034 (.012)	−.001 (.012)	1	−.640 (.120)	.136 (.120)			.0536	3.5 (8, .90)	12.8 (3, .007)	9.9 (3, .02)
	(9)		−.035 (.012)	−.002 (.014)	.027 (.013)	.001 (.012)	.745 (.202)	−.509 (.233)	.188 (.129)			.0506	2.3 (7, .94)	15.8 (3, .002)	0.2 (2, .90)

Δ(PPI) (10)	.000					1			.1424	16.6	4.8	38
	(.016)									(10, .09)	(3, .19)	(8, .000)
(11)	−.057	.003	.038	.015		1	−.573	−.316	.1198	5.6	3.0	6.6
	(.027)	(.027)	(.027)	(.027)			(.120)	(.120)		(8, .69)	(3, .40)	(3, .09)
(12)	−.054	−.002	−.033	.016		.841	−.503	−.203	.1172	4.9	3.8	2.2
	(.032)	(.036)	(.035)	(.027)		(.709)	(.720)	(.269)		(7, .67)	(3, .29)	(2, .34)

I: test for inclusion of seasonals, S1–S4

II: test versus inclusion of seasonals plus MA(1)–MA(4) plus unrestricted AR(1)

matters in the theory (in the determination of money demand and for the calculation of the expected real interest rate). Then the extra persistence may reflect the characteristics of this measurement error. This viewpoint may also apply, but probably with lesser weight, to the CPI.

Table 10.2 shows comparable results for the interwar period, 1922.1–1940.4. There is now some indication of predictable movements in the nominal interest rate. For example, in line 2 of the table, the estimated MA(1) coefficient is .24, s.e. = .12, and the likelihood-ratio statistic *I* for the seasonals has a significance level of .04. However, the seasonal coefficients are small in magnitude. These results turn out to be a middle ground between those shown in Table 10.1 for the post-1954 period and those examined below for the pre-1914 period, which reveal substantial predictable movements in the nominal interest rate.

The growth rate of the monetary base, considered in line 5 of Table 10.2, again exhibits pronounced seasonality, although the pattern differs from that for the post-1954 period. Possible explanations for this shift are the change in composition of the monetary base away from bank reserves and toward currency held by the public, and the substantial variations in reserve requirements. (I have not yet investigated these possibilities.) The ARMA (1, 2) process with the AR(1) coefficient restricted to unity appears satisfactory for the interwar period; the *Q*-statistic on line 5 has a significance level of .25 and the likelihood ratio statistic *II* has a significance level of .68. However, the estimated MA(2) coefficient of − .28, s.e. − .12, differs significantly from the hypothesized value, which is small and positive. One possible story is that this "error" in the structure of the monetary process for the interwar period explains why some short-term predictability remained in the nominal interest rate.

The ARMA (1, 2) processes appear satisfactory now for the CPI and PPI inflation rates (lines 8 and 11 of Table 10.2). However, there is some possibility that the AR(1) coefficient for CPI inflation is less than one (line 9), and the estimated MA(2) coefficient for PPI inflation is significantly negative (line 11).

Table 10.3 shows results for the period 1890.3–1913.4, which applies to the gold standard and precedes the founding of the Federal Reserve. For this period the nominal interest rate appears to be stationary and an AR(1) coefficient of zero is satisfactory (lines 2 and 3 of the table). There is now substantial short-run predictability of movements in the nominal interest rate; in line 2 the likelihood-ratio statistic *I* for seasonality has a significance level of .001. In addition, the first three MA coefficients are positive and significant (.49, s.e. = .11; .21, s.e. = .11; and .25, s.e. = .11).

Table 10.3   Regression Results for 1890.3–1913.4

Dep. Var. Y_t		C	S1	S2	S3	S4	Y_{t-1}	MA (1)	MA (2)	MA (3)	MA (4)	$\hat{\sigma}$	$Q(10)$ (degrees of freedom, significance level)	Likelihood-Ratio Tests I	II
R	(1)	.000 (.001)					1					.0110	24.5 (10, .008)	17.6 (3, .001)	55 (8, .000)
	(2)		.057 (.002)	.055 (.002)	.055 (.002)	.062 (.002)	0	.492 (.107)	.211 (.107)	.252 (.108)		.0088	11.8 (7, .11)	17.5 (3, .001)	8.2* (6, .23)
	(3)		.045 (.025)	.045 (.023)	.045 (.023)	.052 (.023)	.186 (.408)	.318 (.422)	.113 (.234)	.210 (.138)		.0088	11.3 (6, .08)	17.0 (3, .001)	7.8* (5, .17)
Δm	(4)	.001 (.011)					1					.1069	41 (10, .000)	48 (3, .000)	96 (8, .000)
	(5)		.048 (.014)	.011 (.014)	−.009 (.014)	.104 (.014)	0	.280 (.106)				.0668	7.2 (9, .62)	38 (3, .000)	2.5 (4, .65)
	(6)		.072 (.039)	.022 (.022)	−.007 (.014)	.101 (.014)	−.227 (.357)	.516 (.373)				.0666	6.6 (8, .58)	37 (3, .000)	1.5 (3, .64)
Δ(PPI)	(7)	.000 (.017)										.1608	26 (10, .006)	24 (3, .000)	85 (8, .000)
	(8)		−.036 (.024)	.002 (.022)	−.024 (.022)	.088 (.022)	.238 (.098)				−.381 (.107)	.1058	6.9 (8, .54)	27 (3, .000)	1.0 (3, .80)

* Test versus model with 8 MA terms and unrestricted AR(1).
I: test for inclusion of seasonals, S1-S4
II: test versus inclusion of seasonals plus MA(1)–MA(4) plus unrestricted AR(1)

Given the absence of interest-rate smoothing, the behavior of the monetary base and the price level before 1914 should differ from that found in the later periods. The results suggest that the growth rate of the monetary base before 1914 (which coincides in this period with currency in circulation) is stationary, and an AR(1) coefficient of zero is satisfactory (lines 5 and 6 of Table 10.3). There are significant seasonals in monetary base growth, as shown on line 5 by the significance level of .000 for the likelihood-ratio statistic *I*. (I have not yet examined whether these seasonals show up as gold flows or as variations in the domestic component of the monetary base.) In any event, the seasonal in the monetary base did not eliminate the seasonal in the nominal interest rate. In fact, since the United States was on the gold standard, the behavior of the monetary base (and the U.S. price level) would have been largely constrained to be consistent with the world price level (including its seasonal pattern if it had one). Therefore, it would not generally be possible under this type of monetary system to choose a seasonal in the monetary base that removed the seasonal in the nominal interest rate.

Aside from the seasonals, the results for the growth rate of the monetary base on line 5 indicate a positive MA(1) coefficient, .28, s.e. = .11. The simple specification that monetary base growth is an MA(1) with seasonals appears satisfactory according to the *Q*-statistic and the likelihood-ratio statistic *II*.

Viewed jointly, the results for the nominal interest rate and the monetary base in Tables 10.1–10.3 are consistent with the viewpoint (expressed recently by Mankiw, Miron, and Weil 1986) that shifts in monetary policy after the founding of the Federal Reserve in 1914 were responsible for the elimination of predictable temporary movements, including seasonals, in the nominal interest rate. In the present analysis these shifts in monetary policy are identified with specific changes in the structure of the process for monetary base growth. Namely, the growth rate became non-stationary, a substantially negative MA(1) coefficient appeared, and the seasonal patterns changed. Moreover, the results for the interwar period suggest that the Federal Reserve did not get the monetary process right immediately. Only in the post-1954 period does all the short-term predictability of nominal interest rate movements seem to disappear. On the other hand, the results are also consistent with the idea that the elimination of a serious gold standard—also occurring in 1914—was responsible for the changed behavior of nominal interest rates. The elimination of the gold standard may have been a prerequisite for the implementation of a monetary policy that successfully targeted nominal interest rates.

The PPI inflation rate from 1890 to 1913 shows significant seasonality and appears to be stationary (the estimated AR[1] coefficient on line 8 of Table 3 is .24, s.e. = .10). The estimated MA coefficients are insignificant, except for a negative MA(4) ($-.38$, s.e. = .11), which might reflect stochastic variation in seasonals. The CPI is unavailable for this period, except for rough estimates on an annual basis.

V. Extensions of the Analysis

The empirical results for the United States that I have discussed are preliminary and are part of an ongoing research effort. One important issue that I am considering is the implication of international interactions for the feasibility and desirability of interest-rate smoothing. Also, is it possible for different countries to target interest rates independently, or is it feasible only for the world economy to coordinate such policies?

With a classical gold standard, monetary policies are constrained by fixed exchange rates and by a fixed nominal price of gold. In such an environment, central banks—even if acting jointly—can target nominal interest rates only if they can systematically affect at least one real variable, namely the relative price of gold. The policy is not a purely nominal one, as may be true in a regime of fiat money and flexible exchange rates. However, especially with variations in central banks' reserves of gold (which constitute one part of the world's demand for gold), it seems that such real effects would be possible. Although it may be impossible to affect the relative price of gold permanently (depending on the conditions of gold production), it would probably be realistic to have the temporary influences that are necessary to eliminate seasonals and other short-run predictable movements in nominal interest rates. On the other hand, this proposition may conflict with the evidence, cited recently by Clark (1986, p. 85ff.), that the industrialized countries eliminated the main short-term predictability in nominal interest rate movements (including seasonals) more or less simultaneously and roughly around 1914. For the world as a whole, the ending of the classical gold standard may have been the main force that allowed for this new policy. In particular, it may be that the elimination of this commodity standard was a prerequisite for central banks (including the newly formed Federal Reserve) to follow policies of interest-rate targeting.

Suppose now that fixed exchange rates are maintained but the pegged nominal price of a commodity is dropped. Then the remaining nominal degree of freedom allows for interest-rate targeting—say in one country such as the United States—as a purely nominal world policy. However, such a policy calls for coordination across governments in the sense that—given the values of the fixed exchange rates—the other policy-makers have to accord with the interest-rate path set by the selected country. Possibly this regime applies to parts of the interwar period, as well as to the interval from the end of World War II until the early 1970s.

Even in the absence of rigid purchasing-power parity, fixed exchange rates impose constraints on the relative price levels and expected real interest rates across countries. Therefore it would generally be infeasible under this regime for countries to pursue independent policies of interest-rate pegging. At least, the pursuit of such policies would require substantial interference with relative prices and expected real interest rates. Hence such policies tend to go along with restrictions on international trade in goods and capital.

In order to pursue independent policies of interest-rate targeting, while avoiding major repercussions on real variables, it is necessary to have fiat currencies with flexible exchange rates. Moreover, in this type of setting the successful implementation of (independent) interest-rate targeting does not require coordination among the various central banks. Conceivably, the period since the early 1970s fits in with this framework.

In effect, then, the choice among alternative international monetary arrangements involves a tradeoff. Regimes with greater external constraints—including the pegging of a commodity price and the maintenance of fixed exchange rates—have the desirable features that follow from the superiority of rules over discretion. But such settings generally preclude independent monetary policies; in particular, independent policies that would be guided by the targeting of nominal interest rates. To the extent that such independence is worthwhile—and public finance arguments provide one (perhaps minor) reason for this value—there is a case for the superiority of a regime that features fiat money and flexible exchange rates.

References

Barro, R.J. 1976. Rational Expectations and the Role of Monetary Policy. *Journal of Monetary Economics* 2: 1–32.

————. 1981. Unanticipated Money Growth and Economic Activity in the United States. In Barro, R.J. *Money, Expectations, and Business Cycles.* New York: Academic Press.

————. and Gordon, D.B. 1983. Rules, Discretion and Reputation in a Model of Monetary Policy. *Journal of Monetary Economics* 12: 101–121.

————. and ————. 1983. A Positive Theory of Monetary Policy in a Natural Rate Model. *Journal of Political Economy* 91: 589–610.

————. 1987. Interest-Rate Smoothing. Working Paper No. 82. Rochester, NY: Rochester Center for Economic Research.

Brunner, K. 1968. The Role of Money and Monetary Policy. Federal Reserve Bank of St. Louis *Review* July: 9–24.

Clark, T.A. 1986. Interest Rate Seasonals and the Federal Reserve. *Journal of Political Economy* 94: 76–125.

Fair, R.C. 1979. An Analysis of the Accuracy of Four Macroeconometric Models. *Journal of Political Economy* 87: 701–718.

Friedman, M. 1960. *A Program for Monetary Stability.* New York: Fordham University Press.

————. 1968. The Role of Monetary Policy. *American Economic Review* 58: 1–17.

Fuller, W.A. 1976. *Introduction to Statistical Time Series.* New York: Wiley.

Goodfriend, M. 1987. Interest Rate Smoothing and Price Level Trend-Stationarity. *Journal of Monetary Economics* 19: 335–348.

King, R.G., and Plosser, C.I. 1984. Money, Credit and Prices in a Real Business Cycle. *American Economic Review* 74: 363–380.

Kydland, F.E., and Prescott, E.C. 1977. Rules rather than Discretion: the Inconsistency of Optimal Plans. *Journal of Political Economy* 85: 473–491.

Lucas, R.E. 1973. Some International Evidence on Output-Inflation Trade-offs. *American Economic Review* 63: 326–334.

Macaulay, F.R. 1938. *The Movements of Interest Rates, Bond Yields and Stock Prices in the United States since 1856.* New York: National Bureau of Economic Research.

Mankiw, N.G. 1986. The Optimal Collection of Seigniorage: Theory and Evidence. Unpublished. Cambridge, Mass: Harvard University.

————, Miron, J.A., and Weil, D.N. 1986. The Adjustment of Expectations to a Change in Regime: A Study of the Founding of the Federal Reserve. Unpublished. Cambridge, Mass: Harvard University.

McCallum, B.T. 1983. On Non-Uniqueness in Rational Expectations Models: An Attempt at Perspective. *Journal of Monetary Economics* 11: 139–168.

————. 1986. Some Issues Concerning Interest Rate Pegging, Price Level Determinacy, and the Real Bills Doctrine. *Journal of Monetary Economics* 17: 135–160.

Poole, W. 1970. Optimal Choice of Monetary Policy Instruments in a Simple Stochastic Macro Model. *Quarterly Journal of Economics* 84: 197–216.

Shiller, R.J. 1980. Can the Fed Control Real Interest Rates? In Fischer, S., ed., *Rational Expectations and Economic Policy.* Chicago: University of Chicago Press.

Warren, G.F, and Pearson, F.A. 1933. *Prices.* New York: Wiley.

11

Towards the Implementation of Desirable Rules of Monetary Coordination and Intervention

Shin-ichi Fukuda and Koichi Hamada*

I. Introduction

Nowadays people often claim the existence of misalignments of exchange rates among major currencies, and they grope for macro-economic coordination and intervention rules. At the Tokyo Summit in May 1986, the leaders of seven countries agreed to request their finance ministers to review their economic objectives and forecasts collectively, using indicators such as gross national growth rates, inflation rates, interest rates, and so forth.

It is one thing to name important indicators; quite another to implement an effective policy rule based on these indicators. In the present world economy, where there are various kinds of disturbances—supply or demand, monetary or real, domestic or foreign, and temporary or permanent—policy authorities are obliged to rely on some form of monetary rules and intervention rules if they wish to turn the declaration of the summit into an operational scheme.

The purpose of this paper is to characterize the nature of simple, appropriate rules for monetary management in the world economy under uncertainty. We will confine our attention to choices among simple feedback rules. Even though sophisticated discussions of complex dynamic rules, contingent both upon various state variables and upon the reaction of the other player, are intellectually fascinating, we consider that the examination of simpler rules is at least as important as that of sophisticated ones. Simpler rules have a strong advantage in

* We are very much indebted to Willem Buiter, whose suggestions and comments stimulated our research throughout our study. We are also thankful to Hideo Hayakawa, Michael Jones, Masahiro Kawai, and T.N. Srinivasan for their helpful discussions.

that they can be more easily explained to policymakers and more easily understood by them, so that the possibility of adopting one of the simpler rules is much higher.

We must distinguish two types of policy discussions in international macroeconomics on two issues. The first issue is the need for global monetary coordination, as addressed in the proposal by McKinnon (1974) that the monetary authorities of the major countries should agree to provide stable aggregate monetary growth to the world economy in order to stabilize the world price level. The second issue is possible remedies for exchange misalignment, emphasized by Williamson (1983). The discussion of misalignment is concerned with the relative prices of currencies, and, accordingly, with differences among national economies. McKinnon (1984) proposes a program incorporating both of these two aspects.

We will primarily rely on a stochastic two-country version of the model with sluggish price movements developed by Dornbusch (1976), and also on the neoclassical flex-prices model, in which output varies due to the discrepancy between the actual and the expected price level (e.g. Weber 1981). We shall adopt the method of Aoki (1981) for decomposing variables into their sums and differences in a two-country model, following Miller (1982) and Buiter (1986).[1] In order to keep our analysis transparent and focus on the qualitative nature of desirable rules, we will deal with a two-country situation with a symmetric economic structure, assuming identical parameters of characterizing economic behavior between the two countries. Only stochastic disturbances, and policy reactions to these disturbances, can differ.

Under these assumptions, we will show that the subsystems of the Dornbusch model with sluggish prices, as well as those of a neoclassical model, have structures similar to the closed Keynesian model under disturbances that was analyzed by Poole (1970). In the system of average variables of our two-country model, Poole's original results naturally hold. The world average or global money supply target is more desirable when synchronized disturbances in the IS curve dominate; the target for the average interest rate is more desirable when synchronized disturbances in money demand, such as a worldwide financial innovation, dominate. More interesting is the fact that this analogy holds in the difference system as well. No or little intervention is more desirable when country-specific disturbances are mainly in the IS curve, including disturbances due to changing competitiveness in trade; extensive intervention, in such a way as to slow down the

---

[1] See also Jones (1987) and Ueda (1983) for different uses of similar models.

movement of exchange rates, or to reduce the difference in interest rates, is more desirable when the difference, or country-specific, disturbances in the LM curve dominate.

There have been many contributions on optimal intervention rules under uncertainty (notably Boyer 1978, Turnovsky 1983, Weber 1981, and many articles in Bhandari 1985). By adopting a symmetric structure between countries, our paper focuses on the interaction of overall disturbances and country-specific disturbances. Thus the results of Weber (1981) are generalized and set in a more symmetric framework. We also show the effectiveness of feedback rules on interest rate differentials. Such rules have been relatively neglected compared with those that feed back from exchange rates. The link between this kind of model and Poole's analysis was already suggested by Buiter and Eaton (1985), but our analysis shows that the link is much stronger than one might imagine. Some regularities found in the simulation analysis by McKibbin and Sachs (1986) can be better understood by our complementary, analytical approach.

In Section II, we will develop the basic framework of the two-country Dornbusch model, and in Section III we will characterize the optimization problem in the decomposed subsystems of the sum and the difference. In Section IV, we will compare the results of the Dornbusch model with a neoclassical model in which prices clear the goods market instantaneously while the supply of output depends on unexpected price changes. Section V summarizes the results, and the Appendix sketches the possible extension of our approach to n-country cases.

II. The Basic Framework

In order to illustrate the advantage of decomposing the system into averages and differences, consider a simple two-country version of the Dornbusch model. Every parameter is symmetric between the two countries, but disturbances and policy variables may differ. Here m, p, y, and s refer respectively to the logarithm of nominal money supply, price level, real income, and nominal spot exchange rate (the price of the foreign currency in terms of the home currency). Also, i is the nominal rate of interest. All the variables with asterisks indicate variables for the foreign country. Subscripts refer to time periods. There are three types of random disturbances to the system: an LM shock ε_t, an IS shock η_t, and a price shock μ_t. Throughout the paper we shall assume that ε_t, η_t, and μ_t (similarly ε_t^*, η_t^* and μ_t^*) are mutually and time-independent. On the other hand, we do allow positive or negative correlation between ε_t and ε_t^*, η_t and η_t^*, or μ_t and μ_t^*. Let us denote $E(\varepsilon_t^2) = \sigma_\varepsilon^2$, $E(\eta_t^2) = \sigma_\eta^2$, and $E(\mu_t^2) = \sigma_\mu^2$, and so forth.

The model can be described as follows:

$$m_t - p_t = - \alpha i_t + y_t + \varepsilon_t \tag{1a}$$

$$m_t^* - p_t^* = - \alpha i_t^* + y_t^* + \varepsilon_t^* \tag{1b}$$

$$y_t = -\beta(i_t - E_t p_{t+1} + p_t) - \gamma(p_t - s_t - p_t^*) + \eta_t \tag{2a}$$

$$y_t^* = - \beta(i_t^* - E_t p_{t+1}^* - p_t^*) - \gamma(p_t^* + s_t - p_t) + \eta_t^* \tag{2b}$$

$$p_{t+1} - p_t = \delta(y_t - \bar{y}) + \mu_t \tag{3a}$$

$$p_{t+1}^* - p_t^* = \delta(y_t^* - \bar{y}^*) + \mu_t^* \tag{3b}$$

$$E_t s_{t+1} - s_t = i_t - i_t^*. \tag{4}$$

Here $E_t p_{t+1}$, for example, indicates the price in period $t + 1$ forecasted in period t.

Equations (1a), (1b) and (2a), (2b) are respectively the standard LM and the standard IS curves with the simplifying assumption of the unitary income elasticity of the demand for money. Equations (3a) and (3b) indicate that price levels adjust only slowly, that is, δ is small—the crucial assumption in the Dornbusch overshooting model. We do not dare to defend this formulation ourselves, but rather will contrast the characteristics of the optimal feedback rules in this sluggish price model with those in a neoclassical flex-price model in Section IV. Equation (4) indicates the uncovered interest parity through perfect capital mobility.

Under the normalization that $\bar{y} = \bar{y}^* = 0$, the price equation becomes

$$p_{t+1} - p_t = \frac{\delta}{\alpha + \beta} \{ -\beta(1+\alpha)p_t + \alpha\beta \, E_t p_{t+1}$$
$$- \alpha\gamma z_t + \beta(m_t - \varepsilon_t) + \alpha\eta_t \} + \mu_t \tag{5a}$$

and

$$p_{t+1}^* - p_t^* = \frac{\delta}{\alpha + \beta} \{ - \beta(1 + \alpha)p_t^* + \alpha\beta \, E_t p_{t+1}^*$$
$$+ \alpha\gamma z_t + \beta(m_t^* - \varepsilon_t^*) + \alpha\eta_t^* \} + \mu_t^* \tag{5b}$$

where $z_t \equiv p_t - s_t - p_t^*$ denotes the real exchange rate. Notice that there is no counterpart with an asterisk to z_t but it enters with different signs in (5b). There is an element of arbitrariness in what one assumes about the information set on the basis of which private agents make decisions (see Weber [1981] and Canzoneri, Henderson, and Rogoff [1983]). For simplicity, we assume that private agents at time t possess full information on all current variables y_t, p_t, i_t, s_t and on the value of expected exchange rate $E_t s_{t+1}$ that is embodied in the forward exchange rate. This means that private agents can infer exactly the values of ε_t and η_t. However, they cannot observe p_{t+1} at time t nor, accordingly, the value of μ_t. Therefore,

$$p_{t+1} = E_t p_{t+1} + \mu_t \tag{6a}$$

$$p^*_{t+1} = E_t p^*_{t+1} + \mu^*_t \tag{6b}$$

III. Optimal Feedback Rules in Decomposed Systems

Utilizing the method of Aoki (1981), we denote the additive variables with the superscript a and the difference variables with the superscript d.[2] That is, for any variable (or disturbance) X, define

$$X^a_t = X_t + X^*_t,$$

$$X^d_t = X_t - X^*_t.$$

Then the real exchange rate can be written $z_t = p^d_t - s_t$, and the interest parity becomes $E_t s_{t+1} - s_t = i^d_t$.

As the objective of the system we will take the minimization of the unconditional output variances in the two countries. By the following argument, we will show that the objectives of minimizing unconditional output variances can be reduced in this symmetrical world, to the minimization of the unconditional variance of both average output and difference in output.

Consider the following two-country linear systems of variables (or vectors) X and X^* that depend on (vectors of) disturbances ε and ε^* as well as policy parameters π and π^*:

$$X = F(\varepsilon, \varepsilon^*; \pi, \pi^*) \tag{7}$$

$$X^* = F^*(\varepsilon, \varepsilon^*; \pi, \pi^*). \tag{8}$$

---

[2] The structure of our model is almost identical with Buiter (1985), except that our model does not contain the expected current growth rate of the money stock as an augmentation term in the price equation and is formulated in discrete time.

Suppose they are decomposed into two separate systems such that

$$X^a = F^a(\varepsilon^a, \pi^a), \tag{9}$$

$$X^d = F^d(\varepsilon^d, \pi^d), \tag{10}$$

where as usual $X^a = X + X^*$, $X^d = X - X^*$, and where π^a and π^d can be independently chosen. Then we can state:

PROPOSITION 1. If the variances of X^a and X^d are minimized with respect to π^a and π^d, then the sum of the variances, Var (X) + Var (X^*), will be minimized. In particular, if the two countries are completely symmetric such that Var $(x; \hat{\pi}^a, \hat{\pi}^d)$ = Var $(x^*; \hat{\pi}^a, \hat{\pi}^d)$, where $\hat{\pi}^a$ and $\hat{\pi}^d$ are respectively the maximizer of Var (x^a) and Var (x^d), then the minimization with respect to π^a and π^d will achieve both the minimization of Var $(x; \pi)$ and Var $(x^*; \pi^*)$.

Proof   Since

$$\text{Var}(X^a) = \text{Var}(X) + \text{Var}(X^*) + 2\text{Cov}(X, X^*),$$

$$\text{Var}(X^d) = \text{Var}(X) + \text{Var}(X^*) - 2\text{Cov}(X, X^*),$$

it follows

$$\text{Var}(X) + \text{Var}(X^*) = [\text{Var}(X^a) + \text{Var}(X^d)]/2.$$

By assumption Var$(X^a; \pi^a) \geq$ Var$(X^a; \hat{\pi}^a)$

$$\text{Var}(X^d; \pi^d) \geq \text{Var}(X^d; \hat{\pi}^d).$$

Therefore Var(X)+ Var(X^*) are minimized when π^a and π^d are chosen in such a way as to minimize X^a and X^d, respectively. Thus the minimization of Var (X^a) and Var (X^d) amounts to minimizing the sum of variances of X and X^*. By assumption, π^a and π^d can be chosen independently. The second half of the proposition automatically follows from the hypothesis that Var $(X; \hat{\pi}^a, \hat{\pi}^d)$ = Var$(X^*; \hat{\pi}^a, \hat{\pi}^d)$.∥

Thus, we can consider separately the minimization of the variance of the sum of outputs in the additive system and the variance of the difference of outputs below.

A. The Analysis of the Additive System

Under assumption (6a) and (6b), equations (5a) and (5b) lead to the following difference equation:

$$p_{t+1}^a = \frac{\alpha + \beta - (1 + \alpha)\beta\delta}{\alpha + \beta - \alpha\beta\delta} \, p_t^a + \frac{\beta\delta}{\alpha + \beta - \alpha\beta\delta} \, (m_t^a - \varepsilon_t^a)$$

$$+ \frac{\alpha\delta}{\alpha + \beta - \alpha\beta\delta} \, \eta_t^a + \mu_t^a. \tag{11}$$

Thus the additive system is completely separated from all endogenous and exogenous difference variables such as nominal and real exchange rates. Equation (11) indicates that the average world price level depends on the aggregate money supply, and is independent of the exchange rate in this symmetric setting. This may be viewed as giving a supporting ground to McKinnon's proposal that the countries of the world should agree to provide a stable growth rate for the global money stock (McKinnon 1984).[3] In this symmetric system, neither the variation of aggregate output nor the optimal monetary feedback rule depends on the exchange rate. That is, the average unemployment rate in the world does not depend on exchange rates or the rule of intervention.

Based on our previous discussions of the decomposition of objectives, we take the target of minimizing the unconditional variance of average output fluctuations for the objective function for the average system:

$$\mathrm{Var}(y_t^a) = \mathrm{Var}(E_t p_{t+1}^a - p_t^a) \, / \, \delta^2.$$

That is, we are interested in minimizing

$$V^a = E[(E_t p_{t+1}^a - p_t^a)^2]. \tag{12}$$

If monetary authorities were able to observe all the current variables, and thus to infer exactly ε_t^a and η_t^a, and if they were able to react without lags, then they could reduce the expression in (12) to zero except for the influence of μ_t^a. For example, from equation (11) the V^a is minimized if they set

$$m_t^a = \varepsilon_t^a - \frac{\alpha}{\beta} \, \eta_t^a.$$

However, it would be unrealistic to assume that the monetary authorities can not only observe but also react to all the current variables and disturbances inferred from them. For example, price index data usually come with some lags, while interest rates are known more readily.

---

[3] For a similar result in a flex-price model with many countries, see also (Hamada 1985, Ch. 7).

Moreover, the spirit of our approach is to find some simple feedback rule that can be implemented by monetary authorities, without extensive information requirements. Thus we follow Poole (1970) and consider the case where the monetary authorities observe and jointly react to the sum of the interest rates or, equivalently, to the world average interest rate. In particular, we focus on the following feedback rule:

$$m_t^a = \pi \, i_t^a. \tag{13}$$

The aggregate money supply is assumed to be controlled jointly through a McKinnon-type scheme.

Then, one obtains:

$$p_{t+1}^a = \frac{\psi(\pi)}{f(\pi)} \, p_t^a - \frac{\beta\delta}{f(\pi)} \, \varepsilon_t^a + \frac{(\pi + \alpha)\delta}{f(\pi)} \, \eta_t^a + \mu_t^a, \tag{14}$$

where $\psi(\pi) = \alpha + \beta - \beta(1 + \alpha)\delta + (1 - \beta\delta)\pi$, and $f(\pi) = (\alpha + \beta) - \alpha\beta\delta + (1 - \beta\delta)\pi$.

In this sluggish price model, (14) has a nonexplosive (backward) solution if and only if

$$|\psi(\pi) \, / \, f(\pi)| < 1. \tag{15}$$

If the price movement in the goods market is sluggish, δ takes a small value. Accordingly, let us assume that

$$\delta < \min\left[\frac{\alpha + \beta}{\beta(1 + 2\alpha)}, \frac{1}{\beta} \right]. \tag{16}$$

Then one can easily check that $|\psi(0)/f(0)| < 1$ and, accordingly, that the system is stable in the absence of a feedback rule ($\pi = 0$). Also, the stability condition is satisfied if $\psi(\pi) > 0$.

It is rather difficult to consider optimal policies encountering various kinds of shocks at the same time. Therefore we will consider one-by-one the optimal feedback rules that will be appropriate for each type of shock individually. Define:

$$\phi_1(\pi) \equiv \psi(\pi)/f(\pi), \quad \phi_2(\pi) \equiv \beta\delta/f(\pi), \quad \phi_3(\pi) \equiv (\pi + \alpha)\delta/f(\pi),$$

then

$$p_{t+1}^a = \phi_1(\pi)p_t^a + u_t^a + \mu_t^a, \tag{17}$$

where $u_t^a \equiv - \phi_2(\pi)\varepsilon_t^a + \phi_3(\pi)\eta_t^a$.

By using a lag operator L, (17) will read

$$E_t p_{t+1}^a - p_t^a = (1 - L) p_{t+1}^a - \mu_t^a$$

$$= (1 - L)(1 + \phi_1 L + \phi_1^2 L^2 + \dots)u_t^a$$

$$+ (\phi_1 - 1)(1 + \phi_1 L + \phi_1^2 L^2 + \dots)\mu_{t-1}^a, \qquad (18)$$

so that given the stability condition (15), and given the mutually independent white-noise property of ε_t, η_t, and μ_t,

$$\mathrm{Var}(E_t p_{t+1}^a - p_t^a)$$

$$= \frac{2}{1 + \phi_1(\pi)}\left\{[\phi_2(\pi)]^2 \sigma_{\varepsilon a}^2 + [\phi_3(\pi)]^2 \sigma_{\eta a}^2 + \frac{1 - \phi_1(\pi)}{2}\sigma_{\mu a}^2\right\}, \qquad (19)$$

where $\sigma_{\varepsilon a}^2$ is defined as $E[(\varepsilon_t^a)^2]$ and so forth. We will consider consecu-
tively the following cases:

(i) (LM disturbances) $\sigma_{\varepsilon a}^2 > 0$, $\sigma_{\eta a}^2 = \sigma_{\mu a}^2 = 0$.

To minimize V^a implies

$$\underset{\pi}{\mathrm{Min}} \; \frac{\{\phi_2(\pi)\}^2}{1 + \phi_1(\pi)} =$$

$$\underset{\pi}{\mathrm{Min}}\left[\frac{(\beta\delta)^2}{\{\alpha + \beta - \alpha\beta\delta + (1 - \beta\delta)\pi\}\;\{2(\alpha + \beta) - \beta(1 + 2\alpha)\delta + (1 - \beta\delta)\pi\}}\right].$$

Under assumption (16), the optimal feedback rule that retains the
stability should be $\pi \to +\infty$. Thus the optimal monetary policy is to
fix the world nominal interest rates.

(ii) (IS disturbances) $\quad \sigma_{\eta a}^2 > 0 \qquad \sigma_{\varepsilon a}^2 = \sigma_{\mu a}^2 = 0.$

Min V^a implies

$$\underset{\pi}{\mathrm{Min}} \; \frac{\{\phi_3(\pi)\}^2}{1 + \phi_1(\pi)} =$$

$$\underset{\pi}{\mathrm{Min}}\left[\frac{\delta^2(\alpha + \pi)^2}{\{(\alpha + \beta - \alpha\beta\delta) + (1 - \beta\delta)\pi\}\;\{2(\alpha + \beta) - \beta(1 + 2\alpha)\delta + (1 - \beta\delta)\pi\}}\right].$$

Therefore $\pi = -\alpha$ will give the solution. We also obtain $\phi(-\alpha) > 0$
if $\delta < 1$, so that the stability condition is satisfied. Thus this feedback
rule is effective if the price movement is sufficiently slow in this Dornbusch model. If the interest elasticity of money demand α is small,
then the global monetarism that proposes a constant world money
supply will be a proper prescription.

(iii) (Price disturbances) $\quad \sigma_{\mu a}^2 > 0, \qquad \sigma_{\varepsilon a}^2 = \sigma_{\eta a}^2 = 0.$

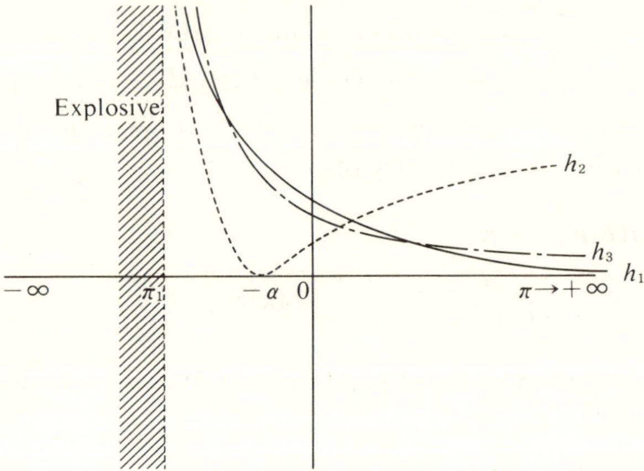

Figure 11.1
Output Variance with LM, IS, and Price Disturbances.

h_1: LM generated disturbance $= \{\phi_2(\pi)\}^2\, \sigma_{\varepsilon a}^2/\{1 + \phi_1(\pi)\}$
h_2: IS generated disturbance $= \{\phi_3(\pi)\}^2\, \sigma_{\eta a}^2/\{1 + \phi_1(\pi)\}$
h_3: Price equation generated disturbance $=\{1-\phi_1(\pi)\}\, \sigma_{ua}^2/\{1+\phi_1(\pi)\}$
π_1 is given by $1 + \phi_1(\pi_1) = 0$

Min V^a implies

$$\operatorname*{Min}_{\pi} \frac{1-\phi_1(\pi)}{1+\phi_1(\pi)} = \operatorname*{Min}_{\pi}\left[\frac{\beta\delta}{2(\alpha + \beta) - \beta(1 + 2\alpha)\delta + (1 - \beta\delta)\pi}\right].$$

Since $\lim_{\pi\to\infty}\psi(\pi) > 0$, the optimal rule is $\pi \to +\infty$ as in the case of (i).[4]

What happens if all the kinds of disturbances coexist? Figure 11.1 roughly illustrates how three components of output variance due to LM, IS, and price equation disturbances vary with respect to the value of π. The relative heights of these curves, of course, depend on relative magnitudes of various disturbances. LM and price disturbances will be eliminated if π approaches plus infinity. The effect of IS disturbances increases and approaches $\delta\sigma_{\eta a}^2/(1 - \beta\delta)^2$ if π approaches infinity. Whether the system should adopt a rule close to that of fixing the average interest rate $(\pi \to +\infty)$, or that of the global monetarist proposal, depends on the relative magnitude of three kinds of shocks.

Thus the additive system behaves almost exactly as the single-country Keynesian system analyzed by Poole (1970). If aggregate disturbances in the LM equation dominate, then it will be desirable to try to stabilize the average world interest rate. On the other hand, if aggregate

---

[4] However, the variance of price level becomes infinity in this case.

disturbances in the IS equation dominate, monetary policy should make the average world interest rate fluctuate slightly. In particular, if the interest elasticity of money demand is negligible, it will be desirable to stabilize the aggregate world money supply. The McKinnon (1979) proposal naturally makes more sense if money demand in each country is relatively more stable and interest-rate inelastic.

B. The Analysis of the Difference System

Recalling the definition of difference variables $X_t^d = X_t - X_t^*$, we obtain the following pair of dynamic equations in terms of p_t^d and s_t:

$$(\alpha + \beta - \alpha\beta\delta)p_{t+1}^d = \{\alpha + \beta - (\alpha\beta + \beta + 2\alpha\gamma)\delta\}p_t^d + 2\alpha\gamma\delta s_t$$
$$+ \beta\delta(m_t^d - \varepsilon_t^d) + \alpha\delta\eta_t^d + (\alpha + \beta - \alpha\beta\delta)\mu_t^d, \quad (20)$$

$$-\beta p_{t+1}^d + (\alpha + \beta)E_t s_{t+1} = (1 - \beta - 2\gamma)p_t^d + (\alpha + \beta + 2\gamma)s_t$$
$$- (m_t^d - \varepsilon_t^d) + \eta_t^d - \beta\mu_t^d. \quad (21)$$

At first we will consider the feedback rule $m_t^d = -\tau s_t$. An increase in m_t^d is a relative increase of money supply in the home country. Our feedback rule can be implemented easily by an unsterilized intervention in the foreign exchange market in such a way as to stabilize the spot exchange rate. Unsterilized interventions in the form of purchase of foreign currencies, for example, increase the home money supply and reduce the foreign money supply. The change in m^d is twice as large as the amount of foreign currency purchased by the home country. Needless to say, m^d increases when the home country expands its money supply by domestic credit creation, without any action on the part of the foreign country.

Under this feedback rule, (20) and (21) become

$$\begin{bmatrix} p_{t+1}^d \\ \\ E_t s_{t+1} \end{bmatrix} = A \begin{bmatrix} p_t \\ \\ s_t^d \end{bmatrix} + \Lambda \begin{bmatrix} \varepsilon_t^d \\ \eta_t^d \\ \mu_t^d \end{bmatrix} \quad (22)$$

where

$$A = \begin{bmatrix} \alpha + \beta - \alpha\beta\delta & 0 \\ -\beta & \alpha + \beta \end{bmatrix}^{-1} \begin{bmatrix} \alpha + \beta - (\alpha\beta + \beta + 2\alpha\gamma) & (2\alpha\gamma - \beta\tau)\delta \\ 1 - \beta - 2\gamma & \alpha + \beta + 2\gamma + \tau \end{bmatrix},$$

and

$$A = \begin{bmatrix} \alpha + \beta - \alpha\beta\delta & 0 \\ -\beta & \alpha + \beta \end{bmatrix}^{-1} \begin{bmatrix} -\beta\delta & \alpha\delta & \alpha + \beta - \alpha\beta\delta \\ 1 & 1 & -\beta \end{bmatrix}.$$

Let us denote the characteristic roots of A as λ_1 and λ_2 such that $|\lambda_1| \leq |\lambda_2|$. The characterization of a system like (24) was given by Blanchard-Kahn (1980). The system has (1) a unique saddle-path solution if $|\lambda_1| < 1 < |\lambda_2|$, (2) no solution that satisfies non-explosion conditions if $1 < |\lambda_1| < |\lambda_2|$, and (3) an infinite number of convergent solutions if $|\lambda_1| \leq |\lambda_2| < 1$. Moreover, if $|\lambda_1| < 1 < |\lambda_2|$, the unique convergent solution of (22) can be written in the following for m, where λ_1 is the characteristic root of A with the smaller norm:

$$p_t^d = \lambda_1 p_{t-1}^d + \phi_1 \varepsilon_{t-1}^d + \phi_2 \eta_{t-1}^d + \phi_3 \mu_{t-1}^d, \tag{23}$$

$$s_t = \psi_1 p_t^d + \psi_2 \varepsilon_t^d + \psi_3 \eta_t^d + \psi_4 \mu_t^d. \tag{24}$$

Either by appealing to the expressions near the end of Blanchard-Kahn (1980), or by the method of undetermined coefficients, one obtains the following expression for ϕ_1, ϕ_2 and ϕ_3:

$$\phi_1 = \lambda_1 \frac{\delta(\beta + 2\gamma)}{H\tau + J}, \quad \phi_2 = \lambda_1 \frac{\delta(\tau + \alpha)}{H\tau + J}, \quad \phi_3 = 1, \tag{25}$$

where $H = -[1 - \delta(\beta + 2\gamma)]$ and $J = -[\alpha + \beta + 2\gamma - \delta(\beta + 2\gamma)(1 + \alpha)]$. If the price is sufficiently sluggish, i.e., if δ is small, H and J are likely to be negative. We assume that H and J are negative.

Define the characteristic polynomial of A as:

$$g(\lambda) = \lambda^2 - (\text{Trace } A)\,\lambda^2 + |A|. \tag{26}$$

Then, the necessary and sufficient conditions for saddle point stability are either (a) $g(1) < 0$ and $g(-1) > 0$, or (b) $g(1) > 0$ and $g(-1) < 0$ (see, for example, Sargent 1979).

If $\tau = 0$, then $g(1) < 0$ and $g(-1) > 0$ for a small value of δ. Thus, for a sufficiently small value of δ, the system has the saddle-point property in the absence of any feedback. Now we shall turn to the minimization of the objective function through policy reactions to various kinds of shocks, considering the optimization of the following objective in terms of differences:

Minimize $V^d = \text{Var}(E_t p_{t+1}^d - p_t^d)$,

which can be written by calculations similar to (19) as

$$V^d = \frac{2}{1 + \lambda_1(\tau)} \{[\phi_1(\tau)]^2 \sigma_{\varepsilon d}^2 + [\phi_2(\tau)]^2 \sigma_{\eta d}^2\} + \frac{1 - \lambda_1(\tau)}{1 + \lambda_1(\tau)} \sigma_{\mu d}^2$$

where $\sigma_{\varepsilon d}^2 = E[(\varepsilon^d)^2]$ and so forth.

Again consider the following cases of individual differential shocks.

(i) (LM disturbances) $\sigma_{\varepsilon d}^2 > 0, \sigma_{\eta d}^2 = \sigma_{\mu d}^2 = 0$.

Minimization of V^d implies

$$\operatorname*{Min}_{\tau} \frac{\phi_1^2}{1 + \lambda_1} = \operatorname*{Min}_{\tau} \left\{ \frac{\lambda_1^2}{1 + \lambda_1} \left[\frac{\delta(\beta + 2\gamma)}{H\tau + J} \right]^2 \right\}.$$

$\tau \to \pm \infty$ are the solutions. It is also possible to show that

$$\lim_{\tau \to \pm\infty} g(1) = \pm \infty \text{ and } \lim_{\tau \to \pm\infty} g(-1) = \pm \infty,$$

provided that δ is sufficiently small so that H is negative. Thus if price levels are sluggish enough, this feedback rule keeps the saddle-point property intact. However, τ makes economic sense only if it approaches positive infinity. Moreover, during the process in which the monetary authority decreases the value of τ from zero to $-\infty$, explosive solutions are easily produced, as is illustrated in Figure 11.2. The best way to cope with differential LM disturbances is to fix exchange rates.

(ii) (IS disturbances) $\sigma_{\eta d}^2 > 0, \sigma_{\varepsilon d}^2 = \sigma_{\mu d}^2 = 0$.

Minimization of V^d implies

$$\operatorname*{Min}_{\tau} \frac{\phi_2^2}{1 + \lambda_1} = \operatorname*{Min}_{\tau} \left\{ \frac{\lambda_1}{1 + \lambda_1} \left[\frac{\lambda_1 \delta(\tau + \alpha)^2}{H\tau + J} \right]^2 \right\}.$$

Thus the best policy is again $\tau = -\alpha$. When $\tau = -\alpha$, $g(1) < 0$ if $\alpha < 1$ and $g(-1) > 0$ for a small value of δ.

Accordingly, this policy keeps the saddle-point property intact. Thus, the best way to cope with differential IS disturbance is to intervene slightly in such a way as to lean *with* the wind. In particular, if the interest elasticity of the demand for money is negligible ($\alpha=0$), then the best regime will be the flexible exchange-rate system without any intervention, i.e., the clean float.

(iii) (Price disturbances) $\sigma_{\mu d}^2 > 0, \sigma_{\varepsilon d}^2 = \sigma_{\eta d}^2 = 0$.

Minimizing V^d implies

$$\operatorname*{Min}_{\tau} \left[\frac{1 - \lambda_1}{1 + \lambda_1} \right].$$

Apparently, the value of τ that generates $\lambda_1 = 1$ would be the solution. However, this definitely violates the stability condition of price dy-

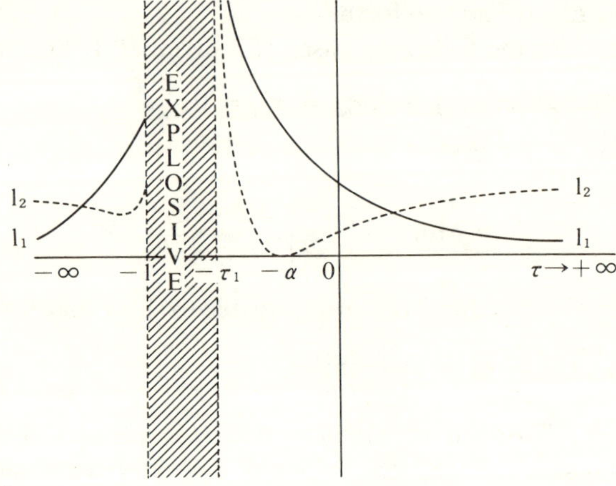

Figure 11.2
Output Variance with LM and IS Disturbances

l_1: LM-generated disturbance $= \{\phi_1\}^2 \sigma_{\varepsilon d}^2 / \{1 + \lambda_1(\tau)\}$
l_2: IS-generated disturbance $= \{\phi_2\}^2 \sigma_{nd}^2 / \{1 + \lambda_1(\tau)\}$
τ_1 is given by $1 + \lambda_1(\tau_1) = 0$.

namics because λ_1 is A's characteristic root with the smaller norm. Thus, there is no well-defined optimal solution.

Figure 11.2 roughly illustrates how two components of output variances due to LM and IS disturbances vary, in a typical case, with respect to the value of π.[5] Again the relative heights between h_1 and h_2 depend on the relative magnitudes of differential disturbances in LM and IS curves. (The effect of price equation disturbances is omitted because the optimal policy is undefined.) Thus, to cope with differential shocks to money demand or money supply functions, the best regime is the fixed exchange-rate regime. To cope with differential shocks in IS curves, interventions leaning slightly with the wind are desirable. In particular, if the interest elasticity of money demand is negligible, clean floating is optimal.

Similarly, one could work with interventions responding to the forward exchange market, namely

$$m_t^d = \tau' E_t s_{t+1}, \tag{27}$$

which would give the following A in equation (22):

---

[5] Depending on values of parameters multiple solutions may appear adjacent to the explosive region. It can be easily seen that τ must pass at least one explosive region corresponding to $\tau = -J/H$ if τ decreases from zero to minus infinity.

$$A = \begin{bmatrix} \alpha+\beta-\alpha\beta\delta & -\beta\delta\tau' \\ -\beta & \alpha+\beta+\tau' \end{bmatrix}^{-1} \begin{bmatrix} \alpha+\beta-(\alpha\beta+\beta+2\alpha\gamma)\delta & 2\alpha\gamma\delta \\ 1-\beta-2\delta & \alpha+\beta+2\gamma \end{bmatrix}.$$

The solution to the price equation is again written as equation (23), in which λ_1 is the characteristic root of A with a smaller norm and

$$\phi_1 = -\lambda_1 \frac{(\beta + 2\gamma)\delta}{(\alpha + \beta + 2\gamma) - (\beta + 2\gamma)(1 + \alpha)\delta},$$

$$\phi_2 = \lambda_1 \frac{\alpha\delta}{(\alpha + \beta + 2\gamma) - (\beta + 2\gamma)(1 + \alpha)\delta} \tag{28}$$

$$\phi_3 = 1.$$

Then, in order to stabilize V^d against both kinds of shocks ε_t^d and η_t^d, the best policy is to minimize the absolute value of λ_1. This would be achieved by setting $\tau' \to \pm\infty$ because the product of the two characteristic roots, i.e., the determinant of A, approaches zero. However,

$$\lim_{\tau' \pm \infty} g(1) = \frac{2\gamma\delta}{\alpha + \beta - \beta\delta} > 0$$

$$\lim_{\tau' \to \pm \infty} g(-1) = \frac{2\{1 - (\beta + \gamma)\delta\}}{\alpha + \beta - \beta\delta} > 0$$

for a reasonably small value of δ. Thus, the saddle-point property is not satisfied by this feedback rule (27). Moreover, the economic meaning of the feedback rule is not clear. In order to stabilize the forward exchange rate by intervening in the spot market, τ' seems to be only meaningful when negative. But under the assumption of $\alpha + \beta - \beta\delta > 0$, if one reduces the value of τ' from zero to minus infinity, at one time $|A|$ and Trade A will explode. For these reasons, interventions in response to the forward exchange-rate market cannot necessarily be recommended, even though the same therapy seems to apply to both kinds of shocks in this feedback scheme.

Finally, let us consider the following intervention scheme responding to interest rate differences:

$$m_t^d = \theta(E_t s_{t+1} - s_t) = \theta\, i_t^d. \tag{29}$$

Then A in equation (22) can be written as

$$A = \begin{bmatrix} \alpha + \beta - \alpha\beta\delta & \beta\delta \\ -\beta & \alpha + \beta + \theta \end{bmatrix}^{-1}$$

$$\cdot \begin{bmatrix} \alpha + \beta - (\alpha\beta + \beta + 2\alpha\gamma)\delta & (2\alpha\gamma - \beta\theta)\delta \\ 1 - \beta - 2\gamma & \alpha + \beta + 2\gamma + \theta \end{bmatrix}.$$

The solution to the price equation is again written as:

$$\phi_1 = \lambda_1 \frac{\delta(\beta + \gamma)}{H\theta + J}, \quad \phi_2 = \lambda_1 \frac{-\delta(\alpha + \theta)}{H\theta + J}, \quad \phi_3 = 1,$$

where H and J are defined as before.

(i) (LM disturbances) $\sigma^2_{\varepsilon d} > 0$, $\sigma^2_{\eta d} = \sigma^2_{\mu d} = 0$.

Minimization of V^d is achieved by setting $\theta \to \pm \infty$. But when $1 > (\beta + \gamma)\delta$,

> $\lim_{\theta \to \pm\infty} g(1) = \mp 0$ [meaning $g(1)$ approaches zero from the negative or positive side],

$$\lim_{\theta \to \pm\infty} g(-1) = \frac{2\{1 - (\beta + \gamma)\delta\}}{1 - \beta\delta} > 0.$$

Thus, only the feedback rule $\theta \to + \infty$ satisfies the saddle-point property for a small value of δ.

(ii) (IS disturbances) $\sigma^2_{\eta d} > 0$ $\sigma^2_{\varepsilon d} = \sigma^2_{\mu d} = 0$;

$\theta = -\alpha$ is the solution which minimizes V^d. When $\theta = -\alpha$, $g(1) = -2\gamma\delta/\beta < 0$, and $g(-1) = 1/\beta(\beta + \gamma)(2 - \delta) > 0$ if $\delta < 2$. Thus, this feedback rule keeps the saddle-point property.

This feedback rule based on interest-rate differentials has the attractive property that the product of the two characteristic roots remains finite in any case. Again, the intervention policy that keeps interest-rate differentials from changing is desirable against LM shocks; leaning with the wind, or a little intervention when money demand is interest inelastic, is desirable against IS shocks specific to a particular country.

IV. The Comparison with the "Eclectic" Neoclassical Model

In this section, we will consider optimal monetary rules in the "eclectic" neoclassical model in which output fluctuates, and compare them with our previous results. In fact, the analysis is much easier in this model, and the analogy carries through with a few reservations. Let us start from the macroeconomic model where prices clear in any period, but output decisions depend on the discrepancies between the actual and expected price level; for example, due to the nature of wage contracts lagging behind for a period (see Fischer [1977] and Gray [1976]). Then the system of symmetric two-country economies can be written exactly as in the 7 equations (1a)–(4) in the outset of Section II, except that the price equations (3a) and (3b) are replaced by supply functions (and implicitly by goods-market-clearing equations in which aggregate demand equals the aggregate supply), as follows:

$$y_t = \bar{y} + \delta(p_t - E_{t-1}p_t) + \mu_t, \tag{3'a}$$

$$y_t^* = \bar{y}^* + \delta(p_t^* - E_{t-1}p_t^*) + \mu_t^* \tag{3'b}$$

The economic meaning of δ is different from δ we used in the previous sections, but for the economy of notation, we will use the same symbol.

Here again, we can decompose these equations into the additive system and the difference system. In the additive system, if the feedback rule of money supply is $m_t^a = \pi\, i_t^a$, the dynamic equation of the sum of prices is written

$$-(\alpha + \pi)\beta\, E_t p_{t+1}^a + \{\beta(1 + \delta) + (\beta + \delta)(\alpha + \pi)\}\, p_t^a$$
$$- (\alpha + \beta + \pi)\delta\, E_{t-1}p_t^a = u_t^a, \tag{30}$$

where $u_t^a = -\beta\, \varepsilon_t^a + (\alpha + \pi)\, \eta_t^a - (\alpha + \beta + \pi)\mu_t^a$.

It is easy to show (see Taylor 1977) that (30) has a unique solution if $\pi > -\alpha - 1/2$, and multiple solutions if $\pi < -\alpha - 1/2$. If (30) has a unique solution, (30) can be solved as

$$p_t^a = \frac{1}{\beta(1 + \delta) + (\alpha + \pi)(\beta + \delta)}\, u_t^a. \tag{31}$$

Since

$$V^a = E[\delta(p_t^a - E_{t-1}p_t^a) + \mu_t^a]^2$$

$$= \left\{\frac{1}{[\beta(1 + \delta) + (\alpha + \pi)(\beta + \delta)^2]}\right\}^2$$

$$\cdot \{-\beta\delta\sigma_{\varepsilon\alpha}^2 + (\alpha + \pi)\delta\sigma_{\eta a}^2 + \beta(\alpha + 1 + \pi)\sigma_{\mu a}^2\},$$

we obtain the feedback rule that minimizes V^a as follows:[6]

(i) LM disturbances $\quad (\sigma_{\varepsilon a}^2 > 0,\ \sigma_{\eta a}^2 = \sigma_{\mu a}^2 = 0), \quad \pi \to +\infty;$

(ii) IS disturbances $\quad (\sigma_{\eta a}^2 > 0,\ \sigma_{\varepsilon a}^2 = \sigma_{\mu a}^2 = 0), \quad \pi = -\alpha;$

---

[6] In a similar type of model, Aizenman and Frenkel (1985) proposed the objective function which minimizes the dead-weight loss in the labor market. In the absence of supply shocks, our criterion in this neoclassical model would be justified by their microeconomic consideration. (See also Kawai 1986.)

(iii) Price disturbances $(\sigma^2_{\mu a} > 0, \sigma^2_{\varepsilon a} = \sigma^2_{\eta a} = 0)$, $\pi = -\alpha - 1$.

Not surprisingly, these feedback rules are exactly the same as those of Section III-A, except for the case of (iii), in which a finite value of π is prescribed.

However, in the case of (iii), $\pi = -\alpha - 1$ will induce multiple solutions.[7]

In the difference system, if the feedback rule is in the form $m^d_t = -\tau s_t$, the difference equations of p_t and s_t are derived as follows;

$$\beta E_t p^d_{t+1} - (\beta + 2\gamma + \delta)p^d_t + \delta E_{t-1}p^d_t$$
$$- \beta E_t s_{t+1} + (\beta + 2\gamma)s_t = -\eta^d_t + \mu^d_t \tag{32}$$

$$(1 + \delta)p^d_t - \delta E_{t-1}p^d_t - \alpha E_t s_{t+1} + (\alpha + \tau)s_t = -\varepsilon^d_t - \mu^d_t \tag{33}$$

These difference equations have a unique solution if $\tau < -(2\alpha + 1)$ or $\tau > -1$, and multiple solutions if $-(2\alpha + 1) < \tau < -1$.

When the above difference equations have a unique solution, we can obtain $E_{t-1}p^d_t = E_t p^d_{t+1} = E_t s^d_{t+1} = 0$, and therefore,

$$p^d_t = \frac{1}{\Gamma}\{-(\beta + 2\gamma)\varepsilon^d_t + (\alpha + \tau)\eta^d_t - (\alpha + \beta + 2\gamma + \tau)\mu^d_t\}, \tag{34}$$

where $\Gamma = (\beta + 2\gamma + \delta)(\alpha + \tau) + (1 + \delta)(\beta + 2\gamma)$.

Thus, the feedback rule which minimizes V^d is

(i) LM disturbances $(\sigma^2_{\varepsilon d} > 0, \sigma^2_{\eta d} = \sigma^2_{\mu d} = 0)$, $\tau \to \pm \infty$;

(ii) IS disturbances $(\sigma^2_{\eta d} > 0, \sigma^2_{\varepsilon d} = \sigma^2_{\mu d} = 0)$, $\tau = -\alpha$;

(iii) Price disturbances $(\sigma^2_{\mu d} > 0, \sigma^2_{\varepsilon d} = \sigma^2_{\eta d} = 0)$, $\tau = -(\alpha + 1)$.

These results are also exactly the same as those of Section III – B except for those in case (iii). Since α is usually less than $1, \tau \to \pm \infty$ and $\tau = -\alpha$ satisfy the uniqueness conditions. Here again, setting the value of τ at minus infinity does not make much economic sense. Also, in the process the variance of p^d_t explodes because Γ becomes zero. $\tau = -(\alpha + 1)$ will produce multiple solutions as in the additive system.

Similarly, other feedback rules such that

$$m^d_t = \tau' E_t s_{t+1}$$

$$m^d_t = \theta i^d_t = \theta (E_t s_{t+1} - s_t)$$

---

[7] Of course, this statement can be relaxed to some extent if the economy chooses a minimum variance solution when $|\lambda_1| < |\lambda_2| < 1$. See Taylor (1977) and McCallum (1983).

could be considered. But, since $E_t s_{t+1} = 0$ if there exists a unique solution, there is no optimal value of τ' and the optimal values of θ are exactly the same as the optimal τ.

Thus, we find that the nature of the optimal feedback rules is quite robust regardless of whether the structure of two economies are either Keynesian or neoclassical. Interest rate targets are desirable if LM curves are more unstable, and the combination of global monetarism and little intervention is desirable if IS curves are more unstable.

V. Concluding Remarks

The main findings are summarized in Table 11.1. By distinguishing the additive from the difference system, as well as additive from difference disturbances, one can clarify the relationship between the global monetarist proposal and the discussion of misalignment of exchange rates. It is quite natural that the analogy of the discussion of Poole (1970) applies to the additive system as a whole. More interesting is the fact that a similar analogy prevails in the difference system, and the fact that the feedback to interest rate differentials can be as effective as the feedback to exchange rates.

In the appendix, we discuss the possible extension of our results to n-country cases. The analogy is not perfect where scales of national economies differ, but there is a case for decomposing the system into the world average variable and the divergence of a country variable from the world average.

These results in our text are derived in a simplified model in which economic structures of the two countries are symmetric and disturbances are time-independent white noises. Therefore, we should recognize the gap between such theoretical exercises and the appropriate policy proposal to implement desirable regimes. Among many necessary modifications and reservations, we shall mention only relatively important ones.

First, in the actual world, disturbances are not necessarily time-independent but serially correlated. Moreover, we do not know exactly which disturbances are permanent and which are transient. Economic agents and monetary authorities engage in guessing games as to which are permanent or transient. The simple policy recommendation obtained under the assumption of white noises may be modified. Presumably, more adaptive rules should be implemented when there are serial correlations in disturbances, and less rigid or drastic rules should be

Table 11.1

Dominant Disturbances	Closed Economy Keynesian (Poole 1970)	Two-Country Dornbusch	Neoclassical
Additive (Coordination rule)			
LM	Interest-rate target	Average interest-rate target	
IS	Money target (if $\alpha = 0$), slightly leaning with the interest rate (otherwise)	Global money target (if $\alpha = 0$), slightly leaning with the interest rate (if $\alpha > 0$)	
Price		Average interest-rate target	
Difference (Intervention rule)			
LM		Feedback to exchange rates, or feedback to interest rate differential (both leaning against the wind)	
IS		Flexible exchange rates (if $\alpha = 0$), feedback to exchange rate or interest differential, both slightly leaning with the wind (if $\alpha > 0$)	
Price		Undefined	Leaning with the difference in interest rate

Note: α is the interest elasticity of money demand.

applied when we cannot identify the nature of disturbances as permanent or transient. Secondly, the optimal rule will depend on the lag structure of the system and on the information set upon which private agents and monetary authorities take action and formulate expectations on future variables.

Finally, if we are to apply the feedback process to the current world situation, we need to modify our conclusions, taking into account the ongoing process of international credit accumulation due to differences in saving behaviors among countries, which could be based on possible differences in the pattern of time preferences, the stage of technological development, and the given historical datum of resource endowment. The two-country model developed in our paper does not take into account these long-run factors, so that the stationary state of the model corresponds to the equilibrium where the current account will be equated to zero. In reality, however, equilibrium may consist of a path that allows some trend, in the current account, of the balance of payments.

Appendix

In this appendix we will consider the generalization of the two-country model in the previous sections into an *n*-country setting. First suppose the world consists of *n* symmetric countries that have identical parameters. Taking the Dornbusch model as an example, we have for country j (omitting time subscript t) with subscript j:

$$m_j - p_j = -\alpha i_j + y_j + \varepsilon_j,$$

$$y_j = -\beta(i_j - Ep_{+1,j} + p_j) - \sum_{k \neq j} \gamma(p_j - s_{jk} - p_k) + \eta_j,$$

$$p_{+1,j} - p_j = \delta y_j + \mu_j,$$

and for $k \neq j$,

$$Es_{+1,jk} - s_{jk} = i_j - i_k,$$

where s_{jk} indicates the exchange rate of k's currency measured in terms of j's currency.

Define the *average* variable such that $X^a = \sum_{j=1}^{n} X_j/n$. Then the average system is written as

$$m^a - p^a = -\alpha i^a + y^a + \varepsilon^a,$$

$$y^a = -\beta(i^a - Ep^a_{+1} + p^a) + \eta^a.$$

Note that $\sum_{j=1}^{n} \sum_{k \neq j} s_{jk} = 0$ because $s_{jk} = -s_{jk}$. Also

$$p^a_{+1} - p^a = \delta y^a + \mu^a.$$

Thus the analysis for the average system just goes through as for the two-country case.

Define also the *difference* (from the average) variable for country j as

$$X^d_j = X_j - X^a.$$

Then the system for difference variables can be written

$$m_j^d - p_j^d = -\alpha i_j^d + y_j^d + \varepsilon_j^d$$

$$y_j^d = -\beta(i_j^d - EP_{+1,j}^d + p_j^d) - n\gamma(p_j^d - s_j) + \eta_j^d,$$

where $s_j = \sum_{k \neq j} s_{jk}/n \, (= \sum_{k=1}^n s_{jk}/n$, since $s_{jj} = 0$ by definition) indicates the effective exchange rate for country j relative to all the other countries. Similarly, interest parity will read

$$Es_{+1,j} - s_j = i_j^d.$$

Thus discussion of the difference system carries through just as in that of the two-country model.

Next we will turn to the case where there is a difference of scale among countries even though the parameters are still symmetric. We modify the IS curve, taking account of the effect of different scales

$$y_j = -\beta(i_j - Ep_{+1,j} + p_j) - \sum_{k \neq j} \gamma_{jk}(p_j - s_{jk} - p_k) + \eta_j,$$

where $\gamma_{jk} = \bar{\gamma} w_k$, w_k being the relative scale of country k in the world such that $\sum_{k=1}^n w_k = 1$. Then noting $\sum_{k \neq j} w_k (p_j - s_{jk} - p_k) = \sum_{k=1}^n w_k(p_j - s_{jk} - p_k)$, the average system and the divergence system can similarly be defined in terms of

$$X^a = \sum_{k=1}^n w_k X_k, \quad X_j^d = X_j - X^a.$$

For example, IS equations are

$$y^a = -\beta(i^a - Ep_{+1}^a - p^a) + \pi^a$$

and

$$y^d = -\beta(i_j^d - Ep_{+1,j}^d - p_j^d) - \bar{\gamma}(p_j^d - s_j) + \eta_j^d.$$

The interest parity will also hold if we define

$$s_j \equiv \sum_{k=1}^n w_k s_{jk} = \sum_{k \neq j} w_k s_{jk}.$$

Then how can Proposition 1 be generalized to an n-country case? We can state the following proposition for the case of identical scale.

PROPOSITION 2. Suppose the world system of n symmetric countries with an identical scale can be decomposed into an average variable, which depends only on an average disturbance, and $(n-1)$ difference variables, which depend only on difference disturbances. Moreover, suppose that the average, as well as all these difference variables, can be controlled by parameters that can be independently chosen. Then the minimization of variances Var (X^a) and Var (X_j^d) $(j = 2, \ldots, n)$ is equivalent to the minimization of the sum of variances, i.e., $\sum_{j=1}^{n}$ Var (X_j).

Proof. Define:

$$
N_0 = \begin{bmatrix}
\dfrac{1}{n} & \dfrac{1}{n} & \dfrac{1}{n} & \cdots & \dfrac{1}{n} \\[2mm]
\dfrac{1}{n} & \dfrac{1}{n}-1 & \dfrac{1}{n} & \cdots & \dfrac{1}{n} \\[4mm]
& & & & \\[2mm]
\dfrac{1}{n} & \dfrac{1}{n} & \dfrac{1}{n} & \cdots \dfrac{1}{n}-1
\end{bmatrix}
$$

and

$$
N = \begin{bmatrix}
\sqrt{n} & 0 & 0 & \cdots & 0 \\[2mm]
0 & \sqrt{\dfrac{n}{n-1}} & 0 & \cdots & 0 \\[4mm]
& & & & \\[2mm]
0 & 0 & 0 & \cdots & \sqrt{\dfrac{n}{n-1}}
\end{bmatrix} N_0.
$$

N_0 and N are orthogonal and normalized orthogonal matrices. Define

$$
X = [X_1, X_2, \ldots, X_n]^T, \text{ and}
$$

$$
Y = NX = \left[\sqrt{n}\, X^a, \, \sqrt{\frac{n}{n-1}}\, x_2^d, \ldots, \sqrt{\frac{n}{n-1}}\, X_n^d \right]^T.
$$

Then $Y^T Y = X^T X$.

Therefore,

$$
\text{Var}(\sqrt{n}\, X^a) + \sum_{j=2}^{n} \text{Var}\left[\sqrt{\frac{n}{n-1}}\, X_j^d \right] = \sum_{j=1}^{n} \text{Var}(X_j).
$$

By the same reasoning as in the proof of Proposition 1, this proposition follows. ‖

Unfortunately, when there are differences in the relative scales of national economies, the same reasoning does not apply because

$$
N = \begin{bmatrix}
w_1 & w_2 & w_3 & \cdots & w_n \\
w_1 & w_2^{-1} & w_3 & \cdots & w_n \\
w_1 & w_2 & w_3^{-1} & \cdots & w_n \\
w_1 & w_2 & w_3 & \cdots & w_n^{-1}
\end{bmatrix}
$$

is no longer an orthogonal matrix. Only when $\text{Cov}(X_i, X_j)$ is zero for any $i \neq j$ can a result similar to Proposition 2 be obtained.

Thus, in the real world, where scales of countries differ, the average rule combined with the difference rule conducted by $n - 1$ countries falls a little short of the overall optimization of the system. However, this exercise shows that the division of labor involved in the average policy rule and the difference policy rule could have the advantage of simplicity and informational economy.

Let us now come to the question of how to implement this decomposition rule. To implement the average rule, it is natural to consider a coordination body for the aggregate or average money supply. Some international arrangement should be made or institution created to coordinate the control of the global money stock according to a principle similar to the McKinnon plan. The proposal to stabilize the aggregate money supply should be adopted if disturbances in IS curves dominate; the rules aimed at stabilizing the average interest rate should be adopted if disturbances in LM curves dominate. In order to implement the difference rule, unsterilized interventions in the spot exchange market in response to exchange rates or to interest differentials, are the natural choice. By intervening (keeping domestic monetary policy intact) in the exchange market in such a way as to purchase k's currency with j's currency, the country increases its money supply and reduces the money supply of country k without changing the total world money supply. Thus, the combination of the coordinated money supply reacting to aggregate disturbances, and the non-sterilized market intervention policies reacting to differentiated (or country-specific) disturbances is the right assignment of policy instruments. Needless to say, coordination and interventions are called for only when the nature of disturbances, for example IS or LM, requires them. One can compute back from the values of m^a and m^d the appropriate values of m and m^*. An international organization or a surveillance body consisting of finance ministers may compute those assignments of monetary policies for participating countries by specifying the average interest rate and the divergences from it.

Some readers will notice here the classical policy assignment proposal by Mundell (1971). If difference monetary disturbances dominate, and, accordingly, the optimal management of exchange rates should come close to fixed exchange rates, why not let a leader country such as the United States take care of the aggregate price level, and let another leader say Europe, adjust their exchange rates? In a more generalized framework for n countries, this kind of proposal would work. A large country like the United States—a hegemony, if we use the favorite word in political science—would be the natural choice for such a country. Suppose an aggregate disturbance without any differential disturbance strikes the system. If only a single country, say country 1, expands its money supply, then m^a will increase satisfactorily. However, at the same time, the divergence of money supply from the world average will increase by the same amount even in the absence of differential shock. Then other countries will have to adjust their money supplies to stabilize their exchange rates or interest rates through intervention, by purchasing the currency of country 1 with their own currencies. As long as the differential rule reacting to exchange rates or interest rates functions well, the optimal rule will be achieved.

References

Aizenman, J., and Frenkel, J.A. 1985. Optimal Wage Indexation, Foreign Exchange Intervention, and Monetary Policy. *American Economic Review* 75: 402–23.

Aoki, M. 1981. *Dynamic Analysis of Open Economies*. New York: Academic Press.

Bhardari, J.S., ed. 1985. *Exchange Rate Management Under Uncertainty*. Cambridge, Mass.: The MIT Press.

Blanchard, D.J., and Kahn, C.M. 1980. The Solution of Linear Difference Models Under Rational Expectations. *Econometrica* 48: 1305–11.

Boyer, R.S. 1978. Optimal Foreign Exchange Market Intervention. *Journal of Political Economy* 86: 1045–55.

Buiter, W.H. 1986. Macroeconomic Policy Design in an Interdependent World Economy: An Analysis of Three Contingencies. *IMF Staff Papers*, September 1986.

———, and Eaton, J. 1985. Policy Decentralization and Exchange Rate Management in Interdependent Economies. In Bhandari, J., ed., *Exchange Rate Management Under Uncertainty*. Cambridge, Mass.: The MIT Press.

Canzoneri, M.B., Henderson, D.W., and Rogoff, K.S., 1983. The Information Content of Interest Rate and Optimal Monetary Policy. *Quarterly Journal of Economics* 98: 545–56.

Dornbusch, R. 1976. Expectations and Exchange Rate Dynamics. *Journal of Political Economy* 84: 893–915.

Fischer, S. 1977. Long-Term Contracts, Rational Expectations, and the Optimal Money Supply Rule. *Journal of Political Economy* 85: 191–206.

Gray, J.A. 1976. Wage Indexation: A Macroeconomic Approach. *Journal of Monetary Economics* 2: 221–35.

Hamada, K. 1985. *The Political Economy of International Monetary Interdependence*. Cambridge, Mass.: The MIT Press.

Jones, M. 1987. IMF Surveillance, Policy Coordination, and Time Consistency. *International Economic Review* 28: 135–58.

Kawai, M. 1986. *Kokusai Kinyi to Kaiho Makurokeizaigaku (International Finance and International Macroeconomics)*. (In Japanese.) Tokyo: Toyo-keizai-shinposha.

McCallum, B.T. 1983. On Non-uniqueness in Rational Expectations Models: An Attempt at Perspective. *Journal of Monetary Economics*: 11, 139–68.

McKibbin, W., and Sachs, J.D. 1986. Coordination of Monetary and Fiscal Policies in the OECD. NBER Working Paper No. 1800.

McKinnon, R.I. 1974. A Tripartite Agreement or a Limping Gold Standard? *Essays in International Finance* No. 106. Princeton, N.J.: Princeton University Press.

————. 1984. *An International Standard for Monetary Stabilization*. Policy Studies in International Economics No. 8., Institute for International Economics.

Miller, M.H. 1982. A Theoretical Analysis of Feasible Policy Measures Under High U.S. Interest Rates. Paper presented at the International Seminar on EPA World Economic Model, the Economic Planning Agency, Tokyo.

Mundell, R.A. 1971. *Monetary Theory: Inflation, Interest, Growth in the World Economy*. Pacific Palisades, Calif.: Goodyear.

Poole, W. 1970. Optimal Choice of Monetary Policy Instruments in a Simple Stochastic Macro Model. *Quarterly Journal of Economics* 84: 197–216.

Sargent, T. 1979. *Macroeconomic Theory*. New York: Academic Press.

Taylor, J.B. 1977. Conditions for Unique Solutions in Stochastic Macroeconomic Models with Rational Expectations. *Econometrica* 35: 1377–85.

Turnovsky, S.J. 1983. Exchange Market Intervention Policies in a Small Open Economy. In Bhandari, J., and Putnam, B.H., eds., *The International Transmission of Economic Disturbances*. Cambridge, Mass.: The MIT Press.

Ueda, K. 1983. *Kokusai Makurokeizaigaku to Nihonkeizai, (International Macroeconomics and Japanese Economy)*. (In Japanese.) Tokyo: Toyokeizai-shinposha.

Weber, W. 1981. Output Variability Under Monetary Policy and Exchange Rate Rules. *Journal of Political Economy* 89: 733–58.

Williamson, J. 1983. *The Exchange Rate System*. Policy Analyses in International Economics, No. 5, Institute for International Economics.

Comments

Georg Rich

Let me start by expressing my gratitude to Mr. Suzuki and his colleagues for inviting a representative of the Swiss National Bank to this very interesting and useful conference. I am glad that this conference takes place in 1987 rather than 1787. Had we all lived 200 years ago, among the North American and European participants only our two Dutch friends, Mr. Bomhoff and Mr. Koning, would have been permitted to enter Japan. Fortunately, we live in 1987. Therefore, all of us have an opportunity to visit a friendly and dynamic country that has undertaken enormous efforts to become a major economic power.

The subject of this session is "optimal monetary regime and policy management for economic stability in the future." Considering the difficulties of designing optimal monetary regimes, I am hardly surprised to find that Professors Barro and Fukuda and Hamada do not offer blueprints for monetary policy reform. They focus instead on particular aspects of the issue at hand. Barro explores the question of whether a nominal interest rate target is compatible with price stability, while Fukuda and Hamada attempt to apply the Poole analysis of choosing an optimal intermediate target to the issue of international policy coordination. Let me discuss briefly each of the two papers.

Barro's ingenious analysis departs from the standard literature on monetary targeting insofar as he does not regard the rate of interest as an intermediate target variable. In Barro's model, no intermediate target is required because changes in the monetary base affect instantaneously such ultimate target variables as the price level. Therefore, the central bank may operate directly on its ultimate target variables. Rather, stability of nominal interest rates is an ultimate objective together with price stability. Barro then shows that there exists a policy rule—cast in terms of a central-bank reaction function linking contemporaneous changes in the monetary base to contemporaneous and past deviations of the realized nominal interest rate from its targets—which allows the central bank to minimize the variance of the nominal interest rate and of the one-period-ahead forecast error for the price level. Note that Barro's central bank does not endeavor to keep prices stable; it merely ensures that the public is not frustrated by overly large deviations in realized prices from their expected values.

Considering the time constraint imposed on discussants, I would like to confine my comments to two questions raised by Barro's paper. The first one concerns the choice of ultimate policy objectives. Why should central banks regard stability of nominal interest rates as such an objective? Barro attempts to justify this choice on the grounds of optimal public finance in an intertemporal context, an argument I do not really understand. In the empirical part of the paper, he points to the stability of the financial system as another possible reason. I believe his paper would benefit greatly from a full discussion of this issue.

Furthermore, Barro's paper implies that inflation or deflation entails social costs only to the extent that realized prices diverge from their expected values. An inflation objective of, say, $+100\%$ or -50% would be optimal, so long as the central bank succeeds in minimizing the forecast error of the price level. I realize, of course, that economists do not possess a fully satisfactory explanation as to why central banks are commonly expected to maintain a stable price level, rather than stabilize the rate of change in the price level at some arbitrary positive or negative value. Be that as it may, Barro's rule would not generate optimal central-bank behavior if policymakers were committed not only to render the future price level as predictable as possible, but also to keep the inflation rate near zero.

The second question concerns the feasibility of the policy rule postulated by Barro. At first sight, the rule appears to be strikingly simple. If Barro's model adequately describes the real world, then optimal policy outcomes could be achieved by varying the money supply mechanically in response to target misses in interest rates. Thus central bankers would be out of a job, as they could easily be replaced by computers. A close examination of Barro's analysis, however, suggests that his rule is rather more complicated than he appears to suggest.

One complication arises from a problem not discussed by Barro. The rule—as specified by the central-bank reaction function (5)—would be simple only if μ_t, that is, the permanent component of base-money growth, could be treated as a truly exogenous variable. However, this need not be the case. Suppose that the real rate of interest rate increases permanently, that is, the variable r—which Barro treats as a constant—rises. If the nominal interest rate R is to remain stable, the expected rate of inflation must decline. Therefore, the permanent component of base-money growth must fall. This result also follows from equation (6). Unless we live in a world in which r is in fact constant, the central bank must be able to distinguish properly between transitory and permanent changes in real interest rates in order to ensure that the rule generates optimal solutions.

Further doubts about the feasibility of Barro's rule arise from the empirical part of his paper. He points out that "the CPI inflation rate shows somewhat greater 'persistence' than predicted by the theory." He dismisses these results with the argument that there may be measurement errors in the price index, such as departures between reported and transactions prices. I am not convinced by this argument. If, in a rational-expectations world, the general public knows all the transactions prices, then why do the statisticians insist on publishing false indexes based on reported prices? Could it not be that the evidence is inconsistent with rapid adjustment in prices to monetary and real shocks? However, in Barro's model rapid adjustment in prices is crucial if the central bank is to be able to correct quickly deviations from the interest rate target by changing current prices relative to expected prices.

Let me now turn to the Fukuda/Hamada paper. In my opinion, Fukuda and Hamada have written an excellent piece of work that requires few comments. They show that an extension of the Poole analysis to the open-economy case produces meaningful conclusions as to the choice of optimal policy regimes. Of course, the Fukuda/Hamada analysis hardly represents more than a first step toward tackling complicated and frequently elusive issues. Like Poole, they focus their attention on the implications for policy choices of the stochastic nature of exogenous shocks. Needless to say, uncertainty of this sort is not the only obstacle to designing an optimal international policy regime. Even greater obstacles are conflicts among national policy objectives, an unwillingness to consider the effects of domestic policy on other countries, or uncertainty about such effects.

Comments

John H. Makin

Robert Barro's papers are always a pleasure to read. I especially enjoyed this paper after three years away from active research in the area of monetary theory and policy.

At first, I thought that some radical change had occurred in my absence, since the Fisherian equation for nominal interest rate determination suggests that naive targeting with money growth of a nominal interest rate, like that advertised in Barro's title, carries with it the likelihood of a runaway inflation.

I quickly realized that I had nothing to fear. Barro works out nicely the conditions under which nominal interest rate targeting is both viable and stable. Not surprisingly, such conditions are stringent and, to some, might seem a little counter-intuitive. A rise in money growth in response to a nominal interest rate above the target level will lower the nominal interest rate only if expected inflation falls due to a drop in expected future money growth. Specifically, the lagged reaction of money growth to a nominal interest rate above or below its target level must be greater than, and opposite in sign to, the contemporary reaction.

Barro also shows that contemporary monetary accommodation must be greater the larger is the variance of temporary shocks to money demand relative to temporary shocks to real interest. This result brings to mind Poole's (1970) famous article, yet in Barro's model the trade-off is not between targeting the nominal interest rate and the money supply but only in arriving at a viable rule for using money supply instruments to achieve a nominal interest rate target.

Barro derives some very specific, observable implications from his model. Both money growth and inflation ought to follow an ARMA (1, 2) process. The AR term ought to have a value of 1. The nominal interest rate ought to behave as a random walk. Barro tests the consistency of the data with the nominal interest rate targeting specification over three sample periods. The first, running from 1954 to 1986, fits the data reasonably well. The period from 1922 to 1940, which Barro interprets as a period of transition away from the gold standard, and the 1890 to 1913 pre-Federal Reserve gold standard period do not conform as well with the prediction of Barro's interest rate targeting specification. This latter result is consistent with the notion that under the gold standard with an essentially passive monetary policy, the data ought not to conform to a pattern implied by active targeting of nominal interest rates.

One could quibble that during each period there were departures from a single policy regime, such as the post-October 1979 announced abandonment of interest rate targeting for money supply targeting by the Federal Reserve. But Barro could argue in reply that "actions speak louder than words" and that the failure of the data to contradict his hypothesis casts doubt on the actual extent to which the Fed followed a policy of money supply targeting in the 1979–82 period. It might be interesting to conduct some empirical tests omitting that period to see whether the remaining postwar data conform better to the pattern implied by the Barro interest rate targeting paradigm.

Overall, Barro's paper is really not a repudiation of Friedman's dictum that interest rate targeting is inflationary. Friedman was really arguing that a central bank attempting to lower nominal interest rates with easier money would not conform with Barro's rule that money would subsequently have to be tightened and more stringently than would have been the case had money not been used initially to lower nominal interest rates. The notion that a rise in money growth reduces inflationary expectations implies a central bank ultimately willing to endure the costs of reducing inflationary expectations. The turbulent period after October of 1979 comes to mind as one in which the Fed had to pay the price with extra-tight money for attempting to bring down interest rates with easier money during the pre-1979 period.

The Fukuda-Hamada paper explores the question of appropriate responses to alternative shocks in an open economy, two-country setting. With worldwide shocks and a stringent set of conditions specified by Fukuda and Hamada the rule is exactly the same as that for a closed-economy, IS-LM model as analyzed by Poole (1970). Specifically: if shocks are on the monetary side, control the interest rate; if shocks are on the real (IS) side, control the quantity of money.

Fukuda-Hamada extend the analysis to include consideration of country-specific shocks, where LM shocks suggest fixing the exchange rates while IS shocks suggest floating the exchange rates.

The Fukuda-Hamada paper provides a useful set of reference cases for pure disturbances. It is not clear, however, that it can be of much help to policymakers who face the very real problem of identifying the nature of shocks as country-specific, world-wide, LM, or IS, before they act. Surely it would be very difficult, even if it were possible, say, to distinguish between LM and IS shocks of a country-specific nature, to switch from fixed to floating exchange rates.

Despite its limited application to actual policy, the Fukuda-Hamada paper provides a useful starting point for thinking about the different types of shocks faced by policymakers. Indeed, the paper supports an eclectic approach to monetary policy in an open-economy setting.

Comments

Philippe Lagayette

According to a long-time monetarist credo, it is preferable to stabilize money growth rather than interest rates. One argument, forcefully stated by Friedman, is that targeting interest rates would induce central bankers to lower interest rates in the short run, which would have the long-run adverse effect of money creation being excessive; also, inflation would rise, as well as nominal interest rates.

It is therefore very interesting to see that an economist such as Professor Barro, who cannot be suspected of sympathy for loose monetary policies, advocates (or at least explains the feasibility of) interest rate targeting.

A monetary policy rule which can both target interest rates to their desired levels and minimize ex-ante price volatility at the same time is proposed in the text. It should be noted that the rule advocated by Barro does not take into account the influence of nominal interest rate targeting on real interest rates, and hence on real variables. He does not address the issue, crucial for central banks, of the possible links between the two. As Mr. Makin has, I will not elaborate on this question.

The proposed rule is one which does not monetize permanent disturbances but which can accommodate, in a very specific manner, some transitory disturbances. It is indeed a shift of emphasis with respect to the earlier monetarist credo, according to which no accommodation at all should take place.

If, in principle, the idea can make a central banker more happy than before because it gives him some flexibility, it is not, however, an easy policy to implement. It requires a careful distinction between various sources of uncertainty. It is not a policy as simple as one which would simply require deflating the money supply when interest rates are low and inflating it otherwise. Carelessly implemented, such policies are open to the earlier monetarist critiques that they may increase the volatility of prices. In contrast, the policy advocated in the text is one which requires a strong commitment of the central bank not to accommodate all kinds of shocks. However, in the real world, the distinction between transitory and permanent shocks is not as clear-cut as in the paper. Who can tell, for instance, whether the low price of oil today is permanent or transitory? It is therefore quite interesting that empirical tests do seem to suggest that the Fed targeted interest rates appropriately, in a way which avoided the risk of a large price volatility.

What are the implications of these findings for international cooperation? Professor Barro concludes his paper by indicating that "there is a case for the superiority of a regime that features fiat money and flexible exchange rates," to the extent that independence of policies is worthwhile.

Indeed, if each country targets its nominal interest rate according to its own country-specific shocks, then flexible exchange rates are the only viable international monetary regime. This is a noncooperative system. I would rather ask the question in the following terms: are monetary policies of, say, the Barro type more likely to generate international coordination than monetary policies of the Friedman type? My answer is yes, they make it more likely, to the extent that most shocks are worldwide phenomena. Conventional monetarism calls for a very stubborn money supply growth, disregarding any shocks affecting the economy. We had an insight into such a policy between 1979 and 1982: a very high and volatile interest rate and, as a result, a wide overshooting of the exchange rate followed. The need to accommodate these fluctuations became so strong that, indeed, the U.S. monetary policy had to resume an interest rate targeting policy. It is this policy, I believe, which made it possible to resume the talks on a cooperative management of the world exchange rates. Interest rate targeting, being very close to exchange rate targeting, is indeed a good avenue for international cooperation. The Plaza and the Louvre agreements, and their possible developments, are instances of such cooperation, and they are, I believe, a good thing for all parties.

How can one judge the appropriateness of targeting interest rates or money supply growth in a world economy? It is the purpose of the paper by Fukuda and Hamada to offer a framework of analysis to deal with these questions, and this should certainly be welcome.

The paper offers several rules. I am just going to pick up a few points.

When the shocks affecting the economies are worldwide and disturb the equilibrium in the money markets, then interest rate targeting is the appropriate response. Some aspects of financial innovation which are common to most countries (multiplication of financial products, dis-intermediation, . . .) are certainly good examples of such shocks.

When the shocks are country-specific, the same prescriptions roughly apply. Real shocks should not be accommodated, while monetary shocks should be accommodated with fixed exchange rates. A flexible exchange rate system (with no policy prescriptions) is there-fore the appropriate framework when shocks are real. However, this view ignores the difficulties we met with flexible exchange rates: overshooting, speculative bubbles. . . . A managed floated system is more appropriate when shocks disturb the money markets of some (but not all) countries.

This conclusion, I believe, is particularly interesting. Indeed, we live in a world in which wide fluctuations in the money markets, due, among other things, to large capital movements or widespread financial in-novation, make it necessary to define a set of stable exchange rates (inasmuch as country-specific real shocks are not too large).

Could some implications be drawn from this analysis for the working of a cooperative agreement such as the EMS? It seems crucial to note that it is not enough to manage collectively an average target to which each member country should individually adjust. Both the average and the differences must follow decision rules, the coherence of which must be decided collectively. This is not a surprising idea. Interestingly, the paper shows, however, that a two-step procedure is worthwhile. For instance, for the EMS countries, this kind of analysis seems to indicate that a target for the Ecu-dollar or the Ecu-yen paritics can be defined first, out of which, then, all bilateral parities of the EMS currencies can be collectively determined. It also seems to imply that an agreement on the evolution of the total money supply or liquidity of the EMS countries, together with the definition of national targets, would be suitable.

Comments

J. S. Flemming

In several respects Robert Barro's paper is typical of his work; it is innovative, it represents a conscious change of direction on his part, and it relates an optimizing model of policymakers' behavior directly to the data rather than using the data to estimate model parameters and documentary evidence for the authorities' intentions. Less typically, the exposition is less transparent than I have come to expect, and this may account for some misapprehension on my part. Also the present exercise contains elements of rationalization of what comes naturally to central bankers.

The idea of a target interest rate is very Keynesian. Keynes was aware that he ought to choose between M and r as exogenous variables but he in fact tried to have it both ways. Although most textbook authors have preferred to take M as exogenous I have always found it easier to make sense of the speculative demand for money if r is exogenous. Moreover, Keynes would endorse the view that it has regressive tendencies. UK data on the pivoting of money-market interest rates support the view that the market believes that the authorities tend to smooth a rate of between one and six months' maturity.

My comments relate largely to the theoretical model.

I have two major problems with the model as presented. The first relates to the mixture of normative and positive ingredients in the argument. While some fairly rigorous optimization exercises are performed within the framework presented, the framework itself has a number of apparently arbitrary features designed to enhance the data-coherence of the model's implications. A more consistently optimizing framework would start not only with the need for credible rules but with the authorities' objectives by reference to which the merits of different rules could be assessed.

In particular the random nature of the nominal interest target $\bar{R}_t$

is disturbing. Is the observed variation in R_t not more likely to reflect shifts in perceived policy trade-offs or problems in policy implementation? Indeed the chosen specification is open, as Barro notes in the empirical section, to the technical objection that it does not respect the non-negativity of nominal interest rates. But while a log specification might actually be desirable in its own right in the money demand equation (2) it would not fit into the interest rate equation (1). Barro cites Mankiw in support of a random walk for $\bar{R}_t$. Mankiw's argument is an application of Barro's own tax rate smoothing arguments. As circumstances change so should tax rates (but their expected change should be zero), and the inflation rate $(R - r)$ can be viewed as a tax. There are, however, several problems with this application, although it does seem to make the random walk less arbitrary, as it implicitly depends on factors impinging on public finance, which are likely to make the distribution of $\bar{R}_t$ both asymmetric and heteroscedastic. The inflation tax, like any tax rate, probably has a revenue maximizing rate which should impose an upper bound on $\bar{R}$. A log transformation while excluding negativity would not be adequate to impose this upper bound.

Thus the model is incomplete, contains some (probably inevitable) approximations associated with linearizing a non-linear system, and excludes the (possibly weak) regressive tendencies in nominal interest rates which are clearly indicated by the freely estimated parameters in equation 2 and Table 1.

By making $\bar{R}$ and R follow random walks Barro removes any expectational pressure taking the yield curve away from the horizontal. He thus does not have to distinguish his interest rates by maturity. Are those in the money demand and policy objective functions of the same maturity? A more general, Keynesian, and data-coherent "smoothing" of interest rates would have radically different implications for the yield curve.

My second problem relates to the presentation of the derived policy rule as interest rate targeting; such targeting comes easily to central bankers, but if they were pursuing nominal interest targets they would tend to do so directly rather than via a rule for varying the monetary base.

How then might one explain the observed variation of R? One possibility, alluded to in the paper, is that r itself is stochastic; another is that the authorities might, in principle, be willing to sacrifice the precise control of nominal interest rates to reduce price forecast errors; a further possibility is that if this leads to a money supply rule there might be irreducible errors in its implementation.

As I understand the paper it is the case that nominal interest rate pegging (which could be achieved with $\lambda_1 = 0$, $\lambda_2 > 0$) would raise problems of price level determinacy and not minimize price forecast errors, and that a money supply rule involving accommodating contemporaneous money demand shocks ($\lambda_1 > 0$) would reduce such errors while a lagged interest rate term ($\lambda_2 > 0$) can offset the effect of contemporaneous accommodation on price expectations and nominal interest rates.

Thus the particular form of the money supply rule is a consequence not of nominal interest rate targeting, as the paper's title might suggest, but of minimizing price forecast errors. This is a reasonable objective, but its introduction into the analysis might better precede that of the policy reaction function it rationalizes.

Barro's specification requires a very different attitude to inflation from that underlying his previous work on monetary policy, and this change may well account for the very different conclusion.

It is important to notice that it is only *ex ante* price surprises, and not price changes as such, that are apparently to be avoided; expected inflation is not penalized. Moreover while changing the money supply at time t changes p_t this jump does not enter either $E_{t-1}[(p_t - E_{t-1}p_t)^2]$ or $E_t[(P_{t+1} - E_tP_{t+1})^2]$. A more general specification would relate to *ex post* inflation, probably decomposed into expected and unexpected components $B_1 \cdot E_{t-1}(P_t - P_{t-1})^2 + B_2(P_t - E_{t-1}P_t)^2$, but this would be much less tractable.

Barro himself suggests a somewhat different reason for the form of the rule. His model lacks any price stickiness. If prices are sticky, as is suggested by some features of the results, it would follow immediately from the money demand function that an increase in m reduces R. In Barro's model this is not necessarily true as p can also jump and R depends on expected monetary growth. This, together with the implicit assumption of continuous clearing of all markets accounts for some of the model's counterintuitive properties.

The assumption of continuous market clearing seems to have prevented Barro from rationalizing the aversion to price surprises by allowing them to distort resource allocation and reduce output.

Given Barro's specification of the money supply reaction function it is tempting, at least to me, to admit that even the monetary base is not very easy to control precisely and thus to want to add an error term to the money supply rule in equation (5). If, however, the contemporaneous nominal rate is in the information set to which the money supply reacts, so would the error term naturally be. Thus in this specification the price of introducing an error into the money supply process would appear to be that m_t would have to react to R_{t-1} and R_{t-2} rather than R_t and R_{t-1}. Given the transitory nature of most of the shocks in the model this would appear to rule out the element of contemporaneous accommodation which makes the proposed money supply rule superior to direct interest rate pegging. It might, however, be possible to enrich the stochastics and dynamics in this sort of way at the cost of some greater complexity.

This question is related to Barro's essentially arbitrary assumption, for the purpose of his empirical work, that the information and decision periods of his theoretical model coincide with the quarterly intervals of his data. On the one hand interest rates are observable so frequently that a continuous specification might be in order—perhaps with lagged reactions. On the other hand if prices and interest rates do not follow strict random walks comparison of their variances are sensitive to the intervals over which they are measured.

So far I have taken the model to be a theoretical exercise relating to a hypothetical closed economy, but Barro's intention appears to be to obtain insights into the determination of interest rates in historical economies. His own empirical work relates to a century of U.S. experience. He obtains significantly different results for the periods 1890–1914, 1922–1940, and 1954–1986. These relate in part to different exchange rate regimes. It is not clear to me to what extent the distinct gold points under the gold standard and permitted range (or capital controls) under Bretton Woods might allow more than one country to smooth its interest rate. Certainly in the U.K. exchange rate considerations have been the driving force behind interest rate movements for the vast majority of the period.

Professors Fukuda and Hamada are well aware of the limitations of their paper's analysis for practical policy purposes, and the reluctance of policymakers to use optimal control techniques in any single country suggests that details of the specification and demand feedback rules are of limited relevance. The paper is, however, of great value in other ways, particularly in extending Poole's analysis to the international economy and extending MacKinnon's global monetary approach to other variables.

It is notable that there is no clear intellectual framework for the current attempts to achieve some measure of international policy coordination. This paper goes quite a long way towards filling that gap. This is particularly true of the emphasis on the "sum economy." In the past there has been a tendency for international discussion to concentrate on the symptoms of disequilibrium which relate particularly to the "difference economy."

A greater stress on the need to consider the world economy as a whole, *as well as* the individual economies and their differences, could make a fruitful contribution. An examination of the prospects for the aggregate world economy and agreement on its implications for "world" policy might provide a very useful background against which to discuss the prospects and policies of individual countries.

Comments

John G. Greenwood

By and large the papers and discussion in this conference have focused on the major countries, all of which have independent monetary policies. In other words these countries maintain floating exchange rates which permit the monetary authority to target a monetary aggregate independent of targets set by other countries. The South East Asian economies, by contrast, are mostly small open economies with fixed foreign exchange rates, with no such independence, or at least with very limited discretion. Dr. Suzuki has asked me as a participant from South East Asia to make a statement about the experience of South East Asian economies as they relate to the themes of this conference. Let me first set the scene; then I shall make some observations.

Until 1973 practically all South East Asian economies maintained exchange rates which were rigidly pegged to the U.S. dollar, the only significant exception being the Hong Kong dollar, which was pegged to sterling until June 1972. Since 1973, with the move by major countries towards floating exchange rates, there has been a divergence of behavior among South East Asian economies. Some countries, notably Thailand, Indonesia, and Taiwan, have maintained a *rigid* foreign exchange rate against the U.S. dollar, with occasional revaluations or devaluations. Others, notably Singapore and Malaysia, have operated a *managed* exchange rate system, usually against some unspecified basket of currencies. Korea has recently moved from a rigid peg to a managed rate system. Still others, like Hong Kong, and more recently Australia and New Zealand, have adopted (at times) a free float.

In Australia and New Zealand, where the authorities could control the money supply, monetary policies have enjoyed only limited success because although the authorities have had the *technical* capability to control money growth, and hence bring down domestic inflation, for *political* or other reasons they have so far failed to do so, and therefore have failed to reduce inflation much below double digits. In the case of Hong Kong, the attempt to operate a floating exchange rate proved an unmitigated disaster because, in the absence of a central bank, there was a high degree of monetary instability between 1972 and 1983, and then in 1983 there was a severe foreign exchange crisis resulting in a sudden 30% depreciation of the currency and a sharp rise in inflation. Hong Kong's crisis was only solved by the re-adoption of a fixed exchange rate under a colonial currency board system, i.e., a 100% reserve system.

What can we say about major themes of this conference from the experience of South East Asia? **First**, on the causes of domestic instability since 1973, those countries with rigid exchange rates against the U.S. dollar have generally been unable to avoid the effects of monetary disturbances emanating from the United States being transmitted to their domestic economies. As Parkin says in his paper, the variability of money supply growth under fixed exchange rates depends on the variability in the demand for money.

Second, there is little doubt, in my judgement, that those economies with *managed* exchange rates as opposed to rigidly pegged rates, have been able to avoid the worst monetary instability associated with the pre-1973 period of fixed rates. This does not mean that these countries have not made other mistakes. For example, Malaysia, which is an oil exporter and has observer status within OPEC, pursued a highly expansionary fiscal policy following the second oil crisis of 1979–80, and has subsequently had to restore a measure of fiscal balance with a series of austerity budgets (see Figure 1). Conversely Singapore pursued an overly contractionary fiscal policy in 1982–85, which, combined with a persistent deceleration in monetary growth, precipitated a serious economic downturn in 1985. But, **third**, even those countries with rigid exchange rates have started to develop mechanisms to offset or counteract the domestic impact of external disequilibria. A widely used device of this kind is the practice of central bank sterilization of foreign currency inflows or outflows. First practiced by Japan in the Far East, this technique has been extensively used in Korea and Taiwan. Normally sterilization refers to the sale of domestic assets by a central bank to offset the accumulation of foreign assets. However, in the case of Taiwan, around October 1985 the Central Bank of China exhausted its stock of domestic assets on its own balance sheet and started to create domestic liabilities with which to absorb the excess liquidity which their foreign exchange intervention was creating. These sterilization operations in Taiwan are now very considerable with the total volume of sterilization instruments (Central Bank of China lia-

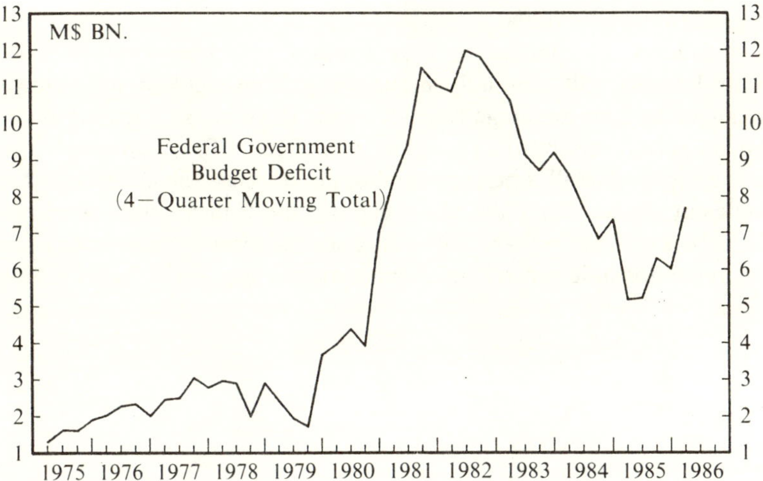

Figure 1
Malaysia: The Budget Deficit

bilities which are not part of the monetary base) exceeding M_{1A}, or equivalent to about one third of M_2, the broadly defined money supply.

As a result of these sterilization operations Taiwan and Korea have been able to delay the adjustment of their external imbalances because on the one hand they have not been forced into large, explicit revaluations to restore external equilibrium and on the other hand they have avoided the large monetary expansion which would have brought about adjustment through raising their price levels. There can be little doubt that this delay in adjusting to their external imbalances is contributing to friction between the U.S. and some of its South East Asian trading partners. My conclusion is that although fixed or managed exchange rates are optimal for small open economies, the extensive use of these new sterilization techniques has significantly undermined the normal transmission channels, and is thereby extending trade and current account imbalances, which in turn contributes to international trade frictions and protectionism rather than reduces them.

This breakdown of the transmission mechanism is analogous to the introduction of central banks and discretionary monetary policies into the 19th-century gold standard regime. The development of activist, discretionary policies ultimately caused the breakdown of the gold standard, and similarly the breakdown of the Bretton Woods system in 1971 because Germany, Japan, and other economies were not prepared to accept the domestic consequences of keeping their currencies pegged to the U.S. dollar.

It follows, in conclusion, that South East Asian economies with central banks will gradually move away from rigid or mechanically managed foreign exchange rates, towards more actively managed rates which permit discretionary domestic policies. Thus, although these economies are small, open economies, nevertheless the authorities have sufficient disdain for passively accepting the transmission of external disturbances that we are witnessing an inexorable move away from the uncomfortable constraints implicit in the adoption of fixed exchange rates.

Program of the Conference

"Toward a World of Economic Stability:
Optimal Monetary Framework and Policy"

Third International Conference
sponsored by
The Institute for Monetary and Economic Studies
Bank of Japan

June 3–5, 1987
Tokyo

Background and Aims of the Conference

When we look back over the last thirteen years, it is evident that the world economy and most national economies have shown enormous instability in prices, growth, and international payments balances. The Bank of Japan convenes this conference in the hope that an in-depth examination of these problems will provide keys to greater economic stability in the future through designing both a more efficient economic framework and better policies, especially in the monetary area.

The decade starting from 1973 was characterized by greater instability in the inflation and growth rates than had previously been experienced in the postwar period. After 1973—a year to be remembered as the beginning of the general floating exchange rate system as well as the year of the first oil-price hike—inflationary pressures that had emerged in the 1960s became more intense and spread to various countries. Many of the countries thus experienced stagflation. Some, however, having adopted sharply different economic policies, were successful in taming recurrent inflation, and subsequently in achieving relative economic stability.

By the early 1980s, this persistent inflation had subsided in most countries. However, large international payments imbalances among major industrial countries constituted a new source of instability. Floating exchange rates, originally expected to play the major role in correcting current account problems, turned out to be much less effective than had been hoped. Has the significant increase in the international mobility of capital flows reduced the efficacy of the hoped-for automatic adjustment mechanism of the floating exchange rates? Or have the transmission processes of one country's economic policy to another altered? It is undeniable that most countries, large and small, have been strongly influenced by the policies pursued by other countries, and that countries can hardly be said to enjoy full autonomy in their economic policies. In this situation, the persistence of large current account imbalances has increasingly threatened the stability of the world economy by fomenting trade protectionism, the dangers of which were made evident by the Great Depression.

These observations lead us to a fundamental question: given the various shocks, does the principal cause of economic instability lie in policy management, or in the prevailing monetary regime itself, which is a combination of the flat money system domestically and the floating exchange rate system internationally? Furthermore, this question compels us to explore, in order to achieve economic stability, the topics of: the optimal monetary regime, the optimal management of policy, and the effective international policy-coordination.

The conference then will seek to identify the causes of the domestic and international economic instability after 1973 and will discuss the optimal monetary regime together with the role and effectiveness of policy management. It is certainly a challenging task to provide answers to these issues, and the discussions by economists from academia, central banks and various international organizations should contribute to the increased understanding of these fundamental and important questions for economic stability.

Wednesday, June 3

Session I (morning)
  Chairman:
    Yoshio Suzuki (Director, Institute for Monetary and Economic Studies, Bank of Japan)

  Opening Address
    Satoshi Sumita (Governor, Bank of Japan)

  Keynote Speeches
    James Tobin (Yale University), "Are There Reliable Adjustment Mechanisms?"
    Allan H. Meltzer (Carnegie-Mellon University), "On Monetary Stability and Monetary Reform"

  Introductory Presentation
    Yoshio Suzuki (Bank of Japan), "The Macroeconomic Performance of Five Major Countries: An Introductory Presentation"

[Coordinator for Sessions II, III, IV, and V: Yoshio Suzuki, Bank of Japan]

Session II (afternoon)

The Causes of Domestic Instability Since 1973

Chairman:
  Hugh Patrick (Columbia University)

Papers by:
  Michael Parkin (University of Western Ontario), "Monetary Policy and Aggregate Fluctuations"
  Stanley Fischer (Massachusetts Institute of Technology), "Monetary Policy and Performance in the U.S., Japan, and Europe, 1973–86"

Leading Discussants:
  Eduard J. Bomhoff (Erasmus University, Rotterdam)
  Choi Yeon-Jong (Bank of Korea)
  William R. White (Bank of Canada)
  John L. Scadding (Federal Reserve Bank of San Francisco)

General Discussion

Thursday, June 4

Session III (morning)
  The Causes of International Imbalances in the 1980s

Chairman:
  P. David Henderson (Organisation for Economic Co-operation and Development)

Papers by:
  Jürg Niehans (University of Bern), "Generating International Disturbances"
  Jeffrey D. Sachs (Harvard University), "Sources of Macroeconomic Imbalances in the World Economy: A Simulation Approach"

Leading Discussants:
  Ryūtarō Komiya (University of Tokyo)
  Edwin M. Truman (Bank of Governors, Federal Reserve System)
  Rainer Stefano Masera (Banca d'Italia)
  Jacob A. Frenkel (International Monetary Fund)

General Discussion

Friday, June 5

Session IV (morning)

Optimal Monetary Regime and Policy Management for Economic Stability in the Future

Chairman:
  Peter Fousek (Federal Reserve Bank of New York)

Papers by:
Robert J. Barro (University of Rochester), "Monetary Policy under Interest-Rate Targeting and Other Arrangements"
Koichi Hamada (Yale University), "Towards the Implementation of Desirable Rules of Monetary Coordination and Intervention"

Leading Discussants:
Georg Rich (Banque Nationale Suisse)
John H. Makin (American Enterprise Institute)
Philippe Lagayette (Banque de France)
John S. Flemming (Bank of England)

General Discussion

Session V (afternoon)

Summary Presentation and General Discussion

Chairman:
Horst Bockelmann (Bank for International Settlements)

Summary Presentation by:
John B. Taylor (Stanford University)
Andrew D. Crockett (International Monetary Fund)

General Discussion

Participants

Robert J. Barro
Professor
University of Rochester

Serge Bertholome
Adviser, Research Department
Banque Nationale de Belgique

Horst Bockelmann
Economic Adviser and Head of Monetary and Economic Department
Bank for International Settlements

Eduard J. Bomhoff
Professor
Erasmus University Rotterdam

Che Peiqin
Member of Council and Director of International Department
  People's Bank of China

Choi Yeon-Jong
Director of Statistics Department
Bank of Korea

Andrew D. Crockett
Deputy Director of Research Department
International Monetary Fund

Daniel M. Doyle
First Vice President
Federal Reserve Bank of Chicago

Peter S. Ferguson
Deputy Chief Manager of Personnel Department
Reserve Bank of Australia

Stanley Fischer
Professor
Massachusetts Institute of Technology

John S. Flemming
Economic Adviser to Governor
Bank of England

Peter Fousek
Executive Vice President and Director of Research
Federal Reserve Bank of New York

Jacob A. Frenkel
Economic Counsellor and Director of Research
International Monetary Fund

John G. Greenwood
Chief Economist
G. T. Management Ltd. (Asia)

Koichi Hamada
Professor
Yale University

P. David Henderson
Head of Economics and Statistics Department
Organisation for Economic Co-operation and Development

Awang Adek Hussin
Assistant Manager, Economics Department
Bank Negara Malaysia

Mats Josefsson
Head of Credit Market Department
Sveriges Riksbank

Michael W. Keran
Vice President and Chief Economist
Prudential Insurance Co.

Ryūtarō Komiya
Professor
University of Tokyo

Jacob Koning
Assistant Deputy Director and Head of Domestic Research
Nederlandsche Bank

Richard Kopcke
Vice President and Economist
Federal Reserve Bank of Boston

Philippe Lagayette
Vice Governor
Banque de France

John H. Makin
Director of Fiscal Policy Studies
American Enterprise Institute

Rainer Stefano Masera
Central Manager for Economic Research
Banca d'Italia

Allan H. Meltzer
Professor
Carnegie-Mellon University

Akira Nambara
Director of Research and Statistics Department
Bank of Japan

Jürg Niehans
Professor
University of Bern

Deddy Nurjaman
Deputy General Manager of Banking Research and Development Bureau
Bank Indonesia

Mitsuaki Okabe
Chief of Research Division 1, Institute for Monetary and Economic Studies
Bank of Japan

Michael Parkin
Professor
University of Western Ontario

Hugh Patrick
Professor
Columbia University

Georg Rich
Director of Economics Section
Banque Nationale Suisse

Jeffrey D. Sachs
Professor
Harvard University

John L. Scadding
Senior Vice President and Director of Research
Federal Reserve Bank of San Francisco

Helmut Schlesinger
Deputy Governor
Deutsche Bundesbank

Kumiharu Shigehara
Deputy Director of Institute for Monetary and Economic Studies
Bank of Japan

Yoichi Shinkai
Professor
Osaka University

Grant H. Spencer
Chief Manager of Economic Department
Reserve Bank of New Zealand

Satoshi Sumita
Governor
Bank of Japan

Yoshio Suzuki
Director of Institute for Monetary and Economic Studies
Bank of Japan

Ryuichiro Tachi
Chief Councillor of Institute for Monetary and Economic Studies
Bank of Japan

John B. Taylor
Professor
Stanford University

James Tobin
Professor
Yale University

Edwin M. Truman
Director of International Finance Division
Board of Governors of Federal Reserve System

Kazuo Ueda
Associate Professor
Osaka University

Hirofumi Uzawa
Professor
University of Tokyo

William R. White
Adviser
Bank of Canada

Index